ONE BILLION

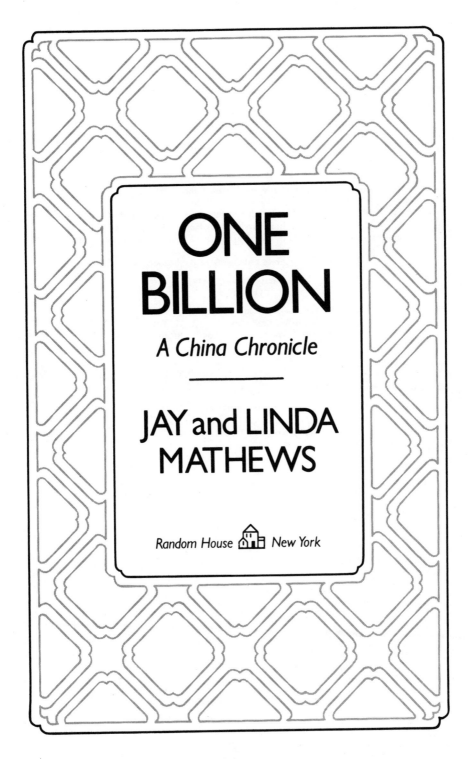

ONE
BILLION

A China Chronicle

JAY and LINDA
MATHEWS

Random House New York

Library of Congress Cataloging in Publication Data

Mathews, Jay, 1945–
One billion.

1. China—Social life and customs—1949–
I. Mathews, Linda, 1946–   . II. Title.
DS777.6.M37 1983   951.05   81–40209
ISBN 0–394–50982–X

Manufactured in the United States of America

2 4 6 8 9 7 5 3

FIRST EDITION

Book design by Carole Lowenstein

To our parents,
Tom and Frances Mathews,
Ralph McVeigh and Edith Eledge

ACKNOWLEDGMENTS

OUR NEWSPAPERS SENT US TO CHINA TO ESTABLISH THEIR NEWS BU-
reaus there, and then gave us the support and freedom which made this
book possible. The editors of the *Washington Post,* particularly Ben Brad-
lee, Howard Simons, Phil Foisie, Lee Lescaze, Rony Koven, Peter Osnos,
Jim Hoagland, Rick Weintraub and Jay Ross, were generous both with
advice and with time; the *Post* granted Jay a leave of absence that allowed
him to devote his full attention to this project. The editors of the *Los Angeles
Times,* while initially wary of having a China correspondent who was
married to a close competitor, were equally supportive. Our thanks go to
William F. Thomas, George Cotliar, Robert Gibson and, in particular, Nick
Williams Jr., Robert Trounson and Don Bremner of the foreign desk.

We would never have undertaken this book had it not been for the energy
and encouragement of our agent, Diane Cleaver. Our editor, Robert Cowley
of Random House, and his assistant, Laura Mathews, inspired us at the
outset and then led us gently through the humbling process of assembling
a book-length manuscript. Several friends, China-watchers and China-lov-
ers all, read parts of the manuscript and offered their comments. We are
grateful to Frank Hawke, Richard Baum, Jean Wong, Perry Link, Stanley
Rosen, Paul Pickowicz, Michael Weisskopf, Susan Shirk, Ezra Vogel and
Deborah Davis-Friedmann. Anne Asplund typed the manuscript.

Our sons, Joe and Peter, were very young when we first took them to
China, but as readers will discover, they were crucial to this book. As a
family, the four of us learned far more about China, particularly about
Chinese families, than would have been possible otherwise; our sons,
frankly, opened doors for us. They were also infinitely forbearing when
picnics at the Ming Tombs and excursions to the Summer Palace were
postponed so "Mommy and Daddy can work." Joe and Peter spent many
chilly afternoons reading wall posters with us at Democracy Wall, when
they would rather have been playing in Zhongshan Park. Someday we hope

they will read this book and appreciate what an adventure China was for us all.

A final word of thanks must be said to Lau Lin, our housekeeper, friend and mentor, who accompanied us from Hong Kong to Peking and then back to Pasadena. For five years, in the grand tradition of Chinese amahs, she tended our children, cooked our meals, introduced us to Peking opera, tried to persuade us of the superiority of all things Chinese and ran our lives. Ah-Lin was really the one indispensable element in this undertaking.

AUTHORS' NOTE

WE HAVE ADOPTED IN THIS BOOK THE *PINYIN* ROMANIZATION SYSTEM for Chinese. It is used on public signs in China and in most American newspapers and magazines. Most of the pronunciations are self-explanatory to English speakers, with these exceptions: *c* is pronounced like *ts* in "its," *zh* like *j* in "jug," *q* roughly like *ch,* and *x* very roughly like *sh*.

In some cases we have used hyphens, contrary to standard usage, in order to help pronunciation. For names made famous long before the popularization of *pinyin* (such as Mao Tse-tung), we have kept the old spellings, as American newspapers often do.

While we were in China, the exchange rate was approximately 1.5 yuan to the dollar. By early 1983 this rate had changed to nearly 2 yuan for each American dollar. To keep prices in perspective, bear in mind that according to Chinese government statistics, per capita annual income for city dwellers in 1982 was $230, and for rural residents only $96.

CONTENTS

ESCAPE

EPILOGUE

BEGINNINGS

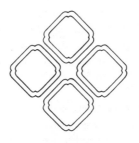

GUANXI

WE CAME UPON THE CHINESE, A NATION OF GENEROUS HUSTLERS, over the course of four years writing about and living in their country. We were an American family, a husband and wife each working for a large U.S. newspaper. At the beginning of our travels in China in 1977, we thought we were seeing a nation like America a century ago. Chinese had lace doilies on their furniture. Their young boys fell in love with the locomotives that whistled past their villages. The condition of the next grain crop was a matter of daily and personal concern for the vast majority of the population. The teen-agers we met seemed almost naïve, untouched by television, dating and cars. Farm youths blushed at questions about love. In the countryside, young men and women still dreamed of joining the army, clearing more land, getting married and having children. We felt the initial rush of astonishment and admiration that affects most visitors from the dissipated West.

We moved to China in the summer of 1979 and lived there for about fifteen months. We had been based in Hong Kong since 1976 and had made eight trips to the mainland before the Chinese invited us to set up bureaus in Peking: Linda for the *Los Angeles Times* and Jay for the *Washington Post.* Along with the *Wall Street Journal* and the *New York Times,* ours were the first American newspapers to establish permanent bureaus in Peking, and we were the first American journalists to bring in small children.

Jay had studied Chinese language, history and politics throughout college, and had a master's degree in East Asian studies; Linda had taken some related courses in college and graduate school before earning a law degree and covering the U.S. Supreme Court for the *Los Angeles Times.* She had put herself through a crash course of China studies, first as a reporter for the Asian *Wall Street Journal* and then as the *Los Angeles Times* bureau chief in Hong Kong.

For us, the chance to travel and eventually live in China was the experience of a lifetime. Our household also included our amah from Hong Kong, Lau Lin, and our two sons, Joe (six) and Peter (two). Peter had bright red hair and spoke Cantonese with Ms. Lau, whom we called Ah-Lin. Joe, who wore his California Angels baseball cap everywhere in China, proved the most reluctant to accept the restrictions of life in a totalitarian state. Once we found him trying to punch out the beefy security guard at the Peking Hotel, who had allowed him to take his bicycle out of the hotel but would not let him take it back in.

As we traveled more we began to see the Chinese, their needs and their troubles, more clearly. They resent—some actively, the majority almost unconsciously—the oppression and inconvenience of their form of government but prefer to finesse it rather than challenge it outright. Like other foreign journalists we looked for underground literature, underground commerce, underground art, and found instead that the whole country operates underground much of the time. People kept their complaints within the family and pursued their goals through the "back door." Only a few openly criticized the practice of circumventing the system. An elderly Chinese novelist, Bai Hua, remarked with disapproval, "Some comrades with children say anxiously, 'My son will surely be put in jail in the future because he does not know how to tell a lie.' Other comrades seem complacent: 'My son has a promising future because he is a young double-dealer.' "

The Chinese obsession with human feelings, their ties to family and neighborhood, their commitment to the simple idea of being Chinese, somehow bind together the world's most populous nation. China is a small town of one billion people. A word we heard often in Peking is *guanxi*. It means "relationships" or "connections," but the English equivalents don't capture its scope. The Chinese use it frequently to refer to face-to-face personal ties and influence with other people. Chinese emigrants we met in Hong Kong enjoyed their release from the political pressures of the mainland, but said they missed "the friends, the personal relationships." One emigrant spoke of his new freedom to say what he thought, to take whatever job he could find, then added, "I miss the people at my village. They knew me, they looked out for me." An emigrant spoke of co-workers at his factory back on the mainland asking after his sick child, something few, if any, of his acquaintances in Hong Kong ever did.

Close bonds of family and friendship helped the Communists win the civil war and run the country in the early 1950s. Then Mao Tse-tung's forces tore human ties apart with the "anti-rightist" campaign, the Great Leap Forward and the Cultural Revolution. The ensuing healing process is sometimes painful, but the relationships of trust that have survived the Cultural Revolution are now all the more precious and important because of that experience.

All of us who have come in contact with Chinese in the 1980s have felt the disappointment and cynicism that followed the brief celebrations and democratic experiments after Mao's death and the fall of the Gang of Four. But has China really gone downhill since that brief period of euphoria?

Probably not. Our cynicism and distress at life in China today is as much a commentary on how we, the foreign commentators, have changed as it is a fair commentary on China. For a totalitarian society, China has shown a remarkable flexibility and willingness to admit mistakes and learn from outsiders in the last few years. The changes have been unprecedented for a Communist government and society, yet as Americans we notice first and foremost the lack of freedom and the submission of the individual. As important and depressing as those conditions are, they lead us to ignore much of what makes Chinese society today so exceedingly complex and vibrant.

Being Chinese in the 1980s, we discovered, is less a commitment to Mao, Marx and the motherland than it is a commitment to one another—billions of small relationships becoming one great whole. Foreigners will continue to misread the Chinese and their future role in the world unless they appreciate this point. What gets done usually succeeds in spite of party directives and *People's Daily* articles. The very idea of being Chinese, doing things in a very personal, Chinese way, wars with Marxist efficiency, factory quotas and train schedules.

As Americans we tended to leap too quickly to the conclusion that the Chinese had finally begun to appreciate the blessings of Western trade and technology and some democratic ideals. For a century we have envisioned the Chinese lining up eagerly to buy Christianity, free enterprise and now the latest in our military arsenal. But we have failed to see the Chinese struggling to gouge just a few bland pieces from this big Western apple, most of which they consider poisoned fruit.

We may have been misled by the similarities between China and America, particularly the sense of geographic distances and isolation. In land area, China is the third largest country in the world, after the Soviet Union and Canada, and just ahead of the United States. The Chinese are at the center of Asia, yet cut off from other major populations by mountains, deserts or seas. Twelve countries—the Soviet Union, Mongolia, Afghanistan, Pakistan, India, Nepal, Bhutan, Burma, Thailand, Laos, Vietnam and North Korea, and two territories, Macao and Hong Kong—touch on China, with varying degrees of apprehension.

The differences in temperature and climate can be as breath-taking as those in North America. At the northernmost Chinese outpost, Manzhouli Pass, there were seven young People's Liberation Army soldiers and a dog shivering in sixty-below-zero weather as they gazed at the Soviet border. On Hainan Island in China's far southeast, we noticed that rubber-plantation workers have to wear huge straw hats or risk fainting in the hundred-degree heat. Flying from Peking to Canton was a treat in fall and spring, for we escaped the chilly, dusty north to enjoy the moist, warm breezes of the south.

The Long March of 1934–1935, the colossal event which marked the painful birth of Communist China, covered a route about three thousand miles long. But Mao's fleeing troops had to zigzag so often that they marched twice that distance—a hike comparable to walking from New York to Los Angeles by way of Alaska. Red Army soldiers saw much of the western part of the country, the two thirds of Chinese land that is semi-desert or mountains. Once they came to power, few wanted to go back; today, as always, the Chinese huddle along their eastern coast. Ninety percent of the people live on one sixth of the land—the fertile eastern plains and deltas. A country that must feed nearly one quarter of the world's population farms only 10 percent of its own territory.

We could never really gracefully and happily assume the ties and bonds which make Chinese life at such close quarters work. Their methods often struck us as corrupt, or at least inefficient. Not being Chinese, we had to remain a little apart. Our next to last night in China we visited a worker and human rights activist who had told us what he could of his own life. He suffered the day-to-day annoyance of having to share a kitchen with two other families in his apartment corridor. He had what seemed to be a monotonous job, and appeared depressed that he could interest so few Chinese in his ideas of democracy. But we felt we had become friends. As a farewell gift he gave us a tiny snapshot of him and his daughter, with a few English words she had written on the back to our son Joe. We gave him a small Chinese-language pamphlet about early-American history. As we left he helped us down the pitch-black stairway with his flashlight and wished us a peaceful journey. None of these warm feelings did much good when the police arrested him five months later. We had no *guanxi* to protect him.

Books on life and government in twentieth-century China go stale very quickly; you find them in remaindered bookstalls, made obsolete by new shifts of policy in Peking. Since 1957 the Chinese have gone through at least seven political and economic policy shifts, in nearly all cases changing lives far more than any of the six Administrations that have passed through Washington in that time. Foreign visitors who marveled at the human-wave projects and backyard steel furnaces of the Great Leap Forward in 1959 found the Chinese grumbling three years later about the Great Leap's phony statistics. Biographers who profiled Mao's heir apparent, Liu Shaoqi (Liu Shao-chi), in the early 1960s found him discredited by 1967. Other potential heirs to Mao, the late Defense Minister Lin Biao (Lin Piao) and the Shanghai politician Zhang Chunqiao (Chang Ch'un-ch'iao) disappeared almost as quickly.

Each dizzying shift seemed to strip away a little more of the patience and good will the Chinese had felt toward the Communists and made their always suspect commitment to Marxism seem all the more shallow. (Mao himself found Marx only a convenient tool.) But some things did not change. The Chinese remained committed to themselves, to the Chinese way of life and to the old Chinese dream of a more prosperous future for their web of family and friends—what the government, in its dry way, calls the four modernizations. So here we have tried to tell the stories, jokes and conversations which illumine these unchanging Chinese needs.

We are fascinated by China's numbers, but more so by the glue that binds the numbers together. If there were not so many Chinese, the world would not be so interested in them or hold them in such awe. If there were fewer Chinese, they would be a stronger, more prosperous and thus in reality a more threatening nation. But that would not change the way the Chinese look at themselves. We cannot think of another country, not even the Soviet Union, where national ambitions and sense of historical mission so outstrip present capabilities. This depressing gap has been a Chinese obsession for more than a century. It explains some of the Chinese discontent that colors this book. Along with the obsession with personal ties, that feeling of resentment at the tricks of fate defines what it means to be Chinese today.

The old Chinese curse "May you live in interesting times" seemed appropriate for our stay in Peking. It fulfilled ambitions we had had for some time, but at the same time it was wearing on our personal lives and on our children. We were forced to live in two hotel rooms, one for us and one for our sons and amah. Nothing else was available. The demands of news gathering and child rearing in that situation sometimes drove us a bit crazy. Individually the Chinese could be wonderful, but collected together into a bureaucracy they were exasperating. At age six, Joe took to ending every conversation with the statement "I won't STAND for it!" When we asked him where he had heard that, he answered, *Everybody* says it." *Guanxi* can wear you down. We arranged lengthy luncheons and teas to try, unsuccessfully, to establish rapport with the men who would give us an apartment. Meanwhile a driver quit because we had not established rapport with *him*.

So we want to wrap together the most heartening and annoying parts of Chinese life, the obsession with self and history, the weary contrasts between city and country life, the obligations to older generations that touch on birth, marriage, death and even college exams, the grinding bureaucracy and callousness about personal rights, the lust for amusements, and the frequently betrayed optimism about the future.

We miss the place, and the spirit of first-hand human contact, the kind of *guanxi* that makes China work. The Chinese disappointed us when they accepted and promoted bureaucracy and oppression, then surprised us with the fortitude and pluck by which they outwitted it. With some luck at balancing this discipline and spirit, they may make it safely into the modern world. Doesn't modernization, after all, require some flexibility and innovation, which, in turn, weaken the hold of an arrogant government?

We recall, for instance, the moment in Canton when the authorities tried to ban special television antennas that could pick up Hong Kong frequencies. Watching Cantonese comedies and variety shows beamed from the British territory has become immensely popular, but authorities worried that dangerous, bourgeois ideas might spread. Faced with a directive, the Canton residents assumed the proper Chinese stance, quietly bowing to authority and taking down their antennas. Each evening when it was too dark to be noticed they crawled back up to their roofs and temporarily reconnected the equipment so they could enjoy the night's programing. Eventually the officials in charge gave up. A new campaign for sanitation improvement allowed them to direct their energies elsewhere. After a few days people no longer bothered climbing on the roofs to disconnect the equipment each morning. The television antennas had recaptured their place in the sun.

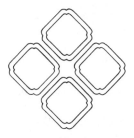

MANDATE OF HEAVEN

THE CHINESE LIVE THEIR LIVES AND RAISE THEIR CHILDREN IN ONE OF the most protected and orderly environments on earth, yet when neighborhood and family ties are broken, people can become violent, even vicious. Personal relations rule their days; and friendships are extremely close and emotion-laden; nevertheless, the country is littered with stories of betrayal. No people have a higher opinion of their own personal integrity, yet petty corruption and favor-trading are second nature to them. Foreign guests coming into a Chinese home are received with a kindness and warmth unrivaled anywhere, yet the Chinese are among the world's most racist people, sneering at and manipulating foreigners behind their backs, fiercely opposed to interracial marriage and inclined to push around the minority peoples living on their borders (many of whom look as Chinese as Chairman Mao). The Chinese are outraged at stories of elderly people in the United States living alone and occasionally freezing to death in their apartments, but are annoyed when American reporters criticize the Chinese practice of sending young rowdies and malcontents off to labor camps for life.

Such contradictions—many of which stymie modernization—could only be managed in a country with a strong sense of itself. Perhaps by the next century the Chinese will have achieved the blend of organization, prosperity and overwhelming strength of numbers to make them a true superpower. But in their own minds they are already special, and only their obsession with the past can explain it.

John Dolphin, an American who directed the University Services Center in Hong Kong, saw the lengths to which this could go when he visited his wife's native village in a remote corner of Henan (Honan) province. He struck up a conversation with the town elders. "Am I the first foreigner ever to visit your village?" he asked. The stooped old men with wispy goatees chuckled at his presumption. "No, no, of course not," one of them finally answered.

"Oh, who came before me? Did you have Russian advisers here in the nineteen-fifties?"

"No, no Russians."

"I suppose the Japanese must have come through sometime during the war."

"No, they never got this far, though they got close enough so that we had to hide what little gold we had."

"Well, then, a foreign missionary perhaps?" Dolphin persisted.

"No," said another old man, "although I recall that for a little while in the twenties there was a Belgian missionary living a few villages away. He turned out to be a spy, though, so the villagers drove him away."

Finally Dolphin lost patience. "Can you tell me who *were* the first foreigners?"

"Well," one of the elders said matter-of-factly, "part of the Mongol army passed right through here during the great invasion, on their way to the capital." And that, as John knew, happened sometime in the early thirteenth century.

The point of this story is not simply that the Chinese take a long view of history—practically a truism by now—but that history is somehow more real, more immediate to the people of China than it is to most Westerners. We found in talking to ordinary Chinese that the thirteenth century at times seems every bit as relevant as yesterday. For a supposedly revolutionary society, China spends an inordinate amount of time looking backward. This does not mean that every conversation is punctuated with historical aphorisms. Many youths, in fact, tend to be ignorant about the details of their country's history. The authorities try to remind them by arranging "speak bitterness" sessions at factories, communes and schools in which elderly workers describe how they suffered before 1949.

The past matters to the Chinese in down-to-earth ways, affecting everything from television entertainment to the tenor of political debates. Political vendettas, for example, last a very long time. Chinese politicians, mindful of their proper place in history, can be obsessive about "settling accounts" with their rivals, and carry on feuds long after Americans would have buried the hatchet. "Let bygones be bygones" is not a sentiment heard much in China. During a trip to Africa in the early sixties Premier Chou En-lai thanked the Sudanese for killing Charles George Gordon, the British soldier of fortune who tried to put down a revolt in Khartoum in 1885. In 1860 Gordon had supervised the burning of the Old Summer Palace of the Qing (Ch'ing) emperor. More than a century later, Peking still considered Gordon's activities an insult to the Chinese.

Stranger still to outsiders is the Chinese habit of adjusting someone's historical standing after he is long gone. Genghis Khan, the nomad chief who sacked Peking in 1215 and cut a bloody swath across Eurasia, was formally rehabilitated in 1980. This obviously mattered not to the Great

Khan himself, but to modern-day Mongolians in China's northwest. Confucius and Puyi, the last emperor, are other one-time villains now at least partially restored to favor.

Odysseys to outer space lure future-oriented Americans to movie houses. In China, historical dramas lead box-office sales, and the more ancient the story, the better. Chinese children so far have no space-age Superman to emulate. At play, they pretend to be the Monkey King, the supernatural hero of a famous medieval epic. Xunxun, the small bespectacled son of Linda's interpreter, Hou Ying, had Monkey's hand gestures down pat and put on his own performances in Ritan (Sun Altar) Park. China has its modern-day soap operas, but the top-rated radio show is the saga of Yue Fei, a combination of Paul Bunyan and Robin Hood, based on an actual Song dynasty warrior of legendary strength and cunning. Each episode was broadcast twice a day (in case someone missed the first). Lao Wang, our driver, tuned in both times on the car radio. Chinese, or more often their children, would turn it on while we were talking with them in their homes. A brief official attempt to cut off reruns ("Well, it wasn't very revolutionary, *was* it?" said one cynical Chinese friend) ended in a minor scandal. A leading novelist wrote an article in the *Peking Evening News* criticizing the censorship attempt, and Yue Fei returned triumphantly to the airwaves. Peasants in the suburbs bought up every available cheap radio when the program resumed.

Chinese scientists look to the past for inspiration. In the national archives, teams of Chinese meteorologists are now combing the voluminous weather records of the last three hundred years in an effort to discover patterns that might help them predict the droughts and floods that still plague the country. Seismologists in charge of improving China's earthquake-prediction methods are doing the same thing. The unique continuity of their historical records makes such research possible. "Nobody but China keeps records like these," a Chinese historian told us, "and nobody but the Chinese has the discipline to sort through them again and again."

The past obsesses the Chinese in part because there is so much of it. The longest continuing civilization in the annals of mankind, China can document its history back to the Shang dynasty, thirty-seven hundred years ago. What came before the Shang had always been steeped in mystery, legend and fairy tales about celestial and terrestrial sovereigns and the great Yellow Emperor, a sort of Chinese King Arthur. Then, in 1978, at a bend of the Yellow River where Henan (Honan) and Shanxi (Shansi) provinces meet, two expeditions unearthed fragments that appear to prove the existence of the semimythical Xia dynasty, four hundred years older than the Shang.

Like the New York Yankees, the Chinese have heard so often of their considerable past—attested to by the foreigners who flock to see their relics —that they find it difficult to see how they can fail to be great again. Rising and falling, rising and falling again, they have survived so many empires, rebellions and invasions that anticipation of change has become an all-purpose national myth and a political philosophy.

Historians call this the dynastic cycle, but it is more than a convenient way to divide textbook chapters. It is a whole system of thought. Americans accustomed to continual material progress may be shattered when their expectations are thwarted, but the Chinese accept calamity, such as the Cultural Revolution they have just been through, and await the next climb up the roller coaster. The philosophy comforts, but also deflates initiative. The Chinese talk so much now about the long-term future that the country's much ballyhooed goals for the next century have inspired jokes. In a Chinese vaudeville routine one comedian asks, "When can you fix this chair?" His sidekick answers, "Come back about the year 2000."

In the classic dynastic cycle, a new empire led by a vigorous tyrant would rise, then fall under the corruption and weakness of the great man's heirs and suffer the rage of mistreated peasants and emboldened foreign invaders. One dynasty might follow another quickly, as happened between the first great unifying dynasty, the Qin (223–206 B.C.), and its successor, the early Han (206 B.C.–A.D. 8). Or the country might experience centuries of intermittent civil war, such as followed the late Han (A.D. 25–221) before a new unified dynasty, the Sui, arose in A.D. 589.

Chinese at every level of society accepted the notion that a ruler governed under a "mandate of heaven." This concept, combined with a brilliantly conceived civil service examination and organization, kept the Chinese political system more or less intact. For two thousand years it also frustrated the efforts of merchants and inventors who wanted something more than just stability.

The Chinese tripped over their self-satisfaction from the outset of their confrontation with the energetic innovators of the West. When a delegation sent by King George III in 1793 petitioned Peking to let in more British merchants, the Qianlong emperor declined, saying, "Our celestial empire possesses all things in prolific abundance." In conversation with foreigners today, Chinese consider it polite to point out China's shortcomings and say they hope to learn from abroad. Still, a kind of "We're number one" mentality permeates the country. China ranks near the bottom on the United Nations charts of per capita income, yet the Chinese blame their economic backwardness on hard luck and bad leaders—nothing that lessens, in their view, the importance of being Chinese or their assumed past and future greatness.

Even Chinese revolutionaries have taken the long view. Sun Yat-sen, the founder of the Chinese republic, once confounded a group of Russian revolutionaries by telling them it might take a hundred years for the Chinese revolution to succeed. Mao Tse-tung was not a patient man, trying to accelerate or divert Chinese history with his Great Leap Forward and Cultural Revolution, but after his experiments failed he would muse about the future, predicting at one point that Marx, Engels, Lenin and Stalin would probably "appear ridiculous" in a thousand years.

Why, the Chinese ask, should they rush? The bird men we encountered in a little grove at Peking's Longtan Lake had achieved the universally desired pace, exercising themselves and their birds by holding a cage in each hand, raising one and lowering the other like a seesaw. Despite appeals to the people to exceed production quotas, life goals for the average Chinese are to find a good job, a good friend, a kind spouse and a long retirement. Most Chinese will tell you that they strive to realize the four modernizations of agriculture, industry, science and the army. But further conversation often reveals that they see modern progress only as a way to achieve those simpler, modest pleasures of home and family.

The government provides food and housing and arranges for almost everyone to take a midday nap. It is nearly impossible to get fired unless one commits a serious crime. Only the brilliant, the ambitious, the politically misguided or unlucky have to struggle for what they want.

A daring historian might suggest that ancient memories have enshrined a national lust for the soft life. The wandering tribes of the Asian steppes that became the Chinese nation found they could easily tend two crops a year of fat wild grains in the well-irrigated valleys of the Wei, the Yangtze and the Yellow rivers. Tribes in Europe had to struggle with drier summers and only one annual crop.

The Chinese imagination remained stuck between these well-worn riverbanks. It became a civilization and government feeding off irrigated agriculture and land taxes. Admiral Cheng Ho tried to break his country out of the trap in the early fifteenth century with a series of adventurous expeditions to the Persian Gulf and the east coast of Africa. Some Chinese peasants and merchants followed him into southeast Asia, but the Ming dynasty court showed none of the interest in foreign riches that would soon entice the kings of Portugal, Spain, France and England. Confucianism looked down on merchant ventures, the Mongols were acting up in the north, and Admiral Cheng himself was unfortunately a eunuch, a sore point for Peking's scholar officials.

Chinese writers obsessed with the missed opportunity to keep up with the West now look back before Cheng's time to the golden age when their ancestors invented paper, rockets, gunpowder, movable type and the compass. Both pride and melancholy enter here. The foreign historian of China whom educated Chinese know best, Harvard's John K. Fairbank, argues that China in the twelfth century was far ahead of Europe in size of population, food supply, ship building, commerce, city life, fine arts, porcelain making and the "civility of upper-class existence." The Chinese lacked the cutthroat business sense and wanderlust that helped the Europeans turn invention into world power, and no historian really knows why. Perhaps the Chinese were too successful too early. In building such a huge, wealthy and politically stable society, they insulated themselves from the international wars that stimulated much of Europe's expansion.

So history in China remains inextricably entwined with politics. Writers argue over modern problems by repeating old stories, a technique that fails to warn ordinary Chinese of how unique and deep their problems are. Fierce debates over current policies are often disguised as seemingly innocuous discussions of ancient history in the scholarly journals. The elaborate historical imagery is too obscure for most foreigners to follow, but Chinese intellectuals advise anyone who really wants to know what is happening in Peking to read the historical journals. We know of one CIA analyst who delighted in pulling small nuggets of intelligence out of the turgid essays in the Peking journal *Historical Research* and other obscure sources. In 1980 the official historians exploded scholarly firecrackers in the face of Mao's beleaguered and since deposed successor as Party Chairman, Hua Guofeng (Hua Kuo-feng). One article described an unscrupulous Tang dynasty eunuch whose ruler expressed confidence in him with words nearly identical to those used by Mao in praise of Hua. A *People's Daily* article criticized a dynastic official who received the blessing of an ailing emperor and afterward took over the country in a manner reminiscent of Hua's succession.

The Chinese understand this tricky game of political backbiting in historical commentary because they have played it for centuries. A Tang dynasty poem may describe a cassia blossom, but some Chinese historians will insist it is actually a comment on the corruption around the emperor. Historians also understand the dangers of the game, for theirs is a hazardous profession. Sima Qian—perhaps the greatest Chinese historian—was castrated for meddling in a dispute between the emperor and one of his generals in the first century B.C. The writer-historian Wu Han endured repeated Red Guard interrogations and "airplane" torture (being forced to bend forward with his arms tied back for long periods) during the Cultural Revolution because his plays on the Ming dynasty seemed to ridicule Mao. He died in 1969 of undisclosed causes.

The Chinese are so wedded to their cyclical thinking that death does not end a man's life story. In 1980 China's former security chief, Kang Sheng, was uncovered as a co-conspirator of the Gang of Four—five years after his death. His family quickly went to the special cemetery for revolutionary heroes, Babaoshan, and removed his ashes for reburial elsewhere. "Otherwise," said a Chinese official, "we would have invited him to leave Babaoshan." In imperial China, bodies of top officials were sometimes exhumed and publicly flogged, a practice that gave rise to the term *bian shi,* "whipping the corpse," still used today. Some Chinese believe that before his death in January 1976, Chou ordered his ashes scattered to the four winds to prevent desecration of his remains by his political foes.

Reputations can also rebound after death, the most noteworthy being

Mao's chief rival, former head of state Liu Shaoqi (Liu Shao-chi). The bogeyman of the Cultural Revolution, Liu was maligned for years as "the archreactionary capitalist roader." The elaborate 1980 rehabilitation ceremony at the Great Hall of the People, complete with those attending in mourning clothes, came too late for Liu, who had died eleven years before in a dingy provincial prison, but its significance was not lost on the history-conscious Chinese. It was designed to restore his family's standing, help his disgraced associates recover their jobs, and most important, breathe life into the pragmatic economics doctrines Liu had preached.

In atheistic China, there is life after death. That is why, despite the urge to build an industrial economy and a modern state, the Chinese still fight old battles over the meaning of history. Could that be what fueled the vehemence of the Cultural Revolution?

During the Cultural Revolution, students, soldiers and other "revolutionaries" were recruited to purge all the bureaucrats and intellectuals who blocked Mao's notions of government by mass movement. It was a Maoist revolt against all the historical notions of how people should be governed, an attack on the idea of a mandate of heaven, and it brought enormous casualties. Former Red Guards we met in Hong Kong told of mass rapes and of rival bands of Red Guards attacking one another with firearms. Torture victims from that era are found throughout the ranks of leading Chinese artists and writers today.

Provincial statistics indicate that at least two hundred thousand people perished—other estimates reach into the millions—as a result of deliberate torture, assault, execution or suicide. The Cultural Revolution was a turning point in the life of every Chinese adult alive today. But it failed, and the idea of a mandate survived, to be bestowed on those who outlasted the torture, heartbreak and economic calamity.

The concept of a mandate of heaven leaves the Chinese government with a fatalistic tinge, a feeling that only survival, not progress, is important. There is much less of the black magic and prophecy which used to surround the notion of heaven's favor, but we still noticed considerable nervousness when unusual meteor showers—one of the old signs of dynastic change— lit up the north China skies in early 1976. The Peking newspapers spoke of unspecified "superstitions" which it indicated were being used to whip up sentiment against what had become a very unpopular government in Mao's last days.

Then, in July, little more than a month before the death of Mao, a massive earthquake at Tangshan killed more than two hundred and forty thousand people. Three years later, as we chatted about this with a well-educated official in Peking, the man paused and then confessed, "No matter what you hear people say, many of us were impressed that we had that big earthquake just before Mao died. Nobody is quite sure what we are going through now, whether this is a new dynasty or just more of the old one."

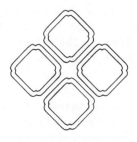

BELONGING

STRANGERS MEETING FOR THE FIRST TIME IN CHINA ARE LESS LIKELY TO ask each other's name than to inquire politely, "What is your unit?" China is organized by units—factories, offices, neighborhoods or rural work teams —and they are all-important. Every Chinese belongs to one, usually the place where he or she works. A unit provides the citizen of China with the necessities of life: employment, ration tickets and housing. It educates the children and pays a pension in old age. Even the decision to bear a child is usually made by the unit; the married women within the group decide whose turn it is to become pregnant. Newcomers to China feel absolutely lost in this system, as we discovered when we arrived in Peking to set up news bureaus. Without a unit, we could not reserve hotel rooms, buy train tickets or apply for ration coupons. "If you don't have a unit, you can't even communicate with other units," fretted Linda's interpreter, Hou Ying.

Only a small percentage of the hundreds of young Chinese who have gone to the United States and Europe to study in the 1980s will stay in or emigrate to the West. Barring another major political upheaval in Peking, most of them will eventually return to China because that's where they find their families and their units. "You shouldn't discount the great emotional and physical security of life in China compared to the helter-skelter in the West," one well-traveled Chinese scholar commented. "As Deng Xiaoping said, it takes days to do things here that would take a few hours in the West, and ironically, there is some comfort in that statistic for us Chinese."

The Chinese unit is a sacrifice to the gods of both Confucius and Marx. Confucius urged his followers to commit themselves to what he called the five great relationships: between ruler and subject, father and son, husband and wife, elder brother and younger brother, friend and friend. Until this century, a person's extended family generally provided him with a job, education, social contacts, recreation and security. The Communists considered this system distastefully feudal and tried to substitute factory, office, street committee and rural work team for traditional family ties. It has not been a wholly satisfactory exchange. Loyalty to the family and loyalty to the unit continue to do battle in China. Still, unless you have a larger group to hang on to, you are left out in the cold. Steve Holder, a young consular officer in Peking, told us of recent emigrants to the United States who had returned to China, shell-shocked. "The pace was too fast, there were too many demands," Holder explained. "They just didn't like having to look out for themselves. In the States, there are no units."

Officials of the Peking Hotel, though at first spurning our request for rooms, kindly suggested that we could get the U.S. embassy to be our unit. That was out of the question. As journalists, we were supposed to maintain a certain distance from the government. Another possibility was the Information Department of the Chinese Foreign Ministry, the agency that accredits all foreign journalists. But if we did not want to become too closely identified with the American government, how could we align ourselves with a unit of the Chinese government?

Hou supplied the solution. Realizing that the essence of a unit is a rubber "chop" (or stamp) that can be used to impress the unit's name on documents and correspondence, she made a chop for Linda's office that said THE LOS ANGELES TIMES OF AMERICA in English and Chinese. It is difficult to overemphasize the importance of the chop in China, so wedded is the country to the trappings of bureaucracy. During the worst upheavals of the Cultural Revolution in the late 1960s, Red Guard youths created administrative chaos and in effect took control of some organizations simply by stealing their chops. They fought bloody battles with knives, swords and sometimes firearms against other Red Guard groups that possessed these symbols of office.

Armed with their handsome new chop, Linda and Hou succeeded in buying plane tickets, renting hotel rooms, even running up sizable bills. It was accepted unquestioningly even by the best units.

And, somewhere in the process, Hou Ying and Linda became a unit, although one that still remained apart from the Chinese system.

Dealing with foreigners remains a sticky and potentially dangerous problem for the Chinese. In some circumstances, acknowledging a friendly relationship with a foreigner has brought official censure and even imprisonment. Even the less cautious Chinese we encountered seemed nervous about meeting with foreigners. One day a young Chinese factory technician telephoned Jay and asked if they could get together. One of Jay's business cards had reached him through the friend of a friend; he wanted to talk about emigrating to America. Could Jay find him a sponsor? Jay picked him up after dark outside Yuetan Park. They drove around Peking for an hour, trying to find a place where they could stop and talk without being observed. Except for the moving automobile itself, no such place existed. American journalists in the Soviet Union cannot be immediately identified on sight as foreigners, but Jay could not easily pass himself off as Chinese. And if the young Chinese had tried to enter our hotel, he would have had to run the gauntlet, identifying himself to the guard, registering his name and unit and declaring whom he was seeing.

Guards at the Peking Hotel wear no uniforms and carry no discernible weapons, but they are armed with the confidence of functionaries in a society where everybody knows the rule against unauthorized dealings with foreigners. They stand outside the hotel's electronically sliding doors and question any Chinese trying to enter. The only exceptions are regular workers at the hotel or overseas Chinese, who are easy to identify by their clothes and haircuts. A deputy mayor of Peking, a seventy-four-year-old woman named Lei Jieqiong, once failed to get through their checkpoint because the guards could not believe she was a ranking city official.

Any Chinese who tries to accompany an acquaintance into a foreign apartment compound will usually be stopped by the armed military guards at the gate. Once inside the building itself, a Chinese visitor cannot escape notice by the ever-present elevator "operators." The elevators are self-operating, but the women assigned to them insist on escorting passengers to their floors. They appear to have little else to do but record who is coming and going. We never found a quiet, untraveled street or park in Peking. A foreigner and a Chinese walking together would immediately attract curious glances.

So Jay and his new friend continued to drive. The young man was afraid that some passer-by might report the unusual sight of a foreigner chauffeuring a Chinese. It was not an idle fear. Jay's government-assigned interpreter, Sun Chongren, well known to the Peking Hotel guards, had been stopped twice and asked to show his identification simply because when the car pulled up to the hotel, he happened to be in the back seat with Jay. The guards considered it suspicious that Sun was not riding next to the driver, where interpreters usually sit.

Finally, that night, tired of driving all over town, Jay barreled into the Jianguomenwai diplomatic compound while the Chinese youth hunched over in the back seat so the army guards would not see him. They stopped in a dark corner of the parking lot and chatted for another half-hour, although the young Chinese looked worried whenever an elevator operator peered out from an apartment building nearby.

If there was ever a day when we felt like noxious weeds in a beautiful Chinese garden, it was the day Hou brought her five-year-old son to play with our boys. We had coaxed her to bring Xunxun to the hotel some Saturday morning. Hou seemed reluctant, but we guessed she had an itch to show off her little boy, who turned out to be very bright and talented.

The appointed Saturday morning came. Hou and Xunxun failed to appear. Jay went downstairs, only to discover them standing outside in the street; the desk clerks had refused to let Xunxun enter the building. The little boy did not seem much of a threat, staring through large glasses like a blue-jacketed owl. "They said he has no business coming into the hotel. It has nothing to do with my work," Hou told Jay as the three of them huddled outside in the cold.

The staff of the hotel manager's office was not much more helpful when Jay went back inside to talk to them. One staff member said, "This is a hotel, not an office building. We cannot make special allowances for guests."

"What has that got to do with inviting somebody over to play with my children?" Jay asked.

One of the office staff, a woman, looked embarrassed. "How old did you say the little boy was?"

"Five."

"Well, you know," said another, "if we let one Chinese child in, there might be thousands coming in soon."

"How could that be? There are only six or seven children living in this entire hotel," Jay said. "Why would they be inviting thousands of Chinese playmates?" The official stared at Jay for about ten seconds, apparently considering the logic of this. It was not good to have the foreign guests screaming in frustration in the lobby. "All right," he said finally, "the little boy can come in."

But when Jay emerged, he discovered that Hou had already solved the problem, quickly and easily, in the Chinese way. While Jay argued with the hotel staff, our driver gave Hou and Xunxun a ride. When they returned, she and Xunxun sailed through the front door and up to our room without a problem: Hou had brought back a letter from her unit.

The only way for a Chinese to briefly escape his own society is to pass for a foreigner. In this little game, played occasionally by some of the Chinese we came to know, absurdities of misidentification abound. One young Chinese artist had worked out a routine. He would arrive at our offices wearing a white trenchcoat pulled tight over Hawaiian shirt, white pants (somewhat soiled), short canvas boots and white socks. He had grown his hair to his shoulders and added a mustache and goatee. He wanted to look like an overseas Chinese, or even a Japanese, and the disguise seemed to work. The guards did not stop him. He could come up to our offices without having to give his name and unit. Eventually, however, the police took notice of him in the Peking neighborhood where he shared a friend's room. We were glad it was not his visits to us that led to his arrest. We hoped he was sent back, as he had been once before, to his wife and child in Heilongjiang (Heilungkiang).

China isolates foreigners for some of the same reasons that other closed societies do: its leaders do not want to expose their own people to ideas and living standards that might disrupt the system. The newspapers occasionally exhort citizens to beware the wiles of foreign music and bell-bottom trousers. But the special handling of foreigners results from more than just fear that the natives will be corrupted. Embarrassment over their poor standard of living, and a simple passion for order, authority and propriety also play a part. Bad feelings and misunderstandings then occur when the Chinese seek to manipulate, usually under cover of sincerity and politeness, the foreigners who remind them of their current shortcomings.

When the menu of the Peking Hotel dining hall became too familiar, we tried our hand at restaurant hunting. There were places where a casual visitor could arrive without a reservation, but often all the tables were taken. Even worse, sometimes Chinese workers who had looked forward to a rare night out were swiftly removed to make room for the ignorant barbarians who arrived without warning.

So we would call ahead and brace ourselves for the Peking squeeze:
"Yes?"
"I'd like to reserve a table for eight for lunch Tuesday."
"What nationality are you?"
"American."
"What is the standard?"
"The what?"
"How much do you want to pay for each setting?"
"Uh—how about ten dollars?"
"Well, you won't get much for that."
"What would you suggest?"
"Oh, sir, you must decide."
"Well, how about fifteen dollars?"
"Hmmm, we'll try."

The question of nationality, which always began such dialogues, was not frivolous. Speed and sometimes price of service depended on the prosperity of and China's official policy toward the nation in question. Hotels, shops and even the Peking Taxi Company wanted to know our nationality. It used to be that Albanians got cabs in five minutes while Americans had to wait much longer. By the time we came to Peking to live in 1979, Albanian relations with China had cooled and the taxi situation had reversed.

Our relations with the Peking Hotel staff also became progressively smoother, mostly because the passage of time without our misbehaving seriously made us more trustworthy in the Chinese system of judging such relationships. We had become, in the Chinese phrase, *lao pengyou,* "old friends." Our amah from Hong Kong was a strict vegetarian who refused to eat anything prepared by the hotel kitchen. Ah-Lin cooked rice and vegetables in her room on the fifteenth floor in flagrant violation of hotel rules, but the floor attendants looked the other way. When Joe's baseball shattered a chandelier, and when Peter knocked over a vase, the damage was accepted with equanimity.

To our children, China was a place where strange grownups bestowed candy and peanuts, bounced you on their knee and pushed your swing for hours without once complaining (as did their short-tempered parents) that it was time you learned to pump. To Peter, every Chinese was a *shu-shu.* That's Chinese for Uncle. Children are encouraged to use it, or the female equivalent, *ai-yi* (Auntie), to address all adults. *"Nihao, shu-shu,"* Peter automatically said to the dozens of room attendants—all of them male— he met during the course of a day. Waiters and waitresses at the hotel dining room would in turn stop by Peter's table to inquire after his health or maybe suggest to his mother that he needed a haircut.

The sheer number of *shu-shu* or *ai-yi* meant that it was impossible for a small red-haired foreigner like Peter to get lost or even hurt. There was always an adult around to keep an eye on him. The first time Peter sped down the hall on his tricycle and failed to reappear, Linda frantically started searching for him, certain he had run afoul of elevators, open windows or other hotel hazards. But she found him in another room, lying on his stomach, showing off his Matchbox cars to an appreciative circle of *shu-shu,* also prone.

After that, when he went off in search of amusement and exercise, we knew he'd likely be down the hall, playing with the *shu-shu,* helping them push their trolleys of fresh linens or cleaning a room for a newly arrived guest. And eventually he always wandered back, his progress checked by the *shu-shu* along the way.

Joe, a baseball fanatic, brought his beloved ball and bat and a tattered old California Angels program to Peking. He succeeded in turning a corner of the Peking Hotel parking lot into a baseball diamond. Batting practice, with Jay serving up the pitches to Joe, sometimes attracted a crowd of a few hundred Chinese. They congregated just behind the evergreens that marked the edge of the parking lot, eager for a glimpse of the clumsy American father chasing balls rapped by his frenzied small son.

Order at the Peking Hotel entrance was preserved by a squad of People's Liberation Army soldiers, and over many months the PLA troopers became enthusiastic and knowledgeable baseball fans. The drivers of the impressive Hong Qi (Red Flag) limousines that lined the hotel driveways also allowed themselves to be drawn into the game. They fetched foul balls and agreed that whenever Joe's ball struck one of their gleaming bumpers it was a ground rule double.

The cultural exchange worked both ways, sometimes in a somewhat dismaying fashion, as in the makeshift garage of the U.S. embassy, which became the Peking American School. It had sixteen pupils, or "little friends" as the Chinese called them, and three teachers, an enviable student-teacher ratio. Joe learned enough Chinese there to make plays on words or offer a few helpful phrases. If Linda was struggling to the elevator loaded with packages, Joe sang out, *"Deng yi deng, wode mama lai!"* (Hold on, my mommy's coming!) A few American children attended local Chinese primary schools as well. Instruction was in Chinese, but in grades above the kindergarten Peter attended, all foreign children were segregated into special classes, so there was little mixing with Chinese youngsters.

Still, the essence of Chinese education filtered through, even its unabashed militarism. "I won an event at our school's athletic games and got to compete in the big city games," the eleven-year-old son of an American diplomat told us with excitement. "What event?" we asked. "The grenade throw," he said. Joe came home one day with an art project, a four-foot-long scroll-like drawing of the Great Wall of China on which he had labored for weeks. Some fierce and ugly-looking figures near the wall were, he reported, "the Russians attacking on horseback." Fighter aircraft clashed incongruously overhead. Atop the wall, repulsing the invaders with cannon and crossbows, were Chinese soldiers. "They're the good guys," Joe said.

With all this flow of good feeling, the most bittersweet aspect of life in China was the realization that the Chinese with whom we were most likely to make friends were those whose job it was to inform on us. A cheerful, bespectacled Cantonese woman in her early thirties, Hou Ying proved herself a conscientious employee. Besides turning out reams of Chinese-English translations every day, she also sparred with the Chinese bureaucracy on Linda's behalf, prescribed Chinese herbs for Jay's colds and tolerated the occasional presence of our two sons in the hotel room that served as the *Los Angeles Times* office.

What especially endeared Hou to us was that she was free of political cant. One day she declared that she intended to have no more children. Linda was curious. She asked Hou whether that was because of the new government policy that offered financial rewards to couples who stopped after one child. Hou laughed, as if Linda were daft. "No—having a baby hurts too much," she said. "Childbirth was the worst experience of my life."

Linda and Hou had some difficulty deciding what to call each other. In the end they opted for an old Chinese custom: When in Peking, do as the Pekingese do. Chinese co-workers address each other by the last name, but soften the effect by appending an adjective that indicates whether the other person is older or younger. Five months younger than Linda, Hou became Xiao Hou (Little Hou), and seemed happy with it. Linda, however, was not crazy about being called Lao Ma, or Old Mathews. Translated literally, it was even worse: Old Horse.

Linda had to keep reminding herself that the woman she was becoming so fond of, who was glued to her side eight hours a day, actually worked for the Chinese government. Seasoned diplomats said we should assume that, in her cheerful way, Xiao Hou was keeping tabs on our family. The same, we were told, held true for the interpreter who worked for Jay.

Linda once put her feelings about this relationship in an article, which Hou read. After a moment's silence, she asked, "Do you think I'm spying on you?"

"Yes, in a way I do," Linda said.

"I'm not a spy."

"Well, perhaps not in the strict sense of the term, but if I ever do something out of the ordinary, something you hear or see, I think you are likely to be asked about it. And you will have to make some kind of a report. Am I wrong?" Hou did not reply.

We, like Hou, had come to assume that both of us were being watched, the fate of foreign journalists in any totalitarian state. The watchers were not as obtrusive as in the Soviet Union, and we rarely thought about it. Our cars were issued special "double O" license plates, which clearly identified us as foreign journalists. Travel outside Peking required special permission from the Foreign Ministry, at least two days in advance. (A general ban on journalist travel had begun to lift by the time we moved to Peking, however, and soon it was possible to visit dozens of Chinese cities being opened to tourists, and even a few, like Fuzhou [Foochow] and Xiamen [Amoy], which were not.)

Some foreign students based in Peking initiated a fad—seeing how far they could get beyond the city limits. They found that if they dressed as Tibetans, Uighurs or other national minorities, the army guards would generally overlook them. Once caught, they would be returned to Peking with a scolding. One Canadian traveled a hundred miles into Gansu (Kansu) province before he was caught. Two Frenchwomen took an unauthorized bus trip to Tibet, lasting several days, and were last seen bicycling on the streets of Lhasa.

Our telephone conversations were—to judge from the strange sounds we heard on the line—monitored occasionally. Calls to the American embassy or to the office of Agence France-Presse, which had closely reported the 1979 democracy movement, were at times almost inaudible. This may have been due to the amount of listening equipment plugged in from outside. A Hungarian diplomat tried to call a friend in Hong Kong from his Shanghai hotel. When the operator learned that the conversation was to be in Hungarian, she apologized and said the call could not be placed at that moment. Three hours later the phone rang in the diplomat's room and a voice said, in passable Hungarian, "You may make your call now." The wife of an East European journalist we know picked up the phone one day to hear a tape of a conversation her husband had had the day before being played back. "They must have hit the 'Play' instead of the 'Record' button," she said.

An American diplomat's wife was distressed when one of her previous night's dinner guests called to say he had found someone else's keys in his coat pocket. The hostess called the owner of the keys on the telephone and said she had found a beautiful new scarf she just had to bring over right away. She picked up the keys from the first dinner guest and delivered them to the rightful owner. Why the ruse? She wanted to disguise the incident on the telephone because she believed that her housekeeper, or the waiters catering the dinner, had made a mistake replacing what they found in the coat pockets of all her guests. She didn't want their superiors to hear about the mistake; good help was hard to come by.

Jay would occasionally open the glove compartment of his car and find a journal of our comings and goings, including our younger son's trips to nursery school, as written by our warm and efficient driver, Wang Fachen. One foreign student at Peking University said that an hour after mailing a letter home in which she complained about the lack of hot water, a Chinese official was at her door, asking if she was happy and reciting her complaints. Perhaps he had read the letter, or perhaps news of what she had told friends had reached him and the sight of the letter home simply spurred him to action.

An official at Canton's Zhongshan University was much more blunt when she turned over to visiting UCLA scholar Perry Link an academic report on Canton youth that had been mailed to him by a colleague in Los Angeles.

"How did he learn all these things about Canton?" the official asked.

"I don't know. I haven't read it yet," Perry said.

"I have," she said.

We acquired a queasy sense of people looking over our shoulders. The Foreign Ministry received copies of our stories from the cable office as soon as we filed them, which we learned when a Foreign Ministry official mentioned to Linda the content of one of her stories that day only two hours after she had sent it off. But our articles were never censored while we were in Peking. The last time anything like that had happened, as far as we could discover, was in 1972 when John Burns, then of the *Toronto Globe and Mail,* dropped off a story at the cable office about a secret, unhappy meeting between Chou En-lai and Pham Van Dong that indicated deterioration of Sino-Vietnamese ties. The minute Burns returned home he was summoned by telephone to the Foreign Ministry. "I knew I was in trouble when Ma Youzhen [probably the best English speaker in the ministry] pulled a statement out of his pocket and began to read it in Chinese," Burns said. An English interpretation followed, informing Burns that his cable had abused the friendship of the Chinese people and sought to sow discord between them and the Vietnamese people. Burns decided the story was not worth losing the *Globe and Mail* bureau in Peking, so he agreed to Ma's demand that he not transmit it to Toronto in any fashion.

After Mao's death in 1976, the Chinese ceased even to give chilly warnings to correspondents who wrote articles their hosts considered unfavorable. Someone in the Foreign Ministry realized that it was best to pay such outrages no notice at all, and let the offending articles be quietly buried under the daily avalanche of other news. The earlier, hypersensitive approach surfaced at least two more times, in 1977 when the Foreign Ministry refused to extend the visa of Burns's successor, Ross H. Munro, and in 1981 when the ministry officially reprimanded Jay's successor, Michael Weisskopf of the *Washington Post*. Both had written stories about labor camps and other Chinese deficiencies in human rights, and in both cases the mild warnings only served to draw more attention overseas to their articles.

The Chinese do find foreigners entertaining, hence the stares and gathering crowds, even in cities like Canton long used to hordes of tourists. In conversation, the Chinese emphasize how much China can learn from the West; at least, that is what they have been encouraged to say by a government that wants to inspire its citizens to catch up with the West. But the most prevalent and apparently honest reactions we saw alternated between deference and contempt.

A prevalent view of Westerners, part of the general disdain for those outside the Middle Kingdom, was expressed in the sixteenth century by one of the first Chinese to meet Europeans: "They understand to a certain degree the distinction between superior and inferior, but I do not know whether they have a proper system of ceremonial etiquette . . . They show their feelings without any self-control . . . They are a people who spend their lives roving here and there." While the deference to foreigners later forced on the Chinese by the opium wars and the various European military victories never set well, the Chinese have failed to shake some habits of deference even today.

In the context of China's socialist commitment to equal treatment for all, the almost feudal courtesies extended to foreigners, such as inviting them into special shops or giving them good seats in theaters, surprise many visitors and irritate many Chinese. Foreign life styles in China in the 1980s in some ways recall the last century, which ended with the Boxer Rebellion and the siege of the foreign legations in 1900. In that year, people probably very much like us—Americans and Europeans drawn to the beauty and mystery of China—mounted walls near our hotel in Peking and fired rifles at mobs of Chinese attempting to break into their compound.

One day in Nanning, in southeast China, a few American journalists stopped at the local Friendship Store, one of the several "foreigners only" shops found throughout China. Jay bought a Coke and was inspecting some of the silk hangings for sale when he heard a commotion near the front door. An old man, wearing shabby blue clothes and a long beard, stood outside and shouted, "Why can't I go in there? All those foreigners can go in!" A store clerk smiled nervously and tried to quiet the man. "Isn't my money good enough? Damn it, this is not fair!" He took a few coins out of his pocket and threw them at the clerk's feet.

At the other extreme, foreigners represent an escape route for the discontented, the desperate, the disaffected. A young American graduate student we met at the Peking Languages Institute told us about a beautiful Chinese woman he met on a bus. He was captivated by her, but thought nothing would come of it until, apparently by chance, he met her again a week later in an antique shop. "I happened to turn around and there she was, smiling at me," he said. "This was Thanksgiving. By December 4 we had decided to get married. She was lovely, and a very different girl. She said she hated Chinese men. She said they were silly, aggressive and stupid. She worked in a factory and she hated her life. After seeing China through her eyes, from the point of view of someone I cared about, the harshness of life here got to me too.

"We made plans. I heard a rumor (which proved groundless) that in a few weeks the Chinese authorities would ban all further marriages of Chinese with foreigners. I began to look into this, but while I was doing that, she missed a date we had had to see each other." He was frightened that something had happened to her. She had never been cautious, even kissing him once at a public bus stop.

When he went looking for her the mystery solved itself. She was at the home of another young man, a Chinese. "Both of them gasped when they saw me. They jumped up, so I knew something was going on. It was like something out of a Chinese melodrama; perhaps that was exactly what it was. I felt angry and spiteful. She seemed to want to try to draw me out about the rumored marriage ban without tipping off her friend. 'Did you check out that little matter?' she asked me. I played dumb. 'What matter?' I said. 'You know, you know, *that* matter,' she said. The man could tell from her face that something was not right. 'Didn't you tell him?' he asked her. 'What *did* you tell him?'

"I spoke up: 'She said she loved me.' He looked like he was ready to take her head off. I decided that as bad as I felt, it was time for me to be gallant or she wouldn't have anything left."

Then they told him their story. The day he met her in the antique shop she had been fired from her factory job. She was already on a one-year probation and had been absent too many times. Without a job, she had no wages, no legal residence and no way to get permission to marry.

"They loved each other, but she saw me as her last chance. If she could get to the States, she could find a way to bring him too, later on."

As much as the Chinese may abuse the chances they have now for friendships with foreigners, an escape from the system denied them in the recent past, they also may use foreigners as a first step in restoring friendship itself as a Chinese institution.

A Shanghai college student, a quiet young woman with an habitually pained expression, asked an American exchange scholar we knew to take a walk with her. The two women strolled the campus for a while. When they were out of earshot of other students, the young Chinese woman began to pour out a long list of personal frustrations. Her life was too dull. Her high school education had been so interrupted by political campaigns that she was struggling in college. Her professors had told her that the best job she could hope for was teaching school in some rural commune. The American, somewhat taken aback, asked if there wasn't some way to work out these problems. Why didn't she talk this over with her close friends? "That would not be wise," the Chinese woman said.

China Travel Service guides usually keep their feelings to themselves, but Tao Yongsheng, whom we met in Nanjing (Nanking), proved unusually warm and friendly. We talked about his job, the price of vegetables, the health of Deng Xiaoping (Teng Hsiao-ping). At forty, Tao had acquired a measure of confidence with foreigners. But he paused when we broached the subject of friendship. "It is hard to say who my best friends are now. Before the Cultural Revolution, many of us found that our friendships were not as valuable as we thought, so people are less willing to confide in other people now." A television technician in Hefei said, "A close friend now, who has passed the test and not betrayed you during the campaigns, that is someone who will be close to you always. You can talk to him without fear of what is in your heart. But such people are very rare." A Peking teacher said, "You might meet people who seem to be the best of friends, but often they don't trust each other at all."

It is thirty years since the word "comrade" *(tong zhi)* became the proper term of address for all Chinese. It symbolized not only new speech patterns but what Communist leaders thought would be a revolution in personal relationships. Instead, the change the Communists sought seriously damaged ordinary day-to-day discourse and ended millions of friendships. What a friend told you of his slightest doubts about new government policies could be—*had* to be—revealed at weekly political study sessions. Small talk over tea could result in a prison sentence.

Political pressures were relaxed after Mao died in 1976. Routine meetings to criticize school friends or co-workers became less common. But the Chinese we know say it is still difficult to be frank with more than one or two people in their lives, and even that is risky. The thirty-year effort to make everyone a comrade, ready for public praise or blame, and outlaw special friends, has made trusting friendships rare. When they occur, as they still do for some Chinese, they are, in the word of one woman, "wonderful." But such friendships provide a quiet, potentially powerful threat to the sort of widespread personal allegiance the Chinese Communist Party must have to survive, so they remain suspect and full of risk.

The novelist Ding Ling once told an interviewer that in China, "when there are only two persons, they talk frankly. When there are three, they tell jokes, and when there are four, they tell lies." University of California Professor Susan L. Shirk, in a study of personal relationships among Chinese high school students, concluded that "under a system in which anyone can gain career advantage by betraying a friend, loyalty to friends becomes more highly valued."

It is enough to worry the *People's Daily.* Commentator Yu Li said in 1980: "Some people do not distinguish between right and wrong and cast aside principles in dealing with their relatives, fellow townsmen, or with persons having an 'old relationship' with them or regarded as their 'friends.' When this type of person has shortcomings, makes mistakes or does evil things, they do not criticize and struggle against him, but treat him leniently and even try to condone and protect him."

Friendship was the last of the five relationships sanctified by Confucius, but it was the one relationship where both parties were equal. It offered relief from the severe obligations to higher authority represented by the more important relationships.

Today, too, people need a respite from having to worry about not offending party supervisors in the party line—and friendships help in an economy plagued by chronic shortages. One Peking worker said, "We really count on our friends, and not just for listening to our thoughts. If my friend sees some good shoes suddenly put on sale at the store where he happens to be, I expect him to buy a pair for me as well as for himself." A long-time foreign resident of Peking, comparing habits in China and the West, said, "The Chinese place intolerable demands on a friend, such as taking care of their kids for long periods, and you best be prepared to reciprocate."

The obsession with friendship is so strong that it spills into China's official dealings with foreigners and foreign governments. A Pennsylvania businessman new to China shook his head as he thought of the photos of Josef Stalin that occasionally adorn meeting rooms in China, a testament to Stalin's early interest in the Chinese Communist Party that overlooked all the harm he did the Maoists during his lifetime. The businessman said with a sigh, "Josef Stalin is a friend. Richard Nixon is a friend. People who first came here seven years ago will be getting the contracts, because they are friends." The Chinese love to quote the late Premier Chou En-lai: "When drinking from the well, remember the well-digger."

Trading favors, the old "back door" network, is a national pastime. But the Chinese say they can usually risk confiding personal thoughts only to a single friend, and such trusting ties are not easy to find. Friendship took a horrible beating in the Cultural Revolution. The stories of betrayal abound, from the very top of the leadership on down. A Peking office worker talked to us once, hesitantly, about the aches and annoyances of working side by side in the post-Mao era with the man whose denunciations had sent him out to a lonely and difficult farm assignment in arid northern Anhui (Anhwei) for several years. The fact that so many other people were sent to the countryside helped heal some of these wounds, but the man told us, "I can forgive, but I can never forget. People like to repeat an old saying: 'Once a snake bites you, you are even frightened by a rope.'"

Friendships usually begin in school. They have the clannish flavor of old-boy networks from American and British private schools. The vivid quality of Chinese writing and Chinese puns makes nicknames very popular. Names like "Bullethead," "Old Devil," "Earthquake," "Football," and even "Cowturd" are fixed to their owners by friends and enemies. Hou weighs barely 110 pounds now, but to friends who knew her in high school she is still "Little Fatty." Another friend acquired the nickname "Lao Jiu" (Old Ninth) when he worked in the Chinese embassy in Sweden. It had a dual meaning made possible by the quirks of the Chinese language: there was a hero named "Old Ninth" in the opera *Taking Tiger Mountain by Strategy,* whose libretto our friend could sing. There was also the derogatory term for intellectuals, the "stinking ninth category." Our friend was certainly an intellectual, a graduate of Peking University, but he said the embassy drivers were just kidding.

The Chinese will select their closest friends from those with the same class background—doctors' sons will befriend professors' sons, daughters of steelworkers will make friends with construction foremen's offspring. Usually the friend will be of the same age and also of the same sex. "If male and female go anywhere together, for the most innocent of reasons, there will be too much talk," a Peking office worker said.

Urban dwellers expect to be working alongside the same people, and often living in the same apartment complex until they die. Gossip becomes a favorite pastime, and information about others accumulates even without benefit of close friendships. "Everybody knows *everything,*" complained one overseas Chinese unaccustomed to such clannishness. A friend told her all of her career plans for next year, quite plausible ones, long before she had made up her mind about them.

In such an atmosphere, friendship sometimes profits from a little distance. Many Chinese, asked who their best friend is, will name a high school classmate who now lives in a different city and can only communicate by letter. "My best friend is a primary-school teacher near my home village," said Xu Xingan, a guide in Hangzhou (Hangchow). "We have been friends since we were sixteen. I liked his temperament, we helped each other and played basketball and ping-pong together. He came to my wedding dinner, and I went to his, but it is a long time since I have seen him."

Having spent such time and thought in choosing who their friends are, the Chinese cringe at the casual ways of Americans. They dislike the volley of personal questions—Where did you go to school? What are your children's names? A special Chinese-language booklet—written by Alison R. Lanier and published by the U.S. government for Chinese visitors to the United States—asks for Chinese understanding: "Americans do not have the time for formalities. They must get to know you today because in a short time they may move to another city far across the country."

Americans in turn are hurt when Chinese acquaintanceships they expect to deepen into friendship never do. The Chinese realize such relationships may lead to questions from their superiors in the future; they may routinely lie about foreign contacts or become habitually forgetful. We can go to China, but we cannot ever really belong, even when we create our own units.

As foreign journalists visiting and then living in China, we experienced both Chinese warmth and coldness, often in rapid succession. To the Chinese government, we were guests, taking a first step toward friendship which should have drawn us into the obligations of *guanxi*. But as journalists, pledged to report events that sometimes made the Chinese look bad, we seemed to our hosts to be simply ungrateful, and ignorant of the rules of Chinese friendship. We were either for them or against them; for many Chinese there was no middle ground except that reserved for opportunists.

It was always jarring to discover this, because so many Chinese are warm and friendly people with whom one could enjoy spending a good deal of time. We were accompanied for two weeks on our first trip to China by Xiong Xirong, a bright, witty doctor's son from Canton with a gift for colloquial English. It was a wonderful, varied trip, the three of us covering the length of the country from Canton to Shanghai, then to Peking and the Shanxi provincial village of Dazhai (Tachai). As a local Canton official, Xiong rarely traveled so far on special assignment, and this trip was made all the more memorable by the fact that Linda was eight months pregnant. We joked about what to name the baby. Xiong talked about his wife, a factory worker, and their daughter, whom he picked up from school each Saturday. We assumed we were beginning a long friendship.

A week after we said goodbye to Xiong and returned to Hong Kong, another journalist, Arnold (Skip) Isaacs of the *Baltimore Sun,* went to Canton and drew Xiong as a guide. "Did he ask about us?" Jay asked Skip when he returned.

"No," said Skip. "Actually it was kind of strange. I asked him if he knew any other American journalists. Do you know what he said? He said, 'No, not one.' "

ONE BILLION

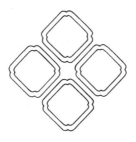

ONE BILLION

DRIVE DOWN THE MAIN STREET OF ANY LARGE CHINESE CITY—PEKING'S Avenue of Eternal Peace or Nanjing's Sun Yat-sen Avenue—and invariably you will have to swerve to avoid large crowds of people who have suddenly materialized on the center line, along the curb or even in the lane ahead of you. This phenomenon excited us the first two or three times we encountered it. Sudden crowds, we reasoned, meant news.

We would pull over and get out of our car to investigate, only to find nothing more exciting than a policeman lecturing a wayward bicyclist. It was our first lesson in what life is like in a nation with the nearly unimaginable population of one billion people. Insect analogies, as applied to the Chinese people, are usually misleading and vaguely racist, but in this case they seemed to fit. Introduce any small event, an argument among friends, a bicycle collision or even an American tourist loading a camera, and the Chinese behave like ants converging on a few spilled grains of sugar.

One billion. It is important to appreciate just what that number means. Every fifth human being is Chinese. At their current rate of population growth, Chinese could march single file into the Yellow Sea forever without causing the slightest decrease in China's total population. If they marched four abreast, day and night, it would still be the next century before the whole population disappeared beneath the waves.

Although China has gathered the largest harvests in world history in the last few years, its people are eating barely more grain now than they did twenty-five years ago. Despite a nearly 50 percent increase in total housing in 192 cities since 1949, the space available for each person has declined from 48 to about 40 square feet. Grain, cloth, soap, light bulbs, bicycles and dozens of other commodities are rationed. Long lines are everywhere. We never boarded a bus in China on which there was an empty seat.

With only 5 percent of the world's arable land to feed about 23 percent of the world's people, the Chinese have stretched the capacity of their fields to the limit. Forests are so depleted that the men who delivered our furniture in Peking argued over who would salvage the packing crates—they use them to make their own furniture. The effects of erosion and drought have been worsened by wholesale cutting of trees and brush to make room for crops.

China has plenty of wide-open spaces. The western parts of the country —the Tibetan highlands, the deserts and mountain ranges of Xinjiang (Sinkiang), Qinghai (Chinghai) and Inner Mongolia, which account for 50 percent of the land—are virtually empty, with only 5 percent of the population living there. Thus the crowding of the eastern port cities and river valleys is even worse than one would expect.

Every year 22 million youths enter the labor market, but few find anything but farm work awaiting them. Many of the city youths go on waiting lists, which have grown very long since the government stopped sending all jobless city school graduates to the countryside.

Chinese cities exist on make-work. Every park employs dozens of ticket takers, some to collect the ten cents for a ticket, some to collect the ticket, some to collect the stub. Even self-operating elevators always have "operators." Hotels smother in room attendants. Even with the most conscientious attention to birth control, these problems will never go away.

How can an American or a European grasp the crowding? Imagine your own office or factory with two or three times as many employees as it has now, working in the same space, with the same volume of work. The inefficiency and sloth that would result are accepted as natural in China. A woman who worked in a Shanghai factory told us she ran out of clerical chores by noon; her co-workers passed the afternoon playing the numbers. Workers at crowded parts of assembly lines jump out of their chairs when visitors pass by and try to look busier than they are.

When a worker gets home, the crush is worse. Parents or grandparents must share beds with their children or grandchildren. The rooms are usually so small that the sleeping platforms or beds half fill them. Dressing and undressing have to be done in turns. Peking, Shanghai and many other large cities have become so stuffed with people that they are using air-raid shelters as dining halls and temporary hotels.

A young Peking violinist told us he had been assigned to share a tiny dormitory room with another student twelve years ago. After graduating and joining an orchestra, both young men remained in the dormitory room. There was no other place to go. Five years later his musician friend was desperate to marry and begged his supervisor for housing. The supervisor was agreeable: "We'll put your roommate somewhere else and your wife can move in with you."

When we met them, the musician and his wife were still living in the dormitory, but they now had a small child. Their kitchen was a small portable gas burner in the common hallway, a dank canyon of cement without any light. They shared a filthy toilet with twelve other people. Still, they didn't feel their situation was unusual.

As we slipped into the routine of Chinese life, we saw more of the inevitable bumping and jostling that comes when there are too many people in too little space. Never in our lives have we witnessed as many fistfights as we did in Peking. Two fights began within the span of ten minutes one Sunday morning at Zhongshan (Central Hill) Park, as we, along with apparently every other couple in Peking, tried to get our children on the park's decrepit but popular airplane ride. Such outbursts usually ended as quickly as they began, for the mob of onlookers made it nearly impossible for the combatants to move.

After years of guessing how many people they had, the Chinese finally counted themselves in July 1982. The total was 1,008,175,288, not including 23 million or so on Taiwan and in the European-governed territories of Hong Kong and Macao. The count took 50 million census takers. They found that one of every four Chinese—a total of 235.8 million—could not read or write. Eighteen of the country's twenty-one provinces had populations greater than Canada's. Of the total, 801.6 million lived in the countryside, in circumstances more typical of the last century than this one.

Chinese officials have been counting noses for two thousand years because they have considered population growth prime evidence that they hold the mandate of heaven. The latest growth spurt, from about 520 million to one billion people in three decades, is only the latest and most impressive sign of the Chinese dynastic cycle. In ancient times, emperors who built efficient dikes and irrigation schemes expected better harvests and more babies. Their successors enjoyed the prosperity which resulted before the inevitable slide into corruption and inefficiency exacerbated by overpopulation. Famine and war eventually wiped out the old dynasty, and opened the way for a new one.

In A.D. 2 the Han dynasty reported a population of 59,594,978, considered by scholars today a fair approximation of the actual number of Chinese alive at the time of Christ's birth. The total equaled the population of the Roman Empire, and subsequent dynasties would be even more populous than the Han. After the fall of Rome, no other single government body in the world was ever able again to claim as many people under its rule as China.

The last Chinese dynasty, the Qing (1644–1911), was the most prosperous of all and laid the groundwork for the huge population of twentieth-century China. The Qing enjoyed a long period of domestic peace and prosperity, which raised the population to a reported 142 million in 1741 and 432 million in 1851. The Qing emperors, Manchus from north of the Great Wall, opened new lands to cultivation. Along with tobacco, seafaring Europeans brought agricultural riches that improved the Chinese diet; maize, sweet potatoes and peanuts were all introduced from abroad in the sixteenth or early-seventeenth centuries. The sweet potato, in particular, became what it is today, a hardy, fast-growing staple which the Chinese don't like to eat but which saves millions from starvation when rice and wheat crops fail.

As in previous dynasties, the Qing imperial civil service could not cope with the population growth. Eventually the military forces proved too small and too softened by barracks life to keep order. The dynastic cycle took its usual downward spin. But this time the whole Chinese system collapsed from the unprecedented seaborne invasion of arms, technology and ideology from Europe.

By 1949, after half a century of internal disruption, invasion, civil war and famine, the old cycle of returning prosperity resumed under the Communists. The marvels of the twentieth century accelerated the whole process. The Chinese had never enjoyed such abundance of modern medicine and improved agriculture. They embarked on a baby-making binge unequaled in human history. The official Chinese census reported 576.049 million in 1953, with few believing that number could nearly double by 1982.

The overwhelming numbers may be old news, but never before have they been so essential to the world's perception of China's importance. The extraordinary reality of one billion people under one government eclipses even the grandeur of Chinese civilization and China's natural resources and historical wonders. The human *potential* for economic, diplomatic and military power brings American Presidents and French arms dealers rushing to Peking. China's numbers have given the country a permanent seat on the United Nations Security Council and pushed China's intricate and often inconclusive internal political struggles onto the front pages of world newspapers. No other underdeveloped country has as many American correspondents based in its capital.

Until recently, the Chinese openly reveled in their numbers with a reckless kind of pride. In 1949 Mao Tse-tung blithely called China's huge population a "good thing" and predicted that it could multiply "many times" without hindering national development. Although the government launched birth control drives in the early 1950s and again in the early 1960s, both attempts failed because of Maoist doubts about any attempt to limit the power of the masses and because of substantial popular resistance to birth control.

Now they are trying again. In 1980 the government rehabilitated Ma Yinchu, a distinguished economist who had been reviled for twenty years because of his commitment to population control. Many Chinese demographers not only call for zero population growth but suggest an eventual *reduction* of the population. Given the Chinese obsession with family life, it is difficult to imagine the government enforcing its one-child-per-family limit for the required several decades, but many Chinese policy makers see no other way out of the dilemma.

The new one-child-per-family rule leads to birth control methods which are not strictly voluntary. Factory officials routinely ask women workers what birth control methods they use, and monitor their menstrual periods. Forced abortions and sterilizations are relatively common for unmarried women or women with two children. Stanford researcher Steven Mosher discovered abortions of fetuses in the third trimester while living in one Guangdong commune. When Stephen Butler, an American researcher living in a remote Hebei (Hopeh) commune, asked what could be done about couples who were not signing the one-child-one-family pledge, a local official answered, with conviction, "All *will* sign the pledge this year."

John Brunner's science-fiction classic, *Stand on Zanzibar,* describes a world of the near future so overpopulated that men with inherited color-blindness are denied permission to have children. Some reputable Chinese are considering this approach. A leading Chinese birth control authority, Zhong Huilan, has proposed active efforts to discourage the color-blind, as well as sufferers of mental illness, hemophilia and other diseases Zhong calls "congenital," from having children. Dr. Richard Ross, dean of the Johns Hopkins medical faculty, found the Chinese intensely interested in gathering information on genetic engineering in the United States. "Since everyone can have only one child, we want to make sure that child is a good one," one Chinese scientist told Ross.

Urban Chinese we met seemed to have mixed feelings about the one-child goal. Few couples have room for more than one child and many seem untroubled by the limitations. Others resent the fact that although birth control is supposedly voluntary, their supervisors act as if it were mandatory. "We are not allowed to have two children any longer," one office worker said flatly.

In the countryside, families still seem to find ways to exceed the one-child limit. Census takers in 1982 were surprised to discover that the population had grown by 1.45 percent in 1981 (higher than estimated) and the second straight year in which the growth rate had gone up instead of down. For a government straining to get the growth rate below 1 percent, it was a bad setback. The official press lectures peasants who resist birth control and threaten stiffer measures, but the emotional toll from forced sterilization and abortion could backfire, forcing the same sort of outrage that shook India in 1975. But for the moment, Chinese demographers assume their programs will work.

One population study team reported: "If the average birth rate begins to drop markedly this year and is reduced to only one child per couple by 1985 and this continues, China's population would continue to increase for 25 years and reach 1.054 billion by 2004, the peak year. China's population would then begin to drop after 2005 and decline to 960 million by 2028, to 613 million by 2060 and to 370 million people by 2080." A Chinese friend of ours, although the father of only one child and a firm advocate of birth control, rolled his eyes at this prediction. "That will *never* happen," he said. "Once we get any room, we're going to fill it up again."

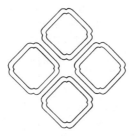

CITY

THE LITTLE CITY OF GUILIN (KWEILIN) IS A GOOD PLACE TO WATCH THE Chinese day unfold, for there city and country are very close. Here in Guangxi (Kwangsi) province, on one side of the Li River, near Liberation Bridge, patchwork fields stretch in front of hills as jagged as pieces of rock candy. On the other side, dusty concrete streets swarm with bell-ringing bicyclists. Morning is the time when Chinese city folk seem closest to their country brethren, getting up with the sun.

You must be up by five or five-thirty or miss the first rush of bicycles, buses and sidewalk vendors jamming the streets. At summer's dawn in Guilin, a thousand miles south of Peking, everyone appears to be eating something. Workers in faded blue pants and short-sleeved shirts hold chunks of steamed bread as they walk toward bus stops. From dank, dark little noodle shops along the avenue come sounds of enthusiastic slurping and clicking of chopsticks. City people linger over their dinners at night, but in the morning fast food is a habit—factory supervisors expect their people at work on time. The commuter bus on Guilin's main street begins to pull away from the curb. Half a block away a woman clutching a cylindrical lunch pail begins to run and yell frantically, "Don't go! Don't go!" She chases the bus for a block, but it does not stop.

Even in an area as picturesque as Guilin, with green mountains in fanciful shapes and blue lakes all around, much of the city life displays all the charm of an office filing cabinet laid on its side. Attractive stores and browsing spots for the early shopper are rare. Signs on nearly every makeshift little clapboard building proclaim serious bureaucratic tasks performed within. "Factory Production Section, Economic Management Division, Guilin City Industrial Bureau," reads the sign on one storefront. Next door is the "Number Two Gate Section of the Guilin City Fruit Products Company," followed by the office of the "Face the Sun People's Commune of New Culture Street."

In similar summer morning heat, we once walked down Liberation Road in Canton, several hundred miles to the southeast, passing dozens of houses with doors left wide open to let in fresh air. Residents performed their morning chores—combing hair, eating breakfast, checking bicycle tires—oblivious to the glances of curious people passing by the small wooden storefrontlike houses. One small boy, about seven, was laboriously copying his homework. He could barely see what he was doing; the tiny room had no lamp, only weak morning light coming through the doorway.

It has become habit, this making do with tiny rooms and few amenities. Only a fifth of China's billion people live in cities, but that number is nearly equal to the population of the United States. Nothing more amplifies the Chinese obsession with *guanxi*, with measuring every action as it will affect the neighbors, than this lack of space. Everywhere people share kitchens and toilets, and envy those friends with a few more square feet of floor than they have.

The lack of adequate housing in the cities readily provides material for comedians. One radio dialogue:

Wang: "My girl friend and I have gone steady for eight years and we registered to marry four years ago, but without a room, how can we wed? I'm so frantic I can't see straight. You've just got to help me."

Li: "How can I, unless I move out and let you have my room?"

Wang: "That would be fine."

Li: "Fine for you, but what about me? Where would I live?"

Wang: "I've got an idea. Doesn't my fiancée work in a packing-case plant? They're selling off extra big packing cases cheap—I'll buy you a couple to live in for the time being."

Life imitates art. Packing-box shanties can be seen on the side streets of Peking and Canton, usually populated by rural people who have received permission to move into town but cannot find any housing.

"At least the floors are nice," said our violinist friend of his converted dormitory housing. He did not have the usual bare or painted concrete floors. Wood planks left over from construction of the Great Hall of the People (the huge party and government headquarters) had been sent over when his building was put up. His shared toilet has a shower; the hot water comes on only for a half-hour at noon, when the orchestra dining room is also open. "You have to choose whether to shower or have lunch," he said.

At least 35 percent of the families in China's cities have housing problems, the official *Enlightenment* (or *Guangming*) *Daily* reported in 1980: 5 to 6 percent are couples with no housing at all, so they stay with relatives or in public reception centers. The average floor space per person often falls below 20 square feet, the basic minimum supposedly guaranteed everyone in China. An official study said total housing floor space in 192 cities in 1978 had gained 46.7 percent since 1949, but at the same time the population of those cities had increased 83 percent, so the average space per person had declined about 10 square feet.

Block 11, Lane 938, Heavenly Mountain Road, part of a workers' housing development on Shanghai's western edge, illustrates how new generations crowd in with the old. In apartment 301 lives Zhou Hounian, a retired rubber worker, with her husband Hu Jinhua, sixty-one, a retired supply clerk, their thirty-six-year-old son, twenty-seven-year-old daughter-in-law and two grandsons, twelve and ten. They share two bedrooms, each about 120 square feet. The grandparents and grandsons sleep in the same room in two double beds. The entire apartment, like most dwellings in China, needs a fresh coat of paint. But the family has decorated it with brightly colored posters of smiling workers. Under glass tabletops they have placed scores of family photographs.

They all step from their bedrooms into a narrow hall that connects them with another family, whose bedrooms are located at the other end. Off the hall is a common bathroom, and a tiny common kitchen. To the Hu family, living like this seems an improvement: before 1960, when they first moved into this block of then brand-new apartments, Zhou, her husband and two children shared a much smaller space—only 72 square feet. The grandchildren, of course, now again reduce the feeling of spaciousness.

The Hus' daughter, twenty-eight, studies and lives at a local university. With four incomes remaining in the family, they have no trouble paying the rent—$5 a month. The apartment building itself is stained and grimy, but there are few cracked windows and no graffiti. Flower boxes adorn the windows. Their home may be humble, but it is a bit of space they can call their own.

For the sake of comparison, we visited a like-size family in a village, the Fangtai Farm Brigade, several miles into the Shanghai suburbs. Living with her husband, their two small children and her husband's parents, Hu Yueceng told us that the family actually owns the house. In collectivized China, peasants are often homeowners. Hu said it cost $1,100 to build. A special crew from the commune did the work with the family's help and materials, in return for a fee. They have three rooms and a back-door kitchen they do not have to share. "We had saved eight hundred and fifty dollars and got a loan of two hundred and fifty dollars from the brigade for the rest," Hu said. The brigade owns the land and charges a nominal rent fee for it.

Higher-level officials, of course, get more spacious quarters than regular workers. He Jingping, the military commander for Peking's western district, took over the villa of a disgraced intellectual during the Cultural Revolution in 1969. The place had ten rooms, and he spent about $11,000 in public funds to add a second bathroom and kitchen. When the intellectual was rehabilitated, the city tried to return the house to him, but the general resisted. He even exaggerated the number of people living there, so that his abuse of privilege would not seem so serious.

Still, China's precious floor space is more evenly distributed now than it was before 1949. Harvard history Professor John K. Fairbank and his wife,

Wilma, a specialist in Asian art, lived in Peking in the early 1930s, and according to Mrs. Fairbank, had "a nice house with plenty of room for us and five servants." We guessed there might be four families sharing those quarters now, but the Fairbanks had already checked: there were seven. By the late 1970s the tenants had constructed so many new rooms that the original house's central courtyard had virtually disappeared.

Every office and factory maintains a list of employees who are seeking better housing; the lists are closely held, but people with special influence can find ways to move their names quickly to the top. "Going in the back door" becomes particularly important in the housing crunch. The official press sporadically scolds officials who trade favors for more space, but the practice seems so widespread and so potentially useful to everyone that most Chinese we know say they accept it as unavoidable.

In the Luwan district of Shanghai, the man in charge of assignment at the Housing Division Bureau forced people appealing to him for apartments to lend their children as unpaid servants in his home. Corrupt housing practices have become common enough for Peking's comedians to incorporate them in routines like this:

Chao complains to Li that he can't get an apartment in a new building because all the units have been allotted to top officials.

Chao: "The health officer in the ministry, she gets an apartment. Vice Minister Wang okayed that."

Li: "Why?"

Chao: "He had to. She's the one who gives him medicine and injections. If he hadn't let her have an apartment and she was peeved, she could jab her needle in so that it hurts."

Li: "Why does Party Secretary Li get an apartment?"

Chao: "He says he's even worse off. Although there are only three in his family, once his son grows up and marries he'll need a room."

Li: "How old is his son?"

Chao: "Already eight."

Chinese find clever ways to create space. After the 1976 Tangshan earthquake shook northern China, thousands of families built "temporary" mud-brick shelters along roads and in courtyards because their high-rise apartments were judged unsafe. Many ignored the dangers and just sent a few family members, usually the newly married couples, out to the shelter to leave more room in the family apartment. The shelters were ordered torn down in 1978, but we have stumbled into out-of-the-way courtyards in Chinese apartment complexes where they still stand. "It helps solve some of the young people's housing problems," said a bus driver whose apartment overlooks four such extralegal shelters, their brown walls brushed clean and neat in the dusty courtyard.

By 1980 authorities in several Chinese cities had begun to try out a device used in the Soviet Union—housing exchanges—in order to ease the widespread unhappiness with living quarters. This is a step beyond the handwritten requests for trades posted on telephone poles in many cities. People wanting to exchange their current apartments for something closer to work meet at special offices with other residents who also want to trade. "It only works if you've got a little more room than you need," one participant said. "A man with a good three-room apartment on the east side isn't going to trade with me—even if he works near where I live—unless I've also got a three-room place, or maybe three rooms and my own separate bathroom." Yet during one of these "fairs" at a downtown middle school, 2,500 people showed up, including a cartographer with three signs around his neck: "Who wants to go north?"; "Who wants to go to Chongwenmen?"; and "Who wants to go to Xuanwumen?" He spent two hours a day commuting and wanted to move closer to work; he also wanted to move his parents closer to him and help a friend find a place. Many at the fair were hoping to find apartments separate from their parents, the dream of many Chinese over age thirty. Some said their children were too hard on the grandparents; others said their mothers and wives clashed. Yet only twenty-five of the families actually managed to arrange moves at the fair.

In 1980 the Western District Housing Office in Peking said it had arranged exchanges for 13,200 families in three years. An office established in Kaifeng in Henan said it solved more than half of the 1,400 cases brought to it. But the arrangements we encountered were often spur-of-the-moment deals designed to avoid the authorities altogether. Some moved into the flat of a friend who was moving out, or who was working in another city, and held on to the place despite official disapproval. Mere possession of the key is often enough to forestall the sluggish housing bureaucracy.

Makeshift solutions abound, though some seem almost more trouble than they are worth. Suzheng, a tall, thin and dour worker in a Peking food factory, was, at age thirty-nine, still unmarried, a situation that caused much gossip and some harsh words from his mother. He got himself a fiancée, but he had no room for her. "I finally found a peasant out in the suburbs who would let me rent a room," Suzheng said, staring down at his faded gray pants and scratching his crew cut. He said this was one of a number of informal arrangements that survive despite official abhorrence for the landlord system. The room was not expensive, but he now spent an hour each way on the bus to work. His bride, a nurse in a hospital near central Peking, had a four-hour commute each day.

Maneuvering for better housing becomes enormously time-consuming and nerve-racking. A construction-company electrician, who chatted with us in his small cement-floored apartment, said he had waited a long time for a room so he could marry. At age thirty he discovered to his horror that the company he worked for was disbanding and that he would be assigned to a new enterprise. His name, near the top of the housing list at his old company, would sink to the bottom at any new company he joined. "My old unit said they would try to find something for me quickly, but our section leader for security had also requested housing and he got priority. They showed him three places and he refused all of them: one because the ceiling was so low he hit his head when he stood on the bed; one because the room had no southern exposure; and the last because, although it had a window facing south and high ceilings, it also had expensive water rates. His wife, who did not work, thought they could not afford it.

"I was getting very anxious, watching him turn down all these places. My fiancée was getting frantic. Finally our unit leadership lost patience with him and I got the third place." The water rates that the section leader's wife had thought so burdensome were thirty-five cents per person, per month. She was used to paying only four cents a month.

Much of Peking's housing consists of old-fashioned bungalows called *hutong,* also the term for the narrow alleys running by them. These are single-story brick huts grouped around small central courts. "People like them because they are quieter and have the court, and there are no stairs to climb, but they don't have central heating, and for that anyone would prefer the multistory apartment buildings," one apartment dweller said. One of the Peking comedy dialogues sums up the perfect abode in urban Chinese eyes: A housing division chief describes a place he has lined up for someone he mistakenly thinks is his boss's son. "I've found an apartment for you. On the second floor of a building, with southern exposure. Three rooms, two large and one small, plus kitchen and bathroom. The rooms are partitioned, with balconies and double windows and doors. How about it? If you don't like it, I'll find you another."

In the cities, people must contend with the sluggish construction industry, often short of materials and skilled workers. The Chinese we know sing a litany of leaky toilets, paper-thin walls, crooked windows, cracked floors, ill-fitting doors and missing window latches. The long row of apartments along Peking's West Qianmen (Front of the Gate) Road, for instance, were supposed to mark a new era: space for 25,000 Chinese in modern one-, two- and three-room apartments, each with a small kitchen, toilet and veranda. A left-wing Hong Kong newspaper boasted that 6,000 Peking families would spend New Year's Day 1979 in their new homes. New Year's came and went and the apartments stood empty, like long rows of huge tombstones. Vice Premier Deng Xiaoping inspected and pointed out some deficiencies. Stories of the lack of water pressure, heat, functioning elevators and other problems spread rapidly. People who had been promised space in the buildings were angry. "No one wanted to live in them. They were just built too high. The garbage chutes would get clogged and cause fires, and it was hard to get out of such high buildings with elevators not working," complained one Peking man who finally moved into the building. "They built them right next to that road so there is lots of noise and air pollution. They did not build enough water towers, so water pressure is not good. Some of these problems are now solved, like the lack of heating pipes in the walls. They've installed new hot-water pipes inside the apartments, not very attractive, but they are wrapped carefully and attached to a radiator."

Much of China would envy the Qianmen residents their radiators. Most of Peking's *hutong* and many apartment residents rely on small air-polluting coal-burning stoves. In the area south of the Yangtze River, which includes the huge city of Shanghai, central heating is simply not built in at all. "You go to someone's home and you shiver," said one foreign resident of Shanghai. "You drink a lot of hot tea and go to bed early. Everyone wears a lot of underwear."

In summertime, the half of Peking's 7 million people who still live in old courtyard houses also find them stiflingly hot by the end of the day. The small apartments in the new housing blocks have tiny windows and no air conditioning. So during the summer months Chinese eat in the street, play in the street, even brush their teeth and shampoo their hair in the street.

China's city folk spill out of their crowded homes like seeds from overripe fruit. Peking's Tiananmen Square, formerly the staging ground for mass rallies, fills on balmy summer nights with courting couples and card players. The young lovers hold hands in the shadows and gaze at the stars. The card players, mostly old men, squat on the pavement and slap down winning combinations in Strive to Get Upstream. Chairman Mao's only remaining public portrait gazes down on the scene from above the Gate of Heavenly Peace.

"Do you suppose Chairman Mao would have approved of this game?" we asked a seventy-year-old player.

"Does it matter?" the old man retorted, delighting his companions. "He's dead and I'm not."

Young women shampoo in the alleys; a bucket of water unceremoniously dumped over the head is the usual method of rinsing out the soap. Those seeking a more therapeutic soak retreat to one of several bathhouses. Few city homes have showers or tubs or hot water; water must be heated in kettles. When Jay visited the Bright and Flowery Bathhouse at 223 Wangfujing Street, and paid his twenty-six fen (sixteen cents) admission, he found the place packed. The ritual was leisurely. Customers stretch out on a towel-covered bench, then soak in one of three huge vats, soaping and showering before reclining once again on the bench with a cup of tea provided by the management. Zhao Zengfu, a retired railcar repair worker, was soaking himself when Jay slipped into the hottest tub, just bearable, beside him. "I'm eighty-one," Zhao said. "I come here twice a week for two or three hours, and that's one reason I've lived so long, I think."

Out on the streets, people fan restless babies, tend to chores or just talk. In the steamy cities of the Yangtze River valley, where temperatures hover about ninety degrees from May until October, many Chinese even sleep in the streets. In Chongqing (Chungking), Wuhan and Nanjing, three southern cities known collectively as the "furnaces of China," families move straw mats and rattan lounge chairs outdoors and hope for a breeze that will freshen their slumber. Street sleeping is discouraged in Peking. The authorities worry about the impression it makes on visiting foreigners. But this does not deter peasants in outlying communes from a roadside snooze. So many of them camp out on the roads that after nightfall motorists are cautioned to slow down and watch for sleeping people, particularly on the sporadically lit twelve-mile highway that links downtown Peking with Capital Airport.

Air conditioning is reserved for foreigners and the political elite. At $200 each, electric fans are beyond the reach of most Chinese, so they cool off in the summer with popsicles, watermelon and beer. Six new ice cream plants went into operation in Peking in the summer of 1980; they turned out some 700 million popsicles during the season, about 100 for every man, woman and child in the capital. In a recent movie, *Those Kids,* the unhappy young lovers drown their sorrows with ten of the little popsicles in one sitting. Available practically everywhere from street vendors, in chocolate or fruit flavors, popsicles (*bing gui,* or "ice sticks") are a real bargain at less than two cents apiece. Children consume so many of the sticky sweet things that mothers and teachers wrote letters requesting that the plants produce flavored ices that are nutritious as well as cooling. The ice cream makers responded with exotic flavors such as sesame seed and green pea, but a vendor in the Xidan shopping district said that the new tastes were not especially popular with the small fry. "Children never choose those flavors if they do the buying themselves," vendor Wu Shitong said.

City residents complain of the chronic shortage of beer. Predictably, the big hotels that cater to foreign tourists are granted top priority, followed by the Friendship Store for resident foreigners. After that, it is every beer lover for himself. An old man waiting in a long beverage-shop line on Peking's Nanwei Street complained, "We have less beer every year." The breweries of Peking produced 52,000 tons of the Five Star and Peking brands in 1980, nearly twice the 1975 output, but new shipments usually sell out by midmorning. The dogged reporters of the *Peking Daily,* beer fanciers themselves, were so alarmed by the situation that they began a full-scale investigation. Their report blamed the breweries for failing to anticipate "the demands and changing tastes of the masses." Stinting on investment was short-sighted, the newspaper argued, because the state gets $150 in tax revenue for every ton of beer sold. Finally the newspaper chided the breweries for ignoring the old Chinese adage: "Prepare before the rain comes and don't sink a well just when you feel thirsty." Although the government announced plans to expand Peking's two breweries and construct another in suburban Xun Yi County, an expenditure of $15 million to increase annual production to 85,000 tons, everyone admitted even that would not be enough.

To squeeze some new amusement from dry urban life, people in Peking and other large cities have latched on to the Frisbee. Foreign tourists frequently brought Frisbees into the country and gave them away, but the plastic discs never made much headway until the Peking No. 4 Toy Factory started mass-producing "flying saucers," as they are known in China. The first 60,000 locally made projectiles sold out quickly in 1980, and now orders from all over the country are backed up. "Frisbee fever has struck," the *Peking Evening News* reported. It recommended a game of Frisbee as a "wholesome pastime" for children and good exercise for their elders. The police, however, are not similarly enchanted by young Frisbee fanatics who commandeer whole neighborhoods and send their flying saucers whizzing in and out of traffic. On a single day in August 1980, police detained 350 wayward disc throwers. Of those, 344 were "criticized" and 6 repeat offenders had to surrender their Frisbees.

With Mao gone, the Chinese have more opportunities to indulge such new pleasures, while destitute workers and peasants may also be more bold, taking advantage of diminished social restraint to bring their grievances into the city. Peking's derelicts huddle in shelters provided by the government, like the barren concrete apartment house located in a back alley near the Yudingmen railway station. During the day they fan out about the city, knocking at the back doors of government agencies they hope will solve their problems. Others squat near railroad and subway stations, offering small items for sale so they can buy food. "I know that if I could only talk with Deng Xiaoping, he would help me," a blind former construction worker named Fu Guanghua told us. He carried in a knapsack all his belongings and the supper he had panhandled from passers-by—a slab of steamed bread *(mantou)*, a half-rotten cucumber and an apple.

Nearby a younger and more openly defiant man vowed, "I've been here two months and I'm not leaving until my case is settled." His wife, grimy and red-eyed, comforted their whimpering baby, who was swaddled in rags. The whole family had hitchhiked on trains from Jiangxi (Kiangsi) province, 750 miles away, to get an old black mark erased from the husband's work record.

Many of these tattered street people, whom the Chinese call "petitioners," were victims of political persecution. Purged or demoted during the Cultural Revolution, they sought to have their reputations cleared and their jobs restored. "I was a teacher of mathematics," explained a quiet, middle-aged vagrant, better dressed than most, who had positioned himself outside the Qianmen subway station. During the Cultural Revolution "I lost everything, my job, my house, even my children. I was labeled a capitalist roader [the title often given intellectuals said to be "taking the capitalist road"] and shipped off to a reform labor camp. Now I can't even get a job, even though

I know China needs teachers." While he waited for his case to be investigated, the ex-teacher spent his days weaving holders for glass tumblers out of small strips of colored plastic. He sold them to passers-by, earning just enough—about forty cents a day—to survive on a diet of *shaobing* (flat buns) and soup.

Like the others, he managed to get to Peking only by evading the usual restrictions on travel. Ordinary Chinese must procure enough money for the fare and a travel permit to leave their hometowns, but the street people, lacking both, walk hundreds of miles, hitch rides with friendly truckers or hop trains to reach the city. Several described the trick of boarding a train without a ticket and managing to stay until the conductor finds them and ejects them. "It's slow, but eventually you get here," said a cheerful but frighteningly thin ten-year-old boy who had come with his father from Heilongjiang.

We were surprised at the benign attitude of the government toward these people. Buses would occasionally round them up and put them back in the multistory shelters near the Yudingmen station. The same buses rounded up sit-down demonstrators in front of public buildings like the Communist Party office compound at Zhongnanhai in central Peking. At times Peking bureaucrats accompanied trainloads of vagrants back to their home provinces to pressure local bureaucrats into moving on their cases. These efforts to put the petitioners out of sight worked, for they are less obvious now than they were in 1979 and 1980. But derelicts and street people linger in nearly every urban area, camping in out-of-the-way places, rummaging through restaurant trash cans for food.

In Guilin, the morning sun reveals much of that grimy, darker side of city life, but after you climb 347 stone steps to the top of the Hill of Many Colors, the harsher tones blur. We see a fairy-tale land, rock-candy hills jutting out of the neat square vegetable and rice patches just outside town. The great height obscures foul odors, crumbling walls, peeling paint and the grind of tractor gears. All seems neat and clean, as if lifted from some feudal paradise and set down there.

By the Li River, at the city end of Liberation Bridge, wait young people in worn blue and gray clothing who seem to have little time for fairy tales. They carry hoes on their shoulders. Stern teen-age girls—Youth League activists at the local middle school—order them to line up for a march across the bridge into the fields. They are the city's future.

"Are you students?"

"Yes."

"But it's summer, so you're not going to school?"

"Oh, but we are. This is the labor part of our course."

The bridge is a thin, well-traveled link between China's two worlds, city and countryside. Peasants trudge into town carrying fruits and vegetables to sell for extra income. Some also bike to city jobs, leaving behind wives or husbands who must live outside the population-controlled city. A few city folk bike out to see relatives or look for hard-to-find vegetables.

The city tinkles with bicycle bells, the same sound we heard in Peking each morning. Everyone is in motion—riding, walking, jogging, talking, spitting, squatting or lining up for a bus. But on the concrete streets the smell of ancient rural life lingers. Small women bend low to the ground to pull 200-pound carts of wood and coal and sand, the slowest things moving in a city going full tilt.

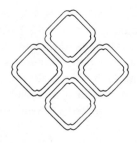

WORKING

DURING A CHAT NEAR THE WATER LILIES IN BEIHAI PARK, LITTLE WANG told us about his routine at the electric motor factory. He worked there as an English translator, apparently a valued one, even though his spoken English was uncertain and our conversations often lapsed into half English, half Chinese. Little Wang translated technical manuals from the United States, working with five other translators at small desks in a bare-walled room with one dirty window. The factory gave him a quota of eight hundred words a day.

"Those eight hundred words usually take me about four hours out of an eight-hour day. After I finish the quota I used to read an English novel. I did it secretly by opening the drawer of my desk a little. But it turned out nobody really checked us, just so we did the eight hundred words. So now we spend half of our time playing basketball in the court outside, or sometimes we play Chinese chess, or go, or bridge. If I did more than the eight-hundred-word quota, the maximum bonus I could earn would be one or two dollars a month."

Translators work without any real supervision. They are technicians and somewhat out of the chain of command. "Some factory leaders have mentioned to us once or twice that they would like us to work harder," Little Wang said, "but we just ignore them."

The revolution is over. Nothing much remains to inspire 100 million city workers. They must cram more work into their days if the country is to pull itself out of poverty and technological backwardness. Nonetheless, many spend their time plotting escape from work. The workers we met look forward only to family events—a fat new baby, a wedding feast with plenty of Qingdao beer, a holiday in the Western Hills, or the purchase of a new Japanese-made television set. They say their jobs give little pleasure or incentive for hard work, all the more irritating to them because they know what hard-working Chinese were able to accomplish during the great dynasties of the past, in Hong Kong and America, and in the early days of the People's Republic. There is a popular saying, ripe with cynicism: "*Zuo i-tian he-sheng, zhuang i-tian zhong*" (Each day be a monk, each day beat the gong).

Urban Chinese workers have few financial worries, though recent inflation has made them wonder a bit about the future. They complain of lack of variety in the market and occasional shortages of vegetables, but they never suffer from famine as peasants in north central China still do on occasion. Their factories charge them nominal fees for housing, sometimes less than $1 a month, on the average no more than $3. Employers hand out monthly coupons good for visits to the bathhouse or barbershop. Workers sometimes sneak personal purchases like umbrellas or bicycles onto expense accounts, leading some stores to demand official letters of authorization before they give receipts. Firings are rare (although 1982 regulations specifically authorize the dismissal of lazy or undisciplined workers). The Chinese sense of community, of *guanxi,* and Communist rhetoric about the power of the working class intimidate any factory managers who might consider dismissing someone. As a practical matter, the Chinese worker is guaranteed a job for life, an "iron rice bowl."

We asked one young factory worker in Peking to keep a diary of his activities and thoughts for one week. He wrote just after one of the country's aged leaders, Wang Renzhong, had pleaded with China's young city workers to reject "unhealthy things from abroad and stick with Communist ideals." Among a lot of contradictions, rumors and petty complaints there is evidence in this diary that the children and grandchildren of the men and women who rescued China from famine, civil war and suffering thirty years ago don't necessarily appreciate their own generation's advantages or find their lives very satisfying.

Friday: Got up at 5 A.M. and went to work at 6 A.M. Discussion of salary readjustment reached its tenth day. We were told that only 40 percent of the factory population will be entitled to salary increases. The past few days have been engaged in heated arguments over who among us should get the pay hike. Although a one-notch promotion only means a few extra dollars, it is still something we ordinary Chinese have long waited for.

Take me, for example: I work my ass off for a measly 40 yuan a month [about $27]. That is hardly enough for myself, not to speak of supporting my family or procuring other things. Not that I'm incompetent. I'm both a technician and a junior administrator, with nine years' experience on the job. The crux of the matter is: the government won't let me earn what I am worth. Besides, there is a group of bureaucrats about me—party secretaries, managers and ass-kissers [in Chinese, *pai ma pi,* those who "pat the horse's rump"]. They've already divided the 40 percent quota among themselves and their protégés.

Want to get a few dollars' raise? Maybe you can, but they'll torture you first with all the meetings, discussions, study sessions . . . Ah, it's frustrating!

Saturday: I went around to the different workshops to inspect the work of transporting some machines. I chatted with some workers and discovered they were grumbling about the salary readjustment plan. The majority of the workers are extremely dissatisfied with the leadership because they have appropriated for themselves the 40 percent quota. All the bureaucrats and some ass-kissers will get a one-notch promotion.

Small wonder that one group of workers just lies down on the job. They read newspapers or chat. The workers are sloppy, the machines are antiquated and noisy. The workshop is messy.

The new government unveiled before the people the bright promise of modernization. But the Chinese saying goes: "Yuchuan Mountain's spring water may taste delightful, but so distant a drink of water cannot quench actual thirst." At present, the workers' salaries are so low that no sweet-talk or high-sounding speeches can possibly rouse them. . . .

The newspapers frequently come out with fabricated reports of "successes" and "achievements." Who the devil will believe them? People are fed up with this talk that capitalism is inferior to socialism. I think the two systems must be treated like two kinds of food in two bowls. Let the people taste both and decide for themselves which one tastes better.

Sunday: After work at 2 P.M. I went window-shopping with a few friends at the Peking Department Store. As we were about to enter the building, our eyes were caught by a huge crowd of people milling in front of the display window on the left side of the building. I squeezed myself in the crowd and found they were all looking at the advertising display for Sanyo Corporation. The window was full of modern household electrical appliances. All the Chinese beside me were raving about them.

Japan achieved such speedy economic development in the past thirty years since the war. China had the same thirty years or so, yet she is way behind. Newspapers sing praises of socialism and deride capitalism, but this is the best proof. You go in the department store and walk up to the counter where they sell cassette recorders and find that the sets are imported from Japan and that the cheapest costs about 1,000 yuan [about $676]. Those goods are exclusively for the bureaucrats. Ordinary Chinese can only gawk at them.

I get a monthly salary of 40 yuan. If I want to buy a cassette recorder, I'll have to save up all of my salary for three years. That is, no food, no drinks for three years.

Monday: The Chongwen Vegetable Market had only one vegetable, garlic shoots, to sell. One has to line up for more than two hours to buy it. . . . People in the line sometimes quarrel over who is ahead of whom to buy those handfuls of vegetables. You are lucky if there is somebody in the family who can line up. If both husband and wife are working, leaving early in the morning and coming back late at night, then just don't expect anything to eat.

However rough and inconsistent the man's language, young Chinese like him often express cautious, vague doubts about the socialist system in private conversations. Fully aware of this, party leaders since Mao's death have tinkered with incentives in factories and farms. They hope bonuses for extra effort will let people identify their own self-interest with the country's. Chairman Mao, of course, feared that incentives to more intelligent and energetic workers would create a new elite, as he felt had happened in the Soviet Union. He is dead now, his side of the issue laughed off with a joke that is heard occasionally in Peking. One day, so the story goes, Chairman Mao received Deng Xiaoping and Deng's small grandson. The old revolutionary had his differences with Deng, whose economic ideas sounded to Mao like neocapitalism, but the grandson seemed like a nice boy.

"Call me Uncle," Mao said.

"Oh, I couldn't, Chairman Mao," answered the boy.

Deng suggested that Mao offer the child an apple. He did, and watched the boy take a big bite. "Thank you, Uncle," he chirped happily.

"See," said Deng, "what a little material incentive will do?"

The story sums up the most sensitive and crucial economic issue for China in the 1980s. Should good deeds and hard work be rewarded with more money, and if so, would that revive the economy without tearing apart the cherished social fabric, a person's close feeling for his fellow worker on the assembly line? Can a nation of one billion really afford to pay material rewards at all?

Those who strive for big money bonuses run into intangible yet powerful obstacles. One worker recalled his first months at a new plant in which, not knowing the others too well, he tried to work at full speed and increase his chances for an extra bonus. A man at the next machine regarded him with a scowl: "Are you trying to make the rest of us look bad?" Chinese women, in particular, seem to lack the desire to push for higher bonuses. We chatted with a woman in a Peking carpet factory who was happy that a cleaning machine at her plant had malfunctioned. She had little work to do and could go home to her one-room apartment early, and escape the noise and the wool particles filling the air, irritating eyes and throat. Her usual monthly bonus for regular attendance was only $3 or so, and she had not gotten any bonus since October because she had been "sick." What would she like to do if she could? She rested her chin on her hands, her elbows propped on the one table in the apartment. "Stay around the house," she said.

A few workers get substantial bonuses, but the system usually works out as might be expected in a land of so many tight communities. Workshops that do hand out bonuses give roughly equal—and generally small—amounts to everyone who shows up regularly for work. The differences in size of the bonuses are often negligible to the Chinese. Some have a saying: "The man who works gets sixteen dollars a month. The man who doesn't work gets seventeen dollars a month because he doesn't have to pay bus fare." When a reporter for one of the Communist newspapers in Hong Kong heard the story of Mao, Deng's grandson and the apple, he was quick to ask the most relevant question: "Was it a large apple or a small apple?"

Incentives lose even more force because the city workers know they are stuck. They cannot change their jobs. Their factories are often so overstaffed that they have little work to do in the first place. At the Bank of China, our checks often passed through the hands of two or three tellers before we could withdraw any money. City streets are dotted with older women armed with megaphones whose only job it is to remind cyclists and pedestrians to obey the posted road signs. Shortages of materials and power cuts caused by inefficiency and droughts leave workshops idle for long periods of time.

The Chinese are bound by lifelong ties to their individual work place, but they display little of the company spirit found in Japan. Company songs and team uniforms are considered damaging to the socialist spirit. Most workers in China do not even know the production figures for their unit. The numbers are rarely made public, and people tend not to trust government statistics anyway. The peasants know much more about their team production rates and returns. Their share of the harvest depends on those figures, so they care.

Foreigners and Chinese from Singapore, Hong Kong, Taiwan and other large overseas Chinese communities are horrified that the Communists have managed to dampen the initiative of a people as inherently ambitious as the Chinese. Still, visitors from the Soviet Union say Peking stores and restaurants are better stocked than those in Moscow. Simple, well-made shoes and toys are readily available. Restaurants actually serve all the dishes on their menus—an unimaginable luxury to any Russian. Chinese have far less cash to spend than the Russians, and so put less pressure on their light industry to meet demand.

On a broad scale, central planning has pulled the Chinese economy into a swamp of inefficiency and sloth. For years factories tolerated shoddy workmanship as long as they met their monthly quotas. Electric power remains so scarce that some assembly lines operate only three days a week. The railroads are overburdened, so raw commodities and spare parts are rarely delivered to factories on time.

By 1980, the Chinese economy had grown so snarled that the government moved to loosen its grip on the nation's 380,000 state-run industrial enterprises and introduce some local autonomy. The National People's Congress in September 1980 formally embraced a so-called self-management system, authorizing Chinese factories to manage their own affairs, establish their own production targets above state quotas, hire and fire their own workers and, in some cases, set their own prices. Even competition, once forbidden, was endorsed by China's top Communists. "Competition among our enterprises should be encouraged," declared Vice Premier Yao Yilin.

"Self-management" was the pet project of Zhao Ziyang, the veteran administrator who was elected premier the same year. Zhao had experimented with the system in Sichuan during his stint as provincial chief there, scoring some early successes in selected key industrial plants. But when he tried to introduce the system nationwide, he encountered immediate, almost overwhelming resistance—from entrenched bureaucrats whose power depended on doing things the old way, from economists and state planners who genuinely worried that local managers were not equipped to take on new responsibilities, and from ideologues concerned that the new premier might be "taking the capitalist road." Zhao pulled back, saying that "self-management" would be phased in slowly. His government remains committed, in theory, to the development of a mixed economy, a hybrid of socialism and capitalism, of central planning and market forces, like those systems already in place in Yugoslavia and Rumania. But it will be a slow evolution.

Another economic experiment, designed to ease the great scourge of Chinese cities, youth unemployment, has proved more durable. Until the late 1970s, China denied that unemployment existed in its socialist paradise; since then it has come clean, reporting that in fact the urban jobless rate has sometimes soared to 10 percent for adults, 35 percent for people under thirty, the *daiye qingnian,* a euphemism meaning "youths awaiting assignment." The antidote the authorities prescribed for this socialist ill, oddly enough, was a big dose of free enterprise. With the blessing of the Communist Party, jobless youths have been going into business for themselves, alone or in small collectives. In nearly every city, young people straight out of high school have revived the service industries dismantled during the doctrinaire days of the Cultural Revolution. They repair furniture and bicycles, cut hair, resole shoes at sidewalk cobblers' shops, carry luggage at railway stations, even run small hotels.

Just south of Qianmen Gate in Peking, the neighborhood committee, worried that local youngsters had too much time on their hands, decided to turn a ramshackle earthquake shelter into a teahouse. "Not to make a profit, but to give our young people something to do with themselves," said Jiang Chenwu, a retired worker who helped keep the accounts. They began with thirteen sidewalk tea vendors; soon eighty people were employed, with a dozen sidewalk stalls selling everything from popsicles to woolen scarfs to pictures of movie stars. Liu Yuzheng, the twenty-year-old buyer for the teahouse, talked like an American business school graduate: "My job is studying the likes and dislikes of our customers and figuring out how to meet their demands. We sell whatever the market demands. As the seasons change and as tastes shift, we move into new product lines."

Other groups of youths have organized sidewalk photo stands outside the Forbidden City. By undercutting the prices of state-run studios and photographers, they win more customers and earn higher salaries. "Our secret is that we are more flexible," said Zhang Jie, eighteen, as he posed a young Chinese tourist against the graceful bridge leading to the Forbidden City. He fussed briefly with her collar and handed her the bunch of artificial flowers he used as a prop. "The government photographers work from fixed locations, but we'll go anywhere a customer wants. We're always looking for unusual sites and poses."

Occasionally we visited what was then Peking's only private restaurant, The Happy Guest, a small one-room apartment with four tables a few blocks north of the Peking Hotel. The place had been crowded since the night it opened, so novel was the idea of a restaurant not run by the state. The proprietor, a Peking woman who once cooked for Politburo member Ye Jianying, was collecting hundreds of dollars in profits with the help of her until then unemployed sons.

The reappearance of entrepreneurs, even on a small scale, is reassuring evidence that the Chinese have not lost that canny business sense renowned in Chinatowns throughout the world. But private enterprises also represent a profound change in the Communist system. Ten years ago, private trade was outlawed as "a tail of capitalism"; anyone who employed someone else was reviled and accused of exploiting the labor of others; even government-licensed peddlers and barbers were regarded with suspicion.

Today, while the government allows neocapitalist experiments to proceed, the official press reports mounting resentment over the idea of restaurant owners and other small businessmen accumulating wealth, earning forty or fifty times the monthly take-home pay of the average factory worker. Chinese still debate, quite seriously, whether a private shopowner can hire outside workers and still be a socialist. The *People's Daily* periodically reassures nervous readers, "It's all right to be rich." There is no doubt that the inequities Mao Tse-tung railed against in his later years are beginning to re-emerge.

One unusual leader of a re-emerging elite can be found in a Peking office with all the hustle and bustle of a modern corporation. Telephones ring nonstop. Secretaries rush by, carrying papers to be signed by the boss. A visiting businessman waiting for his appointment drums his fingers impatiently on the coffee table. A hush falls over the reception room as the suave chairman of the board, a tall, aristocratic-looking man with wavy silver hair, tinted glasses and a chunky gold Swiss watch, strolls past, en route to his chauffeur-driven limousine.

It is easy to forget for a moment that this is China. The man in the tailored Mao suit is Rong Yiren, that rarest of creatures, a Chinese millionaire, a former capitalist whose extravagant life style has survived three decades of Communism. His Shanghai-based business empire once encompassed two dozen factories and eighty thousand employees. Now he works for the government that stripped him of his business holdings, unleashed Red Guards on his family and, for one humiliating year, forced him to work as a janitor.

"Sometimes foreign friends express surprise that people like me still exist in China," Rong told us. "They assume we all fled to Hong Kong or were murdered long ago. That's a complete misconception . . . We have been here all along, many of us." Rong, in his mid-sixties, estimates that there are at least a hundred other millionaires in China—his own net worth has been reckoned at upwards of $6 million—and perhaps fifty thousand less prosperous but still comfortably fixed capitalists left over from the days before the 1949 Communist revolution.

In a land where the average income is extremely low, Rong enjoys a way of life not unlike that of the wealthy anywhere. His world centers on a spacious, courtyard-style house filled with antiques and tended by maids, a driver and a full-time gardener. His hobbies, photography and breeding rare roses, befit a rich man. The Communists treat him like a strange goose laying golden eggs, leading them into the bewildering world of international finance and trade where they must succeed if their economy is to grow. Although thirty years removed from Western-style capitalism, Rong chats casually about the comparative merits of joint ventures, syndicated bank loans and government-to-government credits. The quasi-national company he directs, China International Trust and Investment Corporation, was set up in 1979 to match foreign investors with the multitudes of Chinese corporations, factories and agencies looking for foreign capital and technology.

Rong insists that his goal is not the rebirth of Chinese capitalism, which even before the Communists never really took hold. "We are committed to socialist construction," he said. "And while profits have a place in our system, they must benefit the people and the government, not just individuals. This is not free enterprise."

His organization seems adept at avoiding the red tape that usually ensnares Chinese offices. His employees return phone calls without delay and set up appointments without a fuss, practically unheard of in Peking. "No buck-passing in this office," Rong says, apologizing for his rusty English.

Rong's business day starts at 8 A.M. and often lasts twelve hours. His monthly salary is 400 yuan ($268), about what top leaders like Deng Xiaoping earn. As far as he is concerned, however, the greatest reward is that he finally feels accepted again in a society that for so long scorned him.

Rong was born in Wuxi, near Shanghai, to a large and prominent family that once controlled China's largest milling company. After graduating from St. John's University, a Christian-run school in Shanghai, he went to work managing one of the mills and eventually inherited an empire of twenty-four machinery plants, textile factories and flour mills along the eastern coast. The Communist takeover scattered the family to places like Macao, Rio de Janeiro and New York, but Rong decided to stay.

The Communists, struggling to get the economy under control, let Rong and other capitalists continue working before buying them out in 1956. Rong received $6 million in dividends for his property. Chairman Mao gave him a special audience: "If you want to start a revolution and change the country, better not weep over your lost property." Rong was inclined to look on the bright side until 1966, when Red Guards ransacked his Peking home, smashed the family's priceless collections of porcelain and antique furniture, and beat him and his wife. He spent a year as a janitor, then submitted to a year of study sessions designed to "remold ideology." Rong "retired" for the next decade because he was not permitted to work. Then Mao died and Rong was back in business.

"I could have had an easier, more comfortable life if I had gone abroad," Rong said, "but I thought I would be more useful if I stayed here and worked to overcome China's poverty. That sounds very idealistic, but you have to have ideals, even in difficult times. Only then does your life have any significance."

Zhang Binggui is another man who has reached a certain prominence in Chinese life as he enters his sixties, but in contrast to Rong, he never considered going abroad when the Communists took over in 1949. Zhang was in Tiananmen Square when the red flag of the new People's Republic was raised. "My back straightened and my chest swelled as I listened to Chairman Mao," he said. "He made us believe that the bad old days of war and hunger and foreign exploitation were over. Those of us who suffered much in the old society dared to hope that our lives would improve." As it turned out, Zhang did suffer again, particularly during the Cultural Revolution, but he is now a Communist Party member, a labor hero, a member of the National People's Congress and of the National Party Congress. He is also a clerk at the candy counter of the Peking Number One Department Store. Huge crowds converge on Zhang's counter to watch him scoop up exactly a pound of gumdrops with one sweep of his arm, his trademark.

Zhang's life is what the Communist Chinese revolution was about. If his conservative views fail to square with those of the college-age youths who no longer find his candy trick such a thrill, that does not mean his ideas are not still widely held throughout the country.

"I was essentially a slave, not a human being, before liberation, working sixteen or seventeen hours a day, with never enough rest or enough money or enough food. Now I have security and enough to take care of my family. We don't have to worry about the future." Zhang first went to work as a boy of eight, carrying banners in traditional Peking funeral and wedding processions. He had only one year of formal schooling. His own four children, by contrast, have gone through high school free of charge.

"As a child I was hungry all the time," he told us. "My father was like all working people, he could never get ahead. My mother used to send me off to work with just a single bun that was supposed to last me all day. Once when I was carrying funeral banners, I rushed around so much that the bun fell out of my sleeve and I had nothing to eat that day. My mother must have noticed my hungry look because when I got home she asked me if I'd had enough, and I had to confess I'd lost my bun. I cried. And she cried too. Then she dried her tears and told me I was going to have to find a better-paying job. I was ten."

Now, as a veteran worker of the department store ("hundred products store" the Chinese call it), Zhang earns about $56 monthly. The total family income, counting his wife's retirement pension and the earnings of the three children still at home, exceeds $125.

"If we want something, we can usually buy it," he said. Despite his personal satisfaction and prominence, Zhang knows that many younger people do not share his optimism or approach their lives with his enthusiasm. His own children, ranging in age from seventeen to thirty, apparently display some of this youthful impatience. "Whenever I try to educate them so they can share my happiness at how far China has come, they listen to me, but I'm not sure they understand," he said, shaking his head regretfully. "Sometimes they just say, 'Oh, Papa, we've heard your stories before.' "

In the dark, sooty interiors of China's factories, this clash of young and old plays itself out. Many factories have adopted the self-management system and hope to inspire their young workers with the challenge of making a product that can earn a profit, rather than just fulfill the quota in the state plan. But the resulting pressures on factory managers are great. They are used to the government's buying everything they make; poor quality could be overlooked if they met each month's quota. Managers now must sharpen discipline among their often lethargic work force and also wrestle with lingering doubts that the capitalist experiment can ever succeed under a socialist government.

One of the more beleaguered managers of modern Chinese industry is Li Guisheng, the taciturn director of a workshop at the Peking Electric Motor Factory. Li is a stocky man who relishes working with his hands. He took us around his workshop, fending off the mud of a rainy autumn day with black rubber boots. The Foreign Ministry had cleared our visit and he seemed relaxed and candid. He was an earnest man, somewhat amused by the foibles of his workers as he tried to meet his quota in a situation where the rules were suddenly changing.

Li wakes up a little before six. He and his wife share a bedroom in their apartment on the second floor of a housing complex not far from his workshop. His wife's mother, now eighty-three, sleeps in her padded clothing in the other room. Her feet are tiny, the result of footbinding as a child.

His four sons, aged eighteen to thirty, all work in factories. The eldest, a former soldier, is a deputy party secretary at his plant; the second eldest is a Youth League member and worker at a paint factory; the next is a factory official; and the youngest had just begun work at Li's factory as a pipe cutter.

Li began the morning with his constitutional, a walk up to the nearby railroad tracks and back. He breakfasted on noodles, corn porridge and fried cakes at the factory canteen. By seven he was in the shop, inspecting the work of the night shift. At seven-fifteen he joined fellow workers in morning calisthenics. Twist the hips, twist the neck, squat, move the joints. "It helps my rheumatism," Li said. At seven-thirty the workers divided into production groups. The deadline for the pump-motor quota was approaching. Supervisors spoke of making it on time, but were careful not to rush and violate safety rules.

There had been an accident the day before. Li called a meeting of workshop supervisors to discuss it. The meeting lasted all morning, as the supervisors gently but firmly roasted the two young workers responsible.

A rotor had fallen off a crane, damaging it and several other rotors near it. The man who fastened the rotor to the crane was a thirty-year-old worker with limited experience. He had used a pipe rather than a steel rod as a fastener. The factory has a rule, one of the "five points of attention," which says that the crane operator should not lift if the cargo is not properly fastened, but this time he hit the button anyway. The group had to fix blame precisely, in appropriate measures for the workers' rights, but neither did anyone threaten to fire the culprits. The "major responsibility," the group decided, went to the crane operator. He made a self-criticism. He apologized for failing to remember the rules and for acting rashly. He lost his bonus for the month, about 8 yuan ($5.40). The man who incorrectly fastened the rotor lost 3 yuan ($2) of his monthly bonus. The men suffered no cut in their month's pay, 47 yuan ($31.75). At noon everyone went to lunch.

Li walked home for a meal of steamed bread, porridge and stir-fried pork with green peppers. He drank no liquids. The factory allows only forty-five minutes for lunch, a bit unconventional because that rules out the traditional midday nap.

After lunch, a meeting in the workshop's production section began. Supervisors fretted about the new free-enterprise system being tried in Chinese factories. Li explained, "Every motor must have a fan to cool it. The fans we use are plastic, but our clients—particularly a water-pump factory we sell to—now want aluminum. We do not have any aluminum fans. What should we do? We've decided to keep making the motors, without fans, and wait for the aluminum fans we have ordered. Plastic fans tend to get soft in high temperatures and stop working. Previously our clients had to accept the fans because this was a planned economy. We sold the motors to the government; the clients had to buy them from the government. But now the water-pump factory can shop around for other factories whose motors are better, and they say they will unless we improve ours."

Li went to the different assembly areas and instructed the workers to stop putting plastic fans in the motors and to wait for further instructions. That left him a new problem: how to meet his quota. Li would have to produce another four hundred type-four motors with the corrected fans before the year ended and still turn out a certain quota of motors a month.

Li rates his workers on their monthly production. They begin the month at a slow pace and accelerate only toward the end, rushing to meet their quota. Other workers in other shops do the same, so many of the necessary parts do not arrive until late, and in the last-minute rush to meet the quota, quality suffers.

This has become a very serious matter for Li. "We live and die by quality," says a new slogan on the factory wall. "People want to buy from the Dalian [Dairen] Electric Motor Factory before they buy from us," Li said. "They got the gold medal for quality, while we only got the trusted-products award, which is second place."

Each Thursday afternoon Li studies management in the workshop office, using books and materials supplied by higher-level offices. He thinks it gives him a better understanding of the use of bonuses, regulations and discipline. "We had political management before. We depended on lecturing the workers to do their jobs better, and so we had many ups and downs." A deputy director added, "Senior workers like us have experienced bitterness with the old society, so we know we should work for the state and the people. We work hard and conscientiously. Those workers who started before the Cultural Revolution, they also work quite well. But those who came after 1968, they don't as a rule work as well. Ideological training then was in chaos and they didn't work hard or have good models to follow. We have a kind of forcible education for young workers now. We ask them to study. Their working grades (which determine wages) are arranged according to their skills and attitude toward work."

Like other older workers, Li has served as master for several apprentice workers. He calls them in for regular discussions of their skills and behavior. As Li has prospered in his career, so have some of his earliest apprentices, who are now directors or group leaders. They still consult with him on their problems at work and at home, a tradition that binds the Chinese together almost as tightly as family ties.

Some of his younger workers have been more troublesome. Gao Xianmin, the twenty-six-year-old son of a middle-level party official in a suburban county of Peking, has worked at the factory for almost ten years, and is regarded as a prankster. Li thinks Gao acts as he does because the young man believes—perhaps rightly—that no one will bear down too harshly on the son of a man with high party connections. As a joke, Gao switched the time cards of several workers, causing them to lose pay. When the factory leaders decided to fine him a few yuan, he raised a ruckus. Gao's father makes little effort to control him. Every time the son calls his father and demands tickets for a popular sporting event, the elder Gao comes through.

At four o'clock Li stopped studying and went to meet the night-shift supervisors just arriving. The day shift would quit at four-thirty. He told the incoming men that steel-rod production was slowing down, holding up the whole assembly line. He went to the factory office to read his newspapers, which he has delivered there: the *Worker's Daily,* the *People's Daily* and the *Peking Daily.* At home by six, he dined on noodles with pork, vegetables and sauce, and a little tea. Friday night he would have some wine, since Saturday was a holiday and he could sleep late.

After dinner Li took another short walk. He stopped occasionally to chat with neighbors bringing in their wash from clothes lines strung between buildings. He came back and turned on the television set, a 12-inch "Tianjin" model he bought four years ago for about 430 yuan. "They're cheaper now," he said. He watched a TV movie that night, *Violin Boy,* about a child whose musical education is interrupted by the Cultural Revolution. His mother pleads with the boy to give up the violin, a bourgeois instrument, but suddenly the Gang of Four is arrested and the child is recruited for the big symphony orchestra. "Not bad," said Li. He went to bed at ten o'clock, switching off the fluorescent ceiling light that illuminates his bedroom-living room.

Li's wife works at a rubber factory. Their parents arranged the marriage while Li was working in the northeast. Mrs. Li is not a party member, so she does not accompany her husband to party meetings on Friday nights.

At trade-union meetings, Li often speaks of the need for quality work. Union and management do not have an adversary relationship. On Wednesdays, from four-fifteen to five-fifteen, the workers have political study. That week they discussed the upcoming local elections for delegates to the next national People's Congress and heard announcements of who was to receive special bonuses for good work.

Li is a simple, conscientious worker, the sort who keeps economies afloat all over the world. The Maoist effort to turn such people into supermen, endlessly analyzing their motives and promising more output, brought inevitable disappointments. Now young people often work at half speed, the intensely political years having dulled appreciation of a simple good day's job. Li knows about the laggards who finish quotas early and play basketball or chess, and wonders if something might be salvaged from the Mao years, no matter how unhappy his own memories of them.

In the late 1960s, political study at the factory broke down into a tug-of-war between activists of the "Red Flag Team" and the "Red Flag Rebellion Team." Accepted by neither group, Li lost all authority after an August 1967 fight during which one factory official had his skull fractured by a thick stick. Back in charge now, he seems to supervise his 365 shop members with ease; his family's material needs are met, and he is glad that the "living standard of the people is increasing." Still, Li said he would like to recapture some of the ideological fervor of the old days, if not the factional squabbling. "We should still live a simple life, and not go looking for things that cannot be provided."

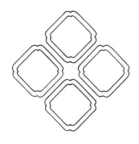

COUNTRY

A DRIVE THROUGH THE CHINESE COUNTRYSIDE SURPRISES A NEWCOMER. In spring the valleys shine as green as new peas. In winter they lie brown and dusty, the topsoil blowing away to annoy housewives in the nearest city. But after soaking in the colors, smells and silences, the newcomer realizes how empty it seems. If this is the home of 800 million peasants, the vast majority of China's one billion, where are they?

They blend into the crosswork rice paddies and terraced wheat fields. They work in small groups and are often some distance from the main roads, so they are easy to miss. A large proportion of the 800 million are children, hidden away in school or helping back at home in the village. The overcrowding and overuse of this clogged countryside do not confront the senses quite the way a walk down Peking's Wangfujing Street does. But notice the little grave mounds, decorated with bits of colored paper on remembrance days, jammed into the corners of grain fields, on steep hillsides or along roadways. Regular graveyards would waste too much good flatland. The dusty village squares overflow with people when they hang up a bedsheet between volleyball poles or basketball hoops to show an evening movie. The skeletons of new houses shoot up on the edges of many villages.

In the Mao era, visitors easily found large concentrations of rural humanity. Mass-work projects were everywhere. In early 1977, before the commune at Dazhai lost its status as a national model ("In agriculture, learn from Dazhai," Mao proclaimed), we marveled at thousands of people there sweating at the bottom of a gully, leveling out a swamp that commune leaders insisted would be cultivated.

Commune. The word has influenced foreign perceptions of China for two decades. At its beginning, it may have been the largest social experiment of this century. Young Americans intrigued by the Chinese—and earlier European—example set up their own mini-communes. Yet the Chinese commune became little more than a collection of clerks and party officials in a set of buildings near the local market town. They inspected fields and production facilities, explained new rules to village leaders and sent reports to Peking. The commune no longer provided new ways to organize such a mass of humanity. It harvested paperwork and red tape, while small units —peasant production teams and families—did the tilling, weeding and harvesting.

When Mao created the communes in the late fifties, pulling the old cooperatives into large administrative units of 50,000 to 100,000 people, he also ordered an end to private property and the beginning of equal wages, nursery care for all children, and communal dining halls. Peasant resistance to this assault on family life weakened most of the reforms. Many communes were eventually reduced in size; by the time we reached China they were mostly administrative shells. More recently, party officials have stripped away the shell altogether and returned to a system of smaller units, administrative districts, brigades and production teams. In 1982 the communes were formally abolished, and collective cultivation was abandoned in many counties. More and more land is worked by small teams, often by families—a change that will have vast significance if it endures. Some commune bureaucrats have been reassigned to field work or to lower-level jobs where they supervise fewer people. Newspapers now expose corrupt former commune leaders, such as the Hunanese officials who drew such high salaries and funded so many pet projects that they wasted an amount equal to half of a village's annual production.

As city people in China, we got the strongest whiff of country life and what the communes meant to us in early winter when rural supplies became important. Cabbages begin to pile up for sale on the streets of Peking in November. The big green-and-white piles darken as the city's soot and grit settle over the leaves. Customers pass by looking for better-quality vegetables inside the markets. Little carts drawn by donkeys, mules or horses pull more produce into town in the early morning. Their wrapped bundles are packed so high and precariously that they overarch and nearly cover the animals. Small mules stagger down the streets looking like huge turtles in burlap and straw shells.

But we found it hard to follow the little animals back to the countryside and see how the precarious balance of land, food and people worked itself out so that we could be fed each winter. Foreigners see very little of the countryside, in part because there are problems there. United Nations relief officials, allowed in the countryside for the first time, found a third of Hebei province's rural population in 1981 hungry and short of grain because of a lengthy drought. Even the Communist Party's theoretical journal *Red Flag* admitted: "Our country is still plagued by a very serious food shortage."

We found beggars from northern Anhui province appearing in Nanjing in winter with special administrative permits authorizing their travel. Even in good years, Anhui peasants do not forget the lean times. On a rare trip through the area, usually off-limits because of its poverty, an American researcher found that many peasants thought the Communist Party's most important recent contribution to their well-being has been the planting of trees with edible leaves.

The two dozen or so rural villages we visited were relatively prosperous, reflecting the government's policy of taking visitors to communes where average incomes top $300, even though per capita rural income for the country rarely exceeds $90.

Some Chinese officials estimate that as many as 100 million peasants are malnourished, but it is difficult for us to verify that. Children out in the country are usually thin, but we never saw bloated stomachs or signs of serious mass malnutrition. Overseas Chinese with relatives in remote parts of China are more likely to see the unadorned rural poor. Most report seeing healthy if meagerly fed people. The local government sometimes supplies special food for the visitor's family in the vain hope that the visiting relative will not find out how plain and meager the usual fare is. One friend of ours visited his wife's village in Shanxi, and although he was well-fed, he found other peasants living on a diet mainly of noodles or porridge, and a few pickled vegetables. Once a month, he said, they could purchase some fatty pork.

Our closest association with peasant life occurred in much more favorable surroundings, in a Peking-area commune where we spent a week. This was Production Team 13, Nanping (Southern Peace) village, Evergreen Commune, whose team leader, Song Duo, showed us how resourceful, cantankerous and individualistic a man could be even in the supposedly communized Chinese countryside.

Song had had his difficult moments. He had resigned in disgust in 1974 after some front-office misbehavior. When we met him, he was sparring with his commune supervisors over a plan to build a new house for his son, who was about to be married. But at age fifty, his close-cropped hair thinning back from his nut-brown scalp, the sometimes irascible Comrade Song talked like a man who had it made. He lived in a house with four large rooms and a charming garden with fruit trees and a fish pond; he expected to receive $650 in profit sharing by the end of the year. "We have so much more money than before—I am eating better, drinking better and dressing better," he told us. The bonds of the commune had loosened, and he was approaching a life that in China could be called comfortably middle-class.

American images of China have probably been forever warped by Pearl Buck's 1930s best seller, *The Good Earth*. The novel portrayed a breed of quiet men and women squeezing a bitter living from ancient, overworked soil. There is still some truth to that picture, but almost all the peasants we encountered—even during impromptu roadside stops—were by turns jovial and querulous, pleasure-seeking and, most recently, working rather hard for a larger portion of the national rice bowl.

Each evening before dinner Song gulped down one or two small shot glasses of *yue gong jiou,* "Moon Palace alcohol," a potent vodkalike brew that comes in white porcelain bottles. Song lined them up on his mantelpiece. We joined him for a meal of fried pork and long beans, noodles and big hunks of steamed bread. "I don't raise pigs," he told us. "It means a lot of chores and who wants to work that hard?" He had the equivalent of $1,380 in the bank, the local People's Bank of China, which pays only 3 or 4 percent interest. His wife and three of his four children work full-time. He had already acquired much of the rock and lime needed to build the new house for his eldest son, Shengli (Victory). A neighbor was willing to share the expense in exchange for some rooms for himself. Soon, Song vowed, he would catch up with many of his neighbors and buy a television set. The *People's Daily* has noted that peasants going to town are now heading first for the television and sewing-machine counters. He expected the prices to come down a bit, since Chinese factories had gone on a television-set production binge.

In the days of Chairman Mao, whose huge portrait stared down benignly from the wall of Song's neat, white-wallpapered living room, such conspicuous consumption would have brought official disapproval, if it had been possible at all. Even today many old revolutionaries in the party express grave doubts about the recent trend of encouraging peasants to work for material gain. One Shanxi newspaper wondered if "the kind of polarization of the rich and poor which existed in the old society" would recur. It said: "Some comrades who engaged in rural work mistakenly believed that being rich meant capitalism and being poor meant socialism."

Mao believed the workers and peasants would be motivated by patriotism and a determination to win the class struggle against exploiters at home and abroad. Individual incentives, he thought, would just dilute that class solidarity. But many of Mao's heirs argue that the only way to keep today's peasants working hard is to pay them more and let them use the money as they wish. Although Song claimed to revere Mao, the back side of the Chairman's portrait served as a place to store the family registration papers. The first four volumes of Mao's *Selected Works* lay on a table below the portrait. When we asked about the somewhat discredited fifth volume, Song's youngest son replied, "We had a copy, but I don't know where it is now."

In China, the Communist Party has always been more of a peasants' party than a vanguard of the urban proletariat. Mao's Red Army built up an enormous fund of good will in the countryside during the years of civil war and in the early years of his regime. Unlike Lenin, the city intellectual who was forced into exile during the years leading up to the Bolshevik victory, Mao shared the same rude village huts and caves with his peasant followers from the beginning of the revolution to its triumph. Later, as the unchallenged leader of the largest assemblage of peasants ever known, Mao grew intoxicated with the possibilities. He forgot the ancient peasant love of family and profit, nurtured in a three-thousand-year-old market system, and tried to mold the Chinese into single-minded warriors with hoes at command arms. By the time of his death in 1976, Mao had spent nearly every last fen of good will he had left in the countryside. Today Chinese peasants retain at most an ambiguous awe for the man who turned their lives around in so many ways, but are looking for ways to weaken the communal ideal which he preached.

It was a perfect evening in Song's garden, with a huge moon illuminating the cabbage rows in his private plot just behind his row of poplar, pear, persimmon, cherry and apple trees. Wang Xunying, a veteran official from the commune office, worked off the heavy meal we had just eaten by swinging her arms and walking back and forth. She was keeping an eye on the foreign visitors, but she had also been listening to Song's plans for the house he wanted to build for his soon-to-be married eldest son.

"It is not easy for you to build six rooms," she said.

"That all depends on whether you approve my plan or not," Song replied.

There was a day when Communist officials would have disapproved of placing such free spirits as Song in leadership roles. It soon became clear to us why they tolerated him. He seemed to be able to grow anything. The thriving fruit trees in his yard were the result of skillful grafting onto the trunks of a particularly sturdy variety of black date tree. He was good at humoring the forty-six men and women of Team 13. In the field he made quick, confident decisions about an incredible variety of crops: eggplant, cucumber, tomato, spinach, garlic, green pepper, radish, scallion, onion, bamboo shoots, lettuce, potato, hot pepper, celery, parsley, fennel, string beans, cabbage and turnips.

The brigade Health and Welfare officer, a slim, chain-smoking woman named Sun Meirong, dropped by seeking permission to use one of Song's team members to dig a well for a new water tower. Song can remember the days when such community projects were attacked en masse, with the whole village or even the whole commune turning out to prove it could put up a water tower, an apartment block or a dam faster than the neighboring communes. The peasants rarely received extra pay. Work projects were organized like athletic contests, produced broken legs and heart attacks, and probably resulted in shoddy, hasty work in the bargain. Nowadays special jobs are more often done by small work details, but Song did not like losing people from the fields even for a few days. Poker-faced, he bristled at Sun Meirong's request and said he could not spare anyone. Then Song and Madame Sun began to trade mild insults, a sparring match which we learned occurred every time she visited and always ended, as this one did, with Song giving in. They dragged in Madame Wang, the senior commune official present, to settle the argument.

Madame Sun: "You served Madame Wang a cup of tea before you served me. Therefore you are flattering her."

Song: "I am flattering Madame Wang so she will promote you!"

A shout came from the gate: "Victory!" The number one son, slouching in his undershirt after a hard day at the commune boiler factory, answered with a loud "Uh!?" In walked a short, pretty young woman in a bright blue blouse and gray slacks, typical of the stylish garb being adopted by many young peasants.

Victory had a gleam in his eye. "This is my . . . uh, wife!" he said. The premature introduction brought laughter and teasing.

"See how the young people are talking today!" said Song in mock disgust. Continuing the tease, he told us about Victory's previous girl friend. "She lived far away and was very tall, maybe five-foot-nine, taller than Victory. I don't know what happened to her, because Victory didn't tell me."

Victory's fiancée is a village girl. Madame Wang, an expert on such matters, explained that "some young girls in Peking think it would be good to marry into this commune. Things are good here, so after a few meetings with a go-between they make arrangements. But they don't know the men well and end up fighting and then get a divorce. So not as many marry here now . . . And, of course, we had the case of a peasant girl who married a schoolteacher from the city. He was a good man, but she was a rough woman, so they could not get along."

"There is a man in our team who got a divorce," Song joined in. "Xu Hui bought a wristwatch and a bicycle for the girl. They registered the marriage and got everything prepared for the feast, but the woman was not a very good woman. She suddenly said, 'Well, I don't want to get married,' and after a lot of complications and explanations, she said she simply didn't like Xu Hui.'" Though unconsummated (Song and Madame Wang blanched at the suggestion the legally married couple might have slept together before the wedding feast), the marriage required an official divorce, swiftly granted. Both parties married again, although Song said the woman's marriage was not a happy one. (He pointed out "the man who got the divorce" the next day. Xu was a husky, energetic man with a sad look on his face.) "At least she returned the wristwatch and the bicycle," Song said.

On a day when we spent much time with Song, he awakened at four o'clock to the sound of raindrops hitting the tile roof above him. Someone had left a small table out in the courtyard the evening before, when we had sat and devoured after-dinner apples and pears, so he dashed outside and rescued the piece of furniture. At five he awoke again, brushed his teeth, washed his face in a basin, and visited the family toilet in a mud-walled, roofless outhouse, where human waste was collected for the private plot. There was no time for a bath, and not much room for one either. "It is easier to take a bath in summer," Song said. "You just wear shorts and bring a basin of water out to the yard and rub the water all over your body with your hands." His wife, Liu, helped wash his back. In winter, perhaps once a week, Song waited until his youngest son and daughter, Winter and Littlehead, had gone to sleep in the adjoining room, then pulled out a big iron basin big enough to stand in and filled it with cold water and some generous helpings from the big teakettle. "I brush my teeth once a day, maybe once every two or three days," Song said. "I'm so busy I can't go off brushing all the time." Young people, we noticed, brush at least once a day, but their strong teeth and good eyesight probably had more to do with diet. The Chinese in this village ate lots of vegetables, and consumed little sugar other than in fruit. The young members of Song's team had excellent teeth and only one young woman wore glasses. "She read too much in middle school," Song said. Her nickname was "Spectacles."

Yu Qiuli, a lanky twenty-year-old woman, weeded in the field under Song's supervision and occasionally scraped mud off her long fingers with her knife. "I envy the eight-hour day the factory workers have," she said. "Some days when I see them leaving their work and going home, and I am still in the fields, I feel jealous." The talk departed only briefly from the young peasants' usual light-hearted teasing. "Your wife really keeps you under her thumb, doesn't she," a deputy team leader said to one of the quieter members. Another member, eavesdropping on one of our interviews, said, "Xiuzhu has now informed all of America she has a boyfriend!"

White flies had returned this season to hover above the fennel, and Song was worried. "They absorb nutrition from the crops. The commune is studying them, but you can see they are everywhere, here, and over near the beans too. I think they come from America"—he glanced at us—"or at least from some foreign country; maybe in some crops shipped here or some shipping crates, because we never saw them until a few years ago. If you sprinkle some insecticide to kill them, some will die, but the eggs last a long time."

Chinese peasants use insecticides, water pumps and other tools of modern farming enthusiastically, but suspect that new ways bring new problems: Would the white flies have appeared without the importation of foreign goods? They also realize that with so many people to put to work, the most efficient tools—tractors and combines—may cost more than they are worth and simply aggravate the already considerable difficulties of finding work for everyone.

Chinese agriculture remains precarious because it is never more than a few steps ahead of population growth, and yet making each peasant more efficient and using fewer workers in the fields would create enormous social problems. To raise living standards and keep the peasants happy, the government increased the prices it pays for crops, allowed peasants to make their own choices about what crops to cultivate (as long as they deliver a specified portion of grain to the state), and encouraged them to invest their profits in small-scale processing plants and farm-machine shops that will create new jobs in the countryside.

In the afternoon the production team enjoyed the luxury of working standing up instead of bent over. They picked string beans from vines growing on tall trestles. Zhao Yongguan, fifty, the team clown, had his undershirt rolled up to his chest. He sang Peking opera love songs: "We know each other *now,* but we *must* know each other *better.*" We asked Zhao what he did in the evening—read the paper, watch television? "I drink," he said. "I sing when I'm happy, but I like to drink first." Song, he noted, consumed six bottles of liquor a month, while he, old Zhao, drank ten. "He is my apprentice in the matter of drinking," Zhao said.

Song was in a philosophical mood: "I have shortcomings because I speak too freely. If I had not spoken so freely at times, I would have been promoted to higher levels." He had first been selected a team leader in 1965, but quit in 1974 when one brigade leader gave a relative easy work and a high pay share over Song's objections. Song had also squabbled with commune leaders over a plan to move the peasants into new two-story apartment buildings costing $30,000 each. They went ahead with the project "to educate me," Song said, but gave up when they ran out of materials and money, leaving only one finished building in the middle of a cabbage field.

The inanities of Chinese rural administration fill peasant conversations. Villages are often supervised by former Red Army soldiers who know little about modern farming and are often abrupt in dealing with the people, particularly when executing commands from headquarters. One American visitor to a remote village in Shanxi received ugly looks from the local people even when he spoke well of the usually popular Deng Xiaoping. Deng, or more likely a local official whom the peasants associated with him, had ordered the village to level its hilly fields so they could be tilled more easily. Unfortunately, the operation was going to destroy fertile topsoil and ruin crops for several years. Families in the village scurried to make sure that at least one relative had a salaried job in one of the few small-scale factories in the area, or in the nearby city of Taiyuan, so they could survive with few crops.

Both of the brigade leaders supervising Song were party members. Song was not. He was picked for his "practical experience," a sign of the decline in influence and prestige enjoyed by party members. At Nanping village, belonging to the party did not seem to matter much to Song or many of the other peasants. When we discussed the only party member in Production Team 13, a forty-eight-year-old woman, Song seemed to dismiss her. "All she does is stay home and take care of her grandchild. Since the policy of one child was passed, she does not like to leave him with the nursery." We said we thought it was odd that the team's only party member took no part in work or labor decisions. Song quoted Chairman Mao on the presence of people with party spirit outside the party and people without it inside the party. "Some people, after they are admitted to the party, lose enthusiasm for working and doing party duties. Although they remain in the party, they are not qualified to be leaders," he said.

Song's sometimes eccentric willfulness manifested itself during the Cultural Revolution when team members were looking for "targets" to criticize in the campaign. They settled on "outsiders" like Song. He was born in Nanping, but his father had come from southern Hebei, which in the insular world of Chinese village life meant that Song was not quite a native. "I had intended to stop at two sons and a daughter," he said, "but when they started looking down on us, I decided to have one more just to increase our numbers a bit in the village." He did not say what his wife thought of this fit of pique. The result was Winter, now a quick-witted, harmonica-playing teen-ager so nicknamed because he was born the first day of winter. During our stay Winter spent much of his time listening to the radio and going out to do the only chore he enjoyed—tending the family goat. It was not the sort of life Song recalled leading when he was thirteen.

"When I was twelve, even younger than Winter, I was working for the Japanese aggressors, repairing the airport," Song said. Song and his father would walk for an hour each day to what is now the military airfield in Peking's western suburbs. They worked until dark, repairing the damage made by Nationalist Chinese and American bombers; Peking was then held by the Japanese. They received as pay one or two cents' worth of corn flour each day, just enough to keep from starving.

Song felt lucky even then, for he understands how much worse things were and are in arid Nangang County, where his father was born. "I have never been to southern Hebei, but this must be a better life than there because we are closer to the big city."

We have seen a few of the people who still wander into the cities from the worst rural areas, as Song's father did in escaping southern Hebei. One rainy April evening Linda and her interpreter, Hou Ying, were leaving a Shanghai theater. Hou was needling Linda about what they had just seen in the movie, one of those made-for-TV American prison yarns that Chinese cultural officials like to offer as true slices of American life. While Linda was considering a reply, an old man dressed in rags, apparently emboldened by the unexpected sight of a foreigner, approached her with his hand outstretched. We had heard of beggars in China, but until then had never encountered one. The man said he was from northern Anhui. A stern look from Hou sent him on his way before Linda could learn more, but to her, the evening was a draw: "That beggar is about as representative of Chinese life as that movie was of American life."

For centuries, destitute farmers have come to the cities seeking help, and in some areas begging has become a tradition with its own rules and castes.

On the streets, beggars sing out to passers-by while shaking a little rattle and pointing to a hat on the ground for contributions. Another American, studying in Nanjing, described his experience at restaurants there. "When the meal was over, beggars would rush to our table and scoop up as much leftover food as they could before the waiters chased them away. Waiters are more tolerant when there are no foreigners around."

In most cities, beggars are a wintertime phenomenon; few stay for the summer. Peking beggars seem less obtrusive. Occasionally they would approach our table gingerly at the end of the meal and inquire, "Is this your dish or someone else's? May I sit down?"

Song's father, who died in 1974 at age eighty, was spared such indignities, as far as Song knows. He had come to Peking in 1909 as the Qing dynasty was collapsing, and found work as a tailor's apprentice. After the Japanese took Peking in the late 1930s, he moved to Nanping, where his wife, Song's mother, had grown up. There he worked as a farm laborer for the local landlords. Song remembered the biggest landlord in the village, Hou Wen. "I tried to gather some crops left over in his fields after harvest one time, when I was about twelve. He saw me, snatched what I had gathered and threw it away, just so I couldn't have it," Song said. Hou was arrested in 1949 and jailed for twenty years, then released and allowed to retire. "Now he just sits and eats," Song said with some scorn.

A nephew and niece of the old landlord belonged to Song's team. We tried to talk to the niece one day as she picked string beans. Song teased her about not being married yet. At thirty, she was a bit old not to be spoken for. Her family background made her a less attractive match because the landlord taint could affect jobs, salary and advancement of her future husband and children. She giggled at Song's taunts, but answered our questions with stock phrases from the *People's Daily*. She dared offer none of the personal impressions and complaints that ordinary Chinese peasants now share openly with visitors.

Song had managed to acquire four years of primary schooling before his family ran out of money. A patriotic-minded young intellectual near his village ran the school. Song now read the newspapers avidly, particularly news of China's activities abroad, and liked to try out his ideas on visitors. During the team's midafternoon break—a half-hour at four—and again after quitting time at seven he quizzed us about American policies toward China. He gave us his low opinion of President Reagan. He usually quoted the *Peking Daily*, the *People's Daily* and the *Peking Evening News*, whose emphasis on crime and light features made it the most popular paper in the city. "Although I am a peasant, I pay much attention to the international news. Why not?" he said. Song discussed U.S. military preparedness ("Some Americans don't want their children drafted. This shows they put their personal feelings above their country. But if there is no country, then you have no home") and dissected U.S. capitalism ("Your total incomes are rather high, but they are controlled by different financial groups. So, like a few years ago there was inflation in the United States and the dollar devalued").

We began to get a feeling what it must be like to be the director at Evergreen Commune and get a lecture from this lean and rough-hewn man. Of those officials who crossed him in 1974, "One was transferred to another place, but the rest are still here," Song said. "When they see me on the street, they get down off their bicycles and greet me, even though they are more important than I. I think it shows they are apologetic, and a little embarrassed."

It was also useful for Song to be older than most other team leaders. Chinese still respect their seniors. The elderly are cared for at home, their eccentricities tolerated. Old Xu, a neighbor of the Songs, told us he was eighty-two. Fearfully tall and thin, Xu spent his days strolling around the village. As we passed by him one day, a villager whispered to us, "He's actually eighty-four." According to a folk saying, seventy-three and eighty-four are hard ages to survive. "He figures he can safely get by this year, when he's eighty-four, by saying he's eighty-two, then next year he'll be eighty-five." Xu lived with his daughter and her husband, a lecturer at the Peking Industrial College. All of his six sons had died in infancy. After the death of the first one, before 1949, an old villager remembered, Xu broke down and wept: "Forgive me, forgive me, that I could not buy enough milk for you!"

Nanping is China at a hazy crossroad, the poverty and drudgery of the countryside evident, but a few goodies of city life slipping in. Planners in Peking would like to believe this is a trend, and perhaps it is—industrializing the countryside bit by bit, keeping the ambitious peasant youths out of the city. The father of Xu Shuxian, another village woman, was a farm hand in the 1960s. He tried to earn a little extra money raising pigs and rabbits in order to feed his wife and three children. Then the commune began to build some small factories to make farm-equipment parts. The factories gradually grew larger. Finally, a factory for boiler parts opened in the commune. Xu's father was hired as a cook. The family now had a guaranteed monthly income and Xu's father had more free time to tend his animals, even though he still could not draw the guaranteed retirement benefits of big-city workers. His children worked in the fields, and they could support him it his old age in the traditional fashion, particularly if, as is likely, one of them eventually got a similar factory job. This new alternative still does not look all that attractive to city people. A couple in a middle-sized Hunan city made their daughter's life miserable when she fell in love with a peasant boy working at a commune factory and finally packed her off to distant relatives to break up the romance.

"We don't have so much yet," Song said, but his team members are better off than peasants in the most remote parts of the country. "The Vietnamese refugees you mentioned who went to America are satisfied because they've got a better life than before. We are something like that. You have to look back at origins."

We noticed a lot of children in the village and asked the commune birth control experts about that. Song's decision in the sixties to have a fourth child would probably have been overruled in the China of the eighties. He and Liu would have been pressured to get an abortion or lose salary, benefits and chances for his other children's education. Li Yulan, a razor-thin, chain-smoking woman in charge of brigade "women's work," made it clear to us that someone was watching every married woman of childbearing age in the village. Of 487 brigade women, Li said, 167 wore intrauterine devices (what the Chinese call "rings"), 40 were on the pill and 147 had been sterilized. Only four husbands had submitted to sterilization.

In 1979, thirty-two babies in the brigade were born. Li anticipated about the same total in 1980, or perhaps one or two fewer. One of those births was not planned. Nine were second children, which would no longer be permitted if the government one-child-per-family rule held firm. Li said she had persuaded all but two of the 101 couples with one child or none to sign the one-child pledge. One of the recalcitrant couples had a child with a blood ailment and were not sure if he would live. The other couple "think this may be another campaign, and when it blows over, they can go ahead and have another child if they want," Li said.

The rule is, Li explained, once a couple are married they can immediately have a child, whenever they like. After that, no more children are allowed. There had already been nineteen abortions in the brigade in the first eight months of 1980, and of these, eleven of the women had been using intrauterine devices. Li planned to look into this more closely, to see if the pregnancies had resulted from carelessness or skulduggery. In other communes, doctors are occasionally caught removing the devices secretly for a fee. "We had one case of a woman who had a second child, without permission, and refused to get an abortion because she wanted a son. After she had the second child, we took away her medical welfare privileges," Li said. She laughed as if to say she could have predicted the outcome. "The second child was a girl too."

Every newborn child is entered in the family registry, a small binder holding a completed form for each member. The police keep one copy and the family keeps another in a safe place, like the space behind the Songs' portrait of Chairman Mao. A family member's vital statistics fill one of the standard pages in the book. It must be shown when applying for permission to travel, marry or undertake any other officially controlled function. Song's page read:

NAME:	*Song Duo*
SEX:	*Male*
BIRTHDATE:	*31-11-2* [November 2, 1931]
BIRTHPLACE:	*Peking*
NATIVE PLACE:	*Peking, Haidian district, Evergreen Commune, Nanping village*
NATIONALITY:	*Han* [meaning pure Chinese]
MARITAL STATUS:	*Married*
CULTURAL LEVEL:	*Primary school graduate*
WORK:	*Pingchuan brigade member, longtime resident*

Song seemed to regard this registration as a badge of place, but also as a trap. In a much poorer and less accessible village in southwestern Fujian (Fukien), American sociologist Victor Nee found growing discontent among peasant youth who saw dreams of city life fading fast. People with a rural registration, the villagers said, were barred by government regulation from being hired in a state-managed factory in an urban area. An old guerrilla activist in the village told Nee, "Urban youths don't even need technical skills to get assigned to a good job, but a rural youth who has a technical skill still can't get ahead." One youth said, "There is no way out." Peasants resented the system by which urban workers retiring from their factory could be replaced by one of their own children. The system, Nee said, "sealed their fate from generation to generation on the farm."

Yet *guanxi* links city and country. Most country people have some relatives who have made it, and they can use those connections to seek out better goods in the city shops while enjoying the spacious housing and better food which their city cousins envy. In many parts of the countryside, like Nanping, country life can be endured, and even improved, particularly if the bureaucrats are not too intrusive.

Song talked of the marriage plans of his eldest son, Victory, and the need to build a house for him. When Jay returned to say goodbye before leaving China, Song was out buying lime for the concrete. His father-in-law, a wiry old man with a five-day growth of beard, was using his skills as a professional carpenter to plane down pieces for a new table. Song had spoken of the project like the traditional Chinese father. He was resigned to pulling his family up to prosperity on his own, without much more help from the government or anyone else. "We have enough land for six rooms, two sets of rooms for two sons, but Victory just thinks of himself and doesn't care what we arrange for his brother." Song smiled with a mix of helplessness and satisfaction. "He thinks the old man can fix that up later."

Song conveyed the belief that his children would always remain in Nanping. Many things would keep them there and they had better make the best of it. Winter had a chance to attend a big, well-run junior middle school near the center of the district. It could enhance his chances to pass the exam for senior middle school, which only a small number of peasant youth ever attempt. Song and his youngest son sparred over transportation. Song said, "If you pass the exam, and really want to go to that school, I would buy you the tickets for the bus." "No," said Winter, "I want a new bicycle." Even if he did well, Song was almost certain his son would not go far. "If they have two students, one from the countryside and one from some city worker's family, the school will take the one from the worker's family. Why? I don't know. After graduation, I guess, they think it's better to assign factory jobs to the worker's family. The child from the countryside, they figure, knows better about the farm job."

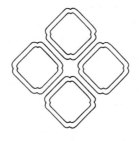

LANGUAGE

CHINESE IS PROBABLY THE OLDEST AND MOST COMMONLY USED LANGUAGE in the world, but it now seems close to a nervous breakdown. As beautiful as the written language is, twentieth-century demands for speed and efficiency have pushed it beyond its capacity. At first we thought our personal troubles with it were what one would expect of foreigners. But the Chinese themselves are embroiled in a debate over whether to reform the whole system or find some way around it.

The Confucianists used to talk about the "rectification of names." They believed that if they changed or eliminated the words that stood for negative aspects of society, those aspects would wither away, a concept given electronic-age trappings by George Orwell in *1984*. Some Chinese also suspect that the current language-reform drive springs from the *1984* impulse to rewrite history: attacking the roots of ancient, feudal Chinese culture by radically changing the writing system.

The Roman alphabet, in use among Western nations today, grew out of an ancient idea originating in western Asia: that written characters should correspond to spoken sounds. The Chinese, who were cut off from most of the world by the Himalayas, produced a very different system; no one knows why. Each character, or ideograph, stands for an object or idea, not its sound.

In one way, this was a very good idea; it helped unify the Chinese empire. In a territory so vast, people naturally spoke many different dialects. Some were as different to the ear as English and German. For example, the Chinese character for "man" looks like a stick figure and is easy to recognize. But in Peking dialect—also called Mandarin Chinese—it is pronounced *ren* and in Canton dialect *yan,* both no closer to each other than the English word "man." (Ask a Chinese to spell his name and he will often begin to trace invisible lines on his palm, like a deaf-mute, since there is no way to spell words orally in Chinese.) Since the writing system conveyed meaning, not sound, people in different parts of the country could read the same books and the same imperial edicts. Most would have had a difficult time understanding if the emperor had spoken to them directly. Chairman Mao himself broadcast very few speeches during his life and none at all in his last years. His periods of silence helped create a mystique, but they also reflected the fact that only a small portion of his audience would have understood his thick Hunanese accent without difficulty.

This ancient Chinese decision to write down concepts rather than sounds left the world's most populous nation with the world's most inefficient writing system (which was later adopted by the unwary Japanese). Each of the 4,000 to 5,000 characters in common use is separate and distinct, sometimes very intricate, and follows few pronunciation rules. Chinese schoolchildren must learn the thousands of characters by rote. Mastering the sound of twenty-six letters in an alphabet and a few hundred combinations of those letters, as Western children do, does not begin to match the requirements for reading Chinese. Memorization has been the only route to literacy, and that appears to have sent traditional Chinese education down into a deep, narrow channel, with little time for developing interest in mathematics, creativity in writing or experimentation in science. Reverence for the past—one of the most spectacular cultural heritages in the world—and the demands of the written language have forced students to spend nearly all their time memorizing the work of others.

During the late 1960s, that tradition along with many others came under political attack, but nothing was really offered in its place. Mao spoke of his distrust for book learning. He told his niece that the boy who sleeps in class is probably wise, for he is looking after his health. The Red Guards were organized in part to criticize their own teachers for the academic burdens placed on them—they had no time for revolution! Writing well became far less important, and the required daily memorization of Chinese characters fell off disastrously. In a short story by Jia Pingao called "Duan Yang," a primary-school teacher embittered by his experiences thinks about the young people he is meeting in the late 1970s: "I seemed to see again the broken windowpanes at school and the battered street lamps. I remembered reading a letter from a boy to his sick uncle. There were only 180 characters in the letter, but more than 100 were written incorrectly."

Students learn Chinese characters by constantly, painfully pounding their odd twists and turns into the synapses of the brain. Like any seven-year-old schoolboy, Jay in his college Chinese class had to practice writing each stroke of each character in a certain order. (This troublesome emphasis on stroke order has now become the key to one of the Chinese systems for computerizing their language). During Jay's recurrent, painful attempts to memorize the ideography, he tried flash cards, word association and mental telepathy. He tried to distinguish one character from another by visualizing sexual fantasies in the convoluted lines and twirls. None of this really worked. His calligraphy—so important to Chinese judgment of personal worth and character—remains hopeless.

One of the less obvious atrocities of the Cultural Revolution was the impact it had on the gritty business of learning the national tongue. Red Guards condemned exams as "surprise attacks" by "stinking intellectual teachers" on poor peasant and worker students. This created an enormous literacy gap when students no longer bothered to put in the long hours mastering the difficult characters. Although the Communists have taught more people to read than any regime in Chinese history, in late 1979 the official news agency reported that 30 percent of the nation's 800 million peasants still could not read and write. Illiteracy actually increased during the Cultural Revolution, the agency said, with about 120 million people under age forty-five now illiterate.

Jiang Liande worked in the Letters to the Editor office at the *People's Daily*. He shook his head ruefully when we asked about the letters the paper received from young people. Dozens of characters were written incorrectly. Army clerks interviewed by one Chinese newspaper confessed they had forgotten so many of the characters they had learned in school that it took them half the night to complete their reports.

The strain the language puts on China's modernization plans became apparent to us after a visit to the Peking typewriter shop at 54 Wangfujing Street. Salesman Hua Xishen told us he did a brisk business selling Double Dove brand Chinese-language typewriters. He was a year behind in filling orders. The Double Dove was considered to be the most efficient Chinese typewriter made. One look revealed why we had never, up to then, seen such a machine in operation. It was an instrument of mental torture. There was no keyboard on the instrument, which was a little larger than an average Western typewriter. A handle moved a clutching device over a tray holding up to 2,300 tiny pieces of type. Each piece was less than one-quarter-inch square and had a single character engraved on it. The operator used the handle to center the clutching device over the proper character. He then struck a key which caused the piece of type to be picked up and struck against the carbon ribbon and paper on a carriage roll similar to that on a Western typewriter.

A typist came into the shop to pick up her new machine. She said she could handle sixty characters a minute. That seemed impossibly fast to us. How long did she train before she could do that? "Three years."

She was the first Chinese we had ever met who claimed to be capable of operating a typewriter at a businesslike speed. An operator clutching type at sixty words a minute had to have an instinctive mental picture of the location of more than 2,000 different characters on the tray. But even that incredible psychic feat didn't solve the whole problem. As many as 4,000 or 5,000 characters, far more than one tray can hold, are necessary to write everyday Chinese. The operator must stop to pick one of the less common characters out of an auxiliary tray and drop it into one of the empty spaces left for that purpose on the typewriter's tray.

"Most typists develop very bad eyesight," a Foreign Ministry official told us. "They really have to squint to pick out the right character, and of course they have to read the image on the type when it is reversed and upside down."

Only a few offices have typewriters. They are hopelessly impractical for home use. We asked Hua, the typewriter-store salesman, why China did not switch to a Roman alphabet, as several Chinese reformers have suggested. The Vietnamese, after all, did this long ago.

"No, that won't work," he said. "People in Shanghai and Canton don't speak like us. They wouldn't understand what we wrote."

This is true, but it is not the only objection we heard to changing the language. Despite its failings, written Chinese has been wedded for more than three thousand years to the history of this particular nation and its development along the Yellow and Yangtze River valleys. The Chinese did not borrow their alphabet from another culture. The beautiful, complex characters were Chinese from the beginning and are difficult to abandon despite their glaring shortcomings.

Eddie Chan (a former Communist judge from Canton who taught Jay in graduate school) introduced us to Chinese language reform and its origins. Early in the twentieth century, forced by the demands of modern times to write faster and teach more people to read, the Chinese developed a short-hand way to write some of the more complicated characters. After the Communists took over in 1949, they organized an official list of these simplified characters and ordered that all publications use the new stream-lined version. *Ji,* meaning "hit" or "attack" (擊) became a much simpler 击 .

In 1978 the list was expanded. John Fraser, the former *Toronto Globe and Mail* correspondent in Peking, noticed that the old character for home, *jia,* which shows a pig under a roof (家), had been altered.

"The pig had been given the boot," Fraser said with some dismay. In its place was the less complicated symbol for a man (叐). Fraser's Chinese teacher had strictly taught him: "An apartment is not a home. An apartment is just a place to sleep and sit. A home has very many people—mother, father, grandparents, children, babies—and a home also has animals, some chickens and a pig. That is why a pig is in the house. It is not a home without a pig."

Many Chinese scholars attacked the 1978 revisions as ugly and confusing. A letter to the *Enlightenment Daily,* the national newspaper for intellectuals, complained that the new character for "face," *mian* (面), looked like a face without nose and eyebrows: 靣. A wave of protest forced officials to suspend the revisions. The pig returned home, at least for a while.

Americans caught a whiff of smoke from the Chinese linguistic battle-ground when newspapers here adopted the official Chinese Roman-alphabet spelling system called *pinyin*. Odd new spellings of Chinese names suddenly confronted American readers—Mao Zedong, Deng Xiaoping, Zhao Ziyang, and so forth. The Chinese hope the system might, among other things, someday enable them to use Western typewriters. *Pinyin*, which means "phonetic spelling," is also designed to help foreigners pronounce the official Peking dialect. For the moment the Chinese use them only on road signs, in advertisements and in schoolbooks, underneath the characters, to help foreigners and non-Mandarin speakers.

There had always been problems with the old Wade-Giles system, created by two Englishmen in the last century. Coming on the same day as official diplomatic normalization with the United States, January 1, 1979, the switch to *pinyin* should have been welcomed with great joy and trans-pacific acclaim—except that it drove people accustomed to the old Wade-Giles spellings absolutely mad. The well-traveled journey from Canton to Peking became, under the new system, an unfamiliar trek from Guangzhou to Beijing.

The old Wade-Giles romanization system was considered unsatisfactory because it made it difficult for the casual foreign reader to pronounce Chinese words correctly, something that gave China watchers much ammu-nition to fire on unsuspecting name-droppers. Before the change to *pinyin*, Linda once had the satisfaction of correcting a distinguished correspondent for CBS News who had spoken the name of Vice Premier Teng Hsiao-ping as it was spelled then. The correspondent pronounced "Teng" like the English word "tongue."

"Actually it's 'dung'—like the stuff cows leave behind," said Linda. The network man was aghast: "But I'm pronouncing it exactly as Walter does on the air!"

The *pinyin* word for the Chinese capital, Beijing, comes much closer to correct pronunciation than the old word, Peking, which was not even, strictly speaking, correct Wade-Giles spelling. It should have been "Pei-ching." Still, there are some troublesome bugs in the new system. For example, two important neighboring provinces of northern China were known in Wade-Giles as Shensi and Shansi, fairly simple to tell apart with practice. Under the *pinyin* system, these two provinces are rendered as Shanxi and . . . Shanxi. The Chinese can tell the difference when they *say* the words because the former calls for a low tone on the first syllable, while the latter has a high tone. The *pinyin* reformers have tried to meet this crisis by spelling the first province "Shaanxi," but that hasn't helped much.

Years ago one of Jay's professors began his first Chinese class by handing out mimeographed copies of a complicated story about a man who ate stone lions. Below the English version Jay found, to his horror, the same story rendered in romanized Chinese. It went: "Shih-shih Shih-shih Shih-shih

shih . . . shih" and so on, an entire story told with one sound. The only way even a Chinese could make sense of the story without seeing the actual Chinese characters was to hear it read aloud by someone who knew which of the four Chinese tones—high, rising, low and falling—to give each sound. A Canadian diplomat in Peking told us about the day he practiced the word *wen* ("to ask") with his attractive young teacher in Hong Kong. *"Wo yao wen ni* [I want to ask you]," he began. His teacher blushed and asked if he really wanted to kiss her. He tried another tone. *"Wo yao wen ni . . ."* "Now you want to *smell* me!"

The new *pinyin* spellings don't alleviate the tone problems—witness the case of the two Shanxi provinces. And how was a layman to know that *pinyin*'s *zh* should be pronounced like *j,* a *q* like *ch,* and an *x* like *s*? But these linguistic puzzles obscure the great secret of spoken Chinese, which is this: If one can master the tones, it is one of the simplest languages on earth to speak. The grammar is spare, perhaps too much so. Nouns don't take male or female articles as French or German nouns do. Verbs do not change their form to past, present or future tense as verbs in most other languages do. The Chinese very often don't even bother to distinguish between plural and singular.

Sidney Rittenberg, an American who arrived in China in 1945 and stayed to work for the Communist government, spent two long spells in Chinese prisons for alleged political offenses. In the process, he became one of the most accomplished American linguists in Peking. He likes the language reform, and thinks the fuzzy grammar should be one of the first things to go. "Take this sentence: 'You should not criticize the *lingxiu.'* The last word can mean 'leader' or 'leaders.' It's ambiguous, and I think the Chinese sometimes make use of this to protect themselves. In this case, it could make a very great difference whether they were attacking one man or a less identifiable group." Rittenberg recalled the old Chinese saying: "The clever bunny has three escape holes."

Rittenberg told us of the difficulty he had persuading a Chinese child that the two words "horse" and "scold," both pronounced *ma,* were the same sound with different tones. "He refused to believe it," Rittenberg said. "To him, there was nothing similar about the words at all, as if we were discussing another dimension."

The tones remain a hard pill for foreigners to swallow. One of Jay's classmates in Chinese was absolutely tone-deaf. He used all the proper Chinese vowels and consonants, but could not make any of the falling and rising tones. The teachers found it difficult to understand him but humored him because he was going to specialize in academic work on Qing dynasty documents, which did not require any real fluency in the spoken language.

In Peking our six-year-old son experienced the joy of approaching the language with the sponge-brain of the very young. He thought it funny that just a slight difference in the pitch of his voice turned the Chinese for "I am seven years old" into "I am an orange soda pop." This had never amused Jay at all. At Harvard he tried to learn the tones through a system so difficult that the college has since discontinued it. Its creator was the brilliant Berkeley linguist Chao Yuan-ren. In Chao's system, each tone was given a slightly different spelling. The four tones of the sound *ma,* for instance, were written "mha, ma, maa, mah"; for the sound *jing,* "jing, jyng, jiing, jinq," etc. One struggling undergraduate called it: "A system created by a genius for geniuses."

As foreigners have struggled to learn basic Chinese, the Chinese themselves have wrestled with whole dictionaries of new terms coming across the border hand in hand with Marxism and the technological revolution. Chinese translators have become alchemists, putting old words into strange new combinations: "rocket" is *huo-jian,* or "fire-arrow"; telephone is *dian-hua,* or "electric-talk." In some cases, the Communists have altered into incomprehensibility a number of old phrases by way of devising their own ideological jargon, taking one character each from a string of two-character words to make abbreviations. *Mei di,* for instance, which literally means "beautiful emperor," is the abbreviation for "American imperialism." The long form is *meiguo diguozhuyi,* or "beautiful country empire principle ruling idea." The Chinese two hundred years ago would have read its literal meaning and twirled their queues in wonderment.

Politics kills old meanings and usages very quickly. For at least a decade Chinese avoided the word "self-study" because it was a favorite term of the late President Liu Shaoqi, the since rehabilitated villain of the Cultural Revolution. "Radical" phrases used by the disgraced Defense Minister Lin Biao, accused of trying to overthrow Chairman Mao in 1971, remained on the proscribed list much longer. At one hospital, it was reported in the press, a patient was given a new type of injection and marveled out loud at its "immediate results." The man in the next bed blanched. "My goodness," he said, " 'immediate results' [one of Lin's favorite slogans] has already been criticized, yet you are still using it!" In 1976, waitresses would chide customers, usually foreigners, who said they wanted to *suan-zhang* (settle accounts). The term, which had been used throughout the Cultural Revolution to denote political revenge, was considered in poor taste. By 1980, memories of that era had faded enough for the term to return to favor, at least in the dining room of the Peking Hotel.

Heartened by such backsliding, some Chinese critics have boldly tried to discredit the language-reform system itself as a temporary aberration. "The written language is not like a car that can be traded in for a new model every year," reasoned Zhou Yuguang, a dissident member of the state council's language-reform committee and a man who has heard about Detroit. "If the written language keeps on changing models, nobody will be able to recognize it." Many Chinese scholars have gradually shed their fears about criticizing the reform, despite its Communist Party backing. The Chinese remain entranced by the beauty of written characters in a way typewriter-bound Westerners find difficult to understand. Artists have used the characters in their work for thousands of years and an expert calligrapher has always been just as much esteemed in China as a painter of the first rank. In the late 1970s the Chinese began to revive the old custom of calligraphy contests for young people. Many older officials also displayed their calligraphy, considered only a few years ago to be a rather backward pastime (except when done by Chairman Mao himself). One clever group of undergraduates at Canton's Zhongshan University gave their literary magazine a shield against official attempts to shut it down by having prestigious scientist and Peking University President Zhou Peiyuan write out the magazine title in his own handwriting, and reproducing that for the cover.

Chinese scholars added to the interest in preserving the old writing style with a raging argument over whether Chinese characters date back six thousand years or only four thousand years. The dispute may seem academic, but it illustrates a fact of overriding importance: ordinary Chinese can read ancient documents without much help. By contrast, English scholars need special glossaries to understand their language as it was written less than a thousand years ago. This gives Chinese characters an enormous sweep over not only time, but geography. Some fifteen hundred years ago, the Japanese perhaps unwisely but irrevocably adopted a huge hunk of the Chinese writing system as their own. So today, without any training, a literate Japanese can get the gist of a Chinese book.

In some mystic fashion the characters hold the secret of the unity of China, and unity is something the historically minded Chinese do not take for granted. The spoken language has eight major dialects, representing several millennia of hostility, bias and distrust. There is the North China, or Peking, dialect, now the official national language, which Westerners call Mandarin. There are the dialects of Jiangsu-Zhejiang (Kiangsu-Chekiang, including Shanghai), Hunan, Jiangxi (Kiangsi), northern Fujian, southern Fujian (Fukien), Guangdong (Kwantung) and Hakka. The Chinese try to paper over regional hostility with humor—their own varieties of Polack jokes. A favorite—and perhaps prehistoric—northern Chinese joke: "I don't fear heaven. I don't fear earth. What frightens me is a southerner speaking northern dialect."

But jokes cannot substitute for the enormous bond of the written language. Our amah, Ah-Lin, grew up in Hong Kong, where everyone spoke Guangdong dialect. In Peking she could not make herself understood. Jay sometimes interpreted the northern dialect for her, using Ah-Lin's own special brand of pidgin English. But if Jay was not around, and Ah-Lin needed something from the hotel staff at the Peking Hotel, she could simply write down what she wanted and be immediately understood.

The language-reform advocates argue that they do not need the old written language to unite the country when everyone learns Peking dialect. But many older inhabitants of southern China consider the northern dialect a foreign tongue best ignored. A teacher in one school in Fujian, the southern province with not one but two distinct dialects, called the northern dialect simply "a waste of time." That was a widespread attitude, to judge from the linguistic talents of Fujian children we talked to, none of whom seemed fluent in the national tongue.

Government officials say all schools now use the northern dialect, but foreigners visiting schools south of Yangtze often find this is not so. One recent British visitor to a Shanghai high school discovered that in every class, except Chinese literature, the teachers were using local dialect. The adherence to local language persists even though local operas are so difficult to understand that theaters in China routinely project the words on a special screen at the side of the stage so that everyone can see the actual characters being sung and spoken. At a Peking divorce trial we attended, the woman suing for divorce was asked to comment on remarks just made by her husband's amateur counsel, a factory supervisor with a Hunanese accent. "Sorry," she said with some sarcasm, "I couldn't understand a word he said."

During our first trip to China in 1977, our official interpreter wrestled with three dialects. Xiong Xirong spoke the northern dialect beautifully, even though he was raised in the far south. He got by with the blurred accents of the Shanxi hill people near the Dazhai model farm brigade. But in the outskirts of Shanghai he broke down completely. During a briefing at a provincial commune, a Shanghainese interpreter listening to Xiong's efforts began to giggle. Xiong sank deeper and deeper into despair, trying to sort out the z and j sounds that so bewilder northern visitors to Shanghai. Finally, and much to Xiong's embarrassment, the Shanghai interpreter took over.

Sidney Rittenberg's interpreter failed him completely on a trip outside Canton, so he tried his own hand at it. "If the village official cadres talked about political and administrative problems, I could follow it. When they talked about everyday life without the easily recognizable bureaucratic and Marxist terms, I couldn't understand them." Hu Sha, deputy editor in chief of the *Enlightenment Daily,* complained that in Guangdong and Fujian, the two southern provinces where the ancestors of most overseas Chinese come from, "people have not only different pronunciation, but different grammar and word order."

Hu supports the reform idea, though with a lingering discomfort he shares with many educated Chinese. "Some people say the intellectuals are the enemies of language reform," Hu said. "They may have something there, for the intellectuals already know the Chinese language well. I am an intellectual, but I am also the deputy chief editor. I should use the simplified versions of characters in my writing, but instead I tend to use the old forms. The young workers in the composing room complain that they can't read my writing."

The Chinese love words and are absorbed in their language. By their very nature, the characters can become works of art. The Chinese used to have a superstition against throwing away anything with writing on it. Dictionaries in Peking are best sellers. Jay would seek help from by-standers when he could not remember a character. Such inquiries often incited animated discussion among waiters or room attendants, or even college-educated officials at an official briefing, on the proper rendering of a particular word.

The Chinese seem resigned to this endless stormy marriage with their language, no matter what it does to their increasingly important relations with the outside world. Foreigners who try to bridge this gap and deal with the Chinese in their own language find many Chinese do not even believe this is possible. There is a story about a British diplomat who had taken honors in Oriental languages at Cambridge and had lived in Peking for years. Driving toward Tianjin, he took a wrong turn and stopped to ask directions in his flawless northern accent from a couple of peasants standing at the roadside: "Is this the road to Tianjin?"

"Eh? What did you say?"

"Which way to Tianjin?"

"Sorry, we don't understand foreign languages."

"Is this the way to Tianjin?"

"Beg your pardon, we only speak Chinese."

The diplomat gave up in disgust and started his car. Then, just before he pulled away, he heard one peasant say to the other, "Wasn't that strange? I could have sworn that foreigner was asking directions to Tianjin."

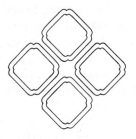

SEX

BY CHINESE STANDARDS, LU PANSHENG WAS A MAN OF THE WORLD. Dispatched to the countryside with thousands of other teen-agers, he had raised rubber trees on the tropical island of Hainan, far from home. Despairing of his future there, he escaped to the big city of Canton and dodged the police for months. He finally made his way to the border and swam across shark-infested waters to Hong Kong.

Despite his self-sufficiency, Lu, a wiry twenty-four-year-old with long locks and movie-star looks, had never attempted and could not even describe the sexual act. Lu's innocence might strike most Americans as improbable, even unbelievable, but the Chinese to whom we have related this story accept it matter-of-factly. "Of course he knew nothing about sex," one said. "He doesn't need to know anything about sex. He's not married."

Although China ranks as the world's leading baby producer, the Chinese are also champions at putting sex in its proper place, the marriage bed. Even there it is a rare indulgence; the government recommends intercourse no more than once a week. Chinese youths, especially the ambitious ones, regard sex as a forbidden zone, a trap that can lead to scandal or a dead-end marriage, and although some plunge in anyway, most feel it is better left unexplored.

The Chinese still cover their furniture with antimacassars and believe that father knows best. They are equally Victorian in their attitude toward sex. Mao and the other idealistic young revolutionaries who came to power three decades ago may have succeeded in reforming many aspects of China's feudal society, but their revolution stopped at the bedroom door.

In a country as crowded as China, where privacy is a luxury, a sexual revolution would have shaken the bonds of family and *guanxi* beyond repair, and perhaps even destroyed the political stability the Communists had painfully reconstructed. More than any other fact of Chinese life, that lack of privacy still affects Chinese sexual expectations, freedom and conduct, and will continue to do so. So many Chinese remain in the neighborhood where they grew up, within shouting distance of their parents' house, or work in the same factory or office all their lives, that they cannot imagine the anonymity which helps make sexual freedom possible in the West. The crush of population also makes the government want to control an individual's sex life, delaying his marriage, requiring reports on a couple's birth control methods, and enforcing abortion and sterilization.

Like residents of any small town, the Chinese have protected themselves from the disruptive emotional power of sex by not talking about it too much, and leaving their young people as ignorant of the subject as possible. We met young Chinese women, students at Peking University, who were convinced they could get pregnant by swimming in a public pool. Some took showers in their underwear rather than appear naked before other women at the university bathhouse. Chinese women of all ages are so fearful of seeming the least bit provocative that they hide their figures with oversized blouses and padded jackets. Anyone who tucks her shirt into her pants or otherwise shows off a curve or two risks being branded promiscuous.

"Does anyone ever get to see your legs?" Linda sometimes asked her interpreter. Hou Ying subscribed to the common view that no respectable woman past the age of thirty should wear a skirt in public. "Just once, before you leave China, I will wear a skirt," Hou promised. She wore pants even on the hottest days, but eventually kept her promise, donning a skirt one night before she welcomed us home from an out-of-town trip. "See," she said gaily, "I have legs."

Pity any woman whose body departs from the boyishly flat ideal. One eighteen-year-old girl complained to a Peking magazine that "people consider me sexually promiscuous because I have a large bosom." The magazine's editors, trying to soothe her and other well-endowed unfortunates, solemnly announced that there was no correlation between a girl's bra size and her morals.

Not surprisingly, among a people so self-conscious about their bodies, misinformation is rife. A Frenchwoman, who had lived a long time in Peking, told us about a twenty-seven-year-old woman who had come to her in some distress a week before she was to marry. "She didn't know whether or not she could get pregnant from kissing—which I think she had only started doing a few weeks before. And she didn't know how to take the pill or understand what good it would accomplish."

Once, at a party, we had some fun at the expense of one of China's most celebrated athletes. Li was a natural cynic with few illusions about anything, an ex-soldier who mingled with movie actresses and high party officials. That evening someone showed him a copy of *Playboy* magazine, which he leafed through with great interest. "So this is something for women to help make themselves more beautiful, right?" he asked.

"No, no, Little Li, it's for men!"

"Well, if it's for men, why aren't there more men in the pictures?" he demanded, leaving his American listeners speechless. He tried to puzzle it out: "The articles—do they contain beauty tips?"

Some foreign tourists find such naïveté intriguing and go home convinced that having banished all overt forms of sexuality, the Chinese have somehow achieved a healthier society. Could it be that the Chinese really have conquered their physical desires in the all-out effort to achieve the four modernizations?

Of course not: public shyness and a strict sense of propriety toward sex often hide deep-seated frustrations that can and do explode. Rape does not appear to be nearly as common as it is in the United States, but it is on the rise in major Chinese cities, as is the incidence of child molestation. Prolonged sexual innocence is not possible without sexual repression. China's social arbiters—the factory supervisors, commune chiefs and neighborhood leaders who enforce the party line—can be heartbreakingly harsh toward anyone caught violating the sexual code. Single women who become pregnant are pressured to get abortions, but are sometimes forced to wait until the sixth or seventh month—when their humiliation will be apparent to everyone and the operation as painful as possible. Teen-age girls who are caught making love with their boyfriends are branded delinquent and packed off to reform schools. The boys, though, are usually excused unless they have also committed some "wrongdoing against society," such as stealing or fighting.

Saddest of all, many Chinese, deprived of the chance to meet informally with the opposite sex during adolescence, end up in unfulfilling, passionless marriages. Forbidden by custom and Communist Party dictum to socialize and date in their teens, the Chinese do not usually pair off until their mid-twenties or later. Even if officials did not frown on such behavior, public teasing and limited privacy would still inhibit teen-age lovers. The usual minimum age for marriage is twenty-seven for men, twenty-five for women, though it varies slightly from place to place. In rural China, marriages are still arranged by go-betweens; even in the cities, where free choice is the rule, marriage brokers are kept busy. The Chinese often end up marrying the first person who strikes their fancy. "Playing the field" is regarded as promiscuity, for men as well as women.

"My parents' marriage is terrible, and nearly every marriage I know about is terrible," one recent Peking University graduate told us. Whether or not her grim assessment was accurate—outsiders can of course only guess what goes on between any husband and wife—her male and female classmates seemed to be in agreement. All of them insisted that they would get to know many members of the opposite sex—socially but not sexually, for they were still too timid for that—before settling on a lifetime mate. That is the extent of China's sexual revolution.

· · ·

The sexual repression that pervades China, oddly enough, departs from some easygoing attitudes of the past. The Christian concept of sex as sinful never took hold in China. Sex was as natural as hoeing the fields, as long as it was carried out in the right time and place, according to the philosopher Mencius, the ancient popularizer of Confucianism. It was assumed that most people would marry, and among the elite, marriage did not automatically mean monogamy: any man who could afford more than one wife or a house full of concubines could have them.

Prostitution was recognized as a necessary occupation. The Ming dynasty maintained scores of brothels, often graded for different ranks of officials. Literary puns were salacious, statues were crude, and many drawings, particularly the "pillow books," intended as instruction for brides and novice prostitutes in the art of love, were openly obscene. The Chinese developed foot-binding as a unique erotic art. The practice originated with the Song dynasty a thousand years ago when growing urban prosperity reduced the need for female labor. The deformed, half-normal-sized feet which resulted from breaking the arch (and crippling the woman) became as sexually provocative to Chinese men as tight jeans are in the modern-day West. Moreover, a wife whose feet had been bound from childhood emphasized the wealth of any man who could afford such a useless bride.

One of the triumphs of Chinese literature, the sixteenth- or seventeenth-century novel entitled *The Golden Lotus,* chronicled the adventures of a Chinese libertine, a wealthy merchant who eventually died of his own excesses. It was a moral tale, which titillated its readers all the same. Chinese pornographers and sex merchants did a thriving business right up until the Communists' 1949 victory, which also ended foot-binding (already in decline) and other lascivious activities. Old Asia hands still reminisce about the supple charms of the Chinese girls who worked on the "flower boats," the floating brothels anchored near Canton and Shanghai.

With the advent of Communism the freewheeling sexual attitudes of China's big coastal cities collided with the sterner peasant values of the Chinese interior, the heart of the Communist revolution. In the countryside, where life was organized around the family and the extended clan, relations between the sexes meant one thing: marriage. Young people were not trusted to make such important decisions on their own. The two families, led by their elders, came to terms, looking out for their future financial security and the assurance of healthy offspring to maintain the family fortunes and observe the proper Confucian ceremonies. Love and sexual attraction were secondary considerations in marriage; what mattered was whether the union was useful to the family and the larger society. Typically, a bride never set eyes on her groom until she was taken in a sedan chair to his parents' home for the ceremony.

The Communists carried over into the new era this idea that the demands of the community should come before the desires of the individual. Sex was to be confined to marriage. Arranged marriages were abolished by a landmark 1950 Marriage Law, but anyone who wants to wed now must have the consent of his factory or brigade chief, surrogate parents. The party also outlawed prostitution, mindful of the impoverished families who had been forced to sell their daughters to brothels in the 1930s and 1940s.

Onto these peasant values the Communists grafted a stiff, Stalinist moral code that was quite alien to China. Like other Marxists, the Chinese Communists saw themselves as ascetics dedicated to the glorious task of remaking an entire country. Love and sex were considered unworthy diversions from revolution. The heart of a true Communist belonged to the cause, not to some other mortal. To encourage young people to give their lives to "national reconstruction," the Communists seized on the idea of prolonging adolescence, delaying marriage until a person had reached his or her late twenties.

China's Communist Party chieftains have not always practiced the sexual asceticism and self-denial that they have preached. In the 1920s some of the young men who later ruled China, such as Mao, dabbled in sexual experiments, just as their counterparts in Paris, London and New York did. The early Chinese Communists of the Jiangxi Soviet were painted as free-love advocates, mostly by their enemies, and subsequent memoirs of those involved confirmed that some strayed from the usual peasant vigilance in sexual matters. Like the emperors of old, many Communist leaders—Mao, Liu Shaoqi, Deng Xiaoping—had several wives, though usually not concurrently. Mao's first wife, Yang Kaihui, has been extolled in the press and on the stage as a great Communist martyr because she refused to betray Mao and was executed by the Nationalists. What the legends about her conveniently overlook is that two years before she died, Mao abandoned her and took up with an eighteen-year-old girl, He Zizhen (Ho Tzu-chen), who eventually became his second wife. He Zizhen was emotionally and physically battered by the travails of the Long March. She and Mao were forced to give away two of their young children to peasants and they never saw them again, then after they ended the march she was replaced in Mao's affections by a Shanghai movie starlet, the now infamous Jiang Qing (Chiang Ch'ing).

A double sexual standard still exists, not so much between men and women (though transgressions are more readily forgiven in men) as between city and country people, and particularly between the privileged elite in the upper ranks of the party and "the masses." Most twenty-five-year-old women will blush furiously and giggle like teen-agers when asked if they have boyfriends. But there are other young Chinese—the offspring of high party officials, with money and time to spare—who could be considered worldly by any standard. An American friend who came to know some of these kids well—they invited her to teach them disco dancing—was unprepared for the kind of entertainment they concoct for themselves.

"They invent sex games," she said. "At parties, they go off to an empty room in their parents' house and lock the door. Then two make love while a third stands by with a stop watch. It was a game: How long could a couple keep one sex act going? How fast could they do this or that? Everyone was quite matter-of-fact about it."

Entertainment for ordinary people is carefully monitored by government censors and film boards who make sure books and movies are wholesome and uplifting, but there are fewer restrictions on the elite. A naval officer we met had attended screenings of X-rated films, imported from the West, at a villa in the western hills of Peking. He had never seen oral sex before and, in fact, had not even known that such practices existed. The films, which party officials had brought home from trips abroad, were shown at regular intervals to soldiers with good connections. Foreign diplomats in Peking say that sure-fire entertainment for Chinese dignitaries visiting their countries is a privately screened film, the raunchier the better. "If word ever gets around that so-and-so saw *Deep Throat,* he can always write it off as a study of Western culture or say he couldn't have walked out without offending his hosts," said one diplomat.

Sexual license is still regarded as one of the privileges of rank. Young girls from the city who were sent off to the countryside during the Cultural Revolution were sometimes convenient targets for unscrupulous rural officials. As the "down to the countryside" program began to disintegrate after Mao's death, tales surfaced in wall posters and even in the party-controlled press about officials who traded extra food or travel permits to girls in return for sexual favors. "We're sure one or two women students in our brigade did something like that to get transfers from the fields to good factory jobs," a student from Guangdong province told us. The Chinese find it easier to discuss such incidents if they have occurred in the past, particularly a discredited period like the Cultural Revolution, but sexual harassment continues in China, just as it does in any other country.

B. Michael Frolic, a Canadian diplomat and scholar, met an emigrant in Hong Kong, a young woman who, with great reluctance, told of being attacked by a commune official. The man had first tried to cajole her: "I can do what I like with women here. Nobody dares oppose me and you'll warm my bed just like the others before you." She eventually fought him off, but he went unpunished while she had to endure stares and more unwelcome propositions. Another man told her, "Why the false modesty? Your affair with the commune cadre is well known here. Take me as your lover now—I'm much better-looking, and I'm younger, too."

This almost feudal pattern of sexual harassment seems widespread. Peasant proverbs—such as "A woman who first resists will then remain faithful forever"—still survive. The *People's Daily* reported that one woman in the Guangxi Zhuang Autonomous Region, the area adjacent to Vietnam, who had rejected an official's proposal was stripped naked and kicked around the local marketplace by him and two cronies.

In outrageous cases like this one, the Lotharios are disciplined. In early 1980 a commune chief who boasted of his harem—he claimed to have slept with nearly every woman who worked for him—was prosecuted, convicted and sentenced to life in prison. Even harsher justice was meted out to a pair of twenty-seven-year-old twin brothers, the sons of a major general in the People's Liberation Army, who were found guilty of seducing or raping no fewer than 106 women in the city of Hangzhou. One brother was sentenced to death and immediately executed by a shot in the back of the head (both his trial and execution were televised); his twin was also sentenced to death, then granted a two-year reprieve, with a chance to escape the executioner if he reformed. The case was widely publicized as an example of China's even-handed justice, but cynics pointed out that the twins' father, a lieutenant of the late Defense Minister Lin Biao, was currently in disgrace. What would have happened, they wondered, if their father had still been in good standing?

China's party-controlled press rarely discusses the private lives of national leaders, but that doesn't stop the masses from gossiping about their superiors. Word of dancing parties and sexual high jinks among the children of top leaders travels fast. Although we never found out whether the rumors were true, most Chinese we met were convinced that the party's second-ranking official, the former Army Marshal Ye Jianying (Yeh Chien-ying), eighty-two, was a roué of enormous sexual appetites. The young nurses who accompanied him everywhere were often referred to as "the concubines."

Appearances mean nearly everything to the Chinese. In most places, walking a young woman home is about the same as putting a wedding notice in the *People's Daily*. Kissing her is virtually a proposal of marriage, or should swiftly lead to one.

Foreigners find out the rules the hard way. When Steve Thorpe, an American college teacher in the southwestern city of Kunming, innocently met a woman student in his office to discuss an assignment, a Chinese colleague warned him not to let it happen again.

Romances occasionally blossom between Chinese and foreigners, and sometimes lead to the altar, but are best pursued only if one has serious intentions. The slightest miscue can offend the opposite sex and lead to severe penalties. As Australian radio correspondent Richard Thwaites, a longtime Peking bachelor, put it, "In China, there is no halfway house between marriage and rape, so you have to be very cautious." The authorities have tried to abort some Chinese-foreign matches on political grounds; they sent to a labor camp a twenty-five-year-old artist who was engaged to

Emmanuel Bellefroid, French attaché and a leading expert on Peking's dissident movement.

Living in a village of one billion, the Chinese are obsessed with appearances. Even small bits of gossip can produce catastrophic results. Unlike Americans, who can move easily from one job or town to another, the vast majority of Chinese grow up assuming they will go on living in the same neighborhood—or attached to their first assigned work unit—for the rest of their lives, with no way to escape whatever reputation is bestowed on them there. In a celebrated case in Peking, warehouse worker Wang Yung-tai, twenty-four, was sentenced to life imprisonment after cracking open the skull of a woman who refused to date him. The prosecutor said Wang lost control only after he came to the erroneous conclusion that the woman had told other people about her refusal.

The sexual code is particularly strict in the countryside. Chinese peasants lead sex-segregated lives and view any pairing off among the young with suspicion. Urban youths accustomed to girl-boy joshing at coeducational high schools and colleges were stunned, during the Cultural Revolution, when they were reassigned to communes and state farms. Many of the perhaps 17 million urban youths dispatched to the countryside quickly adopted the practices of their hosts, however, even to the point of not talking to old classmates of the opposite sex when they passed each other on a tree-shaded rural cowpath.

No one has calculated how many young men and women go to their marriage bed not really knowing what they are supposed to do. In some southern villages, girls reaching puberty are sent to chat with women who are older and "experienced," i.e., matrons with lots of children. The success of these sessions is often thwarted by the pervading peasant reluctance to delve too deeply into the subject of sex.

Some Communist Party leaders have concluded that better-informed young people might have more success at birth control, and so have attempted to shine a little light in this dark corner. One health worker told us of the time the commune delivered a small book to married couples at their wedding ceremony. It described how to raise their baby and discussed all aspects of married life including birth control, but it had no illustrations. It began with a quote from Chairman Mao on the significance of birth control, then discussed contraceptive methods and devices.

A more daring effort, its eventual success unknown, came later, she said. "The commune began to send around a traveling group, going from brigade to brigade to explain birth control in detail with printed pictures. The male team members spoke to the men, the female team members to the women." They met in separate cramped, mud-walled assembly rooms, with colored pictures of Mao staring sternly from the wall. Many prefer, however, to follow the traditional practice of avoiding discussion of sex altogether and hope that will dampen interest in the subject. Few of the hospitals or government license offices we approached, for instance, had any written material on birth control to give out to newlyweds.

Courting and indeed marital relations remain a problem, both in the city and in the countryside. Privacy as we know it does not exist except among the most privileged or fortunate citizens. It is not a human right. In a way, many Chinese welcomed the great north China earthquake of 1976, for the damage and danger of aftershocks forced the construction of mud-brick shelters in the front yards of apartment buildings. Some couples saw a chance for their first night alone in years; they sent children and grandparents to the shelter, gladly accepting the risk for a night by themselves in the crack-walled apartment building.

For young lovers, the chances of solitude are even slimmer. Unmarried Chinese would be stunned at the idea of picking up contraceptives at the local pharmacy, as teen-agers do in America, even though in China they are often free. A young peasant on such a mission would be entering not an impersonal shopping center, but a small shop where he would be known. Word would get around quickly about his unusual acquisition.

In a nation without private automobiles or drive-in theaters, it is difficult to find a place to do much more than chat. The only reliable way a young couple can find a measure of privacy and intimacy in China is to take a long walk. At dusk, on the streets of every Chinese city from Harbin to Nanning, you can see young men and women out strolling in great numbers. They wear faded blue coats and slacks, neither male nor female betraying any effort to dress up for the occasion. Sometimes they hold hands, though usually not; city youths are slightly bolder about this than their country cousins. The couples seem intent on escaping their own neighborhoods, the stares and knowing whispers of their immediate neighbors who spend summer evenings sitting out on the sidewalk. Long bicycle rides, with the love-struck cyclists coasting slowly side by side, are also popular.

At night, while taking a shortcut through a dark and muddy Canton alley, we tripped over a couple embracing on the ground, both apparently fully clothed. There were others in the alley, and we retreated. It was a chilly evening, but there was really no other place the lovers could go. On a much warmer night in Xiamen (Amoy), the city that faces Quemoy (Jinmen) and Taiwan's other offshore islands, we were exploring the Martyrs' Memorial, with its shadowy alcoves, and spotted couples in more compromising positions. The next day we mentioned this to a group of students at Xiamen University, who laughed with some embarrassment. "You should see the beach at night," said one of the young men. "It's worse."

In Shanghai, on steamy spring evenings, lovers carve out a little space on the broad crowded walkways of the Bund—the city's famous riverfront—

by deft use of an umbrella. A China expert from the U.S. State Department, Dennis Harter, became fascinated with this practice and developed what he calls "the umbrella theory of Chinese love." It is possible to judge the intimacy of a relationship, he says, by the position of the umbrellas. If both the man and the woman are holding umbrellas as they perch on a park bench, and there's a space between the umbrellas, then they're just getting acquainted. As the umbrellas draw closer and closer together, so is the relationship. If a couple appears with a single umbrella and huddles behind it, their engagement is imminent. Some then progress again to two umbrellas, curved around so that their activities are completely screened.

These nighttime pursuits have not gone unnoticed by the party. On a bulletin board near Shanghai's People's Park, a former race track now favored for romantic trysts, a printed sign gently counseled moderation. Love is a normal thing, it said, but young men and women should treat it with pure motives. People should not really talk about love during working hours. Too frequent dating might distract them from their work for the state. The sign added an endorsement of late marriage and advised building a happy home life with no more than two children.

"Most people will try to leave them alone," one young peasant woman told us, describing the difficult status of young lovers, "but children follow them just to make jokes, or do other mischief. I know a boy and a girl who went into a sugar-cane field on the way home after work. Another girl walking behind them thought they might try to steal some sugar cane, and she wanted to steal some too. But she came across them making love. She turned around and went on to the village and told everybody. The next day the story was everywhere, and the couple immediately went and registered to marry. In their case, it was just a little sooner than they had planned."

Premarital sex is universally condemned, but when it occurs, the response of families, friends and officialdom is complex—and often difficult to predict.

One official directive, summing up the problem, advised young men that wandering sensual thoughts might be best handled with a cold bath. When two partially clad Chinese students at a Shanghai university were caught making love in the bushes, classmates publicly denounced them because "they let themselves go while others have to hold themselves in." The man was imprisoned and the woman committed suicide, not an unusual response in China to severe public humiliation. Teen-agers who experiment with sex are regarded as deviants, almost as criminals, and are swiftly punished (although a fifteen-year-old girl at a juvenile reformatory outside Peking told us that no one was sent there unless she slept with her boyfriend twice; as the old American courtroom saying goes, every dog is entitled to one bite).

An unmarried woman of any age who finds herself pregnant will be pressured to undergo an abortion even if she intends to marry the father.

The reason for this is that the unplanned pregnancy, which would push her brigade or her factory unit over its annual birth quota, is even more undesirable than the illicit sex act. Abortion is legal and easily available even in small commune clinics. In many clinics and hospitals we visited, the number of abortions almost equaled the number of live births, all for the greater good of controlling the population. From friends in the countryside, we heard of pregnant girls who first underwent an abortion and then were compelled to marry the father, a Chinese variation of the American "shotgun" wedding.

But if the lovers are approaching marriageable age, have formally announced their intention to wed and are savvy enough to avoid pregnancy, people sometimes can be more tolerant of a little pre-wedding lovemaking. "If you make love with your fiancé before marriage, people will understand," a middle-aged Peking woman confided to Linda. "They will not approve, of course, but they will not criticize you. Everyone knows it can be hard to wait." Her younger, unmarried sister, listening to this, was agog. The older woman turned to her, wagged a finger and warned, "But only with your fiancé! And everyone gets only one fiancé!"

Among young people in their twenties, there is a sexual revolution of sorts going on, albeit a hesitant one. Young women in short summer skirts and bouffant hairdos, pretty models on downtown billboards, kisses on the movie screen, couples smooching and groping in the darkened parks, a rising toll of abortions among unmarried girls—all are signs of slowly changing sexual mores.

The personnel officers at the Civil Aviation Administration of China, China's national airline, got a shock when they reviewed the health records of the stewardess applicants who had been judged the most attractive in a preliminary interview. According to the doctors' reports, nearly 90 percent of these unmarried women were no longer virgins. A Chinese woman we asked about this did not seem surprised. "Pretty women have more opportunities to lose their virginity, here as everywhere else, and some do," she said.

By the time we left China in September 1980, the romantic activity in the parks had heated up so much that our amah was embarrassed to walk there. Ah-Lin continued to take Joe and Peter to the Temple of Heaven playground after school, but insisted on leaving before dusk, when the courting couples arrived in droves. Seven-year-old Joe had started asking probing questions about those entwined bodies in the bushes. We mentioned this once to a friend at the U.S. embassy. "Look at it this way," he said. "Most American kids learn about sex in the streets. Someday Joe will be able to tell his friends he learned about sex in the Temple of Heaven."

Oddly enough, the Cultural Revolution of 1966–1976 is probably the single most important factor in today's changing mores. Although ideologically oppressive, the Cultural Revolution was a period of relative sexual freedom and license. Young Red Guards were authorized to traverse the country unchaperoned. Camped out far from home, many boys and girls took advantage of this remarkable, if brief, moment of freedom to share dormitories and sometimes beds. Young adults who passed through the Cultural Revolution as teen-agers reverted to the old behavior norms after the storm passed, but they remain different from their elders. "I was afraid of sex, and even after my marriage, regarded it as a duty I had to perform," said an unusually frank fifty-five-year-old Peking woman. "My daughters look on sex as a pleasure."

As China has opened the door to the West in the past few years, more permissive ideas about sex have wafted in to what was previously a closed society. The authorities, of course, welcome Western tourists, computers and oil rigs; they are far more wary of the accompanying disco music, romantic novels, tight pants and other foreign influences.

A small wave of Western pornography swept into China in the late 1970s. It seemed to us no threat to the village-bred sexual ethos that prevailed, but the big-city media treated it just as small-town papers anywhere would—as a foreign assault on everything that was decent and upstanding. The *Liaoning Daily* complained that the city's youths were being corrupted by imported pinups which showed "foreign actresses with bared chests and exposed backs." The Shanghai press reported, with obvious relish, that a man who peddled 4,700 "extremely obscene" pictures on a busy street corner had been apprehended and jailed.

There was a popular corner of Dongdan Street, near the secondhand shops just off the Avenue of Eternal Peace, where so many young Chinese workers engaged in black-market commerce that we sometimes found it hard to pass on the sidewalk. The knots of buyers around the salesmen were too thick for us to penetrate. When the police finally rounded up about four hundred young people—all, with the exception of a few of the actual salesmen, were eventually released—they reported that the goods included "photos of nude women and foreign sex magazines," as well as Hong Kong–made sunglasses and cassette tapes.

Weak hearts among the authorities in most major cities found all these traumatic signs of a new morality magnified by the return of dance parties, a symbol of the freer, post-Mao era. Foreign television viewers will not soon forget the sight of proper cadres in Sun Yat-sen suits (the Chinese name for Mao jackets) trying out tentative disco steps at 1979 New Year's festivities. They were celebrating a new cultural era—the freewheeling wall posters on Democracy Wall reached their peak at this time—along with a great triumph, the return to full diplomatic relations with the United States. For months after, in small apartments and college halls, dancing remained an obsession, but it produced a troublesome byproduct. Young women, some of them novice prostitutes, began to gather outside the Nationalities Palace and the Peking Languages Institute halls, where public dances were held. This quickly ended the institute dances, and the Nationalities Palace began to swarm with plain-clothes men. Our Chinese-American friends in Peking, always more trusted than we were, received abject pleas to teach the latest disco steps at private sessions. We encountered small impromptu dance parties in parks in Sichuan (Szechwan), and on the Marco Polo Bridge outside Peking. All the while, authorities trembled with indignation. Shanghai police confiscated the sound equipment and detained the young participants at one candlelit dance party. Dressed in bell-bottoms, loosened ties and fedoras, these young Chinese wanted, in an inadvertently humorous way, to both ape the West and taunt the authorities.

In the fall of 1979, we of the newly arrived American press corps were drawn like fruit flies to a bit of journalistic honey, a prostitution ring. Several Westerners in town had discovered the Peace Café, a small beer and soda joint about two blocks from the Peking Hotel. Inside the smoke-filled café were dozens of young Chinese drinking watery beer, sampling chocolate sundaes and letting off steam. On the nights we visited the Peace Café, the clientele seemed fairly innocent. Factory workers en route home from the night shift, unemployed high school graduates, or children of high officials, all seemed eager to rub shoulders with foreigners, to see and be seen in a place that had become a trendy hangout. In staid Peking, where most restaurants closed at seven-thirty and people were in bed by nine, the Peace Café qualified as a nightspot; it stayed open until ten. But there seems no doubt that some of those kids, turned out in outrageous costumes concocted from cast-off Western clothes, were there to make assignations.

Discouraged at our inability to connect with anyone we could prove was a prostitute, Linda urged Jay to go to the Peace Café alone one night. "You'll never get anywhere with me sitting there," she said. "I remind everybody of their mothers." On his own, Jay found a burly, shabbily dressed young man who suggested they meet again at eight the following night to arrange for feminine company. But another man led Jay away from the table and advised against keeping the appointment. "That fellow has no job," he said. "He's in here drinking all the time. I know he arranges for young women to sell themselves. I've even heard him speak in favor of the Republic of China [Taiwan]. We have many good people in China; you should not waste your time on him." Jay kept the appointment, but the man didn't show up.

The Peace Café eventually became too notorious. After at least a dozen stories about it appeared in the foreign press, embarrassed authorities swept through and arrested sixteen men and women. The "hooligans," as they were called, "hung around with foreigners, profited from this and carried out robberies," Radio Peking claimed. "They corrupted public morals and damaged the honor of our country." Three members of the ring were held on criminal charges until they were tried; most of the others were sent off, without trial, to forced-labor camps.

More discreet operators continued elsewhere. For a while one pimp operated a string of prostitutes at some of the universities and hotels with foreign residents, turning up at dances that allowed Chinese women and foreign men to mix. Young Chinese men also attended, but the young women gravitated toward the wealthier foreigners. The prostitutes charged foreigners 10 yuan (about $6.37), slightly less than a week's pay for the average Chinese factory worker. But the university operation, too, was shut down. The problem, as American graduate student Frank Hawke described it, "was that some guys would make a mistake and invite up a girl who had really come to dance. She thought she was just going up to hear the guy's record collection, and when he tried something, there was terrible screaming and trouble. I walked in on one of those scenes."

American researchers Miriam and Ivan D. London, delving into the subject of prostitution, interviewed a refugee from Canton with first-hand experience. In Canton, he said, girls could be found on certain streets wearing Western-style hairdos or colorful badges as identifying marks. "Prostitutes along Pearl Light Road . . . were called 'roadside chickens'— that's a famous culinary dish in Canton," the Londons' informant said. When a friend "saw a few girls answering my description, he called out, 'Motor!' One of the girls, he said, turned and called right back, 'Son of a motor!' Such girls are called motors, I think, because a motor always keeps turning."

An emigrant to Hong Kong from a mining community in the northern province of Hebei told us a different, sadder story about prostitution rings composed of miners' widows who needed to supplement their meager pensions. "They would charge the miners who were not married about one yuan [sixty-four cents] to spend the night, and also do their laundry. The authorities knew about it and just told people not to make it too obvious," the emigrant said.

Officials, realizing there was little they could do about such inconspicuous activities, found comfort in semantics. When an American diplomat asked his opposite number in the Chinese Foreign Ministry about prostitution, the Chinese official said, "There is no prostitution in China. However, we do have some women who make love for money."

In late 1980 the Chinese government made an uneasy attempt to fill the vacuum of information about sex. It published a sex manual, the first in more than two decades, and one official newspaper, the *China Youth News,* started running an occasional column of letters from the lovelorn.

The manual was an immediate best seller. The basic thrust of its advice is that sex should not be overdone. Newlyweds, it says, will have "very frequent sex right after marriage, that is, once every three to seven days." They are advised to settle eventually into a more reasonable routine, "generally speaking, once every week or fortnight." Husbands and wives who keep their bedroom activities within bounds "will not feel tired the day after. In fact, quite the opposite, their bodies will be light, loose and relaxed, and their temperament will be happy." Those who overdo will "feel tired and heavyheaded. Their legs will be tingly and ticklish. Their hearts will beat rapidly, and they will be short of breath and lose their appetite."*

Chinese men, tradition-bound as ever, worry that their fiancées might not be virgins. One young groom, heartsick that his bride had few inhibitions and seemed to like all aspects of lovemaking, wrote to the *China Youth News* for advice on how to confirm his suspicions that he wasn't her first lover. The editor counseled the new husband to apologize to his wife, then explained the nature of the hymen and described how it can become stretched or broken without sexual intercourse.

The *Youth News* has confronted even more sensitive questions, though its advice might not be sanctioned by Western sex therapists. One reader, identified only as Xiao Li from Henan province, wrote to ask about a "problem I am embarrassed to talk about—that is, masturbation. For over a year now, I've wanted to change, but I can't. I feel my strength draining from me. I'd like to see a doctor, but I'm afraid of being ridiculed . . . I'm afraid it will affect my sex life after I marry, or perhaps I won't be potent."

The *Youth News* sex columnist, Professor Ye Gongshao of Peking Medical College, recited the same advice Chinese youths have been hearing for more than two thousand years: "If masturbation happens very seldom, it may not do harm to the health. But if it happens too often, it may cause headaches, dizziness, bad memory, hamper work and study and have a lot to do with impotence and premature ejaculation."

Professor Ye oozed confidence that masturbation could be cured. "Concentrate on study and work and take time for cultural and sports activities," he advised. "Before sleeping at night, go jogging, wash your feet in warm water, and try to fall asleep immediately upon getting into bed. In the morning when you wake up, don't lie around. When sleeping, be careful not to sleep on your stomach, and don't use covers that are too warm . . . Avoid tight underwear."

The authors of the sex manual, perhaps mindful that an earlier edition

---

*The idea that too much sex can be debilitating has been a staple of Chinese culture since ancient times. R. H. Van Gulik, the Dutch author of the popular "Judge Dee" mystery series, quoted a scholar of the Han dynasty, Liu Xiang, who believed that "the art of sexual intercourse with a woman consists of restraining oneself so as not to ejaculate, thus making one's semen return and strengthen one's brain." Liu theorized that if a man could preserve his "vital power" and "male essence," then his "grey hairs will turn black again and new teeth will replace those that have fallen out." Van Gulik noted that "the ancient Chinese arrived, via philosophical considerations, at the erroneous conclusion that while man's semen is strictly limited in quantity, woman is an inexhaustible receptacle of Yin essence."

was canceled in 1959 for being too clinical and "rightist," were more circumspect on the subject of masturbation (or "hand lewdness," as it is called in Chinese). "Where does the strength and inspiration to overcome hand lewdness come from? It comes from the knowledge that the country cares about the well-being and health of its young. It comes from the responsibility you should feel toward your country and the socialist system from the socialist education you have received, and from the vision of your own bright future."

If foreigners consider Chinese sexually inhibited and Victorian, the Chinese often think of foreigners as slaves to their animal instincts. One day Linda received a wedding announcement in the mail from an American friend, long divorced, who remarried at the age of thirty-five. Divorce and remarriage are so unusual in China that Hou's interest was piqued. Linda related the whole story of her friend's life: an early marriage to a domineering, abusive man, a series of secret affairs, then divorce, lots of casual sex, a period living with a much younger man and remarriage to an old friend of her ex-husband's. In short, the life and loves of a fairly typical sexually emancipated American woman. Hou was thoroughly shocked. How could someone conduct herself like that? Weren't her parents humiliated? Wasn't she soundly criticized by her friends and colleagues? Linda said no. Hou frowned and declared staunchly, "Well, that sort of thing could not happen here."

Given this obvious difference in viewpoint, members of Peking's tight little foreign community often chat idly over whether the Chinese are sexually satisfied. Such speculation is essentially pointless, the argument moot, because there is no way to document it. China has few marriage counselors and no sex therapists at all. It has never produced a Kinsey or a Shere Hite to survey the country's sex habits, measure the frequency of intercourse, or homosexuality, and count the extramarital affairs. The Chinese seem to think they can get along without knowing one another's most intimate secrets.

A Chinese friend told Linda that some women are grateful for menopause because hot flashes and insomnia give them an excuse to stop sleeping with their husbands. Undoubtedly there are Chinese men, stuck with frigid wives and barred by convention from extramarital dalliances, who go through life in sexual frustration. But there are many Chinese who marry someone to whom they are physically attracted and, through effort or sheer luck, find enough sexual compatibility and companionship to make married life a pleasure. And though the gaudy, glossy version of sex revealed in Western magazines and books offends the Chinese, we found them sometimes employing the same tricks and white lies that provide the yeast for millions of jokes and hundreds of novels about marriage in libertine America.

One morning, as Linda distractedly dug through her desk, looking for an aspirin bottle, Hou looked up and said, "Why are you taking so much aspirin?"

"I have a headache," Linda answered.

"Oh, are you coming down with the flu?"

Linda, after pausing briefly to contemplate how explicit she should be, said, "No, not flu. I'm ovulating; I always get a headache as I'm ovulating."

"Are you in pain when you ovulate?" Hou asked. "What do you do?"

"Well, for one thing, I don't let Jay anywhere near me."

"Good idea." Hou giggled. "You know, we have a joke in China," she said, about to let Linda in on a secret. "When women don't want to have sex with their husbands, they say they have a headache."

MARRIAGE

FUHUA, SLIM AND ATTRACTIVE, HAD A HUSBAND DOING A TOUR OF DUTY in the army far from their home in southern Hunan. His baggy green uniform and red collar tabs had given the slow-witted village boy a certain allure for Fuhua and her parents. They knew it would be a good match for her, because the Communist Party always takes care of the soldiers of the People's Liberation Army and their families.

Yanlong, one of Fuhua's colleagues in the office of their production brigade, radiated earnestness, with his crew cut and wide-eyed expression, and was known to have intellectual ambitions. His own wife could not live with him yet, for her parents had extracted a hard bargain from his family. The couple had been allowed to marry only on the condition that the girl remain in her home village for another year's worth of work in the rice fields. "We need her work points," her father said, referring to the harvest shares they would receive for her labor.

Eventually some schoolchildren, thrilled at the chance for neighborhood espionage, found Fuhua and Yanlong making love in the canteen kitchen. The news shocked and titillated the villagers, but at the same time there was a bit of sympathy for the lovers. It was a pity, people said. Those two young people suffered because of bad decisions by their parents. Still, the village authorities couldn't ignore what had happened; Fuhua and Yanlong had to be punished.

"The day after they were discovered, the security chief of the brigade called the two of them to the headquarters office and asked them what they had done the night before in the kitchen," a friend of Fuhua's told us. "There were many witnesses, so they confessed." The incident was noted in their personnel records, a step which would affect their salaries and careers for the rest of their lives. Both were transferred to different locations. When Fuhua's soldier husband came home, he demanded a divorce. His family had not written him about the affair. "Perhaps they didn't know how to write," the friend said. "That was lucky because if the husband had learned of the affair while he was still in the army, Yanlong could have faced criminal charges of sabotaging the army."

Over the last three decades, marriage customs in China have changed at least as much as they have in the West. New divorce laws, government-dictated separations, and some tantalizing, if meager, personal freedoms have shaken an institution that is regarded far more seriously in China than in the United States. Still, marriage and family remain the foundation on which Chinese society stands, with or without the Communist Party, and represent the ultimate triumph of Chinese habit and personal inclination over government rule.

The Chinese have come a long way from the days, not so many decades ago, when nearly all marriages were arranged by the couple's parents. Today, young peasants often marry the girl or boy next door. In the past, many families would have resisted this because of old social taboos and a desire to extend family contacts and influence to other villages. But parents still try to steer their children toward certain partners, and marriage remains close to a feudal bond between families.

Indeed, the social pressure and the seemingly innate Chinese urge to marry are so great that our Chinese friends could hardly name one person they knew over thirty who was not married. We talked about this with Chen Wuyong, the motherly director of the Meijiahu Tea Brigade outside Hangzhou. Of 1,300 people in the brigade, none over the age of thirty was single. "We had one man over thirty who was single, but he had been chronically ill and soon died. In the other villages I know of, the only people who stay unmarried are the very sick ones."

Of all the social reforms the Communists promised to make in 1949, the new marriage laws may have been the most far-reaching, though certain customs seem impervious to change. The Marriage Act of 1950 outlawed bigamy and concubinage, apparently with great success, and overturned the old Confucian ban on remarriage of widows. It required the registration of marriages and mandated that women be allowed to retain their own surnames and enjoy equal rights to property ownership and inheritance. Less successfully, it prohibited payment of money and goods as a condition of marriage and declared that marriage must be the desire of the couple involved, without parental compulsion. Divorce by mutual consent was to be available on application to a government office, and in the first few years many unhappy couples married before 1950 took advantage of this. If only one spouse demanded a divorce, the local court was still directed to grant a divorce if reconciliation efforts failed. The act established minimum marriage ages: eighteen for women and twenty for men (raised in 1980 to twenty for women and twenty-two for men). As the population-control drive accelerated after 1972, the party began issuing administrative orders discouraging approval of marriages involving women under the age of twenty-three or men under the age of twenty-five, and recommending even higher minimums for city youth, who could expect less housing space.

In late 1953 the *People's Daily* acknowledged that the campaign for "new style" marriages had not gone far enough. Only 15 percent of local districts had "penetratingly implemented" the law. At least 85 percent had resisted the ban on arranged marriages and the principle of equality between the sexes. Women, the usual party seeking divorce, had particularly suffered. Some had been murdered or committed suicide after being publicly chastised, the *People's Daily* said. The government stopped pushing so hard. Perhaps the more astute party leaders realized that women's heavy contribution to family income would eventually help solidify their rights, without the leaders' having to enforce the law so vigorously.

In courtship and marriage, the Chinese remain confident of their own instincts and small-town customs, no matter what the party decrees. In Hong Kong, American sociologists William Parish and Martin Whyte interviewed sixty-five emigrants from more than thirty southern Chinese villages and found that 89 percent of the villages had some cases of falsifying ages or marriage without registration.

In trying to discourage early marriages, in some ways the government spiked its own balloon. Other policies, especially China's heavy reliance on young female labor, only increased parental concern about finding a marriage partner for their children as early as possible. In rural China, a strong, healthy bride is prized as a wage earner, sometimes even more than as a mate.

Recently the government has tried to discourage discrimination against people whose family ties include such political undesirables as former landlords or rich peasants. But parents who have suffered under these labels, losing jobs, benefits and social standing since the Communists took power, know their children may not have the same cachet on the marriage market as do children of formerly impoverished peasants. Children of soldiers or party officials do even better. So families from the landlord class try to arrange their children's marriages early so as to avoid competing later for a dwindling supply of desirable matches. To manage this, one former women's affairs worker from Guizhou (Kweichow) province said, "Often there are ways of circumventing the minimum-age law. Couples will have the marriage feast, settle down with the acquiescence of village members and local officials, but not officially register the marriage until they are older and ready to have children."

Far more important than governmental decrees are the wishes of parents, who usually maintain veto power over their child's choice of a spouse, even if they no longer make the choice themselves. Their eldest son will invariably continue to live with them after his marriage. A new marriage is not only an agreement between two young people, but part of the village web of relationships. The approval of parents and neighbors is enormously important at the beginning of the marriage and, as Chinese divorce courts attest, at the end of it.

"For young lovers, the main difficulty is the parents," one former government official in Peking told us. "If they are opposed to the person their son, say, has chosen, he will usually be forced to change his mind." In remote parts of the country, parents effortlessly maintained feudal traditions of which the party vigorously disapproves. An official report circulated internally in Peking stated that 43 percent of children under five and 80 percent of children under ten in one Shanxi commune had already been promised in marriage by their parents, a throwback to imperial China. The same report blamed parental pressure on young people to marry for four suicides, four nervous breakdowns and two attempted murders in one Fujian county.

Anyone who has lived in a Chinese village remarks on the amount of time spent in serious negotiations between families before a marriage is decided upon. Usually money and goods exchange hands, even though the marriage law forbids this. In most cases, the groom's family pays the bride's family something for the privilege of her hand in marriage, and the addition of her strong back to his family's labor force.

The negotiations become particularly delicate and painful whenever the prospective groom or bride has some flaw, actual or rumored. A woman in one remote Shanxi village had, through some mischance now clouded by rumor and time, married a man who later became mentally unbalanced. "She abandoned him," a relative told us, "But now their son is of marriageable age, and the family background is a problem. When he was younger, the boy had a fever and was temporarily delirious. The rumor spread fast that he had inherited his father's mental deficiencies." This caused his stock on the marriage market to plummet.

The boy's mother had overseas relatives who sent her about $100 a year. She used some of the money to lure the only prospective bride she could find, a girl from another village. When these relatives arrived for a visit, the girl happened to be there. The boy's mother had asked her overseas sister to help create a good impression by giving the prospective bride a gift. The overseas sister decided the girl was milking the family for all it was worth, and refused. Without a word, the boy's mother went to her sister's suitcase, pulled out the first thing she saw, a scarf, and gave it to her son's intended. "Your aunt brought this for you. It is from Italy." The overseas sister snatched the scarf from the girl's hand, went to her suitcase and returned with another scarf. "Here," she said, "this one was made in Japan."

Once these negotiations have been sealed, woe to anyone who takes that marriage bond lightly. Every village seems to have a tale of violence brought on by the pressure to conform to community standards.

In Canton, the most lurid crime in that city's memory was the New Year Murder Case. The mother of a young woman factory worker named Haihua objected strenuously to her daughter's choice of suitor—a man with a reputation for rowdiness. The mother arranged for an older man, a dull and physically unattractive official with little to recommend him but a regular paycheck, to seek her daughter's hand in marriage. Haihua reluctantly went along, for the sake of family peace and financial security.

Her former boyfriend, Fushan, brooded about the match, then persuaded the bride to see him again. According to the reports later circulated at Canton political meetings as a moral object lesson, the pair had slept together before Haihua's marriage, and this bourgeois indulgence had addled their brains. The lovers conceived a grisly plan. Haihua invited her old boyfriend, posing as a firewood salesman, to her new home. When her husband bent over to inspect the man's goods, Fushan grabbed an ax and chopped his rival into several pieces with a frenzy that left the entire apartment splattered with blood.

This was of course a catastrophe, certain to bring shame to the bride's family, and harsh punishment, probably death, to the young woman and her lover. But the two households reacted in a peculiarly Chinese way: they cooperated to cover up the crime and keep the law out of family business. Several of the dead man's new in-laws were enlisted in the task of cleaning up the apartment and taking his severed parts, wrapped like pieces of meat so that no one on the bus would suspect anything, to scattered parts of the city for hiding. All went well until a farmer in one suburb, wondering at his good luck in finding a large, fresh piece of beef shank in a field, inspected the bundle a little more closely. Convinced it had not come from any farm animal, he turned it over to the police. They made the connection with the case of the missing official and coerced a confession from one of the in-laws.

The results of courtship and marriage in China are rarely so harrowing, but there is less of the light-heartedness and romance that Westerners expect in their own relationships. Young people we spoke to usually put a good disposition and compatibility on the top of their list of things they desired in a mate. Financial security followed close behind, and physical attractiveness came next. The modern class system influences matches in a significant way, to judge from the love stories printed in the magazine *Chinese Women* and other Peking versions of the *Ladies' Home Journal*. A favorite tale, told in many variations, is of the young educated girl from the city who falls in love with a commune swineherd and marries him despite her mother's insistence she wed a party cadre's son. Such stories are published often enough to indicate that the editors would like more young city women to consider marrying swineherds. But marriage in China represents such a crucial investment that few families will stand for letting casual affection produce such an odd match. Courtship occurs with a good deal of kibitzing from outsiders; the generations maneuver constantly, sometimes in cooperation and sometimes not.

An energetic village woman in Hebei province had two problems. She had found a job she thoroughly enjoyed—buying materials for a local clothing factory—but it required much travel and left little time for housework. Also, her husband was from a once rich peasant family, an undesirable class background that seemed likely to hurt their children's marriage prospects. Their eldest son, fifteen, had just flunked the examination for senior middle school, further reducing his value as a future husband.

"She had a relative in a distant village whose wife had died and needed some relief from taking care of five children," the woman's neighbor told us. "So she brought one of the children, a pretty fifteen-year-old girl named Chunhua, back with her to keep house, and to marry the eldest son in a year or so." There was no taboo against the cousins marrying, particularly since they came from different villages.

"Then the girl crossed them up. After working all day, she borrowed textbooks from the woman's husband, who was a teacher, and pored over them at night. She took the senior middle school examination in their district. Unlike the son, she passed. This means she will go off and live in the student dorm, some distance from the village, and probably escape marrying the son." What the Chinese call her "cultural level," her education, will have exceeded that of her betrothed, making this an undesirable match in their eyes: the two should be on a par, or the man a bit ahead.

During the four years we spent reporting on China, we made a point of asking people we met how they got married. Some were city dwellers who found their marriage partners themselves, usually at the university or in their government offices. But many city people, and most of their cousins in the countryside, relied on introductions by relatives or friends living in different, but not too distant, villages, neighborhoods or factories. In nearly all these rural marriages, and in many of those that took place in the city, the parents were actively involved as matchmakers.

Chinese parents, from party members on down, see no harm in trying to arrange romances between their offspring and the children of well-connected families. "Party or government officials in the countryside have great personal influence, even if they might be relatively poor. They will try to take advantage of this by marrying their children into larger families that earn unusual numbers of work points [harvest shares]," one peasant told us. "It becomes a union of political and economic connections."

The ancient practice of marriage brokerage lives on, both in city and rural China. Women in their forties and fifties often take it on as a pastime, almost an amateur sport. Wang Xunying, forty-six, the brigade official we met at Evergreen Commune outside Peking, is a stocky, square-featured woman with just the right blend of romanticism and brass to make a good go-between. She took us on a small raid of the commune apple orchard, and told us of one of her matchmaking triumphs. "The man was thirty, well off enough, but somewhat choosy about women. The woman was twenty-eight and had a good office job. She just did not seem to pay attention to the question of men, but her family began to hound her about it. They met at the woman's house, and agreed to meet some more, and eventually married. That's the way we do it. If she doesn't like the man at the first meeting, she can say she's busy when he suggests a second meeting, and that's it. If he doesn't request a meeting, that's it. Neither side should hide anything. If the man's financial situation is not good, he should say so." The mercenary quality of these negotiations often appalls Westerners, but most Chinese take it in stride. "We have a joke about the 'bride's dream,' " said one young woman. "She wants both of the groom's parents dead"—so the newly married couple will have more room and less in-law friction. "She wants the three wheels"—bicycle and sewing machine. "And she wants obedience to her every command."

Young men and women discovered in the late 1970s that they could broaden their choice of partners by adapting some of the marketing techniques then coming into vogue in the Chinese economy. Some of the more desperate candidates persuaded newspapers like the *Tianjin Daily* to accept personal ads: "MALE, 27, worker, loyal and sincere, father employed, younger brother and sister at university, 5 feet 1 inch tall, spine slightly crooked, seeks to marry employed woman comrade." Several Chinese papers printed articles about Japanese marriage agencies. The idea of sending in names and qualifications for matching by government agencies became instantly popular. One appeal for such a service came to a government newspaper from a complex of factories outside Shanghai where 12,000 unmarried men and only 4,000 unmarried women worked. The men were given traveling privileges only once a year, during spring festival, making it very hard to find a spouse.

At the marriage bureau in Peking's Chongwen district, *Newsweek* correspondent Melinda Liu watched a pretty and unusually tall young woman with crimson gloves, royal-blue socks and upswept hairdo frown over a photo of a prospective mate. The office had a coal-burning stove, a bare concrete floor and pencil marks on the wall to measure height. The significance of the last detail became clear as the young woman, who stood five-foot-seven, regarded all the applicants she saw as too short. Over at another bureau, in Ritan Park, Liu watched in distress as a very tall and handsome young man, who might have been the woman's perfect match, rejected the few photos offered him.

Applicants supply a photograph and are asked to fill out a form giving age, schooling, occupation, salary, days off and housing situation. The last two factors can make or break a budding affair, for the Chinese find it difficult to consider or get permission to marry until they have a room of their own, even if it is just in their parents' home. Days off are fixed at different factories for different days to stagger the load on city transit and power supplies: couples whose days off don't coincide rarely see each other.

The application allows for a certain amount of reasonable choice. Some men have been known to request non-Communist women. That way they can be assured that their future bride will not be so burdened with party meetings that she is never at home.

The staff at the matchmaking bureau set up by the Youth League Committee of the Shanghai Light Industrial Bureau noted that certain industries have severe sex imbalances, making matchmaking essential. Traditionally, most auto workers are male, while plants that produce aircraft components largely employ females. In Shanghai there are more young men in porcelain, thermos-bottle and bicycle factories, more women making clocks, watches and processed foods. The Shanghai party committee managed to persuade a hundred unmarried local women to transfer to jobs at the Xinguang metal plant in neighboring Anhui, not an alluring location for city-bred youth. But this factory had a preponderance of young bachelors—and the committee claimed the young women willingly left the bright lights of Shanghai behind.

We discovered that Zhongshan Park, where our boys liked to play on Sundays, was a favorite meeting place for prospective couples and their matchmakers. We could see the early arrivals, usually an older woman and her young client, waiting nervously on a bench near the entrance. When the other matchmaker and her client arrived, the two go-betweens would launch into a happy chat—often exchanging tales of prior matrimonial successes—while the prospective bride and groom stole glances at each other, and perhaps began their own conversation. One Chinese woman with experience in these matters said she knew of cases where the late-arriving party took one look at his or her intended waiting on the bench and immediately turned around and left. "That was not very tactful," she said. In Peking a young man who has passed this hurdle often seals the bargain by presenting the woman's parents with money—perhaps $100—wrapped in a cloth. Rings are not customary.

The Chinese say about choosing a mate: "The doors and windows should match." To ensure compatible marriages, peasant families throughout China go through a series of rituals that in Western culture might be considered an outrageous invasion of privacy, and in Marxist terms the worst kind of feudal slave trade.

If the prospective bride and groom know each other and have made a tentative commitment, or approve of each other after an introductory meeting, their parents take over. Here enters a feudal custom that has survived Communism—the bride price. "It's not a secret in the village, though also not something you will generally ask about," a peasant youth told us. "Everybody with a son pays a bride price. In our village, it was about ninety yuan to a hundred and eighty yuan." Parish and Whyte heard of only five cases of marriages in Guangdong that did not involve a bride price. The amounts ranged from $60 (90 yuan) to $1,200, the top price charged to a family known to have relatives sending them money from abroad. Such amounts are large for Chinese peasants, but they often save carefully for some time, anticipating a child's coming of age.

The bride's father usually opens negotiations. He delivers to the groom's family a list of the items his family needs before the marriage can take place —usually a new wardrobe for the bride, special foods and delicacies for the wedding feast, jewelry and cash. The groom's father knocks a few items off the list, the other side haggles a bit, and agreement is finally reached. Broken engagements, though rare, often produce heated arguments if goods have already been exchanged and returns are demanded. Local officials may arbitrate, oblivious to the fact that the whole arrangement is outside the law.

The bride's family is invited to visit the groom's village, to make a reconnaissance. They chat with neighbors about the reputation and financial condition of their prospective in-laws. "Many times the groom's family will invite the bride's people to dinner. I attended a meal where the bride's parents went over the house stem to stern, checked the number of pots and pans and inspected the family's private plot," said one Guangdong native. Such prenuptial matters are taken far more seriously than, for example, blood tests, which have been so neglected in much of the country that the government has issued warnings about the health consequences.

The parents of the bride are particularly concerned about acquiring furniture, linens and fabric for making clothes, often purchased with money from the groom's parents. A thick down comforter—an item found on every bed of every home and hotel room we have ever seen in northern China— is a lifetime investment whose purchase is considered the first important decision of the marriage. At Peking's Number One Department Store we often saw young women, with their mothers, carefully picking over the available comforters, debating which pattern to choose. Those who can afford them buy silk covers for the comforters, the only time we ever saw Chinese buy expensive silk. Women try to accumulate a trousseau, enough pants, shirts and shoes to last through the early years of a marriage. There is much hoarding of cotton ration coupons before marriage. Young men scour the town for furniture stores that have received new stocks—an infrequent occurrence—or for scrap wood and packing crates from which they can make tables and chairs.

The mercenary aspects of the marriage arrangements may get out of hand. Chen Baisong, a young man from the famous wine-growing county of Shaoxing in Zhejiang (Chekiang) province, said he was forced to pay $300 just for the privilege of an engagement. The marriage cost another $600. The bride's family demanded: $8 for each year of her life, six jars of wine, eight suits (including three of wool), $7 for the bride's great-grand-mother, a gold ring and the cost of a huge feast. "She threatened to break off the engagement several times when she saw I couldn't meet all the demands," the man told the local party newspaper. "There was nothing I could do about it and we finally broke off." Sadder still was the case of a young man from Shangyu County, so desperate for a bride that he committed suicide after discovering his contracted bride had already been engaged three times, collecting tidy sums each time. He had sold his sow and young pigs and gone deep into debt to meet the bride price.

The government has bided its time in eliminating these old abuses. Huge sums are rather frequently extorted from bridegrooms, with only a few cases publicized. Parents know that whatever the sum they must pay to marry off a son, they'll earn it back from the family of the boy who eventually marries their daughter. Sometimes families simply exchange daughter for son and vice versa, and no money changes hands. One eighteen-year-old Anhui villager complained bitterly of being forced to marry a thirty-four-year-old man she didn't like, just so the man's sister would agree to marry her brother.

All Chinese revel in the color and excitement of a wedding feast. Simply filling out the proper forms with the permission of the couple's work unit makes a marriage official. But few ignore the small ceremonial flourishes and many consider it immoral to consummate a marriage before holding a feast, even though no real vows are exchanged. In the years before Mao's death, when there were severe limits on private commerce, peasants had to resort to the black market for the special trimmings. Now, they say, it is easier to find the extra pork, eggs and vegetables at the local free markets, if you don't mind the higher prices.

Fayong, a young veteran of several wedding feasts in rural Guangdong, filled us in on the current approach.

"The size depends on how rich the family is. The biggest I saw was a two-day feast, a total of four dinners. That family invited the whole village to attend, though usually people have only two dinners, and the poorest people just one. This wealthy family had money because there were nine people in the family who could work. They had a feast in the meeting hall of the production team, rather than at home as most do." We asked the young man if the party officials in the village objected to the extravagance. He laughed. "They were at the top of the guest list!"

The official press periodically denounces these practices, but has had no success in discouraging them. Chinese think of a wedding feast just as many Westerners think of a church wedding. A marriage cannot get under way without one. A progressive-minded young bride in one rural district sent a letter to the local paper complaining that she had been ostracized because she had dispensed with the feast.

Although the official press has kept up its campaign against extravagant weddings, the articles seem only to confirm the popularity of the custom. Three Communist Party officials in Daning, for instance, reportedly extorted $4,800 from subordinates to pay for lavish weddings for their own children. Each feast had up to six hundred guests and stretched out over two or three days. One short-tempered article in the official publication *Women in China* editorialized: "Things were not like this before 1966—the year when China was thrown into turmoil which lasted 10 years. Before 1966, people used to take pride in practicing economy, working hard and serving the people, and regarded extravagance as a disgrace." Many Chinese find this comment hilarious: If anything, big wedding feasts were more widespread in the 1950s and 1960s. These days many guests bring cash gifts up to $15 each at big-city weddings, and this helps defray expenses.

In 1979, newspapers throughout the world began to publish, with captions full of editorial amazement, photographs of Chinese brides in flowing white wedding gowns and their grooms in Western suits. This was not quite what it seemed. In all of China there may be only a few dozen such gowns and suits, but every photo studio has at least one set. Newlyweds enter the studio, and without shedding their blue work slacks, coats, cloth shoes or sandals, simply pull on the Western garments, along with veil, pendant, rhinestone earrings and a bouquet of plastic carnations. They pay $3 to have a photograph made of them in a regal pose, then shed the finery and go on their way.

City couples are quite choosy about how a proper feast must proceed. In Peking and other cities, a bride may think twice about the worthiness of the groom if he cannot activate the personal connections that will produce a taxi to pick her up at her home and bring her to the feast at his place. Taxi fares are not exorbitant, perhaps $2 to $5 depending on the length of the trip, but foreigners and high officials tie up most of the cabs, so the bridegroom must have good *guanxi* with some of the drivers or their friends.

The Chinese love to recount stories about weddings which follow the same pattern for rich and poor alike. Fayong, our best source on Guangdong weddings, told us about one he attended. "The groom and several of his brothers and cousins and some friends headed for the bride's home. They had drums, music-makers and a lion costume. They walked there— it was close enough, but many times the bride is in another village, so they'll use bikes or a tractor borrowed from the production team." The noisy procession stopped at the bride's front door, which was guarded by a pack of giggling sisters and girl cousins. "Sorry, sorry, no entry!" the young women shouted, through fits of laughter. The lion growled at them, setting off more giggles. The women were waiting for the cigarettes, as was the custom. They kept the door shut until the boys produced two or three or maybe four dozen packs of cigarettes, the better brands, Qunying or Yeshu (about thirty cents a pack).

The door opened. The young men stepped warily across the threshold, knowing other dangers lurked within. A water bucket cascaded down from the ceiling, soaking the first intruder. A few smaller cousins, laughing merrily, attacked the rest of the raiding party with sticks. The bride was dressed in her best dark slacks and jacket. She gave her hand to the groom and his escort party. Outside, some of the boys set off a string of firecrackers. In front of the door a middle-aged woman of the village with "rich experience"—many children—observed an essential ritual by sprinkling rice outside the door. It was she, not the groom, who led the bride out by the hand. The rice, a symbol for good harvests and fertility, wasn't wasted—the chickens ate it.

The party moved to the groom's house, a low whitewashed brick building, to greet his parents, and then on to the meeting hall for a dinner. In the fine tradition of wedding banquets everywhere, the party became more raucous as the day wore on. The couple began with an ancient, simple rite. They bowed to a picture of the late Chairman Mao, a substitute for the religious icons that used to decorate Chinese homes. (The practice has fallen off among sophisticated city folk who are aware of Mao's diminished stature, but peasants keep the tradition going.) They bowed to the parents of the groom, to the guests and to each other. The bride served tea to her husband's parents and to the other elders of the family. Then the real fun began. A piece of fruit was pierced clean through by a toothpick; bride and groom were ordered to grasp opposite ends in their mouths and devour the fruit together. "Then we gave them one cigarette, had them put opposite ends in their mouths and someone lit the middle of it," the neighbor recalled. Some of the guests began another ritual—embarrass the couple with lengthy interrogations and silly requests.

A newly married Peking office worker told us about his wedding feast: "We were asked to tell everybody at the dinner where we met and how we fell in love. Then my wife had to sing three or four songs. If she forgot the words, I had to help her. It was hard standing up before all those people, but I'll get my turn to ask questions at my sister's wedding next year." During one such ordeal in Inner Mongolia, the guests refused to toast the marriage until the couple told the story of their first meeting. Drinking continued unabated as the guests enjoyed the couple's embarrassment. The self-appointed master of ceremonies became so drunk that he spent the night sleeping on the marriage bed; his father, who, unlike most Mongols, happened to be a Moslem, would not have understood if he had come home inebriated. The couple meekly accepted separate sleeping quarters with friends.

Peking and Shanghai authorities have tried to encourage mass wedding feasts so as to cut down on family extravagance and demonstrate proper socialist spirit. In the spring of 1980 the Peking government gathered forty-nine couples for a feast at the Working People's Cultural Palace, an old temple once dedicated to imperial ancestors. Each couple was placed at a big round table loaded with candy and tea and seats for twenty of their friends and relatives, a considerable drop from the usual numbers of guests. An official lit firecrackers and showered the couples with confetti. The government introduced some television stars and used the opportunity to deliver a few speeches on family planning and sharing household chores. Many of the brides wore gray pantsuits, with red blouses or sweaters. Peking's chief judge came around to pin on red cloth flowers. The cost per couple was only 20 yuan (about $13.50), but the idea hasn't caught on. Most Chinese still prefer celebrations with lots of guests, and entertainment provided by the couple themselves.

Among some urban couples it has recently become fashionable to dispense with a big celebration and have instead what is called a "traveling wedding," essentially a honeymoon. In Hangzhou, a favorite resort, we stumbled across scores of such couples, delighted that the hotels now let them stay in the same room. Segregated quarters for male and female guests used to be the rule.

Wedding guests find it easy to torment new couples with personal questions because the Chinese, even couples long married, are so instinctively shy and reserved in public. This is even more evident in the countryside than in the cities. In the villages, married couples walking together usually proceed one in front of the other, rarely side by side and never hand in hand. When speaking of one's spouse, husbands and wives still say "Huailing's mother" or "Weiguo's father," using the names of their children. Some couples, particularly young ones, now use personal names for addressing their husbands or wives directly, but this is still considered improper when discussing one's spouse with others.

Country people have three time-honored ways of referring to their marriage partner, each with a colloquial flavor many Americans would find comfortable: *wo de nanren* (my man) or *wo de nuren* (my woman), *wo de laogong* (my old man) or *wo de laopo* (my old lady), and finally, using the name of one's children to refer to little so-and-so's father or so-and-so's mother. Some even use just *jiaren* (houseperson) or *wuli de* (the one in the room). *Wo de airen*—"my lover" or "my beloved"—is making some headway in the cities. It has a daring connotation for some, though it is not considered as risqué as *qingren,* or "darling," reserved for the object of a premarital or secret liaison. Many newlyweds are so shy that they simply say "my whoever" *(wo de na ge shei).*

Despite family separations, despite couples' reluctance or inability to spend much time alone together, despite the lack of privacy, the Chinese say their marriages rarely break up. In the city of Peking, with a population greater than that of Los Angeles, only 490 divorces out of 891 requested were granted in 1981. The Peking courts said 21 percent of the couples reconciled, and 18 percent of the cases were dropped. The main reasons cited for divorce were incompatibility (22 percent), financial problems (16 percent), adultery (13 percent) and hasty youthful marriage (10 percent). Except for high party officials, many of whom changed wives more than once during the revolution, we met only three or four Chinese whom we knew to be divorced. Linda chatted with one of them, a very bright and lively editor at the *China Daily* now in her early fifties. She considered herself lucky to be rid of her husband, who, she said, "was a child." She did not think it likely she would marry again.

The web of family relationships that helps forge the state of matrimony, the participation of parents, neighbors and friends in finding a suitable spouse, and the unusual yearning of the young people to find financial stability and a good disposition rather than romance and good looks seem to put Chinese marriages on a very solid footing. The demands of a socialist government also play a role.

In a short story published in Peking, "The Delicate Scented Rose," author Li Tuo tells of an urban marriage on the rocks. Lu Xiaoling, tall and beautiful but a real fusspot, thinks her steelworker husband has walked out on her. She leaves a note on the door before going to work: "Comrade Li Mingyuan: So you've come back. Please observe that I've waxed the floor. Be kind enough not to trample all over it and ruin my work."

Li Minguan has actually been toiling at the mill night and day to produce a new type of huge steel ingot. He doesn't give much thought to his wife in the excitement of the work until his party supervisor insists that he go home for a while. He stomps all over his wife's shiny floor and can't understand why she throws a tantrum when she returns. To her, this is the last straw. One day soon after, she goes to the steel mill to give her husband the key to the apartment before she goes home to Mother. He is there, addressing an evening physics class for workers furthering their education. "She stood there amazed at her husband's eloquence, and found herself fascinated by what he was saying."

She also hears, to her dismay, her husband invite any workers who have further questions to come back to the apartment with him. "There will be cigarette ashes all over the floor, she thinks." But she goes home to help anyway, forgetting about running off to her mother's, and muses, "How shall we plan our future?"

The demands of work, of community responsibility, press down on Chinese individuals to a remarkable degree, in fiction or real life. They seem to keep many marriages stable but crush those people who cannot cope. A divorce trial we attended in Peking involved a woman in such a desperate situation. Zhou Huixie had moved out of her apartment after, she said, her husband had beaten her seven times, including two occasions that led to miscarriages. Her husband was contesting the divorce. Her neighbors had turned up in court advising reconciliation, and a lower court had denied her request. She had appealed to a higher court, and when we saw her there, she was nearly hysterical.

Zhou wore a red blouse under her purple padded winter jacket and slacks. She was a slim woman with sharp features under ill-cut bangs. She wiped her eyes with a handkerchief and occasionally screamed at the judge and the two civilian assessors, "I want a *divorce*. He beat me *seven* times!" The husband, a chubby truckdriver with a crew cut, was named Han Feli. He was matter-of-fact about the last beating: "My wife said something to my mother that I didn't like, so I kicked her. Then my brother got into an argument with her and boxed her ears. She went home to her mother and wouldn't come back, even though my mother and brother apologized."

The courtroom was full of spectators, mostly neighbors, who strained to hear every word of a drama they could never see on television. All had tickets saying, "Be punctual. No smoking, no noise," and the bailiff later warned, "No spitting." The judge chose to believe the neighbors' version: "They say the husband chased the wife but didn't catch her, so there was no beating." By the time court was adjourned Zhou was in tears and the court seemed unsympathetic, but we were told later the divorce was granted.

It is nearly always the woman who presses for a divorce in China, an ironic aspect of how important women have become. The man doesn't want to lose the investment of his bride price, nor accept the blame for initiating the divorce, which is often more of a stigma than accepting the blame for souring the marriage. The husband and his family either try for a reconciliation or make the wife so miserable that *she* will ask for a divorce.

It is also more difficult for a man than for a woman to find a new spouse in modern-day China, particularly in the circumstances that lead to divorce. People who have lived in Chinese villages say money and food cause trouble. If the husband is eating too much, or is too lazy to earn enough work points, or if his parents did not have as much surplus grain and equipment as the wife was led to believe, she will sometimes seek a divorce in order to find a more economically secure and trustworthy partner.

Political trouble also destroys emotional bonds, particularly when a spouse is demoted or sent away to a work camp for voicing the wrong ideological line or crossing his superiors. There are sexual problems too, and all the abuses of marital life everywhere, such as drinking, gambling and wife beating. In a village of northern Guangdong, a middle-aged farmer with four children kept joining the nightly card games that had become an obsession to many men in his small community. There was little cash to play for. The farmer wagered the wood and bricks holding up the house he lived in, then the bricks he used for flooring.

"Finally he bet and lost the bed for his children, and the bed he and his wife slept on. When the wife complained he beat her, rather regularly," a neighbor said. The local party officials did not intervene. Some of them were playing in the same card game. They were loath, anyway, to interfere in domestic quarrels.

"In the end, the wife just ran off with the children. The husband ended up roaming the streets, trying to pick up vegetables or other food that had been thrown away. It was spoiled, rotten stuff, not fit for pigs."

Until recently, as in most traditional societies, Chinese husbands customarily demanded strict obedience from their wives. The Marriage Act of 1950 was supposed to change that, and to some extent it has. In urban families, more husbands now share the housework, cleaning and cooking chores, although this is still far from the rule. A writer for the official magazine *China Reconstructs* described the reaction of neighbors when a model worker in the large northeastern city of Jilin took over his wife's household chores because her responsibilities at work had increased. "Many people laughed at him," said the writer, who disapproved of the neighbors' attitude. "A man could lose face doing this."

That traditional attitude toward sex roles retains great strength in the countryside. A woman, either the wife or the mother-in-law, is expected to do all the house chores, as well as her share of the field work. Men make the final decisions about education for the children and handling of family finances. Yet a woman expects to be consulted, along with other adult members of the household—grandparents, grown children—on important matters. Women also have responsibilities for many day-to-day decisions such as how to organize household work. They no longer follow the old code of deference, which stipulated that a wife could eat only after her husband had finished his meal. If guests are present, however, there are often no extra chairs, so she will have to wait and eat later.

The modern demands for female labor and the frequent separations of husbands and wives have also added significantly to some women's power in the home and in society. When Xiao Chunying, a forty-six-year-old mother of three, invited us into her home in the Xiangyan Brigade, Hubei (Hupeh) province, she left little doubt as to who was running the family. Her husband came home from his office job in nearby Wuhan only on Saturdays and Sundays. Xiao decided how to divide the family income, who would perform what farm chores on their private plot and when, and whether the young man her eldest daughter had in mind was really suitable. Her husband no longer owned their home—the commune did—and he could no longer command the deference traditionally due the male homeowner or landowner.

And on idle evenings and Sundays, men and women in the villages go their own way. "The men usually prefer to go off and talk with other men, rather than with their wives," said one peasant. "In my village the older men just talk; the younger men play poker." Such pastimes can become bad habits. Rural officials complain of trouble getting the evening meetings started on time. At meetings where next year's crop is to be discussed, women often do not attend at all, leaving such matters to the men, who usually supervise field work.

In the eyes of their neighbors, a peasant couple who might enjoy their own company and refrain from the natural sex segregation would seem out of place. In the evenings, village men often drift into one of the larger homes for long talks over tea or wine. A typical gathering spot is the cottage of a family with several sons, who need—and have been able to afford—a large sitting room. Women take knitting and small children over to another neighbor's home for a long chat, talk being a favorite pastime. A few villages close to the cities have good incomes from the vegetables they sell to city folk, and can afford to build common rooms. A brigade with about 100 to 200 families might have one large meeting room with a television set, where many people congregate in the early evening or on Sunday.

But no matter how much time couples had spent living apart from each other, or how dispassionate they seemed in talking to us about their marriages, rare moments of real feelings did break through. Hou spoke movingly to Linda about how her husband, Yin Anming, a busy and talented Foreign Ministry interpreter, did all the housework for a month after their son Xunxun was born, including washing the sheets and mattress pads following Hou's delivery. He stayed close by her side when the little boy was struck by pneumonia and was not expected to live. "I'll never forget it," Hou said.

Despite all the difficulties of crowded lives and the heavy official restrictions on births, the Chinese remain enormously attached to their children. The rituals of marriage—the painstaking consideration that goes into extending family ties, the little fertility rites such as sprinkling rice on the ground—reflect the old peasant notion that the more children the better. This is perhaps the last and most important battleground between the Communist Party, with its desire for rational population growth, and Chinese peasant tradition.

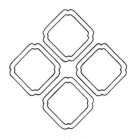

CHILDREN

IN A VILLAGE OF ANHUI PROVINCE, A PEASANT COUPLE WITH TWO daughters found themselves on an official blacklist when the wife became pregnant again. The new birth control campaign had just begun and commune officials wanted to make an example of her. They demanded an abortion. She strenuously refused, and her husband and mother-in-law backed her up because they wanted a male child to carry on the family name.

Finally, under intense pressure, the couple agreed to let the doctors induce early birth at seven months and let the baby die if it was a girl. But when a commune official standing by in the delivery room saw it was a boy, he reneged and insisted it not be saved. The husband and mother-in-law were on their knees at the delivery room door, pleading for reconsideration, but the child died because the nurses were not allowed to put it in an incubator. Some days later the mother-in-law saw the four-year-old son of one of the officials playing by a lake. In a rage, she threw the child into the water, then jumped in herself, and both drowned.

The birth of a baby is special in any country, but in China it has assumed new importance and brought new risks now that the government has endorsed one of the world's most draconian birth control policies. At the moment one baby is acceptable, two are tolerated, and three are grounds for fines and forced abortions. There are so many Chinese of childbearing age that even if each couple starting a family now had only two children, the resulting increase in the population would be devastating. "One is enough," say the billboards in Peking. To the Chinese, this is the curse hanging over their pride at being the world's only billion-member nation.

The Chinese are among the proudest and pushiest parents on earth. During our first impromptu visit to an apartment building in Shanghai in 1977, our hosts would not let us depart until we had listened to their nine-year-old play her *pipa*, heard their four-year-old recite Tang poetry and inspected their twelve-year-old's watercolors. Even middle-class

American parents would be embarrassed at the extent to which Chinese parents put their children through their paces.

That obsession with offspring has successfully crippled government birth control campaigns in the past. The latest campaign, begun in 1979, may also fail eventually, but the Chinese we talked to feel the authorities are more determined this time than ever before. Chinese doctors are trying to improve abortion methods to ensure that only planned children are born, and pursuing genetic research and improved Caesarean-section techniques to guarantee that they have no defects or birth injuries. Some local authorities want to fine couples up to 10 percent of their wages if they insist on having more than two children, or force the parents to pay back bonuses received when they pledged to have just one child. Compulsory sterilizations and abortions have become common.

On the other side of the issue, some party officials have begun to worry that they might be creating unanticipated behavioral problems in a new generation of children without siblings. One Shanghai school study characterized "only children" as unusually impolite, finicky, bad-tempered and selfish, at least in the eyes of the teachers, who rarely encounter unruly children. But such modern psychological concerns will not handicap the one-child policy nearly as much as the obsession with producing male offspring.

Communist Party officials lapse into embarrassed silence when the subject is raised, but the traditional adage "A daughter is like spilled water" still holds for many Chinese. Once married, young women usually move off to live with their in-laws, depriving their families of the harvest shares they earn in the fields. Young men, however, will usually settle near their parents. They earn larger shares than their sisters, anyway, and have the obligation of supporting their parents in old age. The government has only enough money for social security in the cities, and no matter what it says about guarantees for the elderly, it counts on rural sons to observe the ancient Confucian custom of filial devotion.

So the old bias in favor of boys lives on. When we first visited China in April 1977, Linda was eight months pregnant. While the officials we met had the proper, progressive views on nearly everything we asked them, they would still occasionally inquire of Linda, "Do you need sons?," an old way of wishing her success in bearing a boy. An American couple living in Hefei received repeated condolences from their friends when their baby turned out to be a girl. In Anshan a hospital discontinued a special experiment in determining the sex of unborn children after thirty babies were aborted at the parents' request—twenty-nine sets of those parents had been told they had a girl, and they were quick to grab the opportunity given them to hold out for a boy. In 1983 the official press reported alarming increases in drownings and other murders of infant girls, as the conflict between one-child rules and the desire for sons shook the countryside.

Peasants may also increase their chances of producing sons by short-circuiting the birth control program. A doctor in Shanxi, Lin Yigui, was sentenced to two years in prison for removing intrauterine loops from women who wanted more children; the illegal procedure had turned into a thriving business. During a month's stay in a particularly remote village of southwestern Fujian province, American sociologist Victor Nee found that the peasants took advantage of the fact that the IUDs were supposed to be only 80 percent effective: unauthorized pregnancies were blamed on a failure of the devices, even though some of the women were probably taking them out. According to Nee, the Fujian birth control officials were attempting to apply strong sanctions: no grain rations for the first child if the mother refused an IUD after the first birth, or no rations for two children if she balked at sterilization or abortion after a second birth. The local authorities also offered big bonuses for sterilization after one child—a sewing machine, 30 yuan and 500 pounds of grain. But the peasants Nee interviewed said they still strongly preferred to have more than two children.

We detected some skepticism about the chances for this latest birth control campaign to last much longer than the others. The government failed to enforce sanctions during a birth control drive in the early 1970s, and the campaign lost steam. Nee said women in the Fujian village who had aborted children during the earlier campaign quickly became pregnant again. Sterilization also remains unpopular, partly out of superstition. Villagers gossiped that one party secretary was less vigorous and masculine since having himself sterilized as an example to other village men. Another official blamed his sterilization operation for the fact that his wife left him for another man.

In southwestern Fujian, Nee reported, "The most impoverished and pathetic villagers were elderly couples without adult offspring, object lessons for villagers who failed to have sons." A former Guangdong peasant told us with some cynicism, "In many areas the wives of the officials, who are often from big families rich with laborers themselves, are the strongest opponents of birth control. Because they are the wives of the officials, they are more difficult to be persuaded. They dare to object to the policy." Often their husbands encourage them. "One child is prettier than the next," said a bank official from Zhejiang province with seven children. "The more children my wife bears, the younger she looks." Some female officials are no better at setting an example. Wang Danwen, one of the leading women in the Zhejiang provincial government, had a third child without apology and derided colleagues practicing birth control. Many women in her section decided to have more children themselves.

At Shengqiu village in southern China, the women's-affairs officials called a meeting of all village women to discuss their mediocre birth control record. The women were promised some work points—the equivalent of harvest shares—to attend the meeting; the officials had been afraid no one would show up.

"Comrades, we have to set up a birth control plan here," a women's-affairs official said she told them. "Each of you should work out a plan for how many children you plan to have, and how many years between them, and we should make sure no one has more than two."

The wife of a brigade production team leader, an influential woman, stood up and glared at the women's-affairs official. "Go to hell," she said. The room broke into nervous laughter. "I have six children already, but I want at least two more. I refuse to listen to any more of this."

The room buzzed. "I have only four children, but she has six, so I must have at least six," one woman said. Another referred to the wife of one of the most skilled and successful farmers: "She has nine children, the smallest is even younger than one of her grandsons, but she still wants more."

The women's-affairs official despaired of progress. The stubborn resistance to birth control in many parts of the countryside has been dampened by the vigorous campaign of the early 1980s, which produced one of the most remarkable reported birth rate drops in the world. But by 1983 the reported decline in births had leveled off. "Many peasants have started to see how bad it would be if there were too many people in one village," the women's-affairs official said. "But they prefer that other families limit their births, not they."

An old woman anxiously awaits the birth of her son's baby, then spends her days caring for the child, whose mother is likely to go back to her job within days of the delivery. That is the world into which countless Chinese children, particularly boys, are born. Babies are coddled, cuddled, fed at the slightest cry. Frequently grandmothers and grandfathers become their slaves.

Rural villages rarely have day-care centers. Young women must work if the family rice pot is to stay full. Even in large cities, not all working mothers can find spaces in neighborhood nurseries. Maids or housekeepers are out of the question except for a few well-connected government officials in Peking and other large cities.

The government's push for sexual equality and a full-time work force has indirectly fortified the domineering grandmother, an institution progressive-minded bureaucrats, not to mention beleaguered daughters-in-law, would like to see fade away. In the southern village of Dongguan, surrounded by wide, flat green rice paddies, seven-year-old Liang Hailing took her five-year-old brother to the commune pond for some fishing. She didn't return until it was too late to help her mother cook lunch. The mother began to beat the girl with a stick, but her mother-in-law intervened. "These are my grandchildren! I will not allow you to beat them."

"They are my children. I have the right to punish them."

"Oh? Their family name is Liang. You have no right to beat children of the Liang family."

A peasant wife who divorces her husband often returns to her home village without her children, so strong is the assumption that children are born to the father, the paternal grandfather and grandmother, and not the mother's family. One Guangdong villager who knew such a woman said, "She never went back to see the children, and of course they would have been an obstacle to her getting married again. I imagine they disliked her, or at least were taught to dislike her once she left."

In divorce cases it is not the sultry secretary, but the grumbling grandmother who often rocks the marriage. When Wei Jinfeng, a thirty-five-year-old Shanghai woman who eventually sought a divorce, came home from the hospital with her first child, a girl, her mother-in-law held up a boy infant borrowed from a neighbor, both as a good luck charm for next time and as a rebuke. (The Chinese marriage manuals fail to explain that the sex of a child is determined, albeit involuntarily, by the father.) In the ensuing quarrel Wei's husband took his mother's side, and Wei began to lose control. She would smash furniture, rip her husband's clothes and constantly complain about him to his work supervisors. Finally, pregnant again, she had a secret abortion to free herself of the possible shame of another daughter.

In another case a Communist Party member sought unsuccessfully to divorce his wife because she failed to bear him a son. The unfortunate woman had produced one son and three daughters, but the boy had died in an accident. Under pressure from her husband and in-laws, she reluctantly consented to have a fifth baby, but it also turned out to be a girl.

Long days stooped over a hoe, or bent over double planting rice seedlings in mud, begin to wear on a woman in her forties and fifties. A healthy young wife brought home by a son to bear a grandchild provides a convenient excuse for retirement. Lai Zexiong, a Canton trade official, told us about his sister, whose mother-in-law had quickly taken over care of her first child, a boy, in a rural commune of eastern Guangdong. "Many mothers want their sons to marry and have children so they don't have to go to the fields anymore. The retirement age for women is usually fifty-five, but if they have to take care of a baby, they can stop at any age."

In China, there are no televised soap operas, but there is plenty of home-grown drama. The battle of wife and mother-in-law makes family life engrossing. A woman from the rural south told us of a young neighbor, Huang Yun, who married at seventeen and soon became pregnant. She miscarried. It is a common enough tragedy among these hardworking women, but her mother-in-law would not let her forget it. "That was four years ago, and still no second baby," the old woman told the neighbor during one of the endless talks that help pass time in her village of whitewashed brick cottages. "She's a child. How does she know how to take care of herself?" Another neighbor joined in, "It is certainly not your son's fault that they have no child. He fathered the first baby, then she lost it."

At the time of the miscarriage Huang had said nothing about her first pains signaling the trouble—she had not seen an obstetrician and did not know what to expect. Huang heard the neighbors' talk and appeared to be frozen by grief and by the knowledge that the old women might be right. (Such moments of family guilt and frustration run deep; they have inspired several centuries of Chinese drama and literature.) The State Council's latest directive on birth control meant very little to Huang's mother-in-law in Guangdong province. She continued to resent the failure of her son's frail young wife to produce a male grandchild.

To everyone's great relief, after five years of worry and scolding from her mother-in-law, Huang became pregnant again. This time the family was determined to take no chances. She stopped working in the rice fields twenty days before she was due. Many Chinese peasants consider this taking it easy.

"It was a very special case," said the neighbor, "because her husband was the only son in his family, and she had lost one baby. She got very special treatment. Usually women continue to work until a week or so before they deliver." There was no heavy lifting for the mother-to-be. Her housework was done by her mother-in-law, and female cousins and nieces in the neighborhood who could be recruited. Others carried water in and out, a Chinese housewife's frequent chore, or tended the family's private plot.

For the first few months of the pregnancy the family had asked a village woman with experience as a midwife to check in on Huang. At home, Huang's mother-in-law often fixed her a special brew for pregnant women —antaicha. It was a herbal tea, loosely translated "keep baby comfy." (The Chinese soak herbs—different ones depending on the ailment—for nearly everything that bothers them.)

Most Chinese women go into labor for the first time unsure of what precisely is going to happen. "We don't have any childbirth classes," an office worker in Peking told us. "Only at the beginning of labor did the doctor tell me what to do." Anesthetics is very rare except for Caesareans, and husbands are not allowed in the delivery room. "Men would not even think of being around during labor," Hou told Linda.

After a three-day hospital stay, new mothers in the city usually return home for the rest of their guaranteed fifty-six-day maternity leave. For centuries the rule in China has been that following delivery, mothers remain immobile in bed for a month. They are supposed to avoid contact with cold water, since it is widely believed that this will give them arthritis. "Rest, rest, always rest, they told me," said Hou, who admitted that she did not go outside her house for a month after her son was born. "I got lots of good food, chicken and eggs. They kept telling me to stay in bed, but I broke the law. I even washed with cold water." Chinese babies are usually placed on their backs. The infants' heads sometimes flatten a bit as a result of this sleeping posture. Laura Chandler, an American who had her first child while living in Anhui, said, "The nurse we hired tried to put Abigail on her stomach. She knew that was the way we wanted it, but didn't know how to do it."

In the hospital the family, not the short-handed hospital staff, feeds and cares for the recuperating new mother. Laura Chandler's English students at Anhui University, concerned that her relatives were far away in Maryland, organized themselves into teams to watch over her each evening.

Hospital and doctor fees are cheap; in most cases they amount to only about $30, and most of that is paid by the mother's work unit. There is also a considerable amount of folk wisdom being dispensed to young mothers, in a nation that has yet to translate Dr. Spock for general circulation. One new mother was told her early troubles with breast-feeding were caused by wearing a bra for too long during the day. One of Laura Chandler's students asked her why she didn't have a towel around her head to keep her brains from becoming chilled.

All of our Peking friends had their babies in hospitals. Most of the young peasant women we met went to one of the tidy two- or three-room brigade or team clinics when their time came. Some had a "barefoot doctor" paramedic—in many cases a midwife with some medical training—come to their home. Women in the countryside also generally breast-feed, but most city women put their babies on the bottle quickly because of the difficulty of bringing children to work. Not all factories provide convenient nurseries and most offices do not provide day care at all. Mothers can buy a powdered formula, to which they add water, and later milk and eggs. Many of our city friends said that their children did not like milk much. There are few refrigerators, and children more often drink porridge or boiled water.

Huang Yun's village was not far from the district hospital, so she took the regular bus there two or three days before her baby was due. Women in the village normally take their chances with the local midwives, but Huang's in-laws had too much riding on this child. As everyone had hoped, it was a boy. Pleased and excited, the grandmother stayed at the hospital with Huang until four days later, when she brought the child home.

On the thirtieth day of his life, the family held one of the most pleasant rituals of Chinese life, the "full-month feast" to celebrate the baby's initial survival. Villagers usually invite only their closest relatives to the full-month feast, but in this case they invited everyone they were related to, more than thirty people. Special tables were placed inside and outside the house. The baby was brought out and shown around. The menu included meat, normally a once-a-week or once-a-month luxury in many villages, prepared in ways that would bring good luck to the baby: pig's leg with ginger and eggs cooked with red coloring were thought, for reasons now obscure, to be particularly auspicious.

For one month the grandmother cared for the baby while Huang rested. Then Huang went back to the rice fields. The grandmother delegated some of the daily care of the child to the baby's youngest aunt, a bright fourteen-year-old who looked forward to this special family responsibility. She brought the baby to the school with her in the morning and to the fields at noon so his mother could nurse him. When he was about four months old Huang began taking him to the fields with her. She worked until noon and then took her hallowed *xiu-xi,* "noon sleep." Mother and baby returned to the fields in midafternoon, where Huang Yun worked until evening. While working, she put the baby in the shade of some trees, usually strapped in a carrier. The chief of the team assigned her to chores that would allow her to remain close to the baby.

In that tight circle of mother, grandmother, aunts and neighbors, Chinese children are carefully watched. They are accepted everywhere, in restaurants, at movies and concerts, and in some ways very indulged. A group of American child-care specialists led by Yale psychologist William Kessen visited dozens of Chinese homes in 1973, some at scheduled stops and some not. The children, their report noted, were "extraordinarily poised and well-behaved." They greeted visitors warmly. When adults began serious talk, the children resumed play with their books and toys, usually without any prompting. Kessen's group remarked on the amount of physical contact between children and adults. Parents and grandparents often hold children on their knees, smile or exchange glances with them. This creates ties which few children wish to break, so they appear to watch for cues and cause little trouble when adults are near.

"Chinese children simply are better behaved," said a scholar and sometime diplomat who has lived in Taipei, Hong Kong and Peking. He traced this to the Confucian heritage, which insists on moderation, peace and tranquillity in the home, with elders always obeyed. "If you are told from babyhood not to do anything to disturb that," he said, "that means you must disguise any individual feelings."

Over a lunch of onions, string beans, cucumber, eggplant and bowls of steamed bread, a peasant mother near Peking advised us: "We don't spank, we just don't give in. I think in the West whenever a child throws a tantrum, you give him what he wants. Here we don't have the financial means to give the children what they want, and I think they sense that very early. Then, we really have a Confucian tradition. The child should follow the father, and the father teaches the child in a very stern way, so the children become obedient right from the beginning. It is just assumed they will obey."

She thought it was important to introduce the child to sharing and collective living very early, both because the party wanted it and because life in such a crowded country was impossible any other way. She spoke of families with money who bestowed presents on their offspring: "Those children are not so well-behaved." She praised nursery schools and kindergartens like the little brigade nursery school her son attended. "At the nursery, he cannot ask for more. He has to share with the other children, and so he is better behaved now. But foreign children, I understand, when they are not satisfied with something, they cry and kick."

Ruth Sidel, in her book *Women and Child Care in China,* writes that "Chinese children seem to profit from a consensus about how they should be raised. They suffer little of the conflicting advice that bombards American parents." Chinese teachers treat the children just as their parents do, expecting "good behavior, cooperation and obedience." They usually get it, Sidel concluded, after studying several Chinese pre-schools.

Chinese children also are often buffeted by intense clan feeling. Although so often complimented as among the world's best-behaved children, they may not be the most secure; in a curious way, that may explain their good behavior. Psychiatric social worker Carolyn Lee Baum and her husband, UCLA political scientist Richard Baum, found the Chinese families they studied threatening their misbehaving small children with an end to family affection, a denial of their place at the table. It is a dire threat, given how involved all members of the extended family—grandmother, aunts and cousins as well as mother and father—are in raising the offspring in comparison to mother-centered Western children. Being excluded from the family circle is a terrifying prospect. It may have helped create a nation full of adults who cringe at Western ideas of rugged individualism.

We tried to plumb these mysteries with visits to the Peking No. 1 Kindergarten, which tried to transform Peter, then age three, into an obedient Chinese child, at least for the three hours each morning he was there. The school staff did not seem happy to see us; Chinese parents do not usually drop by to observe their children. In fact, all of the nine Chinese children in Peter's class slept there overnight and saw their parents only on weekends. The seven foreign children, assigned to the school because of its good equipment and central location, comprised two Americans, two Japanese, a Nigerian, a Sudanese and a Moroccan.

For the first two weeks Peter cried when we left him off at the school, a collection of tile-roofed buildings in a walled compound that once served as a Buddhist nunnery. This was not uncommon for new pupils, particularly those who spent all week in the dormitory, which was laid out like a miniature military barracks. The sinks were scaled to a three-year-old size, and identical beds were lined up headboard to headboard. The grandmotherly director, Ouyang Man, explained, "We can keep the children occupied during the day with play and other activities, but in the first few weeks many of them cry for their mothers at night. The teachers try to comfort them as best they can."

If you persist in asking urban Chinese why their children are so well-behaved, they will eventually give much of the credit to this early taste of "collective living." They expect it to shape the child for life. Foreigners wonder whether the regimentation and long separation from parents might be psychologically damaging for children so young. But in China, both mother and father almost always work away from home, and the only complaint Chinese parents ever voice about the boarding nurseries is that there are not nearly enough of them.

Sun Yan, director of the Ministry of Education's pre-school division, quoted us a new Chinese saying: "It is more difficult to get into kindergarten than into a university." The whole country has only 16,000 kindergartens, and only a quarter of those board pupils overnight. Chinese workers often commute long distances and without many electric appliances face so many time-consuming household chores that the added burden of picking up a child each day is very troublesome. If couples can prove they have no one else to take care of their children during the day—and have good *guanxi* —they can enroll them at the Peking No. 1 Kindergarten for $11 a month. Director Ouyang said, "We see that the child leads a regular life, gets nutritious meals and learns to care for himself. We supervise everything from laundry to haircuts. If he's sick, he can see the doctor in residence." Pupils often form deep emotional attachments to teachers—in the same traditional way that new workers in factories latch on to old-timers as surrogate fathers in the Confucian style. Deputy Minister Sun said her own thirty-year-old daughter still attends reunions with her nursery-school teacher.

"Primary teachers can tell the difference between those children who have gone to nursery schools and those who have been home with their grannies, who are often illiterate and quite indulgent," Sun said. "The children from nursery schools are more accustomed to mass activities, better disciplined and more knowledgeable about the world."

The experience clearly had some impact on Peter. After the first few weeks of school he was dashing eagerly out the hotel door each morning. In stentorian tones he cited his *laoshi* (teacher), a somber but pleasant young woman named Ren Jixen, as the ultimate authority on everything from how he should eat his soup to how he should wear his toy wristwatch. We wondered what exactly was going on.

By the time we arrived at nine o'clock, the morning routine was well under way. Peter's live-in schoolmates had done their morning calisthenics, eaten breakfast and brushed their teeth.

Ren told the children to bring over chairs and line them up for singing. Peter swiftly complied. He sang heartily the Chinese lyrics, but as the songs grew more difficult he lost interest. A child sitting behind him tried to move Peter's chair and Peter punched him.

During his months at the school he began to switch from the Cantonese dialect he had picked up from Ah-Lin to the harsher syllables of northern, or Mandarin, Chinese. He refused to speak Chinese to other foreigners, including his father, but he and the *Washington Post* driver, Wang Fachen, engaged in dialogues that delighted Wang and indicated how much Peter could soak up from the songs and games at school.

Ren led the pupils through a series of choreographed dance steps and hand gestures that would become a repertoire unleashed on the next group of visiting dignitaries. Peter and his classmates went at it with intense concentration. At home he liked to imitate his older brother; at school he carefully watched the moves of the four- and five-year-olds in the class.

"Who needs to urinate?" Ren asked loudly. Peter and other small boys began to line up in front of enamel bedpans. Girls stood over other pans in a corner of the classroom. No one encouraged privacy or shyness. Juice was served, each child taking his own cup from its appointed hook on the wall and sitting at one of the long, low tables. The Chinese children were dressed so colorfully, in pink dresses and fancy green-and-white shorts-and-shirt combinations, that for a while we mistook some of them for Japanese. At a time of loosened social restraints, children were again leaders in fashion. The little Moroccan girl, with earrings and ribbons in her hair, began to cry. She was new, and an assistant teacher picked her up and carried her outside to comfort her.

To cheer everyone up, the singing resumed. There were no chants about Chairman Mao, as there had been in all Chinese schools during the Cultural Revolution. A more ancient authority had returned to favor, as the next song demonstrated:

> *My teacher is like my mother.*
> *We need not be afraid of her.*
> *She teaches us to sing and dance.*
> *We are always happy.*
> *My parents are very satisfied,*
> *And my kindergarten is my home.*

Two hours had passed. The Chinese pupils continued with orderly songs and games, but discipline among the foreigners began to break down: Peter, the other American, Einar Rowan, and the Nigerian boy engaged in a series of skirmishes. The class had somehow acquired a big-wheeled tricycle, and they battled over it.

Toward the end of the three hours, as time approached for the Chinese children to nap in their well-arranged beds, the noise level and chaos in all parts of the room increased. As we helped Peter into his sweater for the trip home, Ren assured us that this was not up to her standard of discipline. "They are too young, so they cannot control themselves," she said.

Peter gave his *laoshi* a cheery farewell and headed to the car for a chat with Wang. Though Peter acquired a fluency in the language that we envied, he never absorbed the ethic of communal living that seems so easy for Chinese. That night he tried out on his brother one of his favorite Chinese phrases. *"Bu shi ni de, shi wo de!"* (That's not yours, it's mine!)

We did not send Peter to school on Saturdays, but we noticed that Saturday afternoon was a special time for schoolchildren in Peking. That is the time when most of the boarding students are picked up for a night at home. Bicycles with small cagelike enclosures lashed to the sides zip through the streets. Inside, in thronelike splendor, sit toddlers bound for home. The capital's candy shops and fruit and popsicle stands are thronged with small children who have managed to wheedle sweets from their slightly guilt-ridden parents. "I know I shouldn't give her this stuff," said Wang Caomeng, an office worker, as his tiny daughter munched on a bag of caramel corn, "but how can I refuse when we see her only once a week?"

Some workers are lucky enough to have nurseries in their work places if their organization is large enough. From what we have seen, the Chinese children in these factory nurseries may be holding back China's long-awaited modernization, something admirers of such work-place conveniences should keep in mind. In a machine tools factory in Shanghai, a couple of dozen women were crowded into the factory nursery, holding and playing with the children. No one appeared to be nursing a baby, the ostensible reason for female workers to take long breaks. Nurseries seen in other factories from Nanning to Peking attract the same crowds of doting mothers, at a time when low productivity and time-wasting remain national afflictions.

Somewhere, somehow, during these hours spent on adult knees in crowded nurseries and classrooms, the children develop the social sense that Westerners find astonishing. A favorite skit, performed endlessly in Chinese kindergartens, has been dubbed the "big apple" by those who have had to sit through it once too often. The moral is: Give the big apple to someone else and keep only the smallest apple for yourself. The nurseries we have seen have almost no toys. There may be a few simple playthings, wooden wagons or small rattles, but little else. Sharing is essential. There can be none of the Western indulgence of selfish desires in children once they have left the home. Cooperative instincts become second nature. Later on, the Chinese may pay a price for this in their efforts to train their own scientists and build a modern technology. Emphasis on cooperation and conformity limits imagination and independence. But the Chinese talents for tackling group problems are startling.

Child specialists in the Kessen group tried something called the "miners' game" on eight-year-olds at the New China Primary School No. 2 in Peking. The visitors produced a narrow-necked jar with a tube allowing water to be pumped in from the bottom and with three wooden men dangling inside the jar from long strings running out the neck. There was only enough room to pull the men out one at a time. "These men are building a tunnel," said the teacher, following the Americans' instructions. "A leak has started and water is rising. The men must get out before the water reaches them. Three children will each hold a string and must try to pull their men out quickly as soon as I say go." Three girls were selected. They immediately began to whisper among themselves about which man was to go first, second and last, and soon all three were out.

No one is sure how the Chinese become so socially oriented so young, but it affects everything they do. Chinese intellectuals, committed to Marx, not Freud, do not seem terribly interested in exploring this character trait as yet, and, after all, it is not universal even in China. The inordinate attention received by small boys—particularly first-borns—at home may weaken their cooperative attitude in school. When three small boys tried the miners' game, one pulled his man out fast, but the other two were jammed at the exit. One boy wore the red scarf of the Little Red Guards, now called again by their 1950s name, the Young Pioneers, the first stop on a road that leads to the Communist Party membership and fruitful careers. The boy with the red scarf whispered, "This is dangerous. You go first and I'll go after you." Both got their miners out.

In factories where managers have recently tried to encourage better individual effort through bonuses, the emphasis on cooperation, which begins in early childhood, has become a severe drag on productivity. "Are you trying to make the rest of us look bad?" one worker recalls being told by workmates when he began a new job at a fast pace. "Slow down, we're all in this together."

In an art class at an elementary school which Jay observed, the teacher drew the outline of a bus at her easel. She carefully painted it red, beginning from the upper right-hand roof down to the lower left-hand fender. Each child followed her movements exactly, not a line out of place. When you walk down the hall of a Chinese school, it is difficult not to fall in step with the chants of lessons being recited in unison from each room. What the Chinese call creative writing must follow a set theme, such as selfishness or leadership. One American twelve-year-old in a Chinese school dutifully copied from the blackboard the oil derrick and oil trucks everyone in his class was asked to draw. But he added the legends "Exxon" and "Caltex" to the sides of the trucks and stuck an American flag on one. The teacher looked at him sharply and put a mark in her book.

The demands of rote learning in Chinese schools point Chinese adults in limited directions. "In a problem like earthquake prediction, the Chinese operate by training thousands of people and collecting millions of bits of data," an American geologist said, "but there is a real reluctance to try deductions, to create a theory that will get to the bottom of it, to dream and speculate. Still, they've come further in many ways with their approach than we have with ours. They work *together* so well."

Children decorate a Chinese crowd like flower petals in a muddy field. Most adults still wear drab blue or green jackets and baggy pants and blend inconspicuously into the masses. Suppressed desires for pattern and color are unleashed when buying or making children's clothing—the brighter, the better.

Once children in the countryside are old enough to walk, they are free to wander as they please. In the safety net of the Chinese village, everyone knows everyone else and watches out for the neighbor children. Little boys pass their first years peering into doorways and chasing chickens, and ignoring their parents' half-hearted attempts at toilet training. Peasant children are allowed to squat just about anywhere. Even the most thickly padded winter clothing includes a long slit through the bottom of the pants, and sometimes the slit goes through several layers of pants. Diapers, except at night, are unheard of.

"About one third of our first graders, seven- and eight-year-olds, were wetting their pants in the classroom," one rural schoolteacher told us. "Before they went to school, nobody told them they should go to the toilet, so the children would solve the problem then and there." She said the relaxed attitude toward toilet training was particularly evident in families with several children. "The parents have no time to look after them, and the older brothers and sisters don't bother to instruct them, so they just wander around and do it where they wish and it is cleaned up afterwards."

The carefree life of many Chinese babies begins to change by and by. Three-year-olds are often given some responsibility—sweeping the floor, picking up sticks or cutting hillside grass for fuel, weeding or picking vegetables in the private plot, or washing the rice before dinner. Punishments become harsher. Children who misbehave are sometimes cuffed, yelled at or beaten, sometimes with bamboo sticks. City children are used to the more permissive methods of their parents, which are encouraged by government child-care pamphlets. Young people from the cities told us they were shocked when they arrived on assignments in the countryside in the 1960s and saw the harsh discipline imposed by rural parents. In the former model village of Dazhai, as well as several less celebrated hamlets, we heard mothers curse their children in language one would not see bannered in the *People's Daily*. Children who misbehaved had their bottoms smacked. But it was a cold spring, and the small rosy-cheeked toddlers wore padded clothing. The blows injured little more than their pride.

Children who fight or who show willfulness or insubordination disrupt the village *guanxi*. Such lapses receive particularly quick and harsh punishment, for they create great unease among the parents. As a child grows up, the father's role as a disciplinarian becomes more important, and his manner more aloof, quite a change from the way fathers dote on infants. One immigrant told sociologists Parish and Whyte, "My children are scared of me, so I can get them to behave easily. Most children are scared of their father, but not their mother. Fathers are strict—they don't say much, and they don't often lose their temper and curse, though, or the child would get used to it. If the mother spanks the child and he cries, the father will say, 'Why are you crying? Stop that crying!' and the child will stop. Fathers are more venerable, while mothers are more sympathetic. Fathers rarely joke with children or play with them. No father would play ping-pong with his child—we just don't have that custom!"

A firm, fatherly hand prepares the child for the almost military regimen he will follow in school and later at work. All important activities, even matters as personal or private to Western thinking as studying, dating or even writing a book, are regularly done in groups. Outside the Yandang Road No. 2 Elementary School, not far from the site of the Chinese Communist Party's first congress in Shanghai, we watched a routine, a sort of sidewalk gym class which has not varied much in the thirty years since the Communist victory. Forty ten-year-old boys and girls were lined up in four columns, swinging their arms rhythmically to the shouts or whistle blasts of their young male teacher. All were in faded, patched clothing, but about half wore the bright red scarf of the Young Pioneers. Many small faces shone with excitement at the beat and precision of the military play. They marched a little way up the sidewalk and marched back, the teacher continually berating and shifting the sluggards at the end of the lines.

Classrooms we have visited, whether in urban Shanghai or rural Guangdong, all run on an ancient and probably Confucian system of strict discipline. Each child sits straight with both hands behind his back. The teachers are usually warm and cheerful, but a pupil seeking attention must raise only one hand—no wiggling or pleading allowed—and must stand at attention to recite.

"The discipline is really hard in the Chinese schools," said one of the few European parents who have sent children to study in the Peking school system. "Our kids don't talk about it much, but they tend to explode when they get home. We let them; we figure they need to let off steam after a day at attention."

An American Cub Scout den mother would find the organizational structure of the Young Pioneers breath-taking. Each primary school has a Young Pioneer corps, divided into platoons for each classroom and squads for each row of the class. Small children are admitted gradually, depending on their behavior and study habits, which are judged by the Young Pioneer leaders and their teachers. They do occasional outings and work projects, but the organizational setup really serves as an adjunct of school. About half of the third graders appear to belong, perhaps as many as 90 percent of all sixth graders. Corps, platoon and squad leaders wear stripes pinned to their sleeves. The slowest students, the worst-behaved and sometimes those from families with political blemishes never make it.

"In China, the children learn to help each other," said Li Guohua, a tour guide working in Canton. Li herself conscientiously followed the rules at each rung of the ladder and moved up from the Young Pioneers to the Communist Youth League when she turned fourteen. Youth League members can remain active until about age thirty-five, when they are either admitted to the party or told they will probably never make it. Li was admitted to the Communist Party in 1979 at the tender age of twenty-six. "In school we had persons who were very clever, but not very well behaved," she said, "so we tried to help them." Did they resent being kept out? "No, they knew they were not doing well, in their studies or in their attitude, so they just tried harder."

Many teachers also use the "three good student" system. They list seven or eight names on the board and then ask the class to comment on who did the best that week, in studies and comportment. "She steers the discussion toward the conclusion she desires," one foreigner said of his son's Chinese teacher. "That's not so bad, but then they do the same thing to pick the three worst students. Our son kind of liked it. It was fun to stomp on somebody else, as long as it wasn't him. So we had to talk to him about it and point out that he was being manipulated." Some schools announce the three best students in each class at a monthly meeting and present each child with a flower, the prizes ordinarily going to Young Pioneers.

It is generally held that success in the Young Pioneers is necessary for advancement to the Youth League in high school and to the Communist Party in adult life. The cheerful red scarf becomes a source of satisfaction for those who wear it—and a goad for those who don't. Peer pressure is organized and channeled to a degree unheard of even in prerevolutionary China. When a bright student in one elementary class we observed answered questions a little too quickly, the Pioneers went into action. The boy's squad leader and other officers waited outside class to remind him that the slower students would never have a chance to participate and learn if he did not wait to be recognized.

A few squad leaders, even at age nine or ten, go so far as to visit the homes of their members to check on their study habits and make sure that they have a quiet place to read. Young Pioneers fetch home the books of errant students who might have conveniently forgotten them. They line up the rows of pupils and issue shovels when they go out for their spell of labor in the fields. As they get older, many of these young leaders, called "activists," inspire both fear and resentment, for they will have much to say eventually about how to distribute the limited benefits of Chinese society, soft jobs, adequate housing. As adults in offices and factories, holding party memberships and real authority, they often become insufferable busybodies, insisting on the same kind of obedience they received in junior middle school. Much of the cynicism and low morale of Chinese youth comes from a system that rewards the young who display constant enthusiasm for whatever project is at hand, even though everyone knows such enthusiasm is unnatural and self-serving.

Perhaps there is no other way to motivate hundreds of millions of Chinese children than to hitch them to the energies and ambitions of a few. Not very many of China's millions of young people make an issue of it, hoping instead to move along quietly and avoid the activists' attentions. A bright young language student at Peking University confessed that despite his own steady progress through the youth groups, the blandishments of the Youth League activists had begun to irritate him and he had taken a new tack. "We're friendly," he said, "but I think the best thing is just to stay away from them."

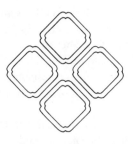

ELDERS

NO GROUP HAS BENEFITED MORE THAN CHINA'S ELDERLY FROM THE guarantees of sufficient food and medical care that followed the Communist victory in 1949. Nearly every Chinese woman we have ever met over the age of sixty tells stories of losing children to disease and malnutrition before the 1949 liberation. Some said they lost as many as seven or eight babies. After liberation, however, children were a bumper crop. Peking's municipal Health Bureau said the city's infant mortality rate dropped from 117.6 to 10.3 per thousand from 1949 to 1978. Nationwide, the rural infant mortality rate has also declined sharply, from 200 per thousand in 1949 to 30 per thousand in 1981. A generation later, many of China's elderly are in what the Chinese consider the enviable position of having several grown sons to feed and house them.

According to Peking's municipal Health Bureau, in 1950 the average life span for city residents was 53.88 years for males and 50.22 for females. By 1975, life expectancies had jumped two decades, to 70.72 for males and 72.72 for females, about the same as in the United States. As with other groups, it is difficult to generalize about living conditions for the elderly throughout China, but when we accompanied former Health, Education and Welfare Secretary Joseph Califano on his visit to a mental health clinic in Shanghai, we noticed far fewer elderly patients than would be found in similar hospitals in the United States. Dr. David Hamburg, director of the National Academy of Sciences Institute of Medicine, told us, "The Chinese seem to be willing to absorb the elderly into their society better than we do." Many retired Chinese still live with their children and undertake responsible work, such as cleaning the streets, looking after grandchildren or minding their private-plot gardens.

But when death approaches, many of the elderly lose their good feelings for what the party has done. Tradition clashes sharply with government regulations for disposing of 70 million dead bodies each year, the end product of the life cycle of a village of a billion. Nearing death, Chinese betray again a desire to be treated as something more than a digit in the state plan.

The man from the little Henan village was eighty-eight years old. He had dark brown skin and a long goatee, and he was crying. "Please help me," he asked a visiting relative. "I don't want to die alone." His wife was the same age as he, but blind and nearly deaf. She had been sent to the nearby big city, Zhengzhou (Chengchow), so that relatives could care for her. Like millions of other elderly Chinese wedded to the old ways, the two of them now faced what to them was a frightening Communist disdain for their belief in the afterlife. The regulations dictated that anybody who died in urban areas had to be cremated.

"We're ready to die, we've been ready for fifteen years to die. But if she dies in the city, she'll be cremated, and I'll be buried here, and we'll never be together," the old man said.

Thirty years of lectures on Marxist atheism and official efforts to stamp out superstition have not erased old fears of improper burial, fortified somewhat by the general Chinese cynicism about any enterprise like cremation turned over to the government. City crematoria give the spouse and children of the deceased small red bags holding the ashes. But Muriel Hoopes, a peppery American in her eighties whose late husband, a Chinese, was cremated in Shanghai, told us she had "a friend working at the crematorium who says they cremate nine or ten people at the same time, then a man there, like a croupier at Las Vegas, rakes from this big heap of ashes into the little bags. You don't know whose ashes you've got."

The old man in Henan had taken his visiting relative into a shed. He pointed to two black coffins, built with wood he had salvaged from a building torn down several years before. He went outside and showed off his burial plot, with trees carefully planted around it. It could not be easily plowed up, as many graves have been, to reclaim crop land. The relative asked the old man what he thought of cremation. He shivered. "I think it must hurt," he said.

People who have preserved a national identity as long as the Chinese often betray deep feelings about ancestors and old times. Proper death and burial rituals in their eyes ensure immortality, both through the annual tending the grave requires and the general belief that the spirit will somehow live on. The party's effort to introduce efficiency in this delicate area has rubbed some emotions raw, and brought acts of creative obstruction typical of modern Chinese attempts to deal with their government.

In ancient times, cremation was considered such a desecration that it was outlawed. Today the hospitals have difficulty persuading relatives to allow even simple autopsies of family members who have died. A number of small black-market syndicates now specialize in smuggling bodies out of the cities so that they can be buried in the countryside. Older peasants say they are reluctant to go to town for medicine for fear they will die there and be cremated, far from where their families are buried. Others try to ensure that medical visits to the city don't force them to stay overnight. They don't take the medicine—what do doctors know?—until they have returned home.

When the American sociologists Parish and Whyte surveyed people from forty-seven different villages in Guangdong province, they found that forty-one had no cremations, five had a few and only one cremated corpses as a usual practice. Cremations that do occur are often special cases designed to set an example. In many areas, the local authorities have not even bothered to build crematoria. Hou, daughter of an upstanding party family with a long record of distinguished adherence to official regulations, said her own grandmother in Guangdong objected to the requirements for cremation. "But you cremated her anyway?" Linda asked. "No," said Hou, looking surprised at such a question. "We buried Grannie just like she told us to."

The prosperity of the early 1950s as the country recovered from civil war produced several social anomalies that subverted the system. For instance, more surviving children, more vigor and longevity reinforced rather than weakened the Confucian traditions of respect and deference toward the old. Today when someone passes a fiftieth, sixtieth or seventieth birthday, special dinners are still held. Friends and relatives come to the "old-age feast" (*shouyan*) and the guest of honor may wear a new suit of clothes sewn by his wife or daughter.

Filial piety survives in a way that also troubles some Chinese Marxists, since it weakens notions of equality. Retired workers often receive a pension equaling 70 percent of their salary after retirement, a substantial contribution to a family's income—often as much as half of the total. This entitles them to determine how the family budget is to be spent, sometimes against the wishes of their fully employed adult children. If the house or apartment is rented by the father, then he decides which grown-up child will stay with him. Some retiring workers in Peking have even been offered an additional bonus if they will agree to leave the overcrowded city and return to their home village: moving to a rural area brings a bonus of $181; just moving from Peking to another city means $95.50. Aging officials are offered additional incentives to retire, if for no other reason than to get them out of the way for the promotion of younger men. Many are reluctant, however, to give up the chauffeured cars, shopping privileges and other badges of rank.

A senior citizen's rather substantial power to determine the living arrangements of children has been augmented by an official decision designed to ease the plight of city youths sent to work in the countryside. An urban worker, when he retires, can now request that one of his children in the countryside be brought back to take over his job, creating some bitterness when one child is chosen over another.

"But I sense relations between the generations are really quite good," said Deborah Davis-Friedmann, a Yale sociologist studying the elderly in

China. "Older people are really quite indispensable in handling the garden, raising pigs, watching kids or taking them to school." She said that older people, particularly women who become grandmothers in their forties, try to retire early. But other peasants may complain if she is a good worker because retirement gives her the time to raise more pigs privately than anyone else. Often the team leader will insist that she wait until she is fifty.

Men retire at a later age. Many male peasants try to remain active as long as possible because, unlike city factories, rural districts offer no guaranteed retirement income for the elderly except for people who have no sons. Though they may work many years, rural elders no longer exercise the overall leadership they did in pre-Communist China. Village elders before 1949 often supervised farm work even though they had ceased to be very active themselves. Today, work-unit leaders are expected to take part in field labor themselves. As men lose their physical stamina in their fifties and sixties they retire from office. This often leaves leadership of basic-level villages in the hands of men in their thirties.

Retirement in the villages remains, by most accounts, a more relaxed time for men than for women. Some grandfathers help prepare meals or baby-sit, and do more household work than they did when they were full-time field workers. But grandfathers often fill their days with visits to a teahouse, or chatting with other retired men, while the grandmothers tend to the baby-sitting and other chores. Rural people argue that because of the rigors of farm work, men deserve rest time at home and a carefree retirement when they grow old, in spite of the fact that many women put in just as many hard hours in the fields as their husbands do.

Yu Meiwang, now in her eighties, has lived in a rural village in Yunan (Yunnan) province all her life, raising seven children, most of whom made it to the big city of Kunming to take jobs as teachers or office workers. She wanted to join them, and they tried to get official permission in the late 1950s, but failed. "It was very strict," her grandson said.

Her life seems typical of aging women in rural China. She's still pretty strong, and she works sometimes, light labor like tending animals or collecting peanuts in the fields. She complains about it, but it is an old person's complaint. "They don't really know what they want," the grandson told us. "When she came to live with us for several weeks in the city as a visitor, she finally asked to leave, to go back to the countryside. All her grandchildren were grown and there was little for her to do in the city, with people she didn't know. She wasn't used to that.

"My mother's second cousin is a peasant in the village, and he takes care of Grandmother. Also, he writes letters for her, to her children. My mother [a teacher with a salary of about 60 yuan, or $40, a month] sends money, about twenty yuan [$13] a month. Her brothers and sisters are supposed to take turns, but if they don't send money, then she does it. The other children say my mother can afford to pay because everybody in her family, my father as well as the grandchildren, is working, but I don't think that's reasonable."

Given the size of Chinese families, elderly without any family to care for them are rare. Relatives with a good sense of the proper rituals are particularly important when death comes. The correct procedures are often so familiar that there is need for little more discussion than when binding up dried wheat stalks.

The funeral, however, remains ceremonious and emotional, a ritual, like the wedding feast, which makes the Communist Party uncomfortable but has survived anyway. Among segments of Chinese society looking for free and lavish entertainment, the old saying still rings true: "It's better to attend the funeral of an eighty-year-old hag than the wedding of an eighteen-year-old." The *Worker's Daily* criticized the expense of a funeral for the head of the Dandong Municipal Catering Company in Liaoning province. It included 117 wreaths from 800 mourners costing $150 in state funds, and $10 to keep the body on ice. The body was cremated, but it took 47 cars, 8 buses and 20 small trucks to transport the coffin and the mourners to the crematorium.

The party attempted to make an example of Hou Peisan, a commune leader in Shandong (Shantung) province, by revoking his party membership for delaying his wife's funeral seven days while extorting gifts from junior officials. Hou had received 814 pounds of wheat, 1,000 bricks, 440 pounds of cabbage, more than 40 wreaths and $487 in cash to conduct the funeral ceremonies. In Hunan province, one county committee reported perhaps the most colossal and calamitous funeral in recent memory. When their father died, two party members, Liu Xinzhu and Liu Xinhou, organized a four-hour, thirteen-mile funeral procession of 300 people with 50 to 60 wreaths in front, and with drums and gongs playing in the rear. The procession followed a circuitous route through fourteen production teams, even though the graveyard was only a mile away. The brothers distributed money to onlookers along the way, provided 112 tables of food and spent about $513, more than fifteen months' wages for an average worker. So much paper and so many joss sticks were burned at the funeral that a fire broke out, sending two people to the hospital.

Funeral arrangements for most Chinese are modest, even in cities like Shanghai, where the average amount spent on a funeral banquet has dropped from $300 to $100. In the countryside, the ritual often seems matter-of-fact, almost callous, but the Chinese do not consider it so.

Long Ansheng, age seventy, had felt uncomfortable for a few days, so his son took him to the local hospital. The old peasant rode on a board on top of the rear fender of his son's bicycle. Long stayed for three days. The doctors decided there was nothing they could do. He had inoperable stomach cancer. They said nothing to the old man, but he knew. "When his son began to give him better food than usual, he understood what that meant," a neighbor said.

Long returned home, not to the bedroom of his neat, whitewashed brick home in a village fifty miles south of Canton, but to a wooden shed, a storehouse for wood and dried-grass fuel. He lay down on some straw and there, without any further discussion of the matter, prepared to die.

"The people in that area think if you die inside your home, that will bring an unlucky fate to your children," the neighbor explained. The Chinese follow different customs in different parts of the country. Some put a bit of earth under the deathbed inside the house; some rebury bones after the flesh has disintegrated underground; others make no special preparations.

Long had gone to town and bought his own burial suit soon after his sixtieth birthday. Elderly Chinese often sew the suit themselves, but Long had his made in town. It was a black suit with a formal Mao jacket (what the Chinese call a Sun Yat-sen suit), and black cloth shoes to match. "In Henan," said a Peking official who worked in a farming village there for several months, "you would live with a peasant family and find the room next door to you prominently occupied by a huge coffin" all ready for the eldest family member years before he died. Elderly Chinese men and women often purchase their own coffins in advance, or at least the wood for them. Long, however, had bought only the suit, not the coffin.

"The old man was in pain and he complained a lot. His son and daughter-in-law brought him food several times a day, but if he didn't eat it, they took it back so someone else could have it," the neighbor said. No one seemed to think much about whether the old man was comfortable in the shed. "His son treated him as Long had treated his own father when he died," the neighbor added. "People follow the old way. They thought he was old enough to die. He was a person who liked to be alone, and did not talk much. He had only the one son. His wife had died three years before."

Basic medical care, so important to older people, has spread far into the countryside with the arrival of the paramedic "barefoot doctors," though for serious illnesses, such as cancer, the Chinese often avoid expert opinion or treatment. Following his trip to the hospital, Long went to the barefoot doctor, who gave him a concoction of herbs called *huang liu xiang,* said to be good for the liver, though Long's trouble was in his stomach. Long said he felt better after taking the medicine in the usual herbal-tea fashion. He was a heavy smoker, but no medical personnel in that nation of smokers warned him against the habit.

A medical worker from another southern village said it was a rare doctor who would reveal to a patient the true seriousness of an ailment such as Long's. "The doctor would tell the patient's family but usually not tell the patient. The patient would know that death was near only when his family began the usual preparations," the health worker explained. "I know of one old woman who was alone when she became ill, with no children or grand-children, so the niece who took care of her did not bother to remove her from her tiny house." But just before her death, she asked people to put her down on the floor beside her bed so that she in some way would not leave an inauspicious spell over a perfectly good bed.

Long died in his little shed, on a hot August night. "Nobody knows exactly when he died; they found him dead the next morning," the neighbor said. Long's son was the first to find him. He called the family and went to inform the chief of the production team. "The chief came to the house —he was a relative of the family, and so the son was seeking his personal help. He needed help cleaning out the old clothes, old goods used by the old man, and he needed people to help him buy a coffin." No one bothered to call a doctor, even the barefoot doctor. They simply covered the body with a clean blanket. No coroner was called in—the local government doesn't require a death certificate as such.

But the team chief had to sign a note verifying that someone had died. With that in hand, a relative went to the office of the brigade and got a coffin certificate. He went to a shop in the commune town, a long bicycle ride away. The shop specialized in farming tools but made prefabricated coffins on the side. The coffin was a set of boards that could be assembled later. It cost about $10. By late afternoon the boards arrived at the village, strapped to the back of the same bicycle the old man had ridden to the local hospital a few weeks earlier.

The son and the production-team chief put a new blanket on the bottom of the coffin, then lifted Long's body, dressed in the new suit, and gently laid it inside. A pillow was placed under Long's head. Following the local custom, a few pieces of jade, the only pieces of jewelry any member of that village could afford, were placed in the coffin beside him. Some of the pieces belonged to the old man himself, some to his relatives who had saved them for just such an occasion. No wreaths appeared; there was no wreath maker nearby. But the circles of white paper flowers are ubiquitous at city funerals. They cost only $3 or $4.

Relatives and good friends had a last look at Long before the coffin was closed. "As usual, the women cried a little," the neighbor said. "The men had some tears for the occasion, but they didn't cry." The men loaded the coffin onto a pushcart. A procession of about thirty adults—most of the adults in a village of about 140 people—followed the cart toward the burial hill a little more than a mile away. Most of the mourners wore plain peasant clothing, in black or some dark color. But the family wore white, with white hoods that did not cover their faces. In other villages, women sometimes wear white wigs. White is a traditional Asian color for death and mourning, perhaps linked to the color of bones. In Chinese cities, some people have adopted the Western custom of black armbands. We watched a funeral procession wind its way down a narrow street in Xiamen (Amoy). Mourners had black armbands in place, but some of the women also wore white scarfs, and men pinned white flowers on their jackets. The coffin was carried on a cart, as in the countryside, with small shrubs in pots beside it.

At Long's funeral, his son led the procession, walking just behind the cart. There was some muted sobbing from the women, but no drums or gongs or music as are sometimes heard at funerals in other parts of the country. (A Peking official who attended a funeral in Henan, far to the north of Long's village, recalled gongs being beaten and firecrackers set off.)

The production team had a hill, actually several hills, and one of them was used as a graveyard. The hill had trees but no plants. "It was too far from the village and the soil was too dry to be really suitable for planting crops," Long's neighbor said.

The villagers in this part of China followed ancient mystical rules for locating the grave, described in a large book called the *Dong-xiong.* Many older people in the village had copies of the book, but the most respected authority on the subject was a blind man, very old, who knew the old Taoist laws about where to place a grave. "This year it might be best turned to the east, next year to the west," he said. When Long was buried, the hill contained about forty or fifty graves, laid out every which way. If the village runs out of room, they will have to find another hill, unless another outbreak of official revulsion against old traditions like the Cultural Revolution forces them to plow some graves under.

By the time the funeral party reached the hill, the gravediggers had finished their work. The production chief had contacted them. The gravediggers had consulted with the Taoist expert on the proper location. They came not from Long's village, but from the commune headquarters. The son paid them a small fee; unlike most of their fellow peasants, they no longer tilled the soil but earned harvest shares from sowing dead bodies.

The diggers rigged ropes to lower the coffin into the six-foot-deep pit. No one spoke, but friends and relatives sang a local folk song as the coffin descended. The family had ordered a headstone, but there had not been time yet to prepare it. They marked the grave temporarily with a piece of wood, with Long's name written on it.

The funeral party walked quietly back to the village. Some women, friends of the family, had been working to prepare a traditional funeral feast. Perhaps sixty people attended, including many village residents who were not members of the funeral party. In some parts of China the solemnity of the occasion is emphasized by forbidding consumption of any meat, but here in southern China the guests were served the usual fare for special occasions—fish, vegetables and a little pork. "By custom, the dishes had to be an odd number, one, three, five, seven or nine," said the neighbor. "This is in contrast to wedding feasts, where there would be an even number of dishes." Again, our informant couldn't explain why—the party does not encourage research into such superstitions.

Each guest received one or two pennies in a red envelope, another southern custom. "There was little loud talk or laughter. The atmosphere was somber," said the neighbor. In most of China, that would be the end of it, except for two special festivals each year when relatives sweep and tend the burial ground. But in Guangdong the families follow a tidy custom of reburial, an ancient practice that may have originated to prevent graveyard congestion. After a wait of about four years, the grave is reopened. In some communities the family gathers around for the ceremony. "It was chilling, I don't ever want to do it again," a young Chinese-American told us after watching a similar rite with her relatives in Hong Kong. In Long's village a hired man specializing in such work was sent out, alone, to dig up Long's body after the required interval and place the bones in a large jar for reburial.

"Usually the body has not completely disintegrated," said another southern Chinese who had seen two such disinterments. "The man will pick out the bones, wipe them clean and put them in the jar. The jar is about two feet high and one foot wide. The bones go in in a certain order, based on a man sitting, feet first, then legs, and so on." Long's jar was carried to another hillside, where about two hundred bone-filled jars were already arranged, half buried into notches in the side of the hill.

In early April each year, families throughout China visit graves at the Qingming festival. It is not a legal holiday—work continues—but family members can leave for a few hours to weed the area around the graves of loved ones. Sometimes they burn play money printed specifically for the purpose, or even light incense and set off firecrackers. Many grave mounds are built with small stone cups at the top for burning the paper offerings. In some localities, relatives have graveside picnics. The old beliefs hold that a person's soul remains near the place of burial for three years, so a share of the meal is set next to the grave. When we traveled through isolated Fujian province during Qingming 1980, small graves at the edge of rice fields were polka-dotted with colored paper, the only markings on the earthen mounds. In Guangxi, along a long hilly road to the Vietnamese border, square granite posts serve as grave markers. Closer to big cities, we found some Western-style tombstones, thin slabs carved with the name of the deceased. At the Babaoshan Cemetery for Revolutionary Martyrs in Peking, huge stone slabs cover graves; the large headstones bear not only the name but a plastic-covered photograph of the deceased.

In the days before 1949 the service for the dead was the main source of income for Buddhist temples. In the reopened temples, incense offerings to the dead now burn again. Lay priests with knowledge of Buddhist or Taoist ceremonies are found performing small graveside rites for their neighbors. In Hunan a friend of ours encountered a ceremony in which a Taoist priest performed a service at a site chosen by the ancient pseudoscience of *feng shui* (wind and water) geomancy, similar to the way Long's grave was selected, with an eye to appeasing dragon spirits who would tolerate burials only in certain areas and in certain directions. People circled the coffin three times as dictated by ancient practice before leaving.

One youth who left Fujian after the Cultural Revolution reported that some Taoist priests had been held up to public ridicule at mass meetings but not long after received renewed requests for their services, even from party officials. Some Hong Kong Chinese believe in "soul passports," a kind of certificate that they obtain from their temples in Hong Kong, then sew into their clothing when they return to China to visit or retire. When the paper is burned, they believe, their soul will return to its proper resting place at their special temple in Hong Kong, or in Buddha's "Western Paradise."

The Chinese in general shiver at some of the funeral customs followed by minority people on their borders, but the party has not interfered with such local practices as the Tibetan funeral rite, which involves taking the corpse to a high, exposed place, chopping it into pieces and leaving it for the birds—vultures—to pick it clean, then crushing the bones to powder so that all traces disappear. That sort of eternal anonymity does not appeal to the Chinese at all.

"My grandmother died several years ago, and I remember my father bringing me during Qingming and watching him burn the paper money on top of the small tablet on the little mound," recalled Wang Guotang, a twenty-four-year-old guide in Xi'an. "But the grave was plowed over during the Cultural Revolution and we don't know exactly where it is now. They had this campaign against the 'four olds'—old customs, old habits, old culture and old thought—and they plowed under many graves to get more land. It made my grandfather feel very bad, but it was not something he could stop. Now they say they are sorry about it, and the government has allocated land to each brigade for graves. My grandfather wants to be buried there, but there is no chance any longer for him to be buried next to my grandmother."

About eighteen miles east of Xi'an, capital of the northcentral province of Shaanxi, sits what may be the biggest grave in China. It looks like a large hill, visible from three miles away across the flat Shaanxi plateau. The mound is more than a hundred feet high, with a circumference of a half mile. Yet the grave has shrunk considerably since the body of the founder of China's first great dynasty, the Emperor Qin Shi Huang Di, was placed in it more than two thousand years ago. Ancient sources say the mound was once over five hundred feet high and one and a half miles around. It is still big enough today to hold its secrets. The Chinese government has so far avoided the mammoth task of excavating it.

A mile from that colossal memorial to the emperor, alongside a corn field in a little grove of apricot and persimmon trees, rest eleven small mounds of earth about two feet high covered by a light blanket of weeds and grass. They look like tiny replicas of the grand mound to the west, but they are relatively new, the graves of peasants of Shanren village, Daiyi Commune, Linteng County. Their shape testifies to the resilience of old forms and customs in China.

A few hundred yards down a dirt road from the little graveyard is the site of one of the most bizarre archaeological finds of the century. Row upon row of life-size terra-cotta soldiers, cavalrymen, charioteers and archers in battle formation have been unearthed in a huge pit, apparently a symbolic burial guard placed underground at the same time as the body of the Qin emperor. Their horses, manes curled and tails knotted, stand four abreast before royal chariots. Only the statues along the sides escaped destruction in an attempted looting and subsequent collapse of the vault's ceiling two thousand years ago. Unearthed down to the waist level, their heads and torsos now project from the sandy soil at drunken angles. Much of the pit resembles the scene of some terrible calamity, with heads, trunks, legs and arms strewn about in confusion. Fortunately for the emperor's real guards, the imperial family only buried terra-cotta statues. In earlier times, slaves and concubines of a nobleman were often buried alive in his tomb.

The government has spent $4 million to erect an enormous hangarlike building over the pit. Heads of state and tourists, sometimes thousands a day, come to see the vault. No one stops at the little village burial ground down the road. The little grave mounds are unmarked, anyway. "Some people put up stone markers, but they are stolen or buried in rainstorms. Anyway, each family knows whose graves these are," said Wang Juwen, a young worker from Xi'an who lives near the gravesite. "Many of the graves contain two people, a husband and a wife. At Qingming, people will sometimes come and bring flowers, or cut the grass."

The mounds are scattered in no recognizable pattern. Crickets chirp and a motorcycle with sidecar clatters by, taking some peasants from the local commune on an errand. The buzz of a crowd at the archaeological dig can be heard faintly in the distance.

Nothing stirred in the grove. A little girl walked by as we watched. She wore one of the bright-colored blouses that symbolize the new, more light-hearted post-Mao era. She glanced without interest at the decrepit little mounds in the rocky ground, and walked on.

THE SYSTEM

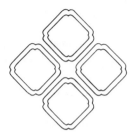

THE SYSTEM

"The Nationalists had lots of taxes; the Communist Party has lots of meetings."

—CHINESE PEASANT

AN AMERICAN BUSINESSMAN WHO SPOKE FLUENT CHINESE WAS VISITING the huge exhibition hall of the Canton Trade Fair and stopped at the exhibit of China's Cereals, Oils and Foodstuffs Corporation. He didn't want to take up their time and asked the Chinese official for one of their sales brochures. "At any other international trade fair," the businessman said later, "that would be like pushing a button—you'd be covered with catalogues."

But the representative at the Cereals, Oils exhibit only smiled warmly and welcomed his new American friend. "Please sit down and tell me how you learned Chinese," he said. The American proceeded to give a forty-five-minute version of the story of his life, prodded by questions. Then he asked again about the printed material. "Come back this afternoon," the Chinese functionary said.

It was a small but revealing moment in the history of the world's oldest, largest and most tenacious bureaucracy, a system that has survived fires, floods, earthquakes, foreign invasions, famines, dynastic declines and revolutions. The system comprises few words, spoken slowly. It exercises maddening caution even in the face of angry speeches and fervent editorials from the leaders of the Marxist political party now trying to modernize China. If the Communist Party is having trouble prodding the bureaucracy along, a Chinese officeholder, like the man at the trade fair, is not going to be hurried by a capitalist upstart from a country only a little more than two hundred years old. No self-respecting Chinese bureaucrat will go to any great lengths to lift the veil that perennially cloaks that system.

The American at the trade fair came back, and after more lengthy pleasantries, finally got his catalogues. But the American decided, for fun, to test the limits of Chinese bureaucratic obfuscation. "Sir, you've asked me some questions; now I'd like to ask you some," he said. "What is your name?" The man paused for a moment, then identified himself as Mr. Wang. "And you work for the Cereals, Oils and Foodstuffs Corporation?"

"Yes."

"Which section do you work for at the moment?"

"That's not too clear."

"You mean to say you can't tell me what kind of work you do?"

"I'm new here."

As we learned from bewildering personal experience, China's wedding-cake government structure and its ancient rules of conduct have become a central issue of the 1980s. Ask any Chinese, from Deng Xiaoping on down to a hotel-room attendant, who the real enemies of the people are these days. In one way or another they will say: The bureaucrats.

Many historians say that the Chinese developed a sophisticated bureaucracy in ancient times because large numbers of people had to be organized to keep the Yellow River from flooding and provide proper irrigation throughout the north China plain. By this theory, the bureaucracies of ancient Egypt and Mesopotamia also grew from mass water projects, in contrast to the smaller, more diversified nations of early Europe which had less formidable geographical conditions and hence less need for man-made irrigation.

But China's tradition of rule by a small aristocracy seems to go back even further, to the Shang dynasty thirty-five hundred years ago, when peasants still depended mostly on rainfall rather than irrigation for watering their crops. Perhaps the many-layered bureaucratic state arose from the Chinese family system, with its natural tendency toward hierarchies, son obeying father obeying grandfather. The early aristocracy, which in time became an educated class supplying young men to the bureaucracy, may have sprung from a group that held the secret of bronze metallurgy—weapon making —or from the need to organize for defense against northern nomads. A few men with experience and education had to direct a great many if such massive projects were to succeed. The Great Wall of China remains the greatest standing monument to this bureaucratic impulse.

By the beginning of the Han dynasty, two hundred years before Christ, the Chinese had moved from a society divided between landed aristocrats and commoners (like Europe a thousand years later) to one divided between educated officialdom and the common taxpayer. The officials had come up from the landowning class, talented landlords' sons placed as advisers to the scattered courts of early, divided China because such bright young men were administratively and politically useful. With help, that family tradition emerged as a system that forged an empire.

Confucius, that itinerant adviser of the fifth century B.C., added the crucial ingredient, the useful idea that an aristocracy had to be accountable.

The government proved it had the mandate of heaven by ensuring that the river dikes were in good repair and fortifications well-manned. Over two millennia this system handled rebellion, foreign invasion, earthquake and drought, accumulating rules that survived even the Communist takeover. For example, by the Qing dynasty, China's last great imperium, the "law of avoidance" had become the rule for administrators. A kind of anti-nepotism law, it stipulated that local officials and their staff of permanent secretaries could not be natives of the district they governed, and thus lessened the opportunities to play favorites with family and friends. Chinese districts today often observe this rule; it serves the party's efforts to standardize administration and legitimizes its assignment of particularly trusted revolutionary veterans, many of them northerners, to leadership positions in the southern provinces.

Like now, the system in ancient times contradicted itself. Chinese officials honored the integrity of the organization more than the search for truth; corruption flourished and weak emperors often heard only what they wanted to hear. Eventually, however, the officialdom developed a system of censors—today we would call them ombudsmen—who were charged with discovering errors and cover-ups of error in the administration of the empire, a role that China's Communist press is playing in a limited way.

By the first century B.C., 130,285 much-sought-after posts were counted in the Chinese bureaucracy, organized into eighteen grades—not so different from the twenty-six grades of officials now in vogue. The Communist Party has a much higher ratio of officials to citizens; these functionaries go much deeper into the countryside than they did in the emperor's day, but the feeling remains of a few men in authority floating on a vast sea of potential problems.

Party secretaries, like local magistrates in the Qing, assume responsibility for what happens in their areas, good and bad. The Qing magistrate tried to keep the lid on and avoid trouble at all costs. The capable Qing administrator, like the party secretary today, did not attack problems, he avoided them. He tried to harmonize or ignore disputes in his area rather than suppress them or change the conditions that caused them. Then, as now, overt action brought unwelcome attention and required a report to higher authorities, which could damage an officeholder's career.

Habits of caution and verbal obfuscation have become imbedded in the manner of nearly all office workers. The Chinese joke about it, which helps ease the frustration, but the old habits remain uncorrected. One official described, in an echo of Francis Bacon, what he did when a directive came down to his desk: "First we look at it. Then we smell it. Then we taste it. Then we chew it a little bit. If the directive is written, giving us this much latitude"—spreading his hands wide—"then we interpret it to give just this much latitude"—bringing his hands together. "That way we won't be criticized in the next campaign!"

Mang Ke, one of the editors of the now defunct nongovernment literary magazine *Today*, described his attempt to acquire official recognition for his magazine after the police, citing the lack of a permit, closed it down. First his group went to a city bureau and was told that yes, they registered publications but only those whose content had been approved by the Culture Bureau. He went to the Culture Bureau and was told that no, they didn't think they could help them, they only approved the content of publications that had already been registered.

The Chinese call it *"ti qiu"*—kicking the ball around—and the problem can often be solved only by going over someone's head. A Chinese-American working in a Peking book publishing company wanted to change her room at the office apartment building, but a series of requests brought no action. Then, on a dare, she called the office of the chief of her bureau, described her problem to a secretary and within an hour her two immediate supervisors were at her door, promising to take care of the matter. Of course this technique can backfire. Yuan Xianlu of the *People's Daily* warned us that a bureaucrat overruled may appear friendly and apologetic, then show his good wishes "by giving you a pair of shoes a size too small." This old phrase means favors that are actually rebukes: a conscientious worker exposes corruption among his superiors and gets a promotion, then discovers his new job is in Tibet.

An American scientist who was exploring a special chemical process worked for several months as an exchange scholar in a Chinese laboratory in 1980. "Old Sun," a bureaucrat recently discharged from the army, had been put in charge of his work. He immediately tried to cut the American off. The Chinese scientists in Sun's section were instructed not to give the American some data he needed from their experiments; he was not told about an important conference that was coming up. Finally the American went to the head of the lab and said, "Either Sun goes or I go!" The head man's solution may have originated in the Han dynasty. Without moving a single test tube he took his organization chart and reassigned the lab section where the American was working to a higher administrative level, different from that to which Old Sun was assigned. "He's still there, harassing other people," the American told us. "He still loves to tell people he doesn't know anything about science and is proud of it."

In the 1980s, Chinese diplomats have taken to bragging about tough-minded new vice premiers and Politburo members who are eliminating the abuse and inefficiency of the Mao years. Their boasts expose the root of the problem. Only one or two dozen men at the very top—those holding vice-premierships on the government side and Politburo seats on the party side—have the confidence to reach decisions on their own. *Everything* finds its way up to them; nothing can be decided quickly.

The government consists of the State Council, a sort of cabinet led by the premier, vice premiers and ministers. The Chinese call their government democratic because citizens elect representatives to the local People's Congresses, which in turn elect delegates to the National People's Congress, China's parliament. The Congress appoints ministers, approves the budget, and in recent years has served as a forum for some interesting, though limited, debate on government policy, but the Congress and the State Council can never be more than an office staff and rubber stamp for the small group that really runs China—the Political Bureau (Politburo) of the Central Committee of the Communist Party.

The Central Committee, a body of several hundred members that is too large to make policy, is headed by a chairman, who presides over the Political Bureau of about two dozen top leaders. The premier and the most important government ministers are usually Politburo members, and it is in Politburo meetings that they forge the policies they will carry out on the government side. A revived secretariat, led by a general secretary, serves as the party's chief administrative arm. One or two factions bound by long-standing personal ties usually hold the most influence on the party Politburo and place their protégés in the key posts. In turn, nearly every small detail is kicked up to them for decision. During our time in China, Deng Xiaoping, as leading vice premier and in consultation with other Politburo members, had to decide everything from the duration of the invasion of Vietnam to permission for official publication of overseas Chinese author Chen Jo-hsi's works to whether a French exchange student could marry her Chinese boyfriend. No matter how much Deng himself complained about how cumbersome this makes the government, he never relaxed his control over decisions, and none of his successors are likely to.

A former Chinese diplomat laughed one day as we rode past the thriving and unauthorized bird market just north of the Avenue of Eternal Peace. Interested bird fanciers there overflowed a construction-materials site. "There was an article in the *Evening News* saying the market should be controlled, but they have still done nothing. Apparently they can't get anyone on the Central Committee interested, otherwise it would be done tomorrow," he said. Appealing to lower authorities often does little good if the desires of higher officials are already clear. A Chinese-speaking American diplomat told us of checking in with his assigned guide in Changsha and asking to see someone at the local Social Sciences Academy. That would be inconvenient, the guide said. So the American went to his room, called the academy and found a researcher who was only too happy to come see him. Carelessly, he told his guide of his success. One half-hour later, the man at the academy called to cancel: something had come up. "Everyone is very busy with the flood," the guide said. The American accepted this. It sounded like a reasonable explanation until the diplomat realized that it was October and the flood had been in April.

. . .

The usual Chinese response to any problem is to call a meeting, *"kai hui."* Further meetings to discuss the previous meetings can carry the issue forward for months. An American businessman who watched this process grind several projects to a halt invented a perfect motto for Chinese bureaucracy. "When in doubt, *kai hui."*

Bureaucrats the world over are cautious, but the political purges of the last twenty years have made Chinese bureaucrats doubly so. While we were in China, the red-tape industry prospered as offices were stuffed to overflowing with officials once purged by the Gang of Four who were now being rehabilitated. A simple request from a foreign collector for a beer-bottle label sent the staff of the Xi'an Brewery into a panic. The letter bounced from the deputy director to the director to the party secretary to the Light Industries Bureau to the provincial headquarters and then back to the brewery. One new staff member told the director, "This is a trifling thing. You have the authority to do it. Why not?"

"Well, young man," the director said, "you never experienced the bitterness of the Cultural Revolution. It may be nothing now, but I don't know what will happen in the future."

"Are you afraid of being accused of illicit relations with a foreigner?"

"When I was denounced during the Cultural Revolution, who came out and spoke for me? Someday this could be trouble."

In one of the lively new plays that opened during our stay, a one-act drama called *Pavilion of the Wind and Waves,* a cowardly local culture bureau director must decide if an opera about the Song dynasty hero Yue Fei can be put on. After much waffling he seems about to announce a decision and an actress in the play-within-a-play pulls out her notebook. "Don't take notes!" he cries. "I had too much trouble during the Cultural Revolution from people recording what I said." The actress holds on to her pen: "In the Cultural Revolution I got into trouble for *not* taking notes. The leaders would order me to perform in some plays, but when the wall posters attacked the production, I got all the blame!" The advertisement for the Yue Fei opera is successively ripped down and replaced as higher-level officials disagree on whether Yue, an imperial aristocrat, should be made a hero. The actress continues to mark her notebook "in case there's another Cultural Revolution in a few years' time."

Chinese bureaucrats, like functionaries everywhere, feel uncomfortable without paperwork. We always had to present requests in writing. In the case of the Xi'an beer-bottle label, the Industry and Commerce Bureau finally called the brewery and approved sending the label abroad, but one of the brewery officials still fretted: "Why doesn't the bureau give us the instructions in writing?" An American business school graduate who was helping to set up a management course in China was admitted to the inner offices of several Chinese factories and said he "saw more forms than I have ever seen in my life. Annual forms, quarterly forms, monthly forms, daily forms, all outlining plans required by supervising agencies. It was an amazing amount of paper." The average manager spent as much as 30 percent of his time immersed in it.

Foreigners we met developed two very different approaches to bureaucratic impediments in China. Some simply lost their temper. But some did it the Chinese way, engaging the Chinese official concerned in long, polite chats. They would take him out to lunch; they would ask if he'd like to try an American cigarette or see an American film. They would sympathize with all his problems. The subtle art of establishing *guanxi* had incalculable importance in a bureaucracy that was very uncomfortable dealing with clear, enforceable rules. The American professor assigned to process applications for U.S. researchers coming to China was asked by the Chinese to screen out all the "undesirable" applications himself: they did not want to have to turn people down. Jack Potter, an American sociologist who enjoyed unusual success in studying a Chinese commune near Canton, did his best to smooth the visit by not making requests he expected would be refused. He realized that he was allowed to live at the Chasang Commune because the commune party secretary was the only one in the area willing to accept the responsibility for whatever calamities might accompany a foreigner's presence. "We exercised some self-censorship," Potter said. "We did not ask to investigate religion, we didn't pry into internal politics. We got some information on the Cultural Revolution, but not a lot because we thought it was sensitive."

American scholars, like American journalists and diplomats, learn the advantages of *guanxi,* of creating mutual obligations by exchanging favors until each side understands what it can get from the other. With this tool, the Chinese have created an underground economy, a system of quasi-legal exchanges without which Chinese society today cannot survive. The Chinese call it *zou hou men,* "using the back door." Every Chinese we met could tell of crucial moments in their lives that depended on finding a rear entrance. Hu Xinglu, now a language student at Peking University, escaped the hard life of an Inner Mongolian commune to return to Peking and study for the college entrance exam. He needed a friendly doctor at the remote commune to certify him eligible for sick leave. "I was sick, in a way," he said. "I was sick of Inner Mongolia." The doctor was glad to oblige, for Hu's father had arranged a good job as an interpreter for the doctor's brother in Peking.

The technician husband of a Peking nurse was abruptly transferred to a newly opened factory in faraway Xinjiang, fifteen hundred miles from the capital. She appealed to a former schoolmate at the Ministry of Metallurgy for help. By pulling strings, the ministry functionary was able to reunite the couple within a year. Later, when his mother fell ill, the nurse repaid the favor. She arranged for the old woman to be admitted to a hospital that had insisted that its beds were full.

The Chinese have become so inured to the back door that they use it even when they could save time going in the front. A Chinese-American woman working in Peking told us about her visit to relatives living near Canton. Her uncle met her at the railroad station and she prepared to take a bus to the family village—a cheap and convenient if bumpy ride. Her uncle would have none of it. While she waited several hours, missing the bus, he searched the town for a truck going their way. To the uncle, relying on official conveniences like ticket offices seemed wasteful, almost impolite, just as placing any hope in the government bureaucracy at any level seemed foolhardy.

Institutions as well as individuals use the back door. American military attachés were under the auspices of the powerful Defense Ministry, which has access to many special shops and services in the city. The attachés got much bigger rooms at the Peking Hotel than those of us hosted by the less influential Foreign Ministry. Teachers at a Canton kindergarten had difficulty locating fresh fruit for their pupils until one of them befriended the middle-aged woman in charge of the neighborhood grocery. In return for a steady supply of apples and pears, and occasionally oranges, the kindergarten admitted the shopkeeper's granddaughter, who was supposed to attend a factory-run school farther from her home.

Back-door dealing has created a de facto social hierarchy, quite unlike what students of the party chain of command are led to anticipate. At the top are "the three treasures"—doctors, butchers and truck drivers. Like certain ambitious parents in the West, the Chinese hope their offspring will wed someone from one of these favored callings. The status attached to them is hardly surprising, considering that they control important goods and services often in short supply. Doctors dispense not only medicine but personal attention, which is even more precious in a society where patients sometimes wait all day long to be examined.

Pork and other meats are only occasionally rationed now, but a friendly butcher can ensure a good cut. Truckers have excellent access to a wide range of consumer goods. Like the peddlers of old China, they can buy merchandise where it is plentiful and sell it where it is scarce. With the loosening of restraints on the free market and moonlighting, other professions may be catching up. We knew one middle-school teacher in Peking who now earns about $150 a month, four times the wages of a factory worker. His language skills are in great demand. Evening schools pay him to teach English, ignoring the fact that his unit has not authorized him to do such work. The English classes are packed with adults who know a foreign language will help their careers, and few qualified teachers are available.

The official press sharply attacks back-door dealing, but the articles have a certain air of futility. Even the *People's Daily* musters humorous sallies on the abuses, which the Chinese enjoy reading while carrying on their own private bargaining. One cartoon from the newspaper's humor supplement shows a patient giving his doctor two fresh crabs. The doctor returns the favor with a slip of paper allowing one week's sick leave.

Another cartoon shows an old Buddhist monk sitting with a young man, apparently a novice. He has the traditional shaved head, but still wears work clothes.

Old Monk: "Can you recite the sutra?"

New Monk: "No."

Old: "Do you know how to beat the wooden drum?"

New: "No."

Old: "What made you a monk?"

New: "Baldness."

Old: "How did you get in?"

New: "Through the back door."

Still, most Chinese are somewhat sensitive on the issue of the back door, particularly those individuals who want to be judged on their own merits, not their connections. One day, months after Hou had gone to work for Linda as interpreter, Linda heard a rumor that Hou's father was an important diplomat. When Linda asked Hou about this, she blushed and refused to say anything about it. "I've never talked about my father," she said. "I don't want people to know who he is." Without a word, Linda reached for her directory of prominent Chinese officials and began to read off the list of Hous. Caught off guard, Hou alternately giggled or denied that this or that Hou was related to her. Finally Linda hit the right name, and Hou fell silent. "I'm not going to say anything," she said.

Foreigners who trade some favors back home are still unaccustomed to conducting the simplest business that way, but they have learned to adjust in China. A Stanford University researcher in Peking studying the banking system found that the Chinese did not begin to cooperate until he arranged for the Hoover Institute to send materials that some of the Chinese faculty were eager to have for their own work. As journalists, we were not above inviting to dinner the officials of the housing bureau who would decide when to assign us an apartment. Some of the Chinese who agreed to speak to us asked how to apply for study in the United States, and we gathered for them what information we could. Others accepted gifts of magazines, or American novels in Chinese translation that the bookstores did not carry.

These were trifles compared to the kind of gifts overseas Chinese and Japanese businessmen sometimes arranged. They knocked much more confidently on the back door than the Americans and Europeans did, though occasionally they overdid it. One Hong Kong businessman, claiming deep concern for the "four modernizations," shipped four station wagons, two minibuses and a sedan to some transport officials in Hubei who had set up a phony tourist service so they could have the cars for their private use. Chinese officials dealing with Japanese traders often received personal gifts of sophisticated tape recorders. In Guangdong province, Hong Kong families who wanted their Chinese relatives cleared for emigration might buy a car for the local commune after the commune officials had approved the relative's application.

Such acts may seem manipulative, if not dishonest, to Americans, but favor trading is often the way Chinese make friends. A Chinese-American working in Peking introduced one of her Chinese acquaintances, a man in the export business, to some visiting Americans. The visitors mentioned they were looking for some jade, and the export bureaucrat insisted on accompanying them to all the dealers he knew. When they suggested after a day of shopping that they could probably make the follow-up visits on their own, he was offended. "He thought it was unethical," his Chinese-American friend said. "Anyway, it made him proud to take them around, even when they ended up buying nothing, because he thought it would please me."

The constant "You scratch my back and I'll scratch yours" draws strength and resilience from the fact that it is so often based on real friendship, not just mutual convenience. Wang Yueling, a Shanghai woman we met, talked about the commune official in faraway Anhui who signed the papers allowing her to join her uncle and aunt in Hong Kong. She had been miserable with farm work, and long before she ever thought of obtaining an exit visa, the head of the commune's security office took a kindly interest in her, perhaps because he was from Shanghai also. His wife listened to Wang's long series of complaints and, sizing her up accurately, decided that the frail city girl would never make much of a farm hand. Since the wife was captain of one of the women's work teams, she arranged for lighter work for Wang and got her a temporary pass to Shanghai to see her sick mother.

Out of gratitude, Wang returned from Shanghai with candy for the children, cold cream and sandals for the wife, and books for the husband. They were enormously pleased and the friendship deepened. Two years later Wang's mother died, eliminating any need to stay in China, and she began to win her friend's favor in a more calculated way. She brought them spareribs, clothes, even a secondhand camera from Shanghai. They shared their food with her. And when she asked for the man's signature on her exit permit, she got it.

Wang never considered giving the man or his family any money. "That would have been insulting!" she said. It might also have been construed as a bribe, landing both her and her friends in deep trouble. As Wang explained, her friends acted out of *ren-qing,* which translates roughly as "human feeling." "In China, everyone assumes that friends must help each other in any way they can," she said. "What's wrong with that?"

It is difficult for foreigners to befriend the Chinese in this way. Foreigners rarely have the time or patience. When the frustrations of life in China grow too great, they throw *guanxi* to the winds. They shout. They scream. They wish that Chinese suits had lapels by which the wearers could be shaken. One Chinese-speaking U.S. businessman we know got into serious trouble when he unleashed a Chinese obscenity at the Peking Hotel manager. Occasionally, though, if the foreigner makes some viable threat and the dispute is not at too high a level, a good old-fashioned tantrum can work.

In June 1979, when American newspapers began to establish bureaus in Peking, many of us asked the Information Department of the Foreign Ministry to set up a teleprinter so we could have immediate access to reports from the official New China News Agency (Xinhua), a vital news source. We tried polite requests, luncheon conversations and ingratiating letters. Nothing happened.

By December, Linda became enraged that she still had to drive and telephone around Peking in search of a European correspondent who might let her look at the latest news from his Xinhua teleprinter. She sent a fiery letter to the boss of the Information Department describing the "evasiveness" of his office in explaining the delay as "insulting." She promised that no future Chinese delegations visiting California would be hosted by the *Los Angeles Times* unless something was done—a severe threat, since a Los Angeles visit gave delegations an excuse for a side trip to Disneyland.

Still believing *guanxi* was the better approach, Jay awaited the reaction to Linda's outburst with great interest. The usually restrained and mild-mannered Foreign Ministry spokesman blew up. Linda received an angry telephone call from a ministry official. He said the accusations in her letter were "unfounded . . . and not helpful to Sino-American relations." He sent the letter back, after someone had unaccountably underlined in pencil some of its stronger language. Linda heard via the grapevine that her outburst would set back our chances for a Xinhua teleprinter by several months.

About two weeks later, while passing the empty Minzu (Nationalities) Hotel room we had rented to house our machine, Jay heard a strange noise. He opened the door and there was a Xinhua teleprinter clicking away. When Jay called Xinhua to order more paper for the teleprinter, the clerk sounded puzzled. "Why is the *Washington Post* calling?" he asked. "That's the *Los Angeles Times* machine."

Some of the difficulties we had dealing with China arose from warfare between Chinese government departments. Foreigners were caught in the crossfire. Our efforts to get a teleprinter had bogged down when the Foreign Ministry could not persuade the Minzu Hotel and the telecommunications office to cooperate. A dresser we had purchased for our children's clothes was stopped at the entrance of the Peking Hotel because the hotel management took a dim view of the increasing number of foreign journalists and businessmen being invited to live in Peking by the Foreign and Trade ministries. The management decided to try to force them out of the hotel by barring their furniture.

When Linda was told that the dresser would not be allowed in the hotel, she again tried the direct approach. She talked Jay into helping her carry the dresser past the startled eyes of the desk clerks and up to our room. Within minutes Mr. Zhang, the chief of hotel-room assignments whom we knew well, came up with an interpreter to politely request its removal. Hours passed, and another, sterner official came to the room. He had no interpreter, so he and Jay discussed the matter in Chinese, a conversation that seemed to Jay much harsher and more direct without the diplomatic buffer. "Mr. Mathews, we don't welcome this kind of behavior at all," he said. "You'll be very sorry." Jay told him to find an interpreter and go see Linda. Two hours later friendly Mr. Zhang and the interpreter came back, found Linda and finally persuaded her to give up. Room attendants came and took away the dresser. Joe and Peter, not yet schooled in the ways of *guanxi,* chased the attendants down the hall, kicking at their heels.

The Chinese we spoke to also had many stories about being squeezed between rival offices. They referred to the sparring government agencies as the "mothers-in-law." The local press in the southwest city of Kunming complained of the long list of offices which had to approve decisions in one local iron and steel plant: the Ministry of Metallurgy, the provincial Party Committee, the municipal Party Committee, the provincial Planning Committee, the Industry and Communications Office, and the Metallurgical Bureau. "It is difficult for a daughter-in-law to serve so many mothers-in-law," Radio Kunming announced.

Occasionally a rare, natural genius found a way to slip out from under all of it. One was Sachi Tooley, a twenty-nine-year-old woman from the Micronesian islands living in Peking with her American husband. She astounded both Chinese and foreigners in 1980 by adopting a Chinese baby. No couple of non-Chinese descent had managed to do that since 1949, as far as anyone knew, but the Tooleys were blessed by naïveté and luck. Through a web of personal connections, the key to all Chinese miracles, they found a peasant couple who had just had a third child and thus, under the new birth control regulations, had to pay a monthly penalty. With the help of a Chinese friend whose daughter worked in a Shanghai hospital, the Tooleys went to Shanghai and returned with Leilani Tooley, formerly Ni Qiuye, age ten months.

When Arthur Tooley's supervisors at the Peking Foreign Languages

Institute heard of this, they exploded. "You kidnapped her!" Tooley's supervisor, Xu Caide, chided him. According to Tooley, "Xu really chewed me out. He said I had to get papers, all kinds of stuff I hadn't gotten. The institute was so hostile. They even tried to fire me. Then, at four o'clock one morning, Sachi wrote a letter to them. It said: 'Please, please, let me keep our baby.' "

Xu read the letter ("I could almost see the tears in his eyes," Tooley said) and took it to the president of the institute, who also read it. At that point the Chinese position changed completely. Xu himself went to Shanghai, met with the natural parents and secured the proper papers: a birth certificate, an agreement from the parents' commune, an agreement from the parents, and witnesses' statements. Then he spent three days guiding them through the Peking City bureaucracy. Finally, the three Tooleys appeared before a matronly administrative judge, who signed the last paper. Tooley had not pulled a single string, had not sought help from the American embassy or anyone else. All it took was a small, anguished letter.

"Generally the soft approach is better," said a Western diplomat who lived in Peking nearly three years. "But you have to be persistent in your softness, and you have to have good intelligence. You have to make sure you are dealing with the right person."

A diplomat shipped his automobile to Peking and took it to the government office for an official inspection. They told him the brakes didn't work right. He had worked as a mechanic in college and did not see what the problem was, but he put in new brakes anyway. "No good," the inspector said. The car had to stop cleanly without swerving at fifty miles an hour. He tried the test, the car worked fine, but he again flunked inspection. Desperate, he asked the inspector, "What should I do?" "Perhaps you should take it to a Chinese garage," the man suggested. The diplomat took the advice. The Chinese mechanics fiddled for a while, then told him it was fixed. He took it out on the road again, stepped on the brakes, and the car swerved about forty-five degrees. Then he took it back to the inspectors, who knew he had taken it to a Chinese garage. It passed.

During our time in Peking such incidents had become frequent enough to lead to a massive campaign against "bureaucratism." At its peak, a court ordered jail sentences for officials responsible for an accident aboard a Bohai Gulf oil rig which overturned, killing seventy-two people. The responsible bureau had ordered the rig moved in the midst of a storm and did not send enough tugboats to accomplish the task. In the aftermath, the government directed the full force of national outrage at the rig supervisors, removed the oil minister and chided the vice premier, but a vivid picture of bureaucratic hubris still emerged. The bureau had ordered the Japanese-made rig six years before, but never bothered to translate the key operating instructions into Chinese. One underling who insisted on better safety preparations for the rig had been transferred. The bureau managers had called for "dashing spirit," one of the watchwords of the Great Leap Forward, and had criticized anyone who pointed out technical problems as being "afraid of difficulties."

The Chinese have managed to cope with this oppressive way of looking at the world, but bureaucracy frustrates and depresses people, and remains a ludicrously convenient target for any new government campaign to improve public morale. In 1982 Premier Zhao Ziyang unleashed a new volley of bureaucratic arrows, abolishing some economic commissions, cutting staffs of some ministries by a third, retiring aged officials, and promising to reduce the ninety-eight ministries, commissions and agencies to a more manageable fifty-two. But as the campaign dragged on, what had been hailed as a new revolution against the bureaucratic monster lost steam, as had all others before it. Most of the deposed bureaucrats were shuffled to new jobs, sometimes disguised as "adviserships," and the wheels of government ground as slowly as ever.

Talented workers seem the most vulnerable to bureaucratic whim, since they often demand the most. A Hefei teacher told us about the veteran head of the English department at a university who held a tight leash on his most accomplished teacher, a woman who often interpreted for visiting foreign dignitaries. He would not give her her teaching assignments until the very last minute, a crucial handicap because it allowed other, less talented teachers to arrange lucrative night jobs teaching English at factories (for about seventy cents an hour, a good wage in China). In mid-1980 we discovered the government was quietly putting similar, vague restrictions on the best university lecturers and researchers seeking fellowships abroad. An unpublished order went out barring such people from going abroad outside regular government exchange programs, which accounted for less than half of study overseas. The instructors were not told directly about the change, one academic said. They just found that government agencies were telling them "there will be delays in issuing passports."

Throughout China, Peking bureaucrats have a reputation for being the worst, particularly in the eyes of people from the southern part of the country. China's Mason-Dixon line is the Yangtze River. Southerners cherish the stereotype of people north of the river, particularly Peking people, being even-tempered, relaxed, passive and vague. Without any real research into the matter, it is generally agreed that this is due to long periods of idleness brought on by cold winters. Southerners, particularly people from Shanghai, are portrayed as emotional, vigorous, aggressive and contentious. "Peking people like things steady and slow. They say, 'Wait, wait,' " observed a man from Shanghai now working in Peking. "Shanghai people like efficiency. They do things quickly, both good and bad. The Gang of Four was from Shanghai, of course. Once the Peking newspapers complained that there was only one private hotel in Shanghai for transients to stay in. People in Shanghai saw that item, and within a month there were a thousand private inns operating in Shanghai—so many that the government had to order several of them closed down."

People find they can get their way with stubborn officeholders by presenting small gifts, cigarettes, theater tickets, or, even better, finding a friend who knows someone in that office. Without such connections, one veteran of the bureaucratic struggle says, "The only thing to do is to go back again and again and make such a nuisance of yourself that they'll help you just to get rid of you."

"We have a bad habit in this country of receiving people who have problems with smiles and promises, and then not doing anything," a Foreign Ministry interpreter told us. Many Chinese see little hope of changing the system, despite the continual upbraiding bureaucrats get in the *People's Daily*. Some Chinese have perfected an ingenious way of disarming foreign critics by throwing up their hands and admitting it is all a mess.

Jennie Dean, an American businesswoman we came to know, tried unsuccessfully to mail a package from the Peking Hotel post office. Her initial annoyance turned to laughter as the postal clerk gently drew her into China's benevolent order of bureaucracy-haters:

"You can't mail that package here," the clerk said.

"Why not?"

"Because we have no customs personnel here."

"But that doesn't make any sense. This is a huge hotel with many foreigners who want to mail packages."

"There are many things in our country that don't make sense."

"Well, what can I do?"

"You could write in our complaint book."

"Well, what good would *that* do?"

"Exactly!"

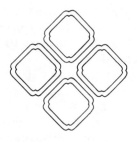

XIU-XI

THE CHINESE *XIU-XI* ISN'T NEARLY AS FAMOUS AS ITS LATIN COUNTER-part, the siesta, but it ought to be. We found its influence reached even an offshore oil rig in the South China Sea, a high-priority project which a visiting American engineer we knew thought was on a tight schedule. He watched astonished on his first day aboard as the Chinese crewmen stopped drilling, shut down all the machinery and vanished for their long midday naps, their *xiu-xi* (pronounced "show shee"). "It costs as much as fifty thousand dollars a day to operate a rig, so in the West we run rigs around the clock," the American said. "It's just unthinkable that you'd ever inter-rupt the drilling." But in China, as he and other foreigners have discovered, it is equally unthinkable that anybody should do without his *xiu-xi*.

A deeply rooted habit that originated in the ancient Chinese countryside, the noontime rest has been adopted enthusiastically by leaders of the Com-munist Party and is now a hallowed institution nationwide, enshrined even in the constitution. There it is, in Article 49: "The working people have the right to rest" *(Laodongzhe you xiu-xi de quan-li)*. And for at least two hours a day—three in the summertime—the people of China exercise that right. Factories, offices, banks, schools and government ministries close down. All shops are shuttered except those that deal with uncivilized foreigners. By one o'clock, a hush seems to fall over the entire country as everyone dozes off. Aged leaders like Deng Xiaoping swear by *xiu-xi*. It is said to increase longevity and cure any number of ills. The term has become so popular and pervasive that railroad waiting lounges are labeled "*xiu-xi* rooms" and whenever a shop or office is closed, even for the whole day, the sign out front will often just say "*xiu-xi*."

It is the rare person who uses his sacred noon *xiu-xi* time to run errands or catch up on paperwork: that would make others look bad and inexcusa-bly violate *guanxi*. For the most part, the Chinese really sleep. Workmen nap on heaps of gravel, peasants slump on sacks of corn, deliverymen doze in the backs of their trucks, and most office workers have beds or couches where they can slumber undisturbed. If nothing more comfortable is available, people will unroll mats and sprawl on their desk tops. So devoted are the Chinese to *xiu-xi* that nothing—planes, trains, national political meetings—is allowed to interfere. We once waited out a rainstorm in the coastal city of Fuzhou, only to be told after three hours that our Peking-bound plane would take off as soon as the cockpit crew members had had their lunch and *xiu-xi.* Three hours later, we finally boarded. When a friend of ours went on a similar flight, his plane landed halfway to its destination so that the crew could have a midday rest.

"I do my best work immediately after my *xiu-xi,*" a senior Foreign Ministry official confided. "My body is refreshed, my mind is clear, I can face anything or anybody." Countless other Chinese also sing the praises of *xiu-xi,* insisting that a nap after lunch aids digestion, restores the spirit, eases tension and even staves off heart attacks. "You should try a *xiu-xi,*" a Peking pharmacist advised an American concerned about his soaring blood pressure. "It's better for you than tranquilizers."

Xiu-xi, which dates from antiquity, has survived because China remains a largely rural nation. Common sense dictates a long rest break at noon to escape the blistering midday sun. Urban dwellers, many of them migrants from the countryside, apparently brought the habit to the city. An American diplomat who worked in Chongqing with the Nationalist Chinese during World War II remembered, "Our staff would also always take a long break at lunch, . . . many of them smoked opium."

Dr. Bruno Calandreau, a physician at the French embassy who ministered to us as well as to other foreigners in Peking, shrugged off the idea that *xiu-xi* is a cure-all, but said that after a heavy Chinese meal, people might as well sleep. "The body is really not capable of much else," he explained. "So much blood is needed simply for the digestive processes."

The need for a post-lunch nap, and the generally low energy levels, may be linked to the Chinese diet, which is short on calories (about 2,700 a day, according to the government) and long on starches. People have a light breakfast, then are so ravenous at lunchtime that they devour huge soup bowls of noodles, steamed bread or *jaozi* (dumplings stuffed with meat and vegetables), washed down with tea, beer or hot water. It is no wonder that such meals leave people drowsy; the effect is like eating a huge platter of pasta.

Many Chinese nap simply out of habit, of course. "On tours of the United States, Chinese are willing to rise early and work late, but if there's no time scheduled for *xiu-xi,* they fade fast," says Eugene Theroux, a Washington attorney who has shepherded Chinese delegations around the country. "An hour or so of sleep makes all the difference." When Chairman Hua Guofeng skipped his *xiu-xi* during a 1980 inspection trip to Tangshan, the city destroyed by the 1976 earthquake, a radio announcer noted with amazement, "After arriving by train at one forty-five P.M., Comrade Hua immediately took a bus to the housing district without taking a rest."

Chinese workers swear they could not last through the day without their *xiu-xi,* but some senior economists and management experts, convinced there should be less sleeping and more working in China, are lobbying for a reduction in *xiu-xi* time. The *xiu-xi,* they say, has become synonymous with idleness, malingering and just plain laziness. "Loafing on the job brought the economy to the brink of collapse in the years when the Gang of Four held sway and remains a widespread social evil," economists Lo Yuanzheng and Xue Yongying declared in the journal *Economic Management.* "Too many workers are not motivated to work hard and do only the minimum work necessary." An economist at the Chinese Academy of Social Sciences is even blunter. "Our biggest problem is the lack of a real work ethic, especially among the young," he said. "Workers are always complaining that the output quotas are too high and clamoring for '*xiu-xi, xiu-xi,* more *xiu-xi.*' People don't care when the job gets done. A manager who suggests that people work overtime usually has a revolt on his hands." Even democracy-movement activists and the government agreed on the need for change. "We must eliminate the problem of laziness, we must work harder," said Xu Wenli of the *April Fifth Forum,* the independent magazine that took the date of the great reformist demonstration of 1976. But like most government leaders, Xu, who has since been imprisoned, still defended the principle of the midday nap.

The main problem with *xiu-xi,* its critics say, is that there is too much of it. Unlike people in Italy, Spain, Mexico and other Latin countries who often return from their afternoon siestas and work until seven or eight, the Chinese insist on going home promptly at six. An urban worker rarely puts in a full eight hours. He typically arrives at work at eight, gets a half-hour exercise break at ten, retires for *xiu-xi* at eleven-thirty, and then works from two-thirty to six with another half-hour break. It is common to extend the break for some shopping. At most, that makes for a six-hour workday.

Xiu-xi also has a way of stretching out beyond the prescribed limits. People duck out a few minutes early before lunch and take extra time at the other end, too. "I was icily informed, when I wanted to take some of my graduate students to the library, that we had to be out by ten-thirty A.M." so the staff could get ready for its *xiu-xi,* observed John Rohsenow, an American teacher at Hangzhou University. The Peking University Library closes for two and a half hours for lunch, and the same for dinner. (Lights go off in the student dormitories at eleven, so students studying late must sit under streetlights outside. Authorities at Shanghai's Fudan University decided that was unhealthy and turned off the streetlights also.)

A sort of "*xiu-xi* spirit" pervades some factories and many offices. Despite a concerted effort by the Communist leadership to restore discipline and schedules, workers tend to be lackadaisical. Assembly lines break down. Deadlines are ignored. Everything moves in slow motion. The leader of a Singapore trade mission, accustomed to the beehive factories of Hong Kong, Taiwan and his own almost entirely Chinese island nation, reported in disgust that he had seen mainland Chinese asleep at their lathes. "Life under socialism has done what I would never have thought possible," he declared. "The Communists have taken a naturally industrious people and made them lazy."

The only other foreigners we knew who had brought a Hong Kong amah to Peking with them—an Australian diplomat and his wife—also hired a Chinese housekeeper, what we called an *ai-yi* (auntie) in Peking. They made a strange pair, the Hong Kong woman busily mopping the floor while the Peking woman sat around and suggested it was time for *xiu-xi,* perhaps a cup of tea. When the U.S. consulate in Canton had to be readied fast for a visit by Vice President Walter F. Mondale, the Americans took no chances and brought in workmen from Hong Kong rather than risk the easy pace of a Chinese crew. Much the same thing happened when the Americans set up a huge trade exhibition in Peking in late 1980; thirty-five imported Chinese workers came from Singapore.

It is unfair to say that all or even most mainland Chinese are lazy. Senior government officials and plant managers typically drive themselves hard. During the sowing and harvest seasons, peasants put in fifteen-hour days in the fields. And like beasts of burden, men and women all over China regularly hitch themselves to carts and pull huge loads of gravel, grain and vegetables to town. But in between the very top and the bottom of China's social ladder, among ordinary office workers and factory hands, there is a lot of inertia.

Resident foreigners who brush up against *xiu-xi* daily often come to cringe at the mention of the word, for it has become an all-purpose excuse for bad service and delays. A Western diplomat waiting to move into an apartment that was being repainted could not understand why it was taking so long, so one morning he dropped in unexpectedly on the painting crew. At ten o'clock one painter was taking a shower and the other two were stretched out on the sofa. "*Xiu-xi,*" they chorused when he asked what they were doing. Five hours later he reappeared to find two of them still napping, and the third playing with a hair dryer. "*Xiu-xi,*" the one with the hair dryer whispered so as not to disturb the others.

It took the three painters, all workers from Peking's Diplomatic Services Bureau, six weeks to paint a five-room apartment. "When I complained about it, I was treated as if I were a nineteenth-century imperialist oppressing the masses," the diplomat recalled. "The man in charge glared at me and said, 'Don't you respect the workmen's right to rest?'"

During a burst of self-deprecation in 1980, the *People's Daily* took the unprecedented step of reprinting a *Los Angeles Times* article written by

Linda which criticized such abuses. Yet when Richard Bernstein of *Time* magazine visited the *People's Daily* the next day, the editors themselves were unmoved, insisting that the midday break was as necessary as ever.

Confronted by suggestions that they eliminate or at least reduce *xiu-xi* time, the bureaucrats tend to be imperturbable. "What are you going to do if war breaks out during your *xiu-xi*? You'd never even know about it!" Linda complained loudly to the Ministry of National Defense after trying, unsuccessfully, to rouse anyone there from one to three on a weekday afternoon. The ministry's spokesman considered that for a moment and then answered serenely, "Your proposition is statistically improbable. Wars nearly always start at night, when everyone's asleep."

The "iron rice bowl"—guaranteed lifetime employment—accounts for the worst abuses of *xiu-xi:* worker apathy and low productivity. Bonuses and material incentives have been introduced nationwide and, in a few places, are hefty enough to account for a third of a worker's annual wages. Plant managers remain reluctant to dock anyone's pay, let alone fire any-one, but at the Shanghai Heavy-Duty Truck Plant and elsewhere, bonuses are withheld from those who loaf on the job or show up habitually late. And in a few plants, *xiu-xi* time is being cut and greater demands imposed on the work force.

"Eventually we're going to have to face up to the fact that *xiu-xi* is a luxury we cannot afford," said the economist from the Chinese Academy of Social Sciences. "It's fine among the peasants, who put in long days no matter what because their livelihood is at stake. But in the cities, *xiu-xi* is a boondoggle. It's a barrier to efficiency."

But if *xiu-xi* goes, it won't be without a struggle. There are millions of Chinese who not only like their *xiu-xi* but are firmly convinced that rest is essential to a well-balanced life. Furthermore, they cannot quite under-stand why Americans and other Westerners drive themselves so hard, at the expense of their mental and physical health. That view, from the other side of the cultural chasm, came through in an April 1980 *People's Daily* com-mentary that warned young Chinese about the drawbacks of the American style of life: "At noontime, the boss of a big American company never lets his staff take a two-hour nap because it would cost him too much money. Americans are extravagant and wasteful, but they do not waste time. They are always chasing after something, except the leisure and carefree style of us Orientals. It is impossible for most Americans even to consider the possibility of simply sitting on the side of a peaceful lake, fishing for an entire afternoon."

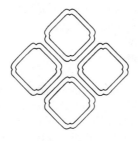

INFORMATION

LONG BEFORE 1949, CHINA'S EMPERORS TREATED INFORMATION as a state resource, to be protected and doled out only when necessary. Historians of the new dynasty always wrote the history of the old, looking at the facts from a view most favorable to their new imperial employers. Information on current events found its way to the Chinese in different forms depending on their status. The Qing emperor Yong Zheng, for instance, made some of his instructions known only to high officials through semisecret documents called palace memorials, while others got empire-wide circulation in an officially sanctioned journal called the *Peking Gazette.*

In their early years, the Chinese Communists required secret communications simply to survive, but once they came to power the old imperial system suited their instinct for confidentiality and had the full weight of tradition besides. So today, as if their government remained a dissident group fearful of discovery, the Communists still operate a vast network of newspapers, books, lectures and other forms of expression that are classified as "internal"—of very limited circulation, unavailable to the Chinese masses or to foreigners. This information system produces a ritualized vagueness that makes some otherwise ordinary conversations seem like extracts from cheap spy novels.

A Peking official invited a Chinese-American we knew who was working for a state publishing house to hear a special, internal report justifying the rehabilitation of the late President Liu Shaoqi. This was a very special privilege, the official made clear, extended only because the American was of Chinese descent and the Chinese he worked with had come to trust him.

The official brought in the document and read it to a small group. He had checked the report out of a special office, after registering his name and office and stating how long he would keep it and to whom he would read it. When the reading concluded, the American realized with some astonishment that he had not heard a single reference to Chairman Mao or the Cultural Revolution, the principal forces behind Liu's purge in 1966 and his death from pneumonia in 1969. Just to make certain he had not missed something, he asked if he could look the report over. "No, it is for the ears, not the eyes," he was told.

"You mean I should just forget it?"

"That is right."

That concern for secrecy creeps like a constricting vine through Chinese official and unofficial life. Even in the relatively relaxed post-Mao era, ordinary small talk has its awkward moments when a subject casually broached turns out to be an "internal" matter, only to be discussed by those with the proper credentials.

While we were in China the official press, as it occasionally does, re-printed China's Official Secrets Act, drawn up in 1951 as a "temporary" measure. It threatens arrest for revealing any internal government information, even weather reports. One friend of ours asked a Chinese soldier the location of the nearest taxi station and had to identify himself and his destination before he got an answer. Even high-ranking Chinese lose track of what is secret and what is not. An editor of the *People's Daily* was once asked why a January 1980 speech by Deng Xiaoping had not been published in his newspaper. He said it was because the speech was too long, but he could give the visitor a pamphlet with Deng's talk in it. A messenger was sent for a copy. After a long wait, the word came back that the speech was still "internal" and could not be released.

For most of the time during our stay in China even the Peking telephone book was an internal document. Julie Munro, a former Canadian resident of Peking who moved to Hong Kong, did a thriving business selling her own painstakingly collected booklet of Chinese telephone numbers to foreign and Chinese organizations alike. It was a sign of a new era in China when, during the last week before we left the country, we were finally allowed to buy two copies of a Chinese-language Peking phone book from an official government distributor.

The system cracked a bit in other ways: the newspapers reported exact casualty figures for a bomb explosion in the Peking railroad station, something they had not done previously, preferring to ignore accidents and most disasters. The national television network began showing nightly world news videotape clips provided by Western agencies, but the broadcasts served only to underscore how much more the Chinese could learn of what was happening in the rest of the world than in their own country.

We got a sense of how difficult extracting fact from impression was going to be the first day we ever set foot in China, April 18, 1977. It was a busy afternoon on Zhongshan Street in Canton. Bicycles filled the street and shoppers jammed the old covered sidewalk when we stumbled onto something we did not understand. A large crowd had formed suddenly, half on the street, half on the sidewalk, blocking traffic. Two men held the arms of a third man. The captive struggled and grimaced. Then all three disappeared into the crowd. As the only foreigners present, we backed up against a wall so we could see without being seen. One of the men appeared again, and handed pieces of twine down to his companion. After a pause, the crowd parted slightly and we could see the two men wheeling away a bicycle with a sidecar holding the third man, apparently bound hand and foot.

A girl in the crowd giggled. Two uniformed soldiers looked on but did not interfere. The three men in the struggle all wore standard faded gray work clothes. No policemen appeared, though one was posted at a nearby corner. We tried to ask bystanders what was going on, but only got nervous smiles in reply. Was it a citizen's arrest of a bicycle thief? A skirmish between political factions? Hospital orderlies apprehending a mental patient? A family squabble? Street theater? We never found out.

Deng Xiaoping became famous for saying, with reference to the Communist tendency to mistrust non-Marxist intellectuals, "It does not matter whether a cat is black or white, just so it catches mice." In our experience, the Chinese still occasionally succumb to the temptation to call black white (or as the Chinese say, call a deer a horse) when faced with the choice of an embarrassing answer or an embarrassing failure to answer. Driving around Shanghai in separate cars, we each asked about the metal shutters used on the fronts of streetside shops. Jay's guide said they were vestiges of the high crime years before 1949; Linda's guide said they were keeping out more contemporary burglars. And for a long time the Chinese refused to admit that they were, in effect, trying to copy the Boeing 707. They confessed only when they had to get some advice from Western technicians as they encountered unforeseen engineering problems in designing a passenger jet so similar to the Boeing plane that wags called it "the 708."

Even after the death of Mao and the arrest of the Gang of Four lessened the number of hysterical political lectures, people remained skeptical of the official press. They could not learn much from their newspapers unless they read between the lines. Some of our Chinese friends were so stunned when the officials occasionally reported real facts about events like the Peking railroad station bombing that they tended to disbelieve them. Their local newspapers were little better, usually reprinting articles from the *People's Daily,* although some publications, such as the *Peking Evening News,* provided some crime stories and other light features that readers found refreshing diversions.

For facts, the Chinese turned by the millions to *Cankao Xiaoxi,* a small tabloid that is unique in the world. Translated, it is called *Reference News,* a latter-day version of the emperor's *Peking Gazette,* but as foreigners we were to hear of it in very roundabout ways.

Early in our stay a Foreign Ministry official complimented Jay on an article he had just written. Jay was pleased and also curious about this rare bit of personal praise, for like any proper Chinese diplomat, the man had never been particularly informative or warm toward us. "Thanks very much," Jay said. "Where did you see the article?" The man acted as if he had not heard. "It was a very good one," he said. At the Peking Hotel billing office soon after we arrived, we leaned over the counter to get a better look at a small Chinese newspaper that did not look familiar. This annoyed the clerk, who quickly snatched it away. A diplomat we knew, out for a stroll, found a copy of the same little tabloid discarded under a park bench, soaked by a recent rainstorm. He told us he was thrilled by the find, and after looking both ways, rolled it up and took it home to dry in front of his apartment radiator.

Such is the awkwardness and mystery generated by what might be called the world's largest-circulation underground newspaper. With at least 9 million daily subscribers, the four-page daily is China's largest-circulation newspaper and still does not meet the demand. In the world, only *Pravda* and the Soviet Young Communist League paper, and perhaps one or two of the Japanese papers, equal or exceed it in circulation. But other Chinese papers do not quote from it. It is not found on Peking newsstands. Until recently, to give, much less sell, a copy to a foreigner was, if not a crime, at least an indiscretion that could bring trouble to the Chinese involved. Under the *Reference News* masthead is clearly printed: "Internal Distribution. Take Care to Hold On To."

Since *Reference News'* back-room editors do not operate under the strict limits of the official press, and since they do not have to consider every article with a view to party policy, they can let the Chinese know more about the outside world, and in an indirect way more about their own government, than any other print medium. *Reference News* provides an example of how the Chinese system of privilege, in this case the demands of bureaucrats for special information from foreign news services, can be stretched so far that much of the urban Chinese society benefits.

Reference News prints only articles taken from foreign publications. The articles, translated into Chinese, are usually used without permission or payment. Keeping the publication "internal"—i.e., not flaunting it—helps avoid sticky questions about copyright. Foreign correspondents like ourselves found it difficult to understand a system that barred us from seeing the one Chinese newspaper that carried our stories, but most of us were flattered to be reprinted there. Who would want to pass up nine million readers?

We collected several dozen copies of *Reference News* from various sources over a three-year period and found its editors bouncing signals back to the Chinese people, using the foreign press as a satellite relay. They printed items so controversial they could never be comfortably raised in the official press, like a *Los Angeles Times* editorial questioning the need to sell U.S. arms to China and a wire-service account of the Dalai Lama asking for more freedom for Tibetans. The newspaper published reports by foreign correspondents, or pro-Communist Hong Kong papers, explaining what

was happening in China—such as challenges to Deng Xiaoping's group—
with a clarity and speculative boldness that was too much for the masters
of obliqueness in the official Chinese press. This way the message got to the
people without anyone being blamed for revealing too much. It seemed clear
to us, after talking to some Hong Kong editors, that Chinese officials
sometimes even intentionally leaked news to them so that it could be printed
in *Reference News*. One night on Anhui's Yellow Mountain a Chinese
journalist, after a few beers, gave Jay a little speech: "Sometimes there are
things we have difficulty criticizing or even noticing in our country. We rely
on you foreigners to write about them. This gets attention. Your pieces
appear in *Reference News*! And that helps us."

Foreigners writing about China must learn how to interpret indirect
information. One time-tested method is to discern and separate current
shortcomings from what is being praised in the official media. If the *People's
Daily* does a series of articles on workers who expose corruption in their
factories and offices, as happens occasionally, then we know the newspaper's official supervisors are concerned that too many workers are winking
at bad practices and that they want to encourage the workers to report
them. The method was summed up by Chou En-lai in a conversation with
Edgar Snow: "Those who come to China for fact-finding don't have to hunt
for any inside information. They can discover our problems from the stage
or from our publications . . . When we encourage the good and criticize the
bad, it means that bad things surely still exist and good ones are not yet
perfect." Sophisticated Chinese use the same method, though they still
complain of their newspapers overdoing *bao xi bu bao you* (reporting only
good news, not bad). The Chinese must rely on their own active grapevine,
called *xiaodao xiaoxi* (alley news), or on publications like *Reference News*.

Several years ago *Reference News* was available only to Chinese officials
and office staff. Now most urban workers have access to it, including some
foreign students and office workers, although our efforts to subscribe were
always rebuffed. Peasants generally do not see it.

To subscribe, one must be a regular member of some factory, university
or office unit. The fee is about thirty cents a month; the impact is sometimes
surprising. At Xiamen University in remote Fujian province, a student
asked us in early 1980 how the race between President Jimmy Carter and
Senator Ted Kennedy was going. We were not surprised by the question,
since official Chinese newspapers had mentioned the Democratic primaries
in the United States. When Jay launched into an analysis of Kennedy's and
Carter's different economic policies, thinking this would interest a Chinese,
the student broke in, "But what about that girl Senator Kennedy drowned?
Hasn't that had an impact?" Readers of the *People's Daily* had not heard
of Chappaquiddick, but readers of *Reference News* had.

Reference News acts like a line of cirrus clouds marking a wave of cool,
invisible air which, although unseen, changes the weather. These cold fronts

moving across the political landscape are the internal books, memos and oral briefings conducted privately in Chinese offices. They are like family stories, not to be repeated to outsiders. They take the form of tape recordings of secret speeches by high party leaders, carefully numbered and logged government statements still in draft form, and short speeches and reminders of occasional political meetings. All are kept "internal," i.e., passed down from one administrative level to the next. The State Council, the highest government body, can issue them, as can ministries and army commands, but the most important come from the Central Committee of the Communist Party. One of the crucial powers of the men who sit on the party Politburo is their right to review these documents before they are dispatched. Some are orders, some reports of secret speeches, some are appeals for debate over suggested new policies. They are usually marked closed to all but certain eyes, and delivered by courier. Central directives, called zhongfa, are numbered sequentially from January to December, with each copy having its own number to avoid theft or loss in distribution.

Higher-level officials may read a much more detailed compendium of foreign news than *Reference News* called *Reference Materials,* published twice a day with as many as seventy-five to a hundred pages. One official told us, "It's rather long and boring. I only read articles which have something to do with my job." Officials at grade 13—bureau directors—and above on the 26-step ladder may read copies of *Internal Reference.* These include a collection of unpublished letters to the *People's Daily,* among the 2,000 or so the paper gets each day, to give officials a sense of what people are complaining about. The *People's Daily* and New China News Agency reporters also write for *Internal Reference* on problems in the bureaucracy. These bits of unvarnished bad news include true casualty statistics for natural disasters and reports of sabotage and crime.

All truths, both internal and external, sooner or later have to undergo processing by the staff of the *People's Daily.* It is the nation's and the party's flagship newspaper. Working in barren and often chilly offices, its reporters and editors have managed to survive years of ideological battering and come out not nearly as punch-drunk as we expected. For years the paper was headquartered in a ramshackle building on Wangfujing Street, visible from the window of Jay's office on the north side of the Peking Hotel. Toward the end of our stay in China, the several hundred editors, writers and press men moved out to remodeled headquarters at what was formerly the Peking Engineering Institute in the Shui Duizi area of east Peking. Visitors drive through a guarded gate to view buildings grouped like lecture halls around a wide campus. Inside, in rooms with bare tile floors and whitewashed walls with little decoration, editors work in offices which rarely hold more than ten staff members each. There are no huge newsrooms, with copy aides dashing about and reporters yelling friendly insults at editors, the usual atmosphere of an American newspaper. The work is done quietly, with a certain insurance-office single-mindedness. The editors we met felt liberated from the tumult of the 1960s and 1970s. The editor in chief was an old party warhorse, Hu Jiwei. He was in the revolutionary base camp of Yenan in the 1930s, as were a surprising number of the upper echelon of China's press establishment. He became an important editor in the northwest after liberation, then moved south to be deputy editor of the *People's Daily* in the mid-1950s and was promoted to editor shortly after Mao's death.

Like many other officials now occupying high posts in China, Hu gains a certain luster from having been severely criticized and temporarily retired during the Cultural Revolution (the worse the treatment received, the more the sufferer must have resisted the discredited ultraleftism of the Gang of Four). Hu spent several years tending cowpens in Henan, International Department director Yuan Xianlu told us. Yuan himself, once an underground Communist youth organizer at the American-funded Yenching University in Peking, has spent thirty years at the *People's Daily.* He is tall, wiry, with huge ears and a weakness for joking about the newspaper's odd twists and turns. The *People's Daily* is one of the few institutions in China not to have closed down completely at one time or another in the tumult of the last twenty years. The overwhelming need to get the paper out every day insulated many people like Yuan, who includes himself in the once dubious category of "intellectual." They kept their jobs even when competence, education and former ties with foreigners were political poison. During the 1960s and 1970s, the radicals around Mao and the surviving champion of the moderates, Premier Chou En-lai, tugged at the paper from both ends. "Quite often the late Premier sent instructions and then the Gang of Four sent quite different instructions," Yuan said. The office sport was to trade stories about the editor, Lu Ying, an appointee of the Gang of Four with little talent for his job. "We called him 'the beautifully embroidered pillow'—nice outside but straw within," Yuan said. Lu challenged his editors to explain the term "Indochina," saying he could find no such country on the map. Persuaded by the similarity of their names in Chinese, Lu insisted at an editorial meeting that Sri Lankan Prime Minister Sirimavo Bandaranaike was the wife of the (allegedly celibate) Panchen Lama of Tibet.

Less humorous moments followed. When letters began to pour into the newspaper protesting editorial slaps at Chou after the Premier's death in early 1976, Lu insisted that the staff turn over the names and units of the complainers, including one person who addressed the editor in chief on the envelope as "Goebbels." Yuan said many people were imprisoned as a result. After Mao died and the Gang of Four fell, "we made investigations and tried to get out of prison all we could find."

Party members like Yuan keep an eye on copy to make sure it does not stray from policy, but official policy is so well known that the editors usually censor themselves. Yuan said he only reads the headlines of most of the articles in his section, saving his time for careful review of the commentaries that have a more official impact. Articles or points of view that seem controversial are sent across town to the offices of the Central Committee for review. Yuan claims a certain independence even from the Foreign Ministry. He said he was not impressed by a protest from the Moroccan embassy, forwarded to him by the Foreign Ministry, about an article on the West Sahara war.

With 6.3 million subscribers, the *People's Daily* still does not print as many copies as *Reference News,* but it is probably distributed more widely because it is available to peasants and because so many local papers reprint its articles. Even as it now moves to expand from the usual six-page format, political articles in the front, foreign news at the back, and publish an English edition, the paper still teaches by indirection. Historical allusions and emulation campaigns still cloud what is actually happening in China.

Rumors naturally thrive in such conditions, as they do in most of the world's closed societies. Typical was the report that Deng Xiaoping had narrowly escaped assassination when General Xu Shiyou, enraged at not being appointed Chief of Staff, fired a pistol at him. "Do you think there is something to it?" one sophisticated Chinese official, with genuine concern on his face, asked when we read him a wire-service report from Taiwan about the alleged confrontation. This was one item that was not carried in *Reference News,* and the Foreign Ministry angrily derided the story as "sheer nonsense."

Over the years the Chinese have learned that such tales assume a life of their own if they are not vigorously nipped in the bud. One story that has refused to die is the "last will and testament" of Mao Tse-tung, which surfaced a month after his death via the respected independent Hong Kong newspaper *Ming Pao.* The story purported to be a transcript of a June 3 meeting between Mao and a few of his likely successors, with the Chairman in a particularly disagreeable mood.

"No one in the world is immortal," the story quotes Mao as saying. "Few can live up to seventy, and as I am over eighty I should have died. Are there not some people among you who hope that I should go to see Marx sooner?"

"No," the alleged transcript quotes Hua Guofeng, Mao's immediate successor, to say in reply.

"Really no one?" Mao replies. "I don't believe it."

Despite a Foreign Ministry denunciation of the story as "sheer fabrication with ulterior motives," in addition to proof that Hua was not even in Peking on June 3, the story was too good for many to resist. The Foreign

Ministry denial was somewhat weakened by the fact that its representatives had often lied outright to reporters during the Mao era.*

Perhaps the most persistent tale of this genre—"the Storm in July" story of 1966—still lives on, much to the frustration and bewilderment of its principal victim, Yugoslav correspondent Branko Bogunovich. The story, which also appeared in *Ming Pao*, provided fascinating details of political maneuvers in Peking in the summer of 1966, when Bogunovich was the Tanjug news agency's Peking correspondent. According to the article, then President Liu Shaoqi had organized a Central Committee meeting to vote Mao out of power, Deng Xiaoping equivocated, and both sides moved troops about the capital. The U.S. consulate in Hong Kong quickly translated the story from *Ming Pao* into English as part of its regular service for China watchers around the world. *Newsweek* devoted a full page to the account. *Time, Le Monde* and some Japanese papers ran it. Scholars called, wrote and visited Bogunovich for years after, seeking further details.

Bogunovich had, however, not written the story. It was a fake, planted in *Ming Pao* by Taiwan or other mischief-makers. Unconvinced by his cries of innocence, the Peking authorities soon threw Bogunovich out of the country. The husky, gray-haired correspondent told us in 1970 that he considered suing the U.S. government for reprinting the story. "It would have been a great socialist act," he said. He was somewhat mollified when a U.S. embassy officer in Belgrade called on him and apologized, but he still lamented that "of all the thousands of stories I've ever written, the only one anyone remembers is one I didn't even write."

During our stay in Peking we detected a more mellow attitude toward other apocryphal reports as the Chinese began to realize that Western journalists considered most of them little more than innocent fun. Yao Wei, perhaps the quickest mind in the Foreign Ministry Information Department, was ready when Chris Szymanski, a U.S. embassy officer, teased him about the report of Xu Shiyou's attempt to kill Deng and the news that Xu was hit by gunfire from a Deng bodyguard. What was Xu doing that week in Nanjing, not his usual place of assignment? Szymanski asked. "He's recovering from his wounds," Yao quipped.

Jokes or not, the government holds on to information as tightly as a fifteenth-century palace eunuch. One day Linda sought to discover how many women were serving in the Chinese army, a small detail for a *Times* wrap-up on the U.S. debate over drafting females. Youthful-looking Li Zhengjun, the Foreign Ministry official who often handled our inquiries, told Linda she should have no trouble getting such a simple statistic from the Defense Ministry's Foreign Affairs office. A man at the Defense Minis-

---

*Parts of the Mao transcript, its uncertain origins explained in footnotes, are included in two new biographies of Mao by scholars Ross Terrill and Dick Wilson.

try asked her to put her request in writing, so she dashed off a letter and hand-delivered it. He promised to call back, but nothing happened.

Usually Linda would assume at this point that she had been rebuffed, and tell her editors that the government had no comment. But the information she desired seemed so trivial that she decided, as an experiment, to pursue it further. Every day for a week she called the Defense Ministry office, without success. She paid another call in person, got a couple of cups of tea —but still no answer. Finally, voicing her exasperation, Linda asked the spokesman why in the world it was so difficult to secure a minor statistic.

Clearly uncomfortable, the ministry spokesman suddenly lowered his voice to a whisper that Linda hoped meant she was finally going to get what she was after. But the man simply said, before hanging up for the last time, "It's a secret."

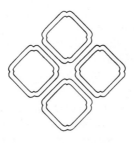

EXAM

LINMEI, A GIRL OF TWENTY-ONE, HEARD ABOUT THE EXAMINATION while visiting her parents in Canton. It is not unusual for young Chinese to remember this moment precisely. The announcement that China's college entrance exams were being reinstituted was a watershed, creating both hope and fear in a generation deadened by lack of adventure and challenge.

For four years Linmei had worked in the rice paddies of northern Guangdong; out of the blue, she had a chance to get into college. If only she could remember enough from her high school lessons. Much had washed out of her memory during years of monotonous loading and planting, digging and carrying, cutting and bailing.

"I did not dare be absent from work during the day, because I thought the work-group leader might bar me from taking the exam. At night there were blackouts. It was a busy harvest season and cold and they needed the electricity for other things than lighting our rooms. Some people just left, went home without permission, back to Canton, but I didn't dare." Linmei and her friends studied textbooks borrowed from their old high schools, or shared with one another. "Usually I studied in my bed—we had no desks —until I fell asleep," she said.

Linmei failed her exam. She became so disheartened at her prospects that she and other unsuccessful candidates rowed a small boat out of China and into Hong Kong. There we met her, and got our first lesson in the price paid for one of the most important reforms in Chinese society since the death of Mao Tse-tung.

When, in the fall of 1977, China gave its first national examination for college entrance in a decade, millions of youths who had been sent to work as field hands in the countryside were suddenly encouraged to rekindle childhood dreams of careers in science, government or teaching. The examination would tax their memory and academic skills. Their political thoughts and activities—or lack of them—had brought grief to many of them in the past. This time they were led to hope politics would no longer be the key factor, but as always, *guanxi* entered in.

A Kunming University student told us, "When they announced the first exam in October 1977, it was like a bomb thrown into the water. The friends I had, they changed a lot in the space of two weeks after the announcement." Access to the grapevine—the network of family and neighborhood contacts bringing confidential news up and down the Communist Party hierarchy—became vital to young people who aspired to enter universities. "Some people heard the news two months before the general announcement, because there was a preparatory meeting for the national educational conference in Peking, and word leaked. Some got the news, and others did not, and that two months of time for preparation made a great difference," the young man said.

If they passed the examination, they would probably be able to spend the rest of their lives in a city—the great hope of young Chinese sick of the drudgery of village life. People with high school diplomas were eligible for teaching jobs; but a university education in English could win them jobs as interpreters, and as one student put it, "If you're an interpreter, you know you'll be working in a place with sidewalks."

It was a century before Christ that young Chinese men first took examinations in the Confucian classics to enter the imperial service and prepare for government jobs. Ever since, passing such examinations has become synonymous with success and security in Chinese minds.

The old three-tier imperial examinations could lead to service with the emperor himself, or at the very least employment as a local official or as a teacher. Early in the Communist era, the examination brought bright young men into power and helped preserve the extraordinary stability and competence of the bureaucracy, which made the system all the more suspect in Mao Tse-tung's eyes. He often spoke of his distrust for book learning. When Mao decided to launch a Cultural Revolution to dislodge the bureaucrats who were challenging his authority, he logically began with an attack on the educational system, including the national college entrance examination. All the high schools (what the Chinese call middle schools) and universities closed for a time. The examination was discontinued, replaced eventually by a recommendation system designed to pick applicants more for their class background and political fervor than for their academic preparation. Young peasants and workers who had labored with particular zeal and enthusiasm were given preference over intellectual youths with good grades, who were often the offspring of deposed bureaucrats anyway.

But the Cultural Revolution students were ill prepared for college work. Courses had to be watered down and university education grew stale, producing near-illiterates and little useful research. Also, without the examinations, it was easier for people with connections to get students into college through the back door. When production units recommended young workers and peasants to fill university slots, they were often the unit leader's own children, or the children of friends who had done him favors.

By 1977, with Mao dead and his ideological acolytes under arrest, reviving a two-day college entrance examination seemed the fair and sensible thing to do, but it was still an alarmingly rigorous blow to young people who had been discouraged for a decade from pursuing academic excellence. In patched clothing and ill-fitting eyeglasses, they hunched over small desks in rural elementary schools where exams were conducted and seemed to greet the chance to get to a university with enthusiasm. But for most, it eventually became a grim nightmare.

Some of the older applicants said they forgot too much in the countryside, or, like Linmei, failed to persuade the dour peasant production chiefs at their farms to give them enough time to study. Others found themselves burdened by family responsibilities that made college impossible and had to disqualify themselves.

Even for the young students fresh out of middle school who now provide the largest pool of university applicants, the examination remains a terrible burden. "Every year after the scores and admissions are published, there are many incidents of suicide among high school students," said the foreign minister's son, Huang Bing, explaining his surprise at the relatively easygoing attitude he found when he went to study at Harvard.

To the Chinese, to fail the college entrance test, or not take the test at all, is to surrender to hopelessness—and only 5 percent of each year's six million senior high school graduates pass the test. An analysis by U.S. experts of the 1978 exam indicated that the science and math questions were easier, and the geography and history questions harder, than what American high school students encounter on the SATs. But many of the candidates have attended schools short on textbooks and trained teachers. Unlike the SATs, there are no multiple-choice questions on the Chinese exam, which requires that answers be written out in full. In most places this exam takes two days, not the single morning or afternoon required of SAT takers. Significantly, a good score in China, enough to qualify for most universities, is 350 points out of 500 possible—only 70 percent.

We stopped by Peking's No. 35 Middle School on a sweltering summer day to see how the 1980 crop of middle-school graduates had reacted to the latest entrance exam. It was a dusty three-story brick building with bare concrete floors and some stunted shrubs growing under the windows. More than eight hundred students from several districts sat at the small desks. The classroom windows were thrown wide open to let in some air. The exam included Chinese literature, geography, history, politics, mathematics, physics, chemistry and foreign languages—principally English. "We've found no cheaters," said Yu Xiufang, a small, slim woman who was the school principal and also head proctor for the exam. Each exam room had two or three teachers to keep watch. The national exam itself had been drawn up by a committee of teachers at a remote mountain resort, to ensure confidentiality.

These were fresh middle-school graduates whose teachers had, in the words of one student, "been preparing us for this for some time." An earlier exam had produced complaints from some youths that a number of questions had never been covered in normal middle-school curricula. The Education Ministry ruled that the exam should closely follow the study outline for all middle schools. Several students began to leave the exam room early. "It was rather easy," said one, "but it all depends on how my score compares with everybody else's."

We examined the history and politics questions. The history exam did not demand much from a well-prepared pupil. Much of it was fill-in-the-blanks, such as "The destruction of opium by Lin Zexu at —— in the year —— was a great victory in the Chinese people's war against opium." The tale of Commissioner Lin's brave effort to stop the British opium trade in Canton in 1839 is as well known to Chinese youth as the Boston Tea Party is to Americans. Harder questions followed about the capitals of obscure dynasties and the names of ancient rebel groups. World-history questions provided a proper revolutionary focus, such as the name of the general who led the American War of Independence, the name of the three main American Indian civilizations destroyed by "the aggression of the Western Europeans" and the name of the "British aggressor" killed by Sudan rebels in 1885. This last was Charles George Gordon, a favorite Chinese villain because of his success in putting down rebellions in China in the mid-nineteenth century. Three essay questions, however, accounted for nearly half of the points on the exam: explaining the emergence of capitalism in the Ming dynasty, the function of the masses in the "three bourgeois uprisings" in France, and the reasons for the Chinese Communists' first united front.

To unreconstructed bourgeoisie like us, the politics exam seemed more difficult, but most students said it was the one for which they were *sure* to be well prepared. They were, for example, asked to explain the socialist legal system and to correct the mistake in the statement "The principle of distribution in socialist society is 'from each according to his ability to each according to his need.' " (Correct answer: "to each according to his *work.*") For 15 points, the students had to "Relate the following viewpoint to theories of philosophy and economy: 'Respecting subjective laws will obstruct the objective initiative to be brought into play, while bringing the objective initiative into full play will create subjective laws and speed the realization of the four modernizations' "! The exam writers saved the most important question (20 out of the total 100 points) for last: "Refute the fallacy that 'our country can realize the four modernizations without the leadership of the Communist Party.' "

. . .

The renewal of the exams has had an enormous impact on China's entire education system, throwing teachers and particularly parents and students into an exam frenzy. "Many schools . . . pay attention to preparing only those students who have the potential to pass college entrance examinations, and ignore the education of all other students in basic studies," Education Minister Jiang Nanxiang told a national conference on secondary and primary schools. A Henan teacher, pressed to increase the success rate at his school, landed in jail after he allowed students to copy from each other's exam papers. (He had also let them smash the bicycle of an outside examiner who objected.) Schools at every level have instituted entrance exams. Even a nursery school catering to the offspring of intellectuals and officials in Peking began giving its own entrance exam. It admitted only 60 out of 400 three- and four-year-old applicants, based on their ability to read some characters, do simple calculations and sing. Hou Ying was unwilling for a while to send her five-year-old Xunxun to a nursery school because she thought she could prepare him better at home for the rigors of an examination-crazed educational system. Xunxun had a regular routine of poems and English words he had memorized at his mother's insistence.

One well-educated official we knew was distraught because he and his wife had only one room to live in and their eleven-year-old son had to board with relatives in Shanghai. He decided to bring the boy to Peking anyway and devoted long hours in the summer of 1980 looking for a school that would have room for him. He wanted a school that was close enough so that the boy could come home each day for parental tutoring. In two years he would have to take an exam to get into a good *junior* middle school, which would then prepare him to take the exam for a good *senior* middle school. A good senior middle school was essential if he were to pass the college entrance exam. "He is doing very well in Shanghai, an eighty-five average, but to get into a good middle school, you need at least ninety-five in each subject," his father said. "In math, I hear, you need one hundred percent. It's frightening. There is lots of competition now, parents spending time helping their children, while I do nothing. When he speaks, he speaks too fast and too vaguely; his thoughts are not well organized. That is something a parent can help with." By summer's end, the father was frantic. None of the schools had an opening. His son returned to Shanghai. The man refused to give up, however. After revisiting a couple of schools he finally found a director who softened and opened a place. The boy came back from Shanghai and his parents rigged a bed in the corner of their room for him.

If urban parents feel harassed by the pressures of the exam, rural parents and youngsters feel completely excluded. The new stiff academic standards appear to end the special access to college some peasants enjoyed in the last years of Mao. At that time a peasant youth, regardless of his scholastic ability, could enter a university if he could demonstrate some political activism—or if his family had useful political connections. American sociologist Victor Nee, permitted a rare visit to a remote commune in Fujian province in 1980, found that since 1977 only one student from the commune had been able to pass the entrance examination for a technical *middle* school. Professors at Fujian universities told Nee they were worried about the very low numbers of peasant youths being admitted to college, fearing an eventual backlash in a nation built on peasant revolution. Today most urban youth, unlike peasant students, can find a senior middle school to attend, giving them an enormous advantage in preparing for college. In fall 1979, only 34 percent of the freshmen at Peking University, China's premier college, were from families of workers and peasants, even though these groups probably represent 90 percent of the population.

Of 4.6 million youths who took the test in the summer of 1979, only 270,000 were admitted to universities, a proportion that has remained fairly constant since. The stories of bizarre and emotionally crippling failures increase each year by the millions. Of the many we encountered, no two were ever quite the same. But each illuminated some unique element of Chinese society, so wide-ranging was the impact of the revival of the examination.

Liang Yiliang had graduated from middle school just a year before the exam was announced in 1977. Most of his schoolmates had gone to the countryside, but he shuddered at the idea of spending a lifetime as a peasant. He told the school authorities that he was in bad health and stayed in town with his parents. Then the national exam came, and he rejoiced: his score was 270, good enough for acceptance to the South China Industrial University in Canton. A happy ending, he thought, until he took the required physical and, without considering the consequences, passed with flying colors.

A sharp-eyed official at the local college enrollment office glanced at Liang's file, then looked again. He called Liang in for an interview, which turned out to be a lecture: "You are cheating the government. You applied to stay in the city because of bad health, but now we find you can pass the physical. You didn't answer the party's call to go to the countryside, so we are not going to let you enroll at the university."

Liang protested. He wrote letters to higher officials. His father sought help from friends with influence. The enrollment officials would not be moved. So Liang gave up, and accepted an assignment in the countryside, determined to come back and try again another year.

Ji Guohua had failed the entrance examination in her district of Fujian province, but her father had friends at the admissions office of Xiamen University. He could not bear to let his hopes for this daughter's future end there, nor did he want her to risk a long wait and another try at the examination the following year. His friend at the university agreed to accept his daughter. The father was overjoyed.

Then, as a friend of the daughter reported, the girl's production-team leader at the commune where she had been working heard of the arrangement and lost his temper. "I will not permit it," he said. "If we give her permission to go, we will have to continue paying her salary [a frequent procedure for workers who go straight from factory to university]. What do we get out of it? And she has not been accepted at the university in a normal way."

The team leader suggested a deal. If the father could find a place at the university for another member of the production team, he would approve both applicants. The extra applicant, it turned out, was the team leader's niece, who had also failed the examination.

The girl's father, headmaster at an important middle school, went to work and persuaded his university friends to open another place in the entering class. The invisible web of *guanxi* now enveloped two families and the university, requiring further favors in the future. But love and malice intervened. The niece of the production-team leader became pregnant. There was no way the university could accept her in that condition. In a fit of bitterness the production-team leader called off the whole deal: "If my niece isn't going, your daughter isn't either."

We encountered a few bright students, like the teen-ager Tang Dajin, who scored over 400 and easily gained a university place. Tang was sent to a prominent technical school in Hefei, where he was unhappy only at being cut off from his best friend back home in Shanghai. "My friend is studying now; he is going to try to pass the next time." If he doesn't? "Well, that will create a very great gap between us," Tang said.

But Tang and others like him are drawn to college life only because of the security it promises them in later life—a city job. Little about Chinese college life itself appeals to the young. College students live in concrete boxes—floors, ceilings and walls a dirty gray, occasionally whitewashed, but always devoid of plaster. The showers, if there are showers, rarely work, and even more rarely have hot water. Free bathhouse tickets are not offered more than once a week. Meat is seldom offered in the cafeteria. Usually students sleep six or eight in a twelve-foot-square room. Randy Stross, an American studying at Nanjing University, noticed that Chinese members of the university basketball team got an extra food allowance, but they were still so lethargic from poor nutrition that practice could last only half as long as it would in an American university.

Some courses are demanding, but professors—particularly foreigners—have found themselves struggling with the notion lingering from the Cultural Revolution that college students should not be taxed too much. To the minds of young Chinese, passing the entrance exam to get into college should be enough of a strain for one life. "When I gave a test each week and a writing assignment at the end of each month, a lot of students complained to the dean," said John Ritter, an American who taught English and history in Anhui province. An American teacher in Canton reported that whenever she asked one student a question, it was considered appropriate for any other student sitting nearby to whisper the answer. "The rule is," one Peking University teacher said, "you design the tests so that everyone can get one hundred percent, and if they don't, *you've* failed."

As happened in the imperial system, the important thing is to pass the entrance exam. That establishes you as an educated person, capable of intellectual service to the nation, and little of what one does or fails to do afterward can remove that label. Imperial examination candidates were locked in small cubicles for several days with paper, brush and mortar to grind the ink. They were expected to have memorized great swatches of classical history and literature and to be able to write poems and essays according to strict rules, but they needed no acquaintance with the sciences, world history, geography or literature. They were expected, once they passed, to nurture a lifelong distaste for manual labor, and grew their fingernails long to prove it.

The Communists have been trying for thirty years to eliminate all traces of that attitude, but much of it lives on. After the exam at No. 35 Middle School we met a quick-witted and frank young candidate, Li Fang. His father works in the Foreign Ministry and speaks some English. His mother works in the Public Security Ministry. Li declined to resort to the usual stock answers to questions about his future—that he would answer the party's call and cheerily accept life as a worker or peasant. Would he be happy as a worker? "Even if I become one, I can still study. Where there is a will, there is a way. Everything depends on self-study and determination."

Would his parents prefer that he become an intellectual? "Certainly," he said, a remarkable answer even in post-Mao China. Why? "Because they are intellectuals themselves."

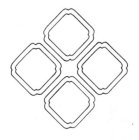

SEPARATION

AS TWO PEOPLE WHO HAVE ALWAYS HAD DIFFICULTY SECURING JOBS IN the same city, we are unusually sensitive to the pain of forced family separation. But we were not prepared for what we found in China—hundreds of thousands of husbands and wives living apart for months or years, casual about it on the surface, but often bitter underneath.

In the summer of 1957 Dulong and Meisong were happy with their lives and their marriage. They had five healthy children, aged seven to thirteen. Both had good jobs. To their minds, the coming of the Communist Party to their city, Canton, eight years before, had been a blessing. A small event at Dulong's factory that summer did not seem cause for concern, though it was about to tear their lives apart.

The printing plant where Dulong served as an accountant had begun to encourage comrades to put up wall posters criticizing any shortcomings in the system. The idea sounded to many like little more than an office suggestion box. Chairman Mao had called for an outpouring of dissenting opinions, for a "hundred flowers to bloom," for a mass-criticism session to shake up the bureaucracy. In that spirit, Dulong wrote a wall poster:

> The gap between the government and the people is growing wider
> and wider. It is very dangerous for the country as well as the
> people if the bureaucracy continues to grow the way it has.

Within a few weeks Dulong had lost his job and was ordered to leave Canton. He could no longer live with his family; his marriage was in shambles. It was little comfort to him, but hundreds of thousands of other earnest critics in China would be sent out to the countryside and suffer a similar fate, the beginning of twenty years of political and economic upheaval that would break up millions of Chinese families.

The story of Meisong and Dulong was not untypical, although many others were separated from their spouses and families even if they had not gotten into political trouble. The revolution required sacrifice. People had to be transferred, deadwood cleared out, malcontents re-educated, skilled workers brought to the underpopulated western provinces. The threat of separation was a useful way to make people conform. Husbands and wives had to adjust to the needs of the state.

A local Communist Party official came to see Meisong a few weeks after Dulong was sent away. He told her she must denounce her husband. "Any good citizen would do the same, particularly one concerned about her children and the lessons they must learn from this experience."

"She really believed that my father had made some mistakes and done something wrong," one of their sons told us. "She thought the punishment was necessary and correct. She told him it would be good for him. But my father insisted he was right. He said he had not done anything wrong."

Dulong had been sent to a collective farm sixty miles from Canton. It was better than the mines, or the work camps reserved for the worst counterrevolutionaries, such as Catholic priests and former officers in Chiang Kai-shek's army. Unlike those unfortunates, Dulong could visit his family once every year or so. "But it wasn't much of a marriage after that," his son said. "I guess they stayed married because of us, the children. Lots of married couples in China, separated or not, stay together because of the children."

Ten years later, the Cultural Revolution reached Canton. The party's troublesome bureaucratic abuses came under public attack, from youthful Red Guards and from Chairman Mao himself. The unremitting political campaign to throw out old officials and install new ones plunged Canton and the rest of China into administrative chaos.

The Cultural Revolution led Meisong to see her husband's "mistake" in a new light. "He was right about the bureaucrats," she told her children. In the meantime, work out at the farm had become easier for Dulong. He became a buyer of supplies for the commune. He could now visit Canton and his family two or three times a year. But his requests to return permanently to the city and live with his family again were turned down, despite the party's promises of a more humane government following Mao's death in 1976.

In the midst of this new era, in 1978, Meisong was visited by another party bureaucrat, this time a local police official. The man demanded that she turn in one of her sons who had illegally fled from his job at a state farm and returned to Canton. She thought for a moment about what the party had done for her, about her original feelings of gratitude and loyalty to the Communists, and what had come of it—and lied. "My son returned for medical treatment," she said. Then she shouted at the policeman, "Why are you bothering us! A person should be allowed to see a doctor if he is ill!"

Since the difficult days of the late fifties, fewer husbands or wives in China have been permanently banished to the countryside for political reasons.

But large numbers of couples continue to be separated by the demands of their jobs, in some cases willingly, in other cases not. Some pharmacies distribute a popular "visiting pill," a powerful contraceptive that women can take during the occasional visits of husbands assigned far away. The official press says that at least 300,000 government officials—civil servants, teachers and scientists—have applied, so far unsuccessfully, to rejoin their spouses.

This figure fails to include the even greater numbers of ordinary workers, peasants and students affected by separation. They have been sent out individually, as a punishment for political trouble or work reassignment, or as part of a mass campaign to learn from the peasants, each generation leaving one more layer of separated families who never managed to reunite. In the early fifties, rapid industrialization pulled many peasants into the cities and many city workers out to new industrial complexes in the interior. In the late fifties, the aftermath of the Hundred Flowers campaign forced recalcitrant critics of the government like Dulong to labor camps for political reform. In the mid-sixties, and particularly after the Cultural Revolution began in 1966, 16 million young people, and a smaller though significant number of urban office workers, were sent off to the countryside to learn the virtues of simple peasant life and relieve overcrowding of the cities.

Most of the office workers and the young people sent out during the Cultural Revolution eventually returned to the cities. The smaller numbers of young people sent to farms these days usually go only as far as the suburbs of their hometowns. But the Cultural Revolution separations created a bitterness, and a crime problem from youths returning without authorization to the cities, which still lingers.

The government promises that it will no longer force mass separations and will try to reduce the numbers of separations caused by new assignments, but promises often fall short. We met an office worker in Peking whose wife had just been assigned to the Chinese embassy in a European capital. The embassy needed more interpreters, and since the man spoke excellent English and had spent two years in London, the Foreign Ministry arranged for an embassy job for him too. But his own office, a government translation service, would not approve the transfer, forcing his wife and him to accept a separation of several years. One official told him, "You've already been overseas. Let someone else have a chance." At Xiangyang village outside the city of Wuhan, peasants told us that one third of the husbands worked and boarded in dormitories in town, and visited their families only once or twice a month. Visitors to other rural villages report similar numbers of families living apart.

About half the Chinese couples we met had endured some lengthy separation. The Chinese have released no overall statistics on this phenomenon, other than to say millions are affected. The term for couples separated in this manner is *niulan zhinü,* "the cowherd and the weaving girl," taken from an old fairy tale about a cowherd who marries a young goddess known for her tapestries and follows her when she is suddenly recalled to heaven. Through divine intervention, the story goes, he is allowed to meet her once a year across the river of stars—the Milky Way—by crossing a magical bridge of flying birds, just as modern separated couples usually see each other on the New Year holiday.

We found it difficult to tell how Chinese couples felt about these separations. In Hong Kong we met a young translator of English who had left his wife in Xiamen soon after their marriage to accept a good job in Peking. "We knew when we were in college that we were probably going to be separated," he said. "It happened to many other couples, so it wasn't too bad." But the translator eventually left China, in part because he and his wife could find no other way to arrange to live together with their three-year-old son, conceived during one of their short annual visits. They had relatives overseas, so they could emigrate legally, although it meant giving up their dream of helping to build a new China.

It became clear to us, two people who also met and married in college, that university campuses provide some of the same romantic temptations in China as they do in the United States. Boys and girls come to live in the same community at the peak of their physical and emotional vitality. One couple we encountered, Chang Duli and Liu Meihua, met and fell in love while attending Shanghai's Fudan University. They looked forward to a long and happy married life pursuing their careers as engineers. Then Chang was transferred in 1969 to a commune in Guangdong province, six hundred miles to the south. He only managed to win a short vacation to return to Shanghai and marry Liu, assigned to a factory in that city. For the next seven years, before he finally fled to Hong Kong, Chang never saw his wife for more than a month each year. They got that much time only by exaggerating the seriousness of what they said was Chang's recurring case of hepatitis. Even when the couple produced a son, Chang's appeals to be reassigned to Shanghai fell on deaf ears.

Convinced of the bad effects of love on studies, and knowing the difficulties of these postgraduate separations, college authorities do what they can to discourage campus entanglements. Even foreigners, usually treated more flexibly, can be affected by the system: Andrew and Lyn Kirkpatrick were already married when they arrived from Britain for a year or two of study at a Shanghai university in late 1976. The college authorities still assigned them to separate dormitories, Andrew with the men and Lyn with the women. A European businessman who allowed them to spend a few nights together at his Shanghai home was reprimanded by the local public security office.

In the late seventies the Ministry of Education attempted to force student love affairs even deeper underground, by prohibiting marriage between university students and ordering the expulsion of any student who married without authorization. But such measures seemed only to increase the tendency of ambitious young husbands to regard their wives as obstacles to future good fortune in the big city. Newspaper columns called it "loving the new and loathing the old," and decried the trend. In a typical story, the *Youth Daily* reported on a woman from rural Anhui whose husband was accepted at the Anhui Medical College, which prohibited married students, after he told them he was single. He told her she had to keep their marriage a secret so he would not be expelled; he insisted that she stay away from the school. Eventually he began an affair with a female student and arranged to be assigned to the same hospital as his new love. When the wife finally showed up to claim support for their child, he tried to throw her out and insisted they weren't married.

The newspapers editorialize about such callousness, but the Chinese we know take it as a matter of course. We encountered a young worker couple who talked happily to us about their new baby soon to arrive. They seemed ideal for each other. But their Chinese acquaintances predicted trouble. The husband had been admitted to the Peking Languages Institute before they were married. One acquaintance said, "Everyone assumed he would not go through with the marriage, since he was learning English and would probably be separated from her. His cultural level is so much higher than hers." She worked at a textile mill. Their friends couldn't understand how come they were still together. They said the marriage would break up.

The Chinese try to accept separations as normal—a necessary sacrifice both for the financial well-being of their families and the needs of the country. Many nonpolitical separations go back to the 1950s, when the newly victorious Communist Party moved whole factories to remote parts of the country in an effort to disperse crucial industries that might be targets of nuclear attack, and to develop the countryside. Husbands or wives who had been assigned to those factories were forced to relocate. Often their spouses could not arrange a job assignment to the same area. Anyway, many of them preferred city life and would not have wanted to move to the remote places even if they could have.

In the past three decades, millions of retired soldiers, considered by the government to make particularly loyal and capable administrators, have been assigned to civilian posts far from their homes. In the suburbs of Peking we visited a construction and repair company set up thirty years ago with veteran combat engineers from all over the country whose families remained in Guizhou, Ningxia (Ningsia) and other provinces. To this day 90 percent of the eight hundred workers' families live away from Peking; the engineers see their families for brief periods during the year. "Children don't recognize their fathers. Old fathers die without having seen their sons for a last time," one worker said. A few of the workers started a slowdown to protest the lack of action on their applications for transfer.

One young worker we knew there, Cui Quanhong, made the best of a bad situation. He had a wife and two children, aged nine and two, living in a rural suburb of Xi'an. His wife managed to visit him for three months in 1980, but he lived in a dormitory where there was no place for her. Finally Cui found an old storeroom, used only occasionally by visiting actor troupes to put on their costumes, and the couple lived there during her stay.

Chinese couples appear to adjust to such separations more easily than Americans might. It makes it somewhat easier for them to know that so many of their friends have the same problem. But one Chinese diplomat, forced to leave his wife and child behind in China for years, warned us against being deceived by the calm demeanor of people who suffer forced separations. "There is an old saying, 'A Chinese is like a thermos bottle, cold on the outside, but hot on the inside.' We will suffer things for a long time, without showing it, then finally the pressure inside is too great and we explode."

In China, what you eat, what you wear and the sort of work you do all depend in part on where you are registered to live. The registration system leads some couples to tolerate separation for fear of something worse. The relatively few people who are registered in large cities like Peking, Shanghai or Canton are guaranteed a steady supply of grain even during bad times, when peasants in some drought-stricken communes must dine on sweet potatoes or roots. Children who grow up in cities are far more likely to get factory jobs, the pinnacle of prestige and job security for most ordinary Chinese. The cities provide schools that will better prepare children for the all-important college entrance examination.

Families will suffer separations to win the advantages of urban life for their children. One immigrant to Hong Kong told of a well-educated Canton woman who had been assigned to rural Hainan Island, married there and bore a child. She sent her small daughter back to Canton to be raised by the child's maternal grandmother, thus avoiding the peasant life that she herself could not escape.

Often, country women with city husbands will leave their communes for two or three days a week to live in the city but cannot get permission to move into town. They take advantage of the liberal leave time given peasant women. (The menstrual period is always a good excuse. It involves a good deal of inconvenience because of the shortage of disposable sanitary napkins.) Of course, they must work some days in the rural commune or risk losing the grain rations and income they and their children need.

Small signs are posted along Sun Yat-sen Avenue in Wuhan, near the Liberation monument in Chongqing, along East Wind Road in Kunming, at Wangfujing Street in Peking and at nearly every other big-city gathering spot we saw. Many are nothing more than perforated, lined sheets torn out of notebooks. At the top, two horizontal arrows point in opposite directions. The signs appeal to anyone in that city who wants to trade jobs and are most often written by men and women stuck in remote factory towns who have wives or husbands living in the bigger cities. "Because my family members and children are all in Nanjing, I have special difficulties," a Mr. Jiang of the outlying town of Jiangdu wrote in a little poster near the Nanjing post office. "My leaders agree that I can be transferred back to Nanjing if someone will exchange with me, so please contact me as soon as possible."

It is no wonder that the most extraordinary holiday in China is the late January or early February Chinese New Year, what the Communists prefer to call Spring Festival, a time when separated couples reunite for as long as two weeks. Many young couples choose it as the time for their wedding. Families serve lots of meat, eggs and other delicacies, ignore work and play cards for money. For the Chinese, it is a celebration with an emotional force and sentimental vibration that surpasses the Christmas holiday in the United States.

As happens occasionally when social tensions become particularly troublesome, China's press has tried to finesse the problem of separation by citing official efforts to bring families back together. Such accounts tend only to confirm the enormity of the problem. An *Enlightenment Daily* article spoke of an engineer, Liu Zigang, at Dalian (Dairen) who "was quite an expert on diesel engines of internal combustion locomotives. In the past, he had family problems because of prolonged separations from his wife. Therefore, his working mood was affected. This time, with his wife transferred to Dalian and his practical family problems solved, he improved the design of the diesel engine and was commended as an advanced worker." After difficult negotiations with other factories and agencies, the Dalian locomotive plant managers helped 115 other engineers and technicians solve family separation problems. But in 1980 the number of top-level officials who had been reunited with their families in one province represented only one half to two thirds of the headquarters staff suffering separations. Applications from separated staffers below that level were not even considered.

Family dislocation in the United States on the scale found in China would generate volumes of learned sociological and psychological studies on the impact of separation on divorce rates and the emotional development of children. The Chinese, however, have only recently re-established sociological and psychological research in Peking. There are no known studies on the effects of long separations, nor is special counseling available. Instead, in yet another example of Communism giving in to the old Chinese system, the government depends on the extended family, the grandmother network, to tide over families suffering the distress of an absent parent or spouse.

The government continues to voice concern for the problem, and since the Chinese are so accustomed to living with it, that may be enough. In 1978

Tian Li, a young railway worker, was reunited with and allowed to marry his fiancée, a Frenchwoman, after intervention by Deng Xiaoping. A French journalist asked Tian why Deng was popular in China. First he mentioned Deng's support for an increase in living standards, but then added, "Deng strongly supports the coming together of couples who are separated by their work throughout the country. The people are especially sensitive about this."

A canny politician and a man who loves wisecracks, Deng did not hesitate to ride this plank of his party platform. He and his men in the leadership showed interest in controlling discontent with at least a few gestures toward modern-day cowherds and weaving girls, even foreigners like Linda and Jay Mathews. In 1979, during Deng's visit to Washington, the *Los Angeles Times* Washington bureau chief Jack Nelson told Deng there was some concern that since we worked for different newspapers, we might not be invited to open up Peking bureaus at the same time. "No, no," Deng said with a grin, "it is against our policy to separate married couples." He could not resist the opportunity to score a small point against his sharpest American critics. "That would violate their human rights!"

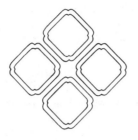

PRIVILEGE

IN CHINA, AS IN THE SOVIET UNION AND OTHER COMMUNIST SOCIETIES, some people are clearly more equal than others despite official doctrine to the contrary. Who you are and whom you know makes all the difference in the quality of Chinese life. Anyone who climbs to the top of the Chinese hierarchy is more or less expected to use his influence to help his friends and relatives. Through string-pulling and favor-trading, party officials can arrange everything from plum job assignments to trips abroad for kith and kin. As an old Chinese proverb says, "When you get to the top, even your chickens and dogs go to heaven."

Privilege and nepotism have been traditions in China since feudal times. Records of one imperial dynasty show that children of nobles, while still in their cradles, were granted honorary posts and salaries because of their fathers' positions. A new privileged class, made up of Communist Party and government officials, whom the Chinese typically call *ganbu* ("manager" or "cadre"), has replaced the old imperial aristocracy. Many Chinese excuse this system as necessary for modernization. In their first five-year plan, 1953 to 1957, the Chinese had to set up a complex administrative structure to run a planned economy that would build heavy industry. This led to privileges and even greater urban-rural differences. But the Communists' impulse to create hierarchies goes back even further. Shadows of the pecking order in the imperial court, particularly the Qing, can be seen in the rationing rules of the Communist base at Yenan, a practice further encouraged by Soviet advisers who followed a similar system back home. (When Wang Shiwei, a Moscow-trained but anti-Soviet Marxist, criticized higher-grade food and clothing for top-level party officials at Yenan in 1942, he was silenced and later shot as a counterrevolutionary.)

Many of China's leaders come from peasant stock and are theoretically committed to the eradication of the bourgeoisie and to the advancement of socialism, but they still live in a manner that for China is positively regal. Like noble Mandarins in the old days, the two dozen or so members of the ruling party Politburo and their families are housed in high-walled villas, mostly in the vicinity of Zhongnanhai, the closely guarded, crimson-walled enclave in mid-Peking where the party and government have their central offices.

Few foreign visitors have been permitted to see this inner sanctum near the Forbidden City. We never made it inside, but three Yugoslav journalists took a special guided tour in 1980. They described two large lakes hidden behind eighteen-foot walls, enclosing an area of about a half square mile. The southernmost lake is lined with tile-roofed mansions, until recently the homes of many of the country's top leaders. Over the last several years, however, all but Deng Yingchao, the widow of Chou En-lai and a Politburo member herself, have vacated Zhongnanhai proper. The mansions had been converted to offices for the Communist Party Central Committee, the Yugoslav visitors were told. Modern office buildings used by the State Council overlook the other lake; trees and flowers are everywhere.

Little Yang, a young Chinese friend of ours familiar with some of the leading families, took us to the villa which houses the family of Deng Xiaoping. We had stopped by an earlier Deng residence at 47 Wide Street, not far north of the Peking Hotel, but the teachers at a neighboring elementary school confirmed that Deng had not lived there since 1977. We could see nothing but willow trees behind the villa's twelve-foot walls, which stretch along close to the sidewalk in Peking fashion. Little Yang said the house now belongs to the family of the late Communist General Luo Rui-qing. Luo suffered greatly in the Cultural Revolution and even attempted suicide once by jumping off a building. He died in 1979, apparently from circulatory problems brought on by the old injury.

Deng's more recent lodgings, at 19 Bright Mountain Street, were not much more visible. The street is busy, taking traffic past the north gate of the Forbidden City at the city's center. An ancient moat, lined with willows, lies just across the road. A twelve-foot-high gray wall encloses this villa as well. Several maples and other trees line the sidewalk outside and poke up from behind the wall. Now and then a large metal gate opens to admit automobiles. We saw no outside guards. (When we happened to pass by at midnight we saw a light in what seemed to be a watchman's office just inside the wall with a window visible above it.) Little Yang preferred to stroll casually on the other side of the street while we inspected the wall. Deng's villa was identified by a small red metal plaque with a white-lettered house number. Like many others in Peking, the plaque was almost obliterated by age and rust. "Next door is another villa, used by the widow of Lu Xun [or Lu Hsün, China's greatest twentieth-century writer]," Yang said. "Deng is not using this place so much now, however." According to Yang, the vice premier increasingly spends his days at still another house, this one in the Western Hills, Peking's exclusive suburb.

Deng's villa on Bright Mountain Street appeared modest compared to a walled residence encompassing a full city block north of Beihai Park. A wall at least twenty feet high, or almost twice the height of Deng's, surrounded this mysterious compound. An overseas Chinese who had lived in Peking several years and agreed to show us around said the place had housed Mao's wife, Jiang Qing, after she and Mao began to go their separate ways. It might still serve as Jiang's occasional prison. Panels have been installed on nearby buildings blocking neighbors' view of the compound, and plain-clothes guards will rush out to inspect any car that pauses too long at the intersection.

To escape the noise of downtown, some leaders, like Deng, choose to live in the suburban splendor of Jade Spring Mountain, a quiet wooded neigh-borhood in the Western Hills which is off-limits to foreigners. It is reached by a side road, off the main road leading tourists and weekend excursionists to the public parks in the Western Hills. The municipal guesthouse-hotel in Tianjin, about seventy miles south of Peking, is another popular weekend retreat and country club for Tianjin and Peking officials. It offers swimming pools, billiard room and sumptuous lounges away from the usual foreign-tourist stops. Red Flag limousines usually jam its entrance.

Many leaders and prominent artists have homes in Beidaihe, a resort on the Bohai Gulf about 165 miles west of Peking. But some have vacated their Beidaihe villas because of the new influx of both foreign and Chinese tourists. "Now most prefer to vacation in Qingdao [a more remote Shan-dong Peninsula resort famous for its beer]," said Lao Zhang, another Chi-nese we knew who was familiar with some of the leading families. "They think it's quieter." In nearly every Chinese city we visited we found a small, usually scenic neighborhood reserved for higher officials. In Canton, it is White Cloud Mountain, with a number of luxurious villas as well as military installations. In Jinan (Tsinan), capital of Shandong province, a taxi driver pointed out the "Hill of One Thousand Buddhas" for us. He indicated the site of a particularly beautiful temple. "Is it open now?" we asked. "Some parts are," he said matter-of-factly, "but this one is for homes for the leadership."

One Chinese we met told us, after extracting a promise we would not identify him in any way, of the time he visited a particularly beautiful Peking villa at the invitation of the son of a general. It had high walls, huge rooms, tiled bathrooms and a beautiful garden full of flowers and trees. But the general's favorite habit after dinner was to lead his son and guests out "to piss in the garden." After his initial shock, our friend saw the experience as a ceremony of honor: "Vice premiers had pissed in that garden. They told me that's the way they did it in Yenan before Liberation."

Such peasant gusto in the Communist hierarchy alternatively enrages and fascinates the Chinese to whom we talked. When leaders venture outside their walled compounds, they travel in shiny black Red Flag limousines, with chauffeurs who honk their way through hordes of bicycles. Lower-level officials ride in slightly less elegant Chinese-made sedans or imported compact cars, mostly Toyotas. One man working in the Trade Bureau told us that by 1980 at least three hundred cars had been sold by the state to private families, though it was hard to distinguish these from the official automobiles which make up most of the auto traffic.

Whatever the make and model of the cars, their side and back windows are usually draped with silk curtains, not unlike the curtains of sedan chairs of the ancient Mandarins. The black or beige silk shields the important travelers from the gaze of the masses. "The curtains are dangerous and a bit ridiculous," admitted a Foreign Ministry official, who professed to be embarrassed that a curtained car came with his recent promotion. "It's the drivers who insist on the curtains. They want the status of driving a curtained car." So great is the craze for curtains among the official Chinese that a new agency head, disappointed at drawing only a secondhand Volkswagen Beetle, insisted on curtains nevertheless.

Privileges extend far beyond this small elite. Anyone who works for the government, including the entire civil service of about 18 million people, is considered a *ganbu,* outranking ordinary men and wielding some degree of authority over others.

Within their "classless" system, the Chinese have devised an elaborate pecking order to decide who gets what. Ordinary factory workers are ranked on an 8-grade pay scale. *Ganbu,* on the other hand, receive their pay and privileges according to a more finely tuned scale of 26 grades. The smaller the peer group, the higher the grade. The dividing line is grade 13, for above that you become a *gaoji ganbu* (high-level cadre), a department head usually. You are then in a position to throw your weight around if you choose. Other professions boast different numbers of grades: 16 for actors, 12 for academics, even 4 for cooks. The army abolished rank insignia in the early 1960s, but people can still identify officers by the four pockets in their jackets instead of the two allotted enlisted men. As one of our more cynical and Westernized acquaintances in the Chinese diplomatic corps said, with an Orwellian wave of his hand, "There are many ranks in the classless society."

An individual's precise standing in this hierarchy determines not only his monthly pay but how many square feet of housing he will be assigned, whether he will travel by car or bicycle, which schools his children will attend and whether he will have access to foreign films and literature. With high enough status, he can call on the expert doctors and medical equipment of Peking Hospital, a restricted facility, or even demand the services of the more exclusive Peking clinic which treated Premier Chou En-lai in his last years. High rank gains access to special flights on British-made Trident jetliners housed at the military airfield in western Peking. We happened to land there by chance on returning from a Defense Ministry tour of Wuhan and Shanghai. At least eight Trident aircraft—with the army marking "8-1" (to denote the August 1 anniversary of the Red Army) inside a red star—sat unused on the tarmac, on call for special trips like ours.

China is a poor country and many of its perquisites seem pedestrian to Americans. Even the availability of telephones and bathtubs is dictated by political position. Only department chiefs and agency heads ordinarily rate either a phone or a tub at home. The more lowly orders must use the public telephone on the corner and are relegated to neighborhood bathhouses for once-a-week soaks.

The bane of a Chinese male's existence—the long wait for a haircut at one of the few available barbershops—does not disturb the ranking *ganbu,* who gets the first available chair no matter how many are waiting. At a shop in Yancheng, Jiangsu (Kiangsu) province, the director of the district Commerce Bureau walked in thirty-five minutes before closing time for his regular trim. He found four chairs occupied, four people waiting and a fifth barber going home, having gotten early leave to take care of some personal business. The barber smiled and asked the bureau director if he would mind coming back the next morning. "So you won't give me a haircut! Let me have your name," the director said, according to the *People's Daily,* which later carried a critical report of the incident. The director stormed out. A few minutes later the shop's immediate supervisor thundered in. "Who the hell are you to turn away the director?" he said. "Have you gone blind?" The barbers quickly offered to cut the man's hair, but it was too late. "This place will be closed tomorrow for a thorough re-evaluation"—meaning, in this case, that the barbers would not be paid.

Even though it would strike most Americans as, at best, comfortably middle-class, the standard of living enjoyed by the average official seems luxurious to most Chinese. A network of special shops and markets carry imported consumer goods and choice foods not available to the general public. Rationing is unknown in these special shops, discreetly tucked away behind unmarked storefronts. Only the Red Flag limousines clustered at the entrance give away the location of Peking's best-stocked grocery store, a five-story building with curtained windows on a side street leading to the Forbidden City. A small sign says: "Peking Food Supply Depot." Admission is limited to those with special passes, who emerge with oranges, chicken and other delicacies. The Hong On clothing shop near the Xinqiao Hotel in the old legation quarter, where special tailoring can be arranged, also admits only special Chinese, as well as anyone with a Western face.

During our time in China three leading government officials, Commerce Minister Wang Lei, Sports Minister Wang Meng and the Foreign Trade Promotion Council Chairman Wang Yaoting, all came to be called, behind their backs, "the three kings of drink." The Chinese pun refers to their huge restaurant bills and the fact that all three were named Wang, meaning "king." Wang Lei got into particularly hot water because he was slow in paying his restaurant tabs. An enraged young cook named Chen Aiwu exposed him. Yet the practice is so widespread that Wang's troubles seemed to cause barely a ripple in the drinks of his high-ranking colleagues. (Wang lost his job in 1982, but the other two "kings" remained in office.)

"People are not happy about privilege, but they feel at a loss, so they save themselves the energy of complaining," one student said. "They are so used to it by now, they sigh and say, 'Well, my *chu shen* [family background] is not good so I can't expect to live like that.' It is so imbedded in everything they do that they think eliminating that part of Chinese society is beyond them."

The government occasionally pursues with some outward diligence its endless campaign against abuse of privilege, but most Chinese shrug their shoulders and joke about it. "The only fat people in China are *ganbu,* at least that's the favorite joke," an American who taught in a northeastern Chinese university told us. "Last winter, when it was so cold, I stuffed all my books inside my thick padded coat and waddled into class. My students had a good laugh. 'I must look pregnant,' I said. 'Oh, no,' they said. 'You just look like a *ganbu.*' "

One day we were leaving the hostel at Yudingmen railway station where hordes of people coming to appeal cases of bureaucratic abuses were put up. A woman tailed after us, desperate to get our attention. "My uncle is a *gaoji ganbu,*" she wailed. Our Chinese companion said to us with a small smile, "If he really is her uncle, I'm sure her problem will be solved very quickly."

Some Chinese blame Confucian tradition for their countrymen's resignation to the continued abuses of privilege. Confucius assigned everyone a place in society and expected each to stay there, accepting all the proper burdens and benefits. Educated Chinese speak of "feudal" influences on society and admit many people are comfortable with them. "The Chinese are the most rank-conscious people I have ever encountered," a Chinese-American scholar remarked to us. "An American notion like 'All men are created equal' is regarded as laughable. Chinese assume that some people are more important than others, and thus are more deserving of special privileges. That's the way it's always been. That's the way it will always be."

During our family's week at the Beidaihe resort on the Bohai Gulf we quickly became accustomed to the pecking order of beaches—one for foreign experts, one for Chinese, and assorted beaches and villas for various government ministers. There was also a special beach for foreign diplomats, including journalists, to be shared with Chinese attached to the Foreign Ministry. Ordinary people who attempted to cross our beach to get to their own received nasty lectures from our Chinese lifeguard. This being the bolder post-Mao era, the beachcombers occasionally cursed him back.

We took careful notice of the people—mostly young Chinese—permitted access to our beach. They laughed and told jokes, dunked one another in the surf and played pirated cassette tapes with sugar-sweet Hong Kong and Taiwan love songs. We struck up a conversation with one young man, assuming he would reveal himself to be the son of a Chinese ambassador posted abroad. "No," he said, "my father is dead. My mother works in a restaurant." He himself was a student in Luoyang, some distance from Peking. How did he get to our beach? Another Luoyang student he had come with had a relative in the Foreign Ministry, and that was all it took. Favors and privilege could be spread around a bit.

Beidaihe is a vestige of imperialist corruption made pure again by passing into Chinese hands. Evan Davis, a tourist from Virginia whom we met at Beidaihe's German-style beer garden, Kiesslings, said he had stayed in Beidaihe in the 1930s when it was still a foreign enclave. Western missionaries like his father and grandfather had built up the place as a summer retreat. The area boasted a posh hotel, the Pine Villa. In that era no natives, not even the wealthy, could enter unless they were part of the staff.

In Lotus Peak Park, a wooded area not far from the beach, we tasted what life is like for the few Chinese prominent enough to enjoy a Beidaihe mansion. The late Lin Biao's mansion is open to visitors. The Chinese want to reveal the shameful luxury he enjoyed, assuming rather naïvely that visitors will not connect his life style with that of current leaders. We saw a huge bathroom and tub, an indoor swimming pool, a sunning room on the roof, and a private screening room. A back door led to a huge underground bomb shelter with a massive steel door protecting access aboveground. What we were being urged to see as obscene opulence seemed shabby (the rugs and furniture had been removed), but a sense of great space, the ultimate Chinese luxury, remained. The house had access to a private beach, as do all the villas scattered about the pine forest that was once off-limits to the public.

In Anhui, during a trip with Maryland's Governor Harry Hughes, we were permitted to view the governor's quarters at Hefei, once used by Mao, and at Yellow Mountain, used by Deng Xiaoping just the year before. Mao's hotel suite included a comfortable set of rooms, with cut flowers and dark paneled walls, but no unusual features except for an enormous, L-shaped bathtub, six feet on each side, and a chaise longue in the bathroom, where he could rest and take a massage before or after a bath. Deng's Yellow Mountain suite was similar—a large living room and four attached bedrooms, with more wood paneling and a chaise longue near the tub.

Three Chinese and a foreign expert told us on different occasions of Deng's reaction when he returned to Beidaihe after Mao's death and found Lotus Peak Park still guarded by soldiers and cut off to all but staff and residents of the villas. "It belongs to the people," Deng declared. So the road was opened to tourists and several villas were assigned to artists and writers, particularly those who had been badly hurt during the Cultural Revolution.

Other privileged areas remain less accessible. Outside Xi'an, the Shaanxi provincial guesthouse sits in a corn- and cotton-growing area. It is closed off to all but visiting officials and foreign dignitaries. We found it during a brief stay in 1979 with the Mondale delegation: a beautiful Chinese Camp David, with graceful little bridges and huge old trees surrounding a pond stocked with fish. Waterfalls cascaded here and there.

Rags-to-riches stories do not occur frequently in socialist China thirty years after its revolution, but there are a few, giving some ambitious souls the idea that they themselves might rise to a position of privilege and ease. We met one playwright who had been an ordinary worker when Mao died. He wrote a play about the ravages of the Cultural Revolution, and after many rebuffs, found an important editor who liked it. He rose to earn $100 a month in royalties, plus his $50 salary—extremely high for someone in his twenties—and had a seemingly limitless expense account. He took trips wherever he pleased in the country, dined in the finest restaurants, shopped at internal bookstores, attended coveted private showings of Western movies and eventually won permission to study abroad.

Three decades of Communism have failed to alter Chinese thinking about the inevitability of privilege. "Communist doctrine may decree that the workers, peasants and soldiers are the vanguard of society, but no Chinese seriously believes that," the young editor of a defunct dissident magazine told us. "We can see who's in the vanguard, and it's not the workers, peasants and soldiers, so people try to get their own privileges."

The area where ordinary people find differences between themselves and the elite most glaring is housing. Former Communist Party Vice Chairman Wang Dongxing, once the bodyguard to Mao Tse-tung, was hounded out of office early in 1980 after it was revealed that he had appropriated $4.2 million in public funds to build himself a palatial residence near Zhongnanhai. The scandal was merely a device of his political enemies, but it did reveal interesting details of his house. The structure, more elaborate than Mao's own house, came complete with gymnasium, cinema and suites for seventeen relatives. Wang's house inspired one waggish Peking bachelor, who could not find himself a wife because he shared a single room with his aged parents, to propose marriage to the Vice Chairman's daughter. "I have never seen your face, but already I am in love with you," the would-be suitor said in a letter, widely reprinted. "Do we get a suite of our own?"

We were never invited to the private home of anyone who could be called a *gaoji ganbu*. Some prominent people we would have thought entitled to large homes, such as star comedian Ma Ji, said they had to make do with two-room apartments like most minor officials. They may have come to prominence too late, after the 1950s, when most of the larger apartments were allotted and further allotments were delayed by political turmoil. One friend of ours, a Chinese-American who enjoyed unusual access to private homes, visited the large Peking apartment of a high-ranking family who had recovered many of these privileges after the Cultural Revolution. The furniture was "reception-room style, some wicker, the sort of things you would buy in the Friendship Store." The upholstery was a little better, however, and fine calligraphy and framed pictures hung on the walls. He saw a small refrigerator and lots of books.

The rule appears to be that *gaoji ganbu* receive at least four or five rooms, while workers are lucky if they get two. A Chinese friend described a Peking apartment which she considered typical for officials of high rank. It had no fewer than three, perhaps as many as five bedrooms and "an enormous" living room. There was a good deal of well-upholstered, almost gaudy furniture, with old chests, antiques, carpets on the floors (some wood floors, some tile), flush toilets and at least two bathrooms (tubs with showers). The extra bathroom fixtures represented extraordinary luxury, since most Chinese usually must heat up the water in kettles and pour it into a wooden tub placed in the middle of the bedroom floor. The apartment had a color television set and a large kitchen. Two elderly women in work clothes were preparing a meal, and although our friend did not ask, he assumed they were paid servants.

Servants are not, in fact, unheard of in Peking. A scholar we knew, working for an archaeological research academy, employed a woman to clean and cook part-time. She was a housewife happy to get some extra money. Several working couples we knew who together earned as much as $100 a month willingly paid the $20 a month to a woman to shop, cook and keep their apartment clean. Many pay a somewhat lower fee to women to watch their children if there are no grandparents at home and no convenient nurseries.

People notice the small signs of special privilege. "The minute I see a bath and shower in an apartment, I know it belongs to a *gaoji ganbu,*" one young office worker in Peking told us. The Chinese become expert at ranking the elite by these visible signs, almost as a game. A Shanghai resident, showing us some of his city, pointed to an apartment building near the U.S. consulate. It was night and we caught a glimpse of color television sets as well as air conditioners. "That means they have to be high officials," our guide said.

No matter how accustomed the Chinese are to this system, there is enough open resentment over official claims of a classless society to cause some *ganbu* and their families embarrassment and make them uneasy. "I heard that a friend had bought a refrigerator, and I made the mistake of asking her about it in front of some other people," one Chinese told us. "She didn't want people to know." Yet a favorite pastime is to take a furtive peek at the watch of any new acquaintance and try to figure out how much it cost: the more expensive, the better. The Chinese cringe at the thought of a cheap watch; it is one of their few status symbols. Jay's successor as

Washington Post Peking correspondent, Michael Weisskopf, had lost his watch, so when he arrived he looked for a cheap, temporary replacement, the Chinese equivalent of the $10 Timex. He visited several shops in Peking but could find no watch, foreign or domestic, for less than $50 and most prices were far beyond that (remember that the average monthly wage for a Peking worker is $40).

A well-connected Chinese who has a fine watch can now find far more exotic status symbols. Since their country made its comeback onto the international scene, Chinese bureaucrats have been seized by a frenzy for foreign travel—but they do not like to go alone. In 1979, for example, the "Sino-Japanese Friendship Boat" sailed to Japan with 600 delegates on board, though, in fact, only 200 were entitled by position to be there. The rest consisted of wives, children and friends who went along for the cruise and a shopping spree in Tokyo. Several were relatives of a prominent Central Committee member, Liao Chengzhi. Unpublicized complaints also arose over Chen Muhua's use of a special plane on a trip to Rumania in 1979. Chen, a vice premier responsible for economic foreign relations, reportedly refused the request for a ride back to China from some touring Chinese athletes who had taken ill.

Abuse of special privileges for officials and their relatives also appears to be rampant in Peking's selection of students for study abroad. A wall poster that appeared early in 1980 on the campus of Peking University charged that of the 268 students chosen from Peking to go overseas, 60 percent were from influential, well-connected families. One Chinese professor familiar with several of the U.S.-bound scholars, including the sons of generals, commented that a number of students in this group were "really stupid. The minute they arrive, it will show."

A few Politburo members have arranged for children and grandchildren to go abroad. Vice Premier Wang Zhen's grandson studied in England. Deng Xiaoping's son-in-law worked at the Chinese embassy in Washington, and Deng's son, Deng Zhifang, studied physics at the University of Rochester. Deng Zhifang managed to acquire a common touch which deflected any criticism. In Peking he was known for his shabby clothes, his ratty book bag and his offbeat sense of humor. After a friend teased him about bringing back a young American wife, Deng said he actually planned to marry a rich widow.

Vice Premier Huang Hua's son enrolled as a Harvard freshman in 1980 and immediately betrayed an unusual upbringing for a citizen of crowded China. He asked his roommates if he could have a room to himself in their suite, because he was not used to sleeping in the same room with other people. He also confessed he had always been taken care of by secretaries and housekeepers, and apologized for being unaccustomed to picking up after himself. His roommates, teen-age American males, smiled and admitted they weren't very good at picking up after themselves either. Huang was also sensitive about his position, asking a *Harvard Crimson* editor, Paul Engelmayer, not to reveal who his father was when the paper published an interview with him.

Some of the well-connected Chinese exchange students, like Huang, are certainly qualified to study abroad. The American professor teaching in Peking who interviewed Huang for Harvard pronounced him a top candidate, with an excellent command of English. But suspicions linger that many unqualified, well-connected students are going abroad. "It is a grave mistake for the Ministry of Education to reserve study abroad for the children of higher-ups," charged a joint faculty-student committee at Peking University in 1980. The group demanded that an independent screening organization be set up to make selections purely on merit. A 1982 regulation banned overseas study by the children of important officials, but U.S. university officials say some still slip through.

In the years since Mao's death, top officials like Deng, through personal conviction or good political sense, appear to have limited special favors for their relatives. Deng Zhifang said he received little money from his father, whom he saw only once a month while in China. The man who became China's new Premier in 1980, Zhao Ziyang, made certain his thirty-one-year-old army officer son, Zhao Jin, was transferred from his comfortable job in Peking to rugged Yunnan near the Vietnamese border, a hardship post.

But many Chinese with important relatives continue to throw their weight around without the slightest bit of self-consciousness. At Zhongshan University in Canton an American teacher objected when several of her students announced that they had tickets to the movie *Zorro* and were going to cut her class. Her department head backed her up, but the student who had gotten the tickets was the daughter of the third-ranking official in the province, and she took the case to a university vice president. The college administrator immediately called a meeting and caucused with other officials for some time. At one point the girl became impatient and stuck her head in the door. "Aren't you finished yet?" she demanded. The meeting adjourned, with the university vice president solemnly announcing that the students could go and see *Zorro*.

Leaders like Liao and the aged National People's Congress president and former General Ye Jianying largely ignored the campaign against special privileges. One or two of Deng's daughters and the daughter of Vice Premier Yu Qiuli were also said to insist on special cars and to encourage fawning admirers. Politburo members Fang Yi and Geng Biao, who have both visited the United States, have been particularly successful at arranging overseas assignments for their children. One of Feng Yi's sons married Geng Biao's daughter and both acquired jobs in Hong Kong, a much-sought-after assignment.

The more extreme and lurid forms of bureaucratic abuse receive more attention in the Chinese press, particularly the sexual exploitation of young women by cadres. The girl friend of one high official's son in Baoding twice had abortions and when she finally suggested marriage, the son said his father would not allow it because she was only an ordinary worker. The father beat up the woman when she complained. The most infamous case, disclosed by the *Observer,* a pro-Peking magazine published in Hong Kong, concerned the male leader of a construction corps in Heilongjiang province which was made up almost entirely of middle-school graduates transplanted from Peking and Shanghai. The corps leader imposed a rule that twice a week the ninety-six girls in his unit would take turns visiting him, their political mentor, so that he could ascertain their "ideological level." His interest, however, did not stop with ideology. He began to boast to friends that "The emperors used to have seventy-two concubines, but I've got ninety-six." The young women were too frightened to complain. Their boss, after all, was empowered to decide when they would return to their families in the city. The racket was eventually discovered and the lecherous boss executed, a sign that Chinese are less tolerant of sexual adventurers than Americans.

The current leadership is clearly disturbed by abuses of privilege, which feed disenchantment with the Communist system. In an editorial, the *Peking Daily* called for "resolute efforts to check and eventually eliminate the unhealthy tendency to seek privileges . . . This tendency is a manifestation of age-old feudalistic ideas and is as incompatible with the character of the socialist system as fire and water. It undermines the party's prestige, weakens its leadership and damages its relations with the masses."

The authorities has backed up this rhetoric with a new disciplinary code that prohibits party members from seeking special housing, job or school assignments for themselves and their relatives. Since those rules went into effect, investigative reporters for local newspapers throughout China have exposed one case of favoritism after another. Several local leaders have been demoted for misusing public funds, and one, who allegedly embezzled $350,000 in state construction funds, was executed. Prosecutors emboldened by the new rules have pressed criminal charges against cadre children for smuggling, rape, assault and other offenses previously ignored out of fear of offending their important fathers. The criminal behavior of the twin sons of a major general who were convicted in Hangzhou of raping more than a hundred women could not have gone on so long without widespread reluctance to report on them.

Any government campaign to clean up corruption and stop privilege will continue to face enormous difficulties. Out of habit, the Chinese help any influential person who can be counted on to return the favor. Even Deng Yingchao, the widow of the upright Premier Chou En-lai, became a soft touch for friends and relatives. And as Zhang Longquan, a young pauper, discovered, anyone cloaked with the aura of a powerful relative finds that doors automatically open, sometimes even without asking.

Zhang's own adventure began innocently enough. He was a penniless but resourceful peasant living illegally in Shanghai. He was dying to go to the theater and see *Much Ado About Nothing*, so he called one of the actresses, identified himself as the director of the Shanghai Communist Party's Propaganda Department and said that the son of Li Da, deputy chief of the People's Liberation Army general staff, needed a ticket. Zhang got the ticket, contrived to meet the cast and officials from the Shanghai Culture Bureau and, a few days later, used the same technique to get into a sold-out musical.

One deceit led to another. Soon Zhang, who was by then calling himself Li Xiaoyong (to conform with Li Da's family name), had ingratiated himself into the city's entertainment and intellectual circles. He frequented the homes of well-known actresses and got himself engaged to the daughter of a former capitalist, moving in with her family just after they recovered part of their fortune confiscated during the Cultural Revolution. The impostor solidified his position by trying a new twist on his old trick. He telephoned the president of Shanghai's Fudan University, and pretending to be Li Da himself, arranged for the use of the university's car. The car opened still more doors to Zhang, for in China, anyone traveling in a private car is by definition a VIP.

Amazingly, Zhang never aroused any suspicion in the high circles in which he was traveling. His joy ride came to an end only when some women who had known him when he was down and out started to wonder about his grand style of living and invisible means of support. They turned him in to the police.

Zhang's exposure inspired a play about his exploits, a television special (canceled at the last moment by Peking officials who had second thoughts about publicizing such *chutzpah*) and a host of fire-breathing editorials. The influential *Enlightenment Daily* denounced Zhang as a "swindler," but reserved its harshest words for the high and mighty he duped. "Those who curried favor, sought patronage, flattered and fawned on this supposedly powerful person and ended up deceived deserve no sympathy," the newspaper said. "Those who were swindled were snobs."

Zhang became a folk hero to many Chinese. Protest marchers and young writers proclaimed support for the great impostor, who maintained that his only crime was that he did not happen to have the right father.

"If I really were Li Da's son," Zhang reportedly told the public security officials who interrogated him, "would any of the things I did be considered a crime?"

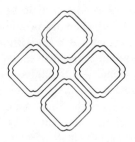

HEALTH

WITH ONE OF THE LEAST EXPENSIVE AND MOST EQUITABLE MEDICAL-care systems in the world, China has become a mecca for foreign health specialists eager to know more about barefoot doctors, acupuncture and centuries-old herbal medicine. But many Chinese carry on a love-hate relationship with their doctors and hospitals. They perceive the medical establishment as indifferent to patients and resort to the old system—*guanxi* and small-scale bribery—to get special attention, special medicines, even sick-leave vacations.

In some parts of Peking, discontent with the medical profession has encouraged individuals who apply herbs, acupuncture or other forms of traditional Chinese medicine to put up small posters advertising their services. The distrust and shortage of regular doctors guarantee them a steady stream of patients, although hospitals also offer traditional medicine.

"Doctors don't take much time to find out what is wrong with you," a Peking University scholar told us. "They just prescribe the first thing that comes to mind—whatever it takes to get rid of you." This is not surprising in a country where so many doctors are poorly trained and underpaid, and see hundreds of people every day in terribly crowded conditions.

Ironically, the cheap, widespread health-care system erected by the Communist Party helped create today's medical difficulties. From 1949 to 1979, life expectancy increased 36 years, to an average of 68.2 years. The death rate declined from 28 to 6.29 per thousand, and the infant mortality rate in Peking plummeted from 117.6 to only 12.8 per thousand. This produced the inevitable: 450 million more people to care for now than there were thirty years ago. The total number of doctors remains little more than half the number in the United States, yet China's population is more than four times as large.

The country has 2.46 million medical personnel, of whom 390,000 are doctors. But the political struggles of the sixties and seventies so disrupted the medical schools that younger physicians have serious gaps in their education. People we met joked about looking for "gray beards or black beards, but never a doctor with no beard." Bolder patients ask the date of their doctor's graduation, and worry if the year is later than 1966, the beginning of the Cultural Revolution.

When struck with serious illness which folk medicine cannot cure, Chinese habitually consult with friends and relatives first, trying to find a clinic where someone knows the doctor and can arrange for them to receive special care and attention. "I had dental problems for a long time, but I could never get the right treatment until I found somebody who knew someone at one hospital. Then they paid attention to me," one office worker told us. A Peking man told the *Enlightenment Daily* what happened when his child contracted a fever while visiting their hometown in Jiangsu. At a hospital where no one knew them, the doctor simply sent the child to a ward without an examination. A day passed before he bothered to examine the child, at which point he diagnosed the illness as meningitis. When the fever soared a week later and the couple could find no doctor on duty at all, they transferred the child to another hospital and, luckily, got much better care.

On the other hand, the Chinese sometimes are so eager to see a doctor that they seem like small children with sniffles and a dislike for school. Many workers will use any excuse for sick leave. Government policy dictates full pay for the first six months of sick leave and 60 percent of pay after that, although factories have begun to check more carefully for false disabilities. When visiting Chinese families, we regularly encountered seemingly vigorous men and women going about their home chores while ostensibly on sick leave. They were happy to be free of the assembly line. A foreign diplomat complained about her own Chinese staff: "For a cold, they take off a week. Of course from their point of view, I'd do the same thing if I was paid so little."

In health, as with other bureaucracies, people have learned to exploit the system and exchange small comforts, which leaves everyone a bit happier. Long-term sick leave requires a doctor's signature. "When you go see the doctor it is best to bring some kind of small gift, maybe a tape cassette with some Hong Kong music on it. He will give you more attention and give you more days off," Linghua, another office worker, told us. Patients in Peking hospitals are often handled by paramedics, who will take them to the doctor's office. These younger aides are susceptible to gifts of cigarettes, particularly foreign brands, and can provide special attention and even sign sick-leave forms. If the illness can be made to seem serious enough, wives or husbands assigned to jobs far from their families can move back home without losing any income. Zheng Lianqun, a Tianjin construction worker, told us that his wife's respiratory ailment allowed her to move down from Jilin and live with him several months of the year. Her factory salary continued to arrive regularly. Use of sick leave declined in some factories after workers with good attendance records began to receive bonuses, but often the bónus was no more than a couple of yuan or so a month, providing no real incentive at all.

Perhaps because of their unpredictable doctors and hospitals, people put great faith in medicines they can administer themselves. Pharmacies are loaded with inexpensive remedies, Chinese herbs as well as Western products. Families hoard whatever prescribed drugs are left over after a family member recovers. Some people trade food or services for additional drugs from nurses and pharmacists who have access to antibiotics and other hard-to-get potions. Dr. Gilbert S. Omenn, a physician who served with the President's Office of Science and Technology Policy in Washington, visited several Chinese medical facilities. "From what I was told and observed, I have little doubt that the Chinese greatly overprescribe medicines of both [Chinese and Western] types," he said.

Chinese patients think Western medicines are unusually potent, with often unpleasant side effects. Their own herbs are gentler, but take longer to effect a cure. Chinese doctors often give massive doses of drugs to foreigners because they want no complaints about inadequate Chinese treatment. However, the Chinese doctors who treated Jay's bronchitis, the product of a severe, freeze-dried Peking winter, appeared reluctant to prescribe strong Western medicine. They seemed relieved when Jay told them he'd like to try some of their herbal remedies for respiratory diseases. The prescriptions called for several herbs to be soaked in water, then drunk like tea. Jay spent several days sipping the bitter potions. Chinese medicine could not change the Peking climate. Jay was not cured until he went to Hong Kong for a spell of warmer, moister air and some Western antibiotics.

Chinese doctors in the last thirty years have been strongly encouraged to experiment with traditional herbal cures. Their successes have led the Chinese to see themselves on the forefront of a great medical breakthrough, all the more satisfactory because they can credit what they have learned to a store of knowledge built up during their illustrious past. The *People's Daily* pointed to 8,000 different volumes on medicine still extant since the Chinese language was invented. The Chinese were even the first, it said, to develop the smallpox vaccine, using human smallpox scabs in the eleventh century.

Accordingly, the Chinese have attracted world attention with their use of acupuncture and medicinal herbs. Chinese hospitals and clinics almost always have at least one room lined with pigeonhole drawer cabinets holding many of the 5,000 herbs in use. Clerks with encyclopedic memories stand by to pluck leaves or roots from the right pigeonhole, just like Chinese typists who must maneuver their 2,000-character trays. Prescriptions include dried gecko lizard for asthma, gallstones of oxen for high fever, dried scorpion or centipede for convulsions and tetanus, dried leech for insomnia, and dried earthworms for high blood pressure. The *Tongrentang,* now 311 years old and one of the apothecaries for the old emperors, survives as a state pharmacy. Here is part of the imperial drugstore's still popular recipe for "tiger bone wine," a medicine with 147 active ingredients prescribed for relief of arthritic pains: "Take 30 special ingredients and steep in sorghum alcohol (such as *maotai*) for ten minutes. Store in cool cellar for six months. Stew tiger bones over slow fire for 88 hours. Mix gelatinous remains with other cooled ingredients, boil for ten minutes, seal into earthen jars and store for 12 months before using."

The Chinese swear by such cures. Western doctors wonder if Chinese treated with herbs might improve simply because they have great confidence in the medicine and the doctors, mind healing matter. The Chinese have been reluctant to test herbal medicines with Western control procedures, such as giving some patients placebos. Many Chinese doctors, firm believers in the herbs, say it would be unethical to deprive patients of genuine treatment. Humane or short-sighted, this attitude hinders Chinese medical research, but some Western doctors see verifiable results from certain herbs. Wood ears, a common ingredient in the popular Chinese restaurant dish mooshu pork, seem to lessen the risk of heart disease. Garlic appears useful in treating meningitis.

Americans throw money at medical and scientific riddles. In their village of one billion, the Chinese throw people. They now have thousands of researchers collecting data on tens of thousands of possible combinations of herbs as cures for disease. In cancer research, the Chinese blanketed key areas like Linxian County with data collectors and interviewers in order to trace a locally based esophageal cancer. More than 10,000 Chinese men are taking an experimental contraceptive made from cottonseed oil. Western scientists have come to admire this research and wish they had such manpower. The Chinese wish they had more Western computers to store and integrate all their herbal data.

There is no shortage of Western admirers of acupuncture as an anesthetic either. In Wuhan we watched a middle-aged woman smile gamely and drink orange juice while a surgeon poked around in her brain. In Canton we saw a surgical team scrape a tumor out of the neck of a male peasant, conscious and talking. The acupuncture needles used in both operations clearly deadened the pain and, we were told, allowed a faster recovery than chemical anesthetics would. David Eisenberg, a Harvard Medical School student who spent a year studying and practicing medicine in Peking, said patients seeking acupuncture cures for ailments such as chronic backaches rarely enjoyed startling improvements. Foreigners we knew who tried acupuncture for head and neck aches said they received only temporary relief, if any. Eisenberg said he was interested in patients who seemed uncomfortable without their acupuncture treatment, suggesting they might be addicted to the needles. Some doctors think acupuncture works by stimulating natural morphinelike substances in the body.

The Chinese accept acupuncture far more readily than foreigners do, but this may be because Chinese doctors are reluctant to use any anesthetics at all, which makes their patients grateful for what they can get. Drugs are expensive and, in the Chinese view, interfere with natural processes like pain. In China, small operations like abortions or tooth extractions are often done without anesthetic.

One Peking office worker we knew had a toothache that would not go away. He decided to see a dentist for the first time in his life, not without some trepidation. His family and friends never went unless they were in pain, and after a few minutes in the dentist's chair he began to understand why. "I can't find anything wrong," the dentist said after examining him. Three or four other dentists were in the same room, working on other patients in various stages of discomfort, all of which he could easily see and hear. Suddenly, without further consultation or anesthetic, his dentist began to drill one of his teeth.

"Why are you doing that?" he asked, when he caught his breath. "I think you have a cavity," she said. "Stop flopping around. This is painless!"

The tooth was drilled and filled, but the pain persisted. The patient vowed thereafter to avoid dental treatments, particularly after overhearing his dentist say to a colleague as he left, "I really didn't see anything wrong, but figured he would feel better if I drilled."

Having heard this story from the victim, Jay did not exactly rush over to the Capital Hospital, a treatment center for foreigners and Chinese living in central Peking, to get a dental checkup. Dr. Liu Cuifeng, a small bespectacled woman who graduated from Shanghai's Second Medical College in 1965 (Jay noted the date with relief), examined him in a small room. The equipment seemed similar to if somewhat older than what we had seen in American and Hong Kong dentists' offices. Jay asked about an anesthetic. "We give it only if we must drill near the pulp of the tooth"—the dentist glanced at Jay's face—"or if the patient is especially nervous." Dr. Liu carefully poked around Jay's teeth. "You have fifteen cavities," she announced. The patient shuddered. "But they are all filled, and the rest seem fine."

There had been no wait to see Dr. Liu, a testament perhaps to the general Chinese aversion to dentists, or as Dr. Liu pointed out, their good teeth. "Chinese teeth are usually better than foreigners' teeth. The Chinese don't have so much sugar in their diet," she said.

The visit cost Jay $1.35, a not negligible amount in terms of average Chinese earnings, but for office and factory workers—almost everyone working in Chinese cities—the larger part of their medical care is free. Medical bills for rural Chinese are paid for them if their communes have sufficient profits.

The system does not always provide for severe or unusual medical problems. Peking worker Xu Wenxiang found that his wife required several operations to treat her tuberculous peritonitis and tuberculosis of a kidney. The medical bills added up to about $2,700. This was at least five years' wages for Xu and his factory would only pay half, though it gave Xu a subsidy to help him through the financial difficulties. We know of no instances in which Chinese were refused care because of lack of money, but these bills may contribute to a complaint often voiced by doctors: people with serious illnesses wait too long to seek treatment.

Just getting to a hospital—particularly in an emergency—presents great difficulties to ordinary Chinese. In the countryside it is next to impossible to move people quickly to a modern medical facility. In emergencies, peasants may transport a patient by cart, hooked up to a tractor. Otherwise they have to wait for the bus or balance the patient on the back of a bicycle. In the cities the situation is not much better. "You can often see people carrying children or old people seemingly near death on a bicycle to the hospital," said Yutai, a Peking factory worker. "That's one reason why we Chinese like to have more children, so you have someone to take you to the hospital."

Once a Chinese patient reaches a hospital, care is often erratic and slow. Often there are long waiting lines similar to those found at emergency rooms in big-city hospitals in the United States. But unlike medical facilities in the United States, Chinese hospitals are poorly staffed and relatively unconcerned about security and disease control, so relatives are usually allowed to stay with the patients and do most of the nursing themselves. Doctors admit that you often cannot tell the staff from the patient's relatives. And hospitals have acquired a bad reputation for being unsanitary. When Hou Ying took Peter to the Capital Hospital for treatment of a bad cold, they had to sit in the waiting room for some time. After collecting his medicine and returning home, Hou insisted that we immediately undress the child, give him a bath and change his clothes. "You can't tell what kind of germs you might pick up in that place," she said.

Not surprisingly, Americans accustomed to the spotless conditions exacted by U.S. medical units are sometimes dismayed to discover that the Chinese put less stock in cleanliness. Aline Mosby, one of the first two United Press International correspondents to live in Peking, spent six days in 1980 at the Capital Hospital being treated for bronchitis. She was in the wing used for foreigners, with the best available care and facilities, yet her sheets, pajamas and one hand towel were never changed while she was there. Hot water was available only two hours each morning, and was never really warm enough for a bath. Patients washed in the sink. Each day a man came to her room to wipe the bed and other furniture clean of dust, the product of the winds from the treeless north that sweep the city each winter. Foreign students complain that they cannot get into even the Capital Hospital but are shunted to the Peking Number Three Hospital, whose facilities, they say, are much inferior, including prevalent cockroaches and infrequent cleaning.

As orderly as the Chinese try to be, old habits and the shortage of electricity and hot water in their homes help spread infection. We saw warnings posted of hepatitis and meningitis outbreaks. Medical authorities declined to give figures, although some admitted that in 1977 they had as many as 30,000 cases of hepatitis in Canton. In universities we saw students quickly lick or wipe clean their own bowls, with no soap or hot water, and put them on a shelf to be used at the next meal. Visiting foreign doctors notice that rural doctors and nurses often used only alcohol to clean instruments such as acupuncture needles. American doctors Frederick Li and Elaine Shiang concluded after a three-month stay in China that this was not enough to protect against hepatitis "B." That disease is associated with the development of liver cancer, cause of about 100,000 deaths annually in China.

For two decades China has boasted that its health-care system has been able to handle more people than any other in history because of the use of "barefoot doctors." These are mostly young people, given three months' training in first aid and diagnosis of common diseases. They take responsibility for preliminary medical care in their villages. Recently, however, the government has admitted that there is room for improvement in the program. "We were told that much of the time the barefoot doctor will just refer a patient to a county hospital, or the patient doesn't trust the barefoot doctor and demands a referral, so now the county hospitals are in a mess," said one U.S. health specialist who toured Chinese medical facilities.

Chinese health authorities say they are now giving these youths more training. Many are being tested to ascertain that they know what they are doing. But most Chinese persist in diagnosing and treating their own illnesses and acquire their own stock of unauthorized antibiotics by exchanging them for movie tickets or special foods with barefoot doctors.

One highly popular self-prescribed drug is tobacco. Cigarettes have a whole range of alleged medicinal uses, such as helping Chinese diplomats "think on their feet." The deluge of colorful cigarette packages—one thousand different brands—puts Madison Avenue to shame. China, Butterfly, Golden Deer, Mudan, Shanghai, Chungchow, Panda, Peony, Golden Orchid and Sailing Boat are just a few of them. Sailing Boat is advertised as impregnated with herbs for "allaying asthma and relieving cough."

As in the United States, Chinese doctors sometimes seem even more wedded to nicotine than their patients are. Five successive "stop smoking" campaigns have gone almost nowhere. Many Chinese point to their long-lived political leaders who smoke, and shrug off the cancer threat. Mao chain-smoked. Deng Xiaoping is rarely seen without a cigarette. High-level government meetings in Peking always generate a blue haze.

This is generally a male pastime, with only a few women taking part. The No. 143 Middle School in Peking reported that 80 percent of its boys smoked before 1978, and that an antismoking campaign eliminated smoking "on school grounds." But their smoking probably continued. A Peking public health official, Sun Yufu, admitted that "adults start smoking again a few days after they give up the habit." When visiting American dignitary Charles Yost declined a cigarette offered by Chou En-lai, the Chinese Premier noted that U.S. cigarette packs carry a health warning. Deadpan, Chou delivered a little advice from Confucius: "A wise ruler never passes a law that he knows his people will not obey." A pair of prominent Chinese doctors, Huang Jiaxi and Li Zhongbu, promised a full-scale campaign against smoking in 1978. They blamed—surprise of surprises—the Gang of Four for sabotaging antismoking campaigns prior to 1978 "for their own crass political motives." But this antismoking campaign too disappeared from sight.

The tobacco industry is big business in China—some years the Chinese lead the United States in production of cigarettes. But the tobacco quality is often poor, and the better brands are far too expensive, in the opinion of many. The doorman at one dormitory of the Peking Languages Institute, like many older Chinese, resorted to smoking marijuana because he could not afford good tobacco. Marijuana grows wild throughout the countryside, mostly ignored by the Chinese but sought out by foreign students who try to overlook its poor quality.

Along with this sanguine attitude toward tobacco consumption comes an increase in cardiovascular disease. Chinese doctors say heart disease has become the leading killer in northern cities, as it is in the United States. Like American physicians, they blame smoking, stress and hypertension.

The tensions of city life are also held responsible for the increased number of psychiatric patients admitted to the few mental hospitals. The Chinese remain very reluctant to treat the mentally or emotionally ill in institutions. They prefer to keep them at home. During a tour of the Shanghai Psychiatric Hospital we met Dr. Xia Zhenyi, a jovial sixty-five-year-old who had worked at New York's Payne Whitney Psychiatric Clinic in the 1940s. As the Shanghai clinic's psychiatry chief, Xia supervises care of 1,000 patients and 500 outpatients who come to get their medication daily. He prescribes the same antipsychotic, antidepressant and antianxiety drugs used in the West, but in smaller doses. "We can do this because we keep the patient longer than you do—two to three months, compared to two to three weeks in your case," he told a group of visiting Americans. Unlike most modern U.S. hospitals, the Chinese use electric shock and insulin shock in severe cases among the 80 percent of patients who are diagnosed as schizophrenic. This is far higher a percentage of schizophrenics than in the United States; more American patients tend to suffer from depression.

In one room of the clinic we saw three men undergoing electro-acupuncture treatment for schizophrenia. Pink wires running from a small machine on the table between them and taped to their foreheads carried six to nine volts. Like most of the patients, they wore rumpled white pajamas turned gray from many washings. They stared vacantly, a sign of the heavy sedation. At the end of our clinic visit, arranged for by then U.S. Secretary of Health, Education and Welfare Joseph Califano, several patients and staff put on a minstrel show, including their rendition of "Oh, Susanna."

The clinic occupied a large pleasant compound of four-story buildings connected by wooden sidewalks. It had been established in 1958, and emphasized modern methods of supplementing drugs with recreation and occupational therapy. We saw patients working at tables making doll faces and matchboxes for sale to state stores.

But relatively few people come to the clinic, for the Chinese, both doctors and patients, would prefer to attribute odd behavior and feelings to something other than mental or emotional illness. Mental illness may be even more of a stigma in China than it is in the West. Disturbed patients prefer home care, for no other reason than to prevent questions from the neighbors about their absence. One patient in Shanghai confessed to us her fear of coming to the clinic. "But now I know everyone is my friend and the doctors take us to see films and television or on long walks and I feel better staying here than staying at home."

Even worse than the dread of being labeled mentally ill is the aversion to any public admission of dissatisfaction with the political or social system. Such confessed inability to adjust can slow job advancement, inhibit friends and relatives and lead to public criticism and ridicule if the moribund Maoist system of singling out misfits revives. As a result, general practitioners we spoke with noted that a common ailment in China these days is "weakness of the nerves," a catch-all phrase for headaches, loss of sleep and vitality, anxiety or irritability. Some doctors who have conversed with such patients find that they have social and political problems such as demanding parents, a spouse working in another city, or an old, unresolved political black mark on their personal record. One doctor said, "If they can turn those complaints into a medical problem, they become easier to deal with because a health problem has nothing to do with criticism of the government or one's family. Patients and doctors go ahead and treat them as physical illnesses, without ever addressing what might be the root cause."

Under the Chinese system, the urge to screen such problems from official notice—a corollary of the *guanxi* system—probably delays help for many. But in recent history the Chinese have had such bad luck with official cures for emotional troubles that their reticence is understandable. Pleading "weakness of the nerves" at least invites the attention of a medical doctor, who can suggest medication or prescribe a rest from work, which may do some real good.

The Cultural Revolution, in temporarily aborting so much of the *guanxi* system which helped the Chinese find realistic solutions to their problems, also ruptured the system for mental health care. At the height of the political madness, mental illness was officially designated an ideological shortcoming, a crime against Mao requiring re-education and persuasion rather than medication and therapy.

A psychiatrist at the Shanghai clinic told two earlier visitors, American University field staff members Dr. James C. Strickler and Norman N. Miller, that he was forced to take this to the logical extreme. By his calculations, he spent months—a total of more than 1,000 hours of therapy by his count—doing nothing but talk about Maoist ideology with one disturbed patient. The patient, he concluded, was in worse condition at the end of the treatment than at the beginning.

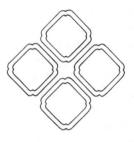

CRITICS

PEKING WAS SLIDING INTO A VERY COLD WINTER THE NIGHT IN 1979 when we met Liu Qing. We had groped our way over small mounds of coal almost invisible in a courtyard lit only by the faint glow from some apartment windows. As usual, we surprised the editors of the unofficial *April Fifth Forum* chatting in their tiny makeshift office. There was no way to call ahead. Few Chinese have home telephones.

Short and stocky, with a mop of black hair brushed back from his forehead, dirty hands and the usual worker's garb of faded blue jacket and slacks, Liu quickly got down to business. "We have more information about the trial," Liu said. He was riding high, gathering information few people in town had access to. China's great dissident hero that season, Wei Jingsheng, editor of the magazine *Explorations,* had just been sentenced to fifteen years in prison for espionage, and Liu had somehow acquired a tape recording of the trial, which had been closed to all but a hand-picked audience of Chinese office workers.

While we sipped hot, bitter tea, holding the old mismatched cups with both hands to keep warm, Liu told us what he knew; he was self-assured, certain that he and other dissidents would have some impact on the Communist Party. We didn't know then that this was the last time we would see him. He was arrested two months later, after he decided to take the blame for the unauthorized release of a transcript of the Wei trial. He did it so that the police would free younger magazine workers who had been arrested for selling the transcript. After we left Peking, Richard Bernstein of *Time* magazine and Michael Weisskopf of the *Washington Post* discovered a "manuscript" by Liu that had been smuggled out of the labor camp in Shanxi where he had been sent. It said he had been kept in solitary confinement in a Peking jail for five months. His long dark hair fell out in clumps and his eyesight deteriorated so badly that he could not distinguish figures in a photograph. But he resisted the persistent advice of his interrogator: "Just admit your mistakes. Being obstinate will do you no good."

Nine months after his arrest he was finally sentenced to three years at the Shanxi labor camp, Lotus Flower Temple. Up to the time that he finished the manuscript he was forced to carry large rocks, working behind the high walls and electrified barbed-wire fences of the enclosure. In the manuscript he still insisted: "I want to fight until the day I can no longer fight."

A year before we met him, when he visited his brother in Peking in 1978, he had got caught up in the excitement of the democracy movement. Many things led him into an infatuation with the ideas of the West. His father had worked in the U.S. embassy before 1949. His own university education at Nanjing had been followed by a dull factory job in Shanxi. He, perhaps more than anyone we met, embodied the spirit of China's little democracy movement. Bored, naïve, ambitious, earnest, reckless—Liu was infected with the growing desire among young Chinese to speak up about where the twentieth century was taking them.

Certain Chinese can be ingenuous about free speech in a way that frightens those who remember what such candor cost them in the past. "We Chinese people want more human rights; we are grateful to your President Carter for this human rights campaign, but you ought to look at China more," a young man once said who thought we were tourists. A note passed to *London Daily Telegraph* correspondent Nigel Wade from a well-known dissident, Yang Guang, expressed a charming enthusiasm: "I love all the people who agree with freedom, happiness, democracy and peace. If you are such a man, not only interested in our activities out of a necessity of your occupation and a legal obligation, but also (more important) out of a heartfelt loving and believing in freedom, democracy and happiness of mankind, I'll be very glad to meet you again." Yang's father had studied engineering at a U.S. school in the late 1940s; the sympathy for Western ways was already there. But the young democracy activists were not just parroting the West. They expressed grievances appreciated by hundreds of thousands of Chinese, at least those living in cities.

We had always considered the democracy movement a small effort with little mass support. But the popular outcry after Wei Jingsheng was given a fifteen-year sentence on what appeared a trumped-up espionage charge astonished us. An unofficial poll of students at Peking University found a majority disagreeing with the severity of Wei's sentence. The letters editor at the *People's Daily* told us he received a deluge of signed protest letters which, fortunately, he decided not to hand over to the police. In the audience of a play extolling youthful 1976 rioters against the Gang of Four, an actor playing a policeman called one of the youths "just another counterrevolutionary." Someone said audibly and sarcastically from the audience, "Just like Wei Jingsheng!"

A few young dissidents such as Wei turned against the Communist Party too harshly and too quickly—their wall posters were too crude and disrespectful—assuming that a groundswell of public resentment toward bureaucratic abuses and political intrigue would make them heroes and give China a new revolution. They were naïve, but they did touch a core of bitterness and political unrest within many Chinese, a desire for more frank talk and fewer orders from above: yearnings a lot of us who had studied China from abroad were not sure still existed. The very existence of the democracy movement gave many people a chance to reveal in some way feelings they found very difficult to express. Frank Ching, the *Wall Street Journal* correspondent, found himself chatting with a worker in the crowd of curiosity seekers outside the trial of another dissident, Fu Yuehua. Fu Yuehua had organized a peasant march by petitioners from the countryside and had complained that she herself had been raped and otherwise mistreated by her construction company supervisor. "What do you think of the trial?" the worker asked.

"I don't know what to think, since I can't get in," Frank replied. "What do you think?"

"It is not convenient to say."

"Is there freedom of speech in China?"

"There is supposed to be."

"As a worker, are you the master of the country?"

"You can say that."

"As the master of the country, don't you have freedom of speech?"

The worker pointed at one of the guards keeping people out of the courthouse. "*He*'s the master of the country."

The hand-picked audience at Fu's trial included legal affairs workers and judges from Peking and elsewhere who might have been expected to support Fu's judge and prosecutors. Instead, they applauded her denial of the charge of leading the demonstration. One judge, observing the trial from the audience, accused the presiding judge of being prejudiced against the defendant. When a government witness testified in support of Fu's work supervisor, an elderly man rose in the audience, said he knew the witness and called him a hooligan. The old man was a member of a powerless but prestigious official group of prominent personalities, the People's Political Consultative Congress, and his comment caused a mild uproar.

We encountered other private expressions of democratic yearning in China that surprised us. In Shanghai an official tour guide, the most cautious of acquaintances, accepted an invitation for a chat in our hotel room. He said bitter things about the Communist Party, all the more astonishing since at the very young age of twenty-six he was already a party member. "People say that if the Guomindang [the Kuomintang, or Nationalist Party] came back and staged a coup d'état, nobody would respond to them. But they also say that if the Communists lead a new movement, nobody will support them either." In Kunming a small group of students latched on to us, and they talked of their displeasure with the late Mao Tse-tung's Cultural Revolution.

We also encountered some dramatic dissents. Suicides, always a common form of protest in Asian nations, flared up again while we were in Peking. The Cultural Revolution had produced uncounted numbers of such politically inspired suicides. They occurred again among the thousands of "petitioners" who came to Peking to ask government officials to remove old taints on their records and restore their jobs, homes and pensions. In the summer of 1979 one petitioner jumped into the canal near the Yudingmen railway station, a temporary living space for petitioners. A young woman on the verge of being arrested at the main tourist gate near the Forbidden City for selling plastic tumblers—a favorite source of income for petitioners—jumped into the old imperial moat and was drowned. The Peking subway, another haven for petitioners, had to close for two hours when a man killed himself by lying down on the tracks in front of an incoming train. A petitioner from Sichuan named Zhao Xinrong unsuccessfully tried suicide by poison after Peking public security officials refused to hear his complaints. We heard about these acts from other petitioners; the official press did not report them.

Out in the provinces, where such protests are not so embarrassing to the central government, suicides even received some official notice from Peking. Two young women workers in Wuxi were praised after both took poison to expose their corrupt supervisor. He had tried to force one of them to marry his son and disciplined the other because she had reported a foreman who had arrived at work late. Fan Xiongxiong, a worker at the fishing company in Ningbo, was posthumously admitted to the Communist Party in 1980 for drowning herself in the ocean, to protest the misdeeds of her boss, who had illegally arranged good jobs at the company for several officials' relatives. We learned during a visit to Shanghai that youths working on state farms near the city had gone on strike. A few had committed suicide when they were told they would not be allowed to rotate back to work in the city as they had expected.

Suicides suggest grievances ignored or too troubling to express. The Chinese always strained to avoid confronting the authorities directly. In 1979 and 1980 what struck us as most remarkable about the wall-poster writers and speechmakers was how few of them attacked the government or party at all. The young Chinese who ventured to express themselves openly in the late seventies and early eighties were the most cautious and overtly pro-government protesters we had ever encountered. A symbol of this oddly patriotic protest might be a light-fixture repairman named Xu Wenli, who in the course of our several long talks also became something of a friend.

Xu (sounds like "shoe") was an endlessly cheerful, youthful-looking man in his thirties with a lock of hair that often fell over his forehead. He told one of the first interviewers to visit him in 1979 that some of the young people in the democracy movement were ignoring "the national condition

of China" in their rush to open the country's borders and remove government restrictions on births. When Washington and Peking were negotiating
diplomatic relations, Xu sounded like a member of the party Politburo:
"President Jimmy Carter was very adept at playing this human rights issue
like a card in his hands. To avoid being placed in a disadvantageous position
in the diplomatic struggle, we hope that some of those childish youths in
our country would refrain from talking about those issues so we can maintain the dignity of our country."

Xu and a staff of about twenty, including Liu Qing, produced seventeen
issues of their magazine, the *April Fifth Forum*. Each month Xu took the
latest issue of the fifty- to sixty-page journal and gave it to his shop supervisor at the Peking Railway Bureau, who accepted the magazine without
comment. At one point he asked Xu if he wasn't working too hard, but there
was never more than that faint suggestion that Xu give up the magazine.
In late 1979 Xu, who suffers from a heart ailment, was on sick leave, like
many other movement activists taking advantage of easy rules for such
leaves at their factories. Later, he said, his heart problem eased and he went
back to work, where his general good will and conscientiousness may have
spared him any harassment. At night and on Sundays he would hole up in
his 12-by-12-foot cubicle, one of two rooms assigned his family in an old,
filthy walk-up apartment building in the southeastern part of the city off
Baiguang Road. There he would compose another gentlemanly attack on
the bureaucratic and legal flaws of the Chinese government.

We had brief, pungent tastes of the salad days of the democracy movement during trips to Peking in January and May 1979, when the government
was still tolerating the wall posters as a way to weaken the position of Mao
holdovers in the government. But we did not move permanently to Peking
until June, after the movement had passed its peak. Only the *April Fifth
Forum* and a few other magazines were still publishing; posters on Democracy Wall, as the young writers called it, had lost their bite. In our last
months in Peking, the movement became even more moribund. Xu and his
colleagues, along with all the other unofficial publishers in Peking we knew,
stopped selling their magazines after police and officials reminded them that
they were not registered, implying that stronger measures might be taken
if they did not desist. They continued to print articles, but only for "internal
reference," distributed free to their friends and old subscribers. That small
bit of defiance apparently brought their eventual downfall. In April 1981 Xu
was arrested, after staying one careful step ahead of the authorities for so
long. Held incommunicado for many months, he was finally sentenced to
fourteen years in prison. Democracy Wall and its successor, an officially
sponsored wall-poster wall in northwest Peking at Yuetan Park, closed
completely when the leadership removed the troublesome, Mao-inspired
clause from the constitution that guaranteed the right to put up such
posters.

Democracy in China was, and is, an odd, contradictory movement. The government and its handful of young critics, quietly backed by some unseen supporters of freer speech in the leadership, play an intricate, political badminton match. They watch each other for any false moves while observing makeshift rules that keep some free discourse flying back and forth. It is, as Xu Wenli was always quick to point out, a situation very different from the harsh adversary relationship between dissidents and the government in the Soviet Union or Poland. In fact, Xu and most other movement leaders did not like to be called dissidents at all.

When we asked about their relationship to party bosses, Xu said, "We are at the grass-roots level, while they are at the leadership level. We look at problems from different angles, but we hope that we can cooperate with them by supervising one another in our common effort to solve the problems of China." Unlike Jews in the Soviet Union, Peking's democracy movement activists do not belong to disadvantaged minority groups. They are ethnic Chinese, with the usual Chinese instinct for keeping disputes in the family. One of the more arresting sights for us was a group of fifty or sixty petitioners from the countryside, dressed in filthy blue and black rags, sitting down in protest before the main automobile entrance to Zhongnanhai, the party and government office compound. The slogan they shouted at the perplexed guards was: "Long live the Chinese Communist Party. Long live the People's Republic." Older protesters, even younger men like Xu, can still remember 1957. Thousands of government critics were sent to labor camps that year; thousands more went in the late 1960s. The cardinal sin committed by Wei Jingsheng, one of the handful of movement leaders to be publicly punished, was to criticize party leaders by name. He suggested in his magazine, *Explorations,* that the party no longer had any business running China, something Xu Wenli never did.

Xu began publishing in November 1978. There was a burst of excitement then after the party reversed itself and said the youthful protesters who had rioted in Tiananmen Square and put up any antigovernment slogans on April 5, 1976, had been justified. Xu and a friend merged their first effort, the *April Fifth Post,* with another small publication, the *People's Forum.* Their staff and readership quickly grew.

When several movement leaders, including Wei, were arrested in late March and early April 1979, Xu's magazine defended them. It argued that socialism could withstand such irritants. Xu remained similarly forthright, though cautious, when the police came around to inspect his tiny, dusty apartment, which served as the magazine's headquarters. "In some respects they exceeded the scope of ordinary inspection, asking all present their names, addresses and work units," he said. "We hope this error was the work of a local police official with insufficient understanding of the political situation, rather than the . . . intent of senior party leaders."

Wei Jingsheng was charged with passing military information about the

Sino-Vietnamese war to an unnamed foreigner and making counterrevolutionary statements. "Before the trial we were very careful in our writing about the case," Xu said, "but after the trial we had a clear understanding that Wei's problem was only an ideological problem and that he should not have been arrested . . . A few of our leaders are incapable of leading the people to attain a higher living standard, so they try to restrain the people. Yet it is precisely the people's never-ending demand for a better life that propels the society forward. The socialist system has many good points, but we must realize that the system has not yet reached the stage of perfection."

Xu and his staff were mostly blue-collar workers, ranging in age from twenty-two to thirty-six. Young men and a few women ran most of the two dozen magazines that bloomed in 1978 and 1979. Xia Xunjian, a forty-three-year-old freelance translator, edited *Reference News for the Masses* (not to be confused with the official *Reference News*) out of his tiny room near Peking University. He said students and intellectuals with office jobs, whom we expected to find running such publications, "are less interested in the democracy movement because they enjoy high social status now and tend to concentrate on their work and their studies," particularly the college entrance examination.

When we stopped by the *April Fifth Forum* office we would often find a peasant from the suburbs, a tall, long-faced and friendly man in his forties. He inked the plastic sheets on which the characters had been scratched and put them on the old wooden frame mimeograph for printing. He was a friend of one of the staff members, and was paid for his work. Xu had bought the mimeograph machines for $3.30 after getting a letter of permission from a friendly supervisor at his Railway Bureau office. Some months the machine would turn out a thousand copies or more of the thick magazine.

The magazine office had been a sitting room and second bedroom for Xu, his wife, a quiet, pleasant woman who worked in a factory, and their seven-year-old daughter, Xingxing. The room was usually littered with stacks of paper. Photos of the late Chairman Mao, a source of controversy within the magazine, as well as pictures of the late Premier Chou and of Xingxing, were displayed on the wall, along with distribution charts for the magazine. We noticed in particular a snapshot of a young couple. "Our first *April Fifth Forum* marriage," said Xu proudly. The two staff members had met and married while putting out the magazine. "Quite a number of people are willing to work for us," he went on, "but if we have too many people, there is not enough room for them to sit down." The young staff, most of whom had full-time jobs elsewhere, put out the magazine in a series of frantic late-night sessions. Some were Communist Party and Youth League members; one or two had fathers who were upper-middle-level officials. Xu insisted that this had nothing to do with the magazine's ability to survive when several unofficial publications were shut down in 1979. The magazine paid the peasant printer a small salary and split whatever few dollars remained among the staff. The magazine sold for only about thirty-three cents a copy, and almost all the revenue went for paper and mailing costs; there were about 200 subscribers. The rest of the copies were sold at Democracy Wall, or to people like us who stopped by the office.

These young people embraced what were to them intriguing notions of democracy and free speech in China. But we sensed, from talking to several, that they also loved working for the unofficial publications because of the rare chance to demonstrate their talent as writers. These were young people who had failed to win one of China's very few university places, and so they had had to suppress their dreams of becoming scholars, novelists or journalists.

Xu's own intellectual ambitions go back to an essay he wrote as a middle school graduate in 1963. "I Demand Self-Study" was the title. He wanted to study social science on his own, despite family demands that he get a job or try to go to college. He did not get into a university. His father, who had been a doctor and an intellectual and might have helped prepare his son for college, had died in an automobile accident when Xu was eight. Instead, Xu joined the army, working as an aircraft mechanic and learning enough to qualify as an electrician when he was discharged and assigned to the Railway Bureau. As a soldier in the 1960s, Xu was protected from the political rampages of the Cultural Revolution. As a demobilized soldier at the Railway Bureau, he enjoyed the special prestige and responsibilities reserved for former army men. This probably gave him some of the confidence he needed to try publishing a magazine. On April 5, 1976, when young rioters stormed through Tiananmen Square in protest of the official removal of wreaths honoring the memory of Premier Chou, Xu was "only an observer." But the purge after Mao's death of the radical leaders who suppressed the riot and an official vindication of the riot in 1978 seemed to many young Chinese a mandate for more open protest. Democracy Wall went into high gear and Xu began writing and publishing.

Xu's family always made him vulnerable. He and his wife were devoted to their little girl, a bright and rather active child whose name means Little Star. Xingxing was good at taking messages. We sometimes found her bundled up and asleep on the office cot when we stopped by in the afternoon. When we brought Joe with us a couple of times, the Xus seemed delighted. Xingxing took Joe off to show him her few toys. In Xu's little office, we once began to leaf through a technical-goods manual, only to find it was the family photo album. The tool diagrams were covered by small snapshots of Xingxing, taken by the photographers who inhabit Peking's parks.

As the democracy movement retreated, Xu seemed to realize that he might be arrested and separated from his wife and child. He betrayed small moments of uncharacteristic nervousness about us. He would carefully tape-record our conversations, often reprinting them verbatim in the magazine or in what he called his own "internal materials." This was no compliment to our questions; he wanted the authorities to know he was hiding nothing, a precaution that did him little good in the end.

We never were able to come up with an accurate count of the active participants in the democracy movement. Xu said he received a hundred letters a month, almost all from democracy supporters. He carried on an active correspondence with editors of small unofficial papers in out-of-the-way cities like Baoding and Hefei, which we foreigners were rarely allowed to visit. Shanghai had active groups of wall-poster makers and unofficial magazine writers. Four unofficial magazine editors were detained briefly in Canton in late 1980 when they tried to organize a national journal. Such activists probably numbered throughout the country no more than a few thousand, but they reflect simmering frustrations felt by millions of educated Chinese. Many people are tired of three decades of clumsy Communist bureaucracy and repression.

There have been other moments of protest in recent Chinese history. In 1898 a few reformers persuaded the twenty-seven-year-old emperor to issue a series of edicts pushing China to emulate the West. They included a broadened education system, more study abroad and a modernized military. But after only a hundred days, the emperor's formidable aunt, the Empress Dowager Tz'u-hsi, put a stop to it. Democratic reformers enjoyed some brief popularity again after mass demonstrations protesting territorial concessions made to Japan by a weak Chinese military government after World War I. When the Communist Party took over, Mao experimented in 1957 with encouraging public criticism of his administration. Then he cut off this Hundred Flowers movement and put thousands of outspoken critics in jail when attacks on the party itself had become too intense.

Each of these brief outbursts helped the Chinese see more clearly the potential for change. But the democracy movement of 1979 and 1980 contained several new elements. The presence of nearly a hundred foreign journalists living in Peking made the demonstrations the most widely publicized in Chinese history. The new government commitment to economic development and pragmatism gave ideas of reform some fertile ground to grow in—if they did not go too far. The government of Deng Xiaoping feared, like its predecessors, a rebirth of the secret societies that used to plague the empire. A close Deng adviser, Hu Qiaomu, even suggested in one speech that secret groups were still operating within the country, contacting one another and foreign agents, but such signs of paranoia were uncommon. The government, instead, did its best to pre-empt the democracy movement.

For instance, in 1980 there were endless discussions in the press about the usefulness of elections in local units to weed out the good supervisors from bad. Some neighborhoods elected delegates to People's Congresses from lists that were not entirely made up by the party. But most of the choices still followed a pattern such as we had encountered in a vegetable commune outside Lanzhou, the capital of Gansu province, in the far northwest.

When we visited the Wild Goose Beach Commune in late 1979, they had just had their first local election in many years. Nobody had campaigned, nobody had put up posters and no names had been listed on the ballot. Yet Ma Xilu, the commune vice director to whom we spoke, and five other candidates had received a stunning 95 percent of the vote, sweeping out of office the entire old leadership. "How could that happen?" we asked, still trying to understand China's supposed return to free elections. Ma, a grizzled, balding veteran of twenty-six years in the Communist Party, smiled and shrugged. "Things are different here," he said.

The commune elections in his part of Gansu province had been held earlier in the year. In his low brick meeting hall near the Yellow River, 166 representatives selected by their production teams (usually comprising forty or fifty families) elected a chairman and five vice chairmen of the commune. Ma said no candidates announced themselves and nobody buttonholed representatives to vote for one man or another. Each person got a blank sheet of paper and "they just wrote what they liked. If they liked the person sitting next to them, they could vote for that person. If they didn't like one of the leading officials in the commune, they didn't have to vote for him." Ma seemed amused as we struggled, through question after question, to understand how five newcomers to the commune leadership could have won all but 5 percent of the votes cast with no announced slates or politicking. "People just know who is best for the job," he said.

It wasn't until the very end of the interview that we, like class idiots playing Twenty Questions, finally stumbled on the secret. What everyone in the commune knew, without any need of politicking, was that the ousted commune leaders had all been lame ducks. Two years before, they had been removed from the commune's Communist Party Committee, the non-elected body that retains the real power in all Chinese organizations, local or national. In the general tidying up after the death of Mao, a new team, including Ma, had been installed in the party committee at Wild Goose Beach, leaving everyone with a firm idea of who should be "elected" to the commune directorships.

In the ancient city of Xi'an we found a few pockets where people had some free choice in running their lives. Chen Yue, a round-faced woman in her forties, explained that in her workshop at the Xi'an Canvas Factory, seventy workers had been allowed to vote and replace their fifty-year-old foreman with a forty-year-old worker. The new foreman was better educated and smoother in dealing with people. The ousted foreman had been a party member and his replacement had not been admitted to the party, but the workers decided, as Chen put it, "the better the leader, the higher our pay." To salve the feelings of the loser, always an enormous concern among the Chinese, the factory arranged a special appointment for him as a "model worker."

This was only a very short step in the direction urged by China's band of democracy activists, but it encouraged them. The spirit and ambitions of the young Chinese we encountered were startling and sometimes comic, no more so than in the case of Cui Quanhong. Cui (sounds like "sway") began to send us copies of a little magazine called the *Four Modernizations,* which he was producing with his supervisors' tacit approval in a storeroom where he worked, a machine shop serving the huge oil refinery in the area. We showed the magazine to Chinese friends. None had ever heard of Cui; we were one of the few on his subscription list. But they were intrigued. "He is a brave man," one commented after reading a copy. China was not moving fast enough for Cui. "We are like Japan in the early sixties when they argued over whether to have rapid economic development. They made it, and we could have a boom too if we tried." Cui had all sorts of ideas for this, such as allowing free hiring of workers without government interference.

After an exchange of letters, Cui invited us to lunch. We arrived at his factory twenty miles outside Peking and could not get past the guard. Cui, incredibly, had not cleared our visit with his bosses. He had stocked up his room with food for our lunch, but we could not go there. Somewhat crestfallen, he led us off to a local restaurant, an authentic workers' hangout, complete with greasy chopsticks and plastic tablecloths. We had beer in soup bowls and all the *jiaozi* we could eat.

Cui had prepared a speech, which he read at the table in a voice so loud that most of the restaurant staff and customers could hear him, even above their loud slurping of noodles. "I would like to take this opportunity to pass my best regards to the friendly American people, to President Carter, Vice President Mondale, Secretary of State Muskie," Cui said. We scribbled notes and tried to keep a serious look on our faces. The restaurant customers looked puzzled.

Cui was thirty-two, a small, stocky man with close-cropped hair and a nearly perpetual grin. He was from a peasant family near Xi'an and had graduated from engineering school there, making him a valuable technician at the Peking plant. He had married a Xi'an girl and unfortunately she was still back home. He could see her only one or two months out of the year. He felt he ought to be able to seek employment in Xi'an without government approval, one of the key reforms in his master plan for China in the year 2000. Writing was an obsession; he sent many articles to Chinese newspapers, scholars, institutes and ministries. He had written to us because *Reference News* reprinted a piece of Jay's critical of Chinese bureaucracy, one of Cui's pet peeves. The *People's Daily* had printed one of his articles, he said, but he still was not getting enough attention to satisfy him. "I hope the government will publish my works, at least as internal publications," he said. "Some of Brezhnev's reactionary articles have been published in China. I should think that my articles are at least better than his!"

We do not know what has happened to Cui; it is very difficult to follow up on such people. One case of dangerous eagerness we did hear about later occurred in Hefei, where Fox Butterfield of the *New York Times,* Mike Parks, now of the *Los Angeles Times,* and Jay were invited by some foreign university teachers to meet their students. We broke up into groups. Mike and Jay were lucky enough to have just two or three students to talk to. The young Chinese spoke frankly because only a few close friends were listening. But Fox was caught in another room with perhaps a dozen students. With that many, one of the teachers explained later, "nobody is quite sure if one of them might report anything unusual that is said." The discussion was listless. Fox asked, as we all did, if the youths disagreed with their professors, if they liked their courses, if the living conditions at the universities were good. He received brightly positive or noncommittal answers. Toward the end one student, clearly frustrated at this, broke into the discussion with a quick, sarcastic remark: "Everything in China is just perfect, isn't it!"

The gathering broke up and we eventually returned to Peking, but several weeks later we happened to meet one of the same foreign teachers, an Australian named Adrian Chan, at the Beidaihe resort. He said one of the other students reported that final, flippant comment to a school official. The student who had made the comment was reprimanded and almost lost a chance to take an examination to study abroad. He was now on his best behavior, avoiding foreigners altogether so there could be no more slips of the tongue.

On several occasions, visitors told us of calling Chinese friends with whom they had had long, unhindered talks in the free and easy days of 1979. When one of these, an American professor of political science, called his Chinese friends to arrange a dinner date, he was told, with some embarrassment, "Maybe you had better go through our office first." He did as instructed, following the bureaucratic procedures which he had been told a year before he could dispense with. Yet the dinner was fine, the talk as lively and revealing as before, including frank comments from his Chinese friends about official harassment and low standards of living. What was going on? It was a delicate balancing act, the Chinese learning to exercise freedom in acceptable contexts.

As we neared the end of our stay in China, the authorities closed down the last unofficial magazine in Peking and were making contacts with ordinary Chinese more difficult. But at the same time, the official press was becoming much more open about China's problems, even admitting that many people were disillusioned with Marxism. Plays and comic dialogues that lampooned Communist Party excesses were often seen and heard.

The National People's Congress in September 1980 removed from the constitution the right to "hold great debates" or "put up wall posters." Yet the Congress itself was the first in twenty years to admit foreign diplomats and journalists as observers. For the first time in the memory of anyone we could find, a few delegates actually recorded opposing or abstaining votes to some of the resolutions. At a concurrent session of the Chinese People's Political Consultative Conference—a powerless, party-selected group of prominent Chinese non-Communists—certain delegates were allowed to voice their arguments against some resolutions from the floor. One man, reacting to a new rule calling for mandatory retirement for older officials, asked how this could work since he could see for himself that most of the leaders on the auditorium stage were older than sixty-five.

These changes are fragile experiments, and we do not expect to find Chinese society and government working just this way when we return in a few years. But our Chinese acquaintances hope that this strange sweet-and-sour democracy will survive. This would be a radical departure from recent Chinese history. In the last thirty years, periods of relatively free self-expression, as we encountered in 1980, always gave way eventually to intense political campaigns which put all expression on a very narrow track. For the moment, the formula seems to be to prohibit direct criticism of the top leadership (except when other members of the leadership are behind that criticism) and restrict dissent to private discussions rather than public wall posters. People may speak freely under those rules.

This is a confusing and not terribly satisfying formula for many Chinese intellectuals, particularly the young men and women with dirty, work-worn hands whom we met at the unofficial magazines. The Communist Party slogan summing up this policy comes from that devotee of contradictions, the late Chairman Mao: "Both democracy and centralism, both discipline and freedom, but unified will and personal ease of mind." These words are no clearer to the Chinese who care about free expression than they are to foreigners. "Which Mao are you quoting," a Peking University student asked, "the nineteen-fifties Mao, the nineteen-sixties Mao? He came out on every side of every question."

The current vague formula, however, appears to be the best this generation of Chinese is going to get. Most have little choice but to try to adapt to it. For its part, the government needs intellectuals' support to modernize the economy, rebuild the universities and re-establish contact with the outside world, and will have to move carefully when limiting intellectual freedoms.

Still, most Chinese who remember the Cultural Revolution, when opinions too freely expressed eventually brought misery, are likely to exercise caution or strong self-restraint. Each chilling act, such as the banning of wall posters or the Wei Jingsheng trial, creates new fears that the latest experiments in democracy are about to end.

Yet events in China today are not proceeding quite the way they have in the past. Most Chinese wait, and no matter what the temporary setbacks, hope for the best. One of the older workers we met, one with a tentative interest in the democracy movement, expressed the guarded feeling of his generation: "We have gone too far this time to retreat so far back."

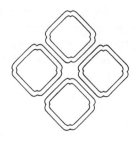

THE LAW

AFTER TWO DECADES OF ACKNOWLEDGED LAWLESSNESS, THE CHINA WE encountered at the beginning of the 1980s was reviving its judicial system and adopting criminal, civil and commercial codes offering protection to defendants in criminal cases and to foreign investors as well. A China that had never had much use for lawyers before suddenly dabbled in Western-style law. Small teams of Wall Street lawyers and Hong Kong solicitors were summoned to Peking to help bring Chinese trade laws into conformity with international practice. The *People's Daily,* which once celebrated the "class struggle" between the proletariat and the bourgeoisie, proclaimed that "all citizens must be equal before the law." The official Chinese media even began to debate the touchy issue of whether the judiciary could ever be independent of Communist Party control.

But then, as the headlines began to fade a bit, we talked to people about their own experiences with the law, how minor crimes could bring lifelong consequences, how young people loitering on street corners were sent to labor camps. For along with all the seemingly Western-style reforms in Chinese law after Mao's death, the government also revived a twenty-year-old regulation allowing persons to be sent to labor camps for crimes roughly equivalent in the United States to disturbing the peace. The regulations had been written in 1957 to silence a number of well-educated, somewhat naïve critics of Mao and the party. This time they were being used to rid the streets of a disruptive, crime-prone youth subculture. The Chinese had never made much of a distinction between political and common criminals anyway—both kinds needed to have their attitudes changed.

The system is called "re-education through labor," and it has emerged as a major loophole in China's widely trumpeted new judicial system. In 1979, to protect citizens against the arbitrary arrest and confinement they suffered during the Cultural Revolution, a criminal code was adopted that guaranteed an open trial to every accused person. But the August 1957 "re-education through labor" regulations, revived and published nationwide in February 1980, allowed local officials to assign youths to labor camps without trial or court review.

Reaffirming the 1957 law gutted the post-Mao legal reforms. Among those "who should be taken in and educated through labor," according to the regulations, are "people with no decent occupation," "those who have behaved like hooligans," "counterrevolutionaries and antisocialist elements, reactionaries . . . not subject to prosecution," those who "refuse job assignments . . . make trouble and refuse to mend their ways." Assignments to the camps are handled by local "control committees" made up of policemen, labor representatives and neighborhood party cadres whose decisions cannot be appealed.

Some Chinese we knew who had proved reliable in the past said that the Peking police, armed with these ordinances, had a quota. At least five thousand delinquents were taken off the streets and put into camps in one six-month period. One former labor camp resident told us that the big Peking-Tianjin area Teahouse Camp had greatly expanded again with a surge of new inmates in their late teens and early twenties.

A young artist we met came from Hunan with the idea of selling his drawings abroad. He found a Hong Kong businessman visiting Peking who was willing to buy. A few days later, six plain-clothes men knocked at the door of the tiny apartment where the artist was staying. It was three o'clock in the morning. "They said they wanted to check the registry of the household," he told us later. "I said I was not registered there, but would be glad to register if they allowed me. If not, I would go. They began to take down my paintings, and I told them, 'Isn't this my property, protected by the constitution? If you want to take it, you should show me some sort of certificate.' But they didn't.

"They put me in a car, and they also had a motorcycle with them. When I asked, they said we were going to the Apple Garden police station, near where I was staying, but after we drove a while I said, 'This is not the way to the Apple Garden.' They told me it was none of my business. The car drove through a big gate to a place I did not know. I was put in a room, thirty feet square, with twenty-one other people. It was very crowded. I had a fever and lay on a cot for two days, without taking any food. 'You will have to eat something or we will have to force-feed you,' they said. So I took some corn cakes and some vegetable soup.

"After two days' detention, six people took me to a house. Three asked questions and three took notes. One said:

" 'You have had contacts with foreigners. Sometimes foreigners do illegal things under the cloak of legality. Write down what you have said and done.' "

He did so, and a few days later was sent back to his home in Hunan, where he was detained for two months at an old Nationalist prison once used by Chiang Kai-shek. After many questions about his contacts with foreigners and students, all part of his scheme to sell paintings, they let him go. He was fortunate to have a wife and child. Their presence reduced the likelihood that he would be declared a vagrant and sent off to a labor camp.

The Chinese don't discuss the widespread detention system officially and simply assume it is hidden from outsiders. But some of the city facilities are not well guarded. In a nation full of neighborhood monitors, the attitude seems to be, Where could anyone safely escape to? One day we drove right up to the gate of one of Peking's main detention centers, "Benevolent Forest." (Prison officials like to give their facilities lyrical names.)

Benevolent Forest is a drab compound off New Virtue Street in northern Peking. A fifteen-foot whitewashed wall with electrical wire on top surrounds the place, but no outside guards kept us from the front gate. We got out of the car and watched about twenty detainees, young men with heads shaved and bedrolls draped over their shoulders, get out of a van and walk into the compound. The gatekeepers, at first speechless at seeing foreigners in the area, told us we could not follow. We would have to make an appointment, they said. Our later efforts to arrange an official visit to the detention center did not succeed.

Based on what we saw published in the official press and on the billboards outside of courthouses we visited, there were at least 198 death sentences carried out from July 1, 1979, to June 30, 1980. Some executions were filmed and shown on television. Most were shot in the back of the head while in a kneeling position. (That style of execution was, ironically, reminiscent of the way thousands of friends and relatives of today's Chinese Communist leaders had been killed by Nationalist Chinese executioners during the civil war fifty years before.)

Those executed included murderers and rapists, but also armed robbers, drug peddlers, gold speculators and those whose crimes would not be capital offenses in North America or Europe. We were almost relieved that the person who picked Jay's wallet out of his airline bag on a crowded street in Nanning was never caught. The wallet contained little money, the credit cards were useless in Nanning, and the thief might well have been executed for a crime against a foreigner. An apparently deranged Chinese was executed for a knife attack on an American tourist in 1976, even though the tourist did not die.

China's large pool of unemployed youth—perhaps as many as 10 to 20 million of them—is the single greatest source of crime. They are no longer automatically sent to jobs in rural communes as they were in the 1970s. Peking's mayor told a local city meeting that many people were afraid to walk the streets at night. While we were in China, youth gangs in Shanghai, Peking and Tianjin went on binges of robbery and vandalism that were publicized to underline the gravity of the situation. Police were authorized for the first time in a decade in 1980 to carry pistols and other weapons on duty. We would occasionally see, when we came out of restaurants late at night, some of the special army patrols that marched down the streets to discourage gangs and robbers.

But we never experienced, and our Chinese friends never described, anything close to the recurrent stories of crime that Americans living in big cities exchange routinely when they meet. This may be because of the way Chinese families, neighborhoods and working places operate. Few people are strangers to those living near them. Everyone keeps track of what everyone else is doing. This discourages even the more reckless members of China's youth culture. At the trial of two young workers in Peking who had committed the first bank robbery to be publicized in the capital in years, defendant Zhang Wenming, twenty-three, described the mounting paranoia that eventually led him to turn himself in. "I kept looking to see who was following me. When I went shopping I always watched the reflections in the windows. I would cross the street to avoid a policeman. Once there was a rally on law and order and I was afraid [although police had not identified him] that I would be denounced and arrested on the spot, so I fled. I was so frightened I couldn't sleep at night."

China's skintight society squeezed him into submission. This is a boon to the police, but a barrier to any attempt to westernize Chinese law. Even before Confucius, the Chinese valued collective harmony more than individual rights. Lawyers could not practice privately in China until after the 1911 revolution, which deposed the emperor. Ancient laws banned the "fomenting of litigation" lest it disturb the smooth fabric of Confucian society. "It is better to enter a tiger's mouth than a court of law," says a Chinese proverb. Even today, the old habits of *guanxi* lead people to avoid officialdom by instinct. They often prefer to punish neighborly wrongdoing on their own, as in a TV movie in which bus riders in Changsha discover a young pickpocket. Instead of turning the culprit over to the police, they beat him up and leave him at the roadside.

When the current Chinese leadership decided they had to modernize their legal system, they had great difficulty summoning the will and intellectual resources to make it work. Lower-level officials, those in charge of implementing the new laws, are accustomed to doing things their own way. In March 1979, just before we moved to Peking, the government unveiled drafts of new rules against arbitrary arrest and detention. No one could be detained by the police for more than a week without the filing of formal criminal charges. But at the same time, police arrested the dissident Wei Jingsheng and several other democracy movement activists, holding them for months with no charges filed at all. At the Gang of Four trial in late 1980, the issues were so important that the authorities gave little pretense of an impartial hearing. They held two rehearsals for the judges, lawyers and some of the witnesses. During the actual trial, cooperative defendant Chen Boda had to stop and search for the proper answer in his script when the prosecutor asked a question out of order.

Chinese officials often told us they needed more lawyers. The universities have turned out a trickle of them since the 1950s, but law has never been a popular field and lawyers were convenient targets in radical political campaigns. There were fewer than ten qualified defense attorneys in all of Peking in 1979. A leading Chinese trade official joked with some American visitors: "The United States has too many lawyers and China has too few. Why don't you export some of yours to us?" Peking University's law school, which had graduated only a thousand attorneys from 1949 to 1978, has begun to turn out about sixty a year, but that is not nearly enough to operate a new criminal code which tries to define crimes, limit detention without charge and increase rights to trial.

Harvard Law School Professor Jerome A. Cohen lived, as we did, in the Peking Hotel. He taught a course in international law for Chinese trade officials and also helped some American clients in negotiations with the Chinese; there he discovered, at first hand, the contradictory Chinese attitude toward lawyers. "At the beginning of the session the Chinese would be saying, 'Oh, Professor Cohen, you are doing so much to build bridges between our two peoples.' Then, the first time I raised an objection to anything, someone would be standing up and shouting, 'You lawyers, always butting in. How can we get anything done with you here?' "

The need to promote international trade, Cohen believes, ultimately will speed the development of a modern Chinese law. That could not come too soon for businessmen, who remember the notorious case of the British firm of Vickers-Zimmer Ltd. A Peking court, apparently influenced by deteriorating relations with Britain during the Cultural Revolution, unilaterally annulled a contract with the firm for construction of a petrochemical plant in Lanzhou. It ordered the company to pay China £650,000 sterling (about $3 million in 1979 dollars) in damages and threw a company executive in jail. The executive, George Watt, accused of being a spy, was not released until three years later, when Sino-British relations had improved.

The Chinese criminal justice system as now reconstructed resembles the Soviet-style system of the 1950s, which had been dismantled by Mao when it got in the way of the Cultural Revolution. The key element is an office called "the procuracy." It blends the functions of grand jury with those of prosecuting attorney and magistrate. It issues arrest warrants, investigates crimes and is the final authority on whether an accused should be brought to trial. At trial an attorney from the procuracy presents the government's case against the defendant, who has his own attorney or some official to represent him.

The party brought back the procuracy to check the authority of the police and guard against the legal atrocities of the Cultural Revolution. But to have a single procurator in every county would require a minimum of 2,300 attorneys, far more than the Chinese have now. Linda, who has a law degree, questioned the legal officials we met closely on judicial issues. Often her questions were not really understood, particularly when we asked about the presumption of innocence, a fundamental concept of American law that remains unknown in China. "Our assumption is that the procuracy does such a thorough investigation beforehand that a case would not be heard if the evidence were inconclusive," said Zhang Chonglin, one of the drafters of China's criminal code. Confronted with such a system, nearly all defendants plead guilty. U.S. District Judge Irving Hill of Los Angeles, who led a delegation of California jurists to China in 1979, concluded after dozens of conversations with Chinese legal experts that the only purpose of a public trial was "to let the defense counsel argue mitigating circumstances and plead for a light sentence." While many members of the U.S. Congress are lawyers, China's leaders are bureaucrats, and they seem prone to file away their most difficult problems. They prefer to send delinquents to labor camps rather than bring them into court and have them confront their accusers.*

Despite all the attempts to reform their legal system in the 1980s, the notion of due process and speedy trial has few friends in China. Like Americans on the old frontier, the Chinese may have to suffer a good deal more of the inconvenience and pain that comes from a legal system without many limits before they are willing to make any real changes.

In December 1979, during a visit to Peking's Yuetan Park, we noticed a large wall poster, written on stiff cloth so it could withstand the cold, gritty winds. The poster began:

A SHOCKING INCIDENT OF MURDER

With deep grief I bring this accusation to all my countrymen. A murder has occurred in Peking, in one of our capital's public security units. At this time, when the Communist Party's policy is being implemented, I believe my countrymen will be shocked and want to know what has happened.

We decided to find the author of the poster, who had taken the unusual step of listing his address. That is how we came to meet Kong Lingliang, and how, over the course of a year, listening to his story and becoming

---

*A particularly interesting case of the law, Chinese style, turned up in the dossier of former Communist Party Central Committee Chairman Hua Guofeng in a detailed study of press reports from Hunan province in the 1950s. University of Michigan Professor Michel Oksenberg and researcher Saicheung Yeung discovered that Hua had permitted the execution of an innocent peasant in 1951. The man, Yang Delun, had brought to light abuses by corrupt party officials in his village and was sentenced to death for his trouble. Like a good bureaucrat, Hua transmitted the order to have the man shot, only two days after he had been informed of the case and long before word of local peasant support for the man could bubble up the chain of command. Hua was in the process of losing his job when we left China, a result of his being the anointed successor of the discredited Chairman Mao; but none of the articles we read about him in the official press ever complained of his hasty verdict in the case of poor Yang Delun.

ourselves a source of local gossip, we learned something about Chinese law and punishment, about bureaucracies, neighbors, police and a father's obsessions.

Kong lived in a muddy back alley of suburban Peking in the Haidian district, an area of vegetable fields and brick-and-plywood huts strung together into shops and small dwelling places. In Kong's neighborhood, reserved for subway construction workers like himself, the residents surrounded their little two- or three-room homes with rickety wooden fences, mud walls, chicken coops, duck pens, vegetable gardens, old motor parts, buckets, sunflowers, dried fruits and bicycles. Few things grew in Kong's yard. His wall posters took up too much room. He wrote the posters with brush and ink on his *kang,* a brick-and-mortar-bed platform that could be heated like a stove. Then he hung them on the clothesline to dry.

We never started a conversation with Kong that did not end with talk of his son, Kong Deyong, age seventeen. His story went like this:

"On July 2, 1978, my son went to see a film—it was *The Kite*—but on the way home our neighbor Feng's son, Feng Beijing, attacked my son with ten friends and knocked him into a ditch. Our two families had a long-standing feud. Deyong climbed out and hit Feng once, then he ran home. Feng's son went to the public security bureau [police station] to complain that my son had attacked him. When I heard that, I was so angry that I took my son to the station to reason with them."

At that point in the story Kong would stop, overcome by the painful memory. He blamed himself for persuading his son to go to the police to straighten the matter out. Instead of listening, the police kept his son. Kong would not see him again for two months, and then only shortly before the boy died.

The morning after the arrest, the elder Kong returned to the police station as he had been asked. He was told that his son had been sent to the Haidian branch of the public security bureau. At first the public security clerk said they had no record of him, and for several days Kong searched for his son. Then it turned out they had the boy. An official named Zhang told him, "Your son injured Feng Beijing, cut his head, broke his nose and four teeth. The case is serious, so we have sentenced your son to three years of forced labor."

Kong demanded a medical check of the victim and Zhang agreed. The next day Zhang said, "Feng's head and teeth are not injured, but his nose is broken." Kong insisted on seeing the report. Zhang said, "It is not necessary. The judgment is made. If you don't agree, you can appeal to a higher office."

Kong went back to Zhang repeatedly, and to the city police headquarters, only to be told the matter was still under investigation. "If you appeal to a higher authority," one local official threatened, "we will punish Kong

Deyong more severely." For more than a month he heard nothing of his son.

Then, on September 1, a police official got in touch with Kong. "Your son is ill and needs an operation. You should go to the hospital at once." Another police official, Yang, met Kong at the hospital and said his son could go home as soon as he recovered if Kong did not make a fuss. "Then he can get a job like anyone else."

"I want his name cleared," Kong said.

Yang snapped, "If you pursue this, your son will still be held for punishment when he gets out of the hospital." He asked Kong to sign an authorization for the operation. "My son was not ill when he left home," Kong said. "I will not sign." Kong said he began to think the police hoped the boy would die on the operating table so the whole thing could be covered up.

Yang ordered the operation anyway. When it ended, at three in the morning, Kong asked the surgeon what was wrong with his son. "No diagnosis has been made," the doctor said; but Yang, the police official, informed him that the boy had gastritis and that it had developed into a gastric perforation.

An hour later Kong was allowed to see his son for the first time in two months. Although terribly weak, the boy gave his father an account of what had happened during his imprisonment. He was sent to a physical-culture school (a college for training athletes) well-known for violence in the Cultural Revolution. Young men, strong and well-trained, hit him with baseball-gloved fists to get him to confess that he had beaten Feng Beijing. They injured his head, nose and teeth. Kong said, "After five days of beatings, my son gave in: they forced him to confess that he used a knife and an ax during the fight."

Kong watched his son die in the hospital bed and then began a relentless campaign to find someone to blame. The police officials began to backtrack. In late September, officer Ma Xuezhong at the police bureau said further investigation showed that "Feng knocked Kong Deyong into the ditch and Kong hit back once. Then a brick was thrown by somebody else and hit Feng. Feng admits his brother forged the three earlier medical certificates." Without Kong's permission, his factory authorized the hospital to cremate his son's body. Kong stopped going to work, but for the next eighteen months his supervisors continued to pay him while Kong put wall posters up on Peking's main street again and again.

We went to the Peking Physical Culture Teachers College, where Kong said his son had been beaten. An unshaven young office worker came out to the gate. He instantly recognized Kong's name. "It is a very complicated case," he said, and added, "We did have juvenile delinquents assigned here for reform during the Cultural Revolution, but not recently, and we have no record of Kong Deyong having been here."

Three police officials visited Kong and promised to pay his expenses, arrange a good job for his daughter, and try Feng's son if Kong would only give up his campaign. Kong said he insisted on a trial for "the highest people involved," but the police said they could not go along on that.

We went to the public security bureau, a new brick building with a chilly little waiting room near the gate. After an hour's wait a man in civilian clothes came out and announced, "We have no authorization from our superiors to answer your questions." At the Haidian hospital a woman official said she was very familiar with the case, "but you will have to ask the Foreign Ministry for any details."

We visited the Fengs. Kong had told us that the Feng boys had harassed his son before, beating him up when he tried to build a rabbit cage on the wall the families shared. The Fengs received us like visiting ambassadors, offering tea and stuffing Jay's bag with peanuts. Young Feng Beijing, twenty-three, showed off a broken tooth and a slight indentation in his nose. The Fengs described young Kong as a bad boy, and his father as a bad neighbor. The Fengs seemed beleaguered. "We have no relatives in Peking since we moved here from Nanjing. No friends, only our family," the father said. "All the neighbors are saying you gave Kong two thousand yuan [$1,350] for his interview."

A big delegation from Kong's unit paid a visit to his home. "Why did you talk to the foreigners?" one woman asked, referring to us. "They came to me," Kong said. "I'll call a press conference if you like." She said, "Don't talk to foreigners, we can deal with this case. Give us ten days." Nothing happened.

Kong continued to write letters and posters. He had become a hero and a resource to other people with grievances. When we came to his house we'd find some of these vagrant peasants and displaced workers staying at his house and working on their own petitions.

At Peking police headquarters Wu Nengfu, a small, balding man, agreed to see us after our second visit. He said, "The facts presented by Kong are not real. That's all I can say."

Before we left China, we went to say goodbye to Kong. His case had gone no further, though he had found an official in the State Council who he thought would help him. His visiting brother told him not to get his hopes up. But Kong would not rest. "Our public security officers are important parts of our proletarian dictatorship," he said, "but if we let them beat up, detain and kill people at will . . . then what is the difference between them and bandits?"

It was a distinction that many young Chinese began to wonder about as the democracy movement unraveled in 1979. The police became bolder about arresting wall-poster writers, but their response was still somewhat restrained. They seemed more interested in frightening their targets than putting them away, so some, like Lu Lin, of the dissident magazine *Explorations,* were released at the beginning and could give revealing first-hand accounts of the public security bureau's interrogation techniques. Lu was arrested by Li Guojin, the security chief at his plant, a man in his forties with teeth so brown that it looked as if they had never been brushed.

"After I was shown the summons," Lu wrote later, "they put me in a Mercedes-Benz like a visiting dignitary. It was my first ride in a Benz sedan, steady but fast and quiet. Another group, led by Ma Danian, searched my house. Ma prosecuted Han Zhixiong, one of the young heroes of the April Fifth [1976] Tiananmen demonstration. Ma was a conscientious worker. He plugged in a five-hundred-watt light bulb and had his men climb through the skylight to search the roof of the house. They crawled around like burglars, finding nothing. It was more polite than the search of Ren Wanding's [a human rights activist] house, when they even dug a hole in the wall. When they left at three A.M., they took with them my nine notebooks, magazines, manuscripts and eight thousand sheets of white paper. Ten more police came the next day, assigned to watch my family and capture anyone who came looking for me. They even assigned a plain-clothes woman to keep watch over my sister when she went to the toilet."

Lu was taken to 44 Banbuqiao, a major prison in southern Peking, and up to the second-floor interrogation chamber in K block. The principal official was Zhang Wenyu, who had interrogated the 1976 Tiananmen demonstrators, later praised for their aborted attempt to turn out the Gang of Four. Zhang had kept his job as an interrogator even after the Gang was arrested, and soon Lu saw why: "Two days convinced me his technique was unique. Instead of resorting to deception, harassment and threats (favored by other interrogators), he chose to lecture me on philosophy, political economy, the causes of poverty in China, the causes of American wealth, American democracy and Chinese democracy.

"The United States did not sustain any substantial loss in either World War One or World War Two," Zhang said. "It made a tremendous amount of money during World War Two while all other countries suffered terrible losses. Later, when the United States invaded Korea and Vietnam and bullied many smaller countries, it took away large amounts of their property . . . Wars made America rich. Can our country do that?

"Elections in the United States, let me remind you, are decided by the amount of property of the candidates. Their democracy serves the interests of the capitalists. It is a fake democracy. Our democracy really represents the greatest majority of the people."

As Zhang paced and talked, sipping tea, Lu said nothing. Zhang took this to be agreement. He winked at an aide, named Liu, who said to Lu, "Tell me who made a film of your printing press." (This appeared to be an attempt to show foreign involvement with the democracy movement.)

"Nobody," Lu replied.

Liu: "You're lying. Take a look. The film is here. How can you deny this?" (Liu displayed a large, bulky brown envelope.)

Lu: "Let me see what is in the envelope."

Liu: "You have no need to see it, because Wei Jinsheng [the editor of *Explorations*] told us everything. Do you still want to cover up the matter?"

Lu: "Can you ask Wei Jingsheng to come over for a cross-examination?"

Liu: "Don't try to play tricks. You know the policy of the party. We'll try to let the matter rest for the time being. You think it over. I don't blame you if you have doubts about the matter. We'll talk about it again when you are sure of yourself."

Lu wrote that this reminded him of a ruse used to get some evidence (which Lu did not describe) from Wei's girl friend, a young Tibetan woman. A policeman told her he had come for something Wei left with her. She admitted she had something, but said she would need Wei's written request to give it up. A police secretary had her sign a written record of what she just said, and with that they forced Wei to admit he had left something with her, something he had not spoken of before.

After two days of interrogation Lu was "exhausted and my eyes bloodshot." The final verdict was that he "did not understand Marxism-Leninism and had been misled by others." The relative leniency of the decision was owing, perhaps, to Lu's age. Zhang called him in for one more private chat:

Zhang: "We haven't beaten you, have we?"

Lu: "No."

Zhang: "How about our attitude?"

Lu: "Not bad."

Zhang: "Are you surprised? People say the public security bureau beats its suspects and never listens to reason . . . When you leave here, don't tell anyone what I have told you. But you may tell them how we treated you. If you have anything to report, give us a call."

Undaunted, Lu returned to 44 Banbuqiao two months later to ask about Wei and Wei's friend Yang Guang, another *Explorations* editor who had been arrested. Liu angrily accused Lu of helping hide Yang in March 1979 by letting him pose as Lu's brother.

Liu: "We were stupid to release you!"

Lu: "If you think you have been too lenient with me, you can arrest me again."

Liu: "Do you suppose we won't do it? Let me tell you, I have seized the [original] manuscripts of the articles you have published. They are pretty reactionary."

Lu: "What do you mean by 'reactionary'? There is no such term in the criminal code."

Liu: "Let me tell you, the activities of you people are counterrevolutionary."

Lu: "Is it a counterrevolutionary activity to publish a journal?"

Liu: "It sure is."

Lu: "How about those who are still putting up big-character posters and publishing journals?"

Liu: "That's none of your business! When the time comes, no one will get away."

To a large extent, he was right. Many of the democracy movement activists were imprisoned—some in Peking, some in provincial labor camps, and some in the bleakest prison camps of China's Siberia—Qinghai.

In the far western reaches of the country, on a bitterly cold and practically treeless plateau, lie the vast empty grasslands of Qinghai (Chinghai) province—disturbed only by the wind and an occasional camel caravan. This wilderness is home to the greatest concentration of prisoners in China. For three decades Qinghai has served as China's black hole, a mysterious place where many were banished but from which few ever returned.

The Chinese learned something about labor camps, as they did about many other things, from the Soviets in the 1950s. But Chinese governments have been sending wrongdoers off to organized hard labor for centuries. A sixteenth-century European adventurer, Fernám Mendes Pinto, wrote of a group of Portuguese who were shipwrecked off the coast of China, arrested and sentenced to a year of hard labor in a camp near the Great Wall.* China's folk literature includes ancient stories and songs of men dragged off to massive work projects, like the Great Wall, because they offended local politicians two thousand years ago.

China has never produced an Alexander Solzhenitsyn to chart the dimensions of its Gulag Archipelago, because a stint in Qinghai has usually meant a life sentence. But while we were in China, so many people were rehabilitated and released from long prison terms that information about this little-known aspect of Chinese society began to seep out.

"The whole province is a sort of prison colony," Daniel Kelly said. Kelly was born in 1941 in China of an American missionary father and a Chinese mother. The father died and his mother stayed after 1949, but when he tried to assert his U.S. citizenship and leave, he was stopped. He tried to swim out to Macao and was caught, which led to twenty-one years in Chinese prisons, including two and a half years in Qinghai. He said it was "bleak and desolate, not the sort of place that would attract ordinary people. You have to be sent." He believes that half of Qinghai's population of 4 million people are prisoners in actual rude penitentiaries or are "enforced laborers" —ex-convicts who have served their time but are forbidden to leave the area or simply cannot find another place to go. "China uses enforced laborers the same way the Russians did, to colonize the wilderness and open up new parts of the country," Kelly said when he talked to us by telephone from

*According to a translation done and brought to our attention by Rebecca Catz.

his current home in Plainfield, Indiana. "In Qinghai, even the waitresses in hotel restaurants are prisoners or ex-prisoners."

Thick walls and armed guards surrounded Singular Beauty Farm, the 30,000-man camp where Kelly was incarcerated from 1959 to mid-1962, but they were superfluous; the whole province was a natural prison. Kelly was transferred from Qinghai to camps near Peking and finally released in 1978 when improved U.S.-China relations made it possible for him to secure an exit permit. Qinghai "was so isolated, so far from civilization, that escape was hopeless. Oh, two or three people made a run for it while I was there, but after a few days a shepherd would come by and report a body out in the brush. The guards would go out on horseback to pick it up."

Physical torture was rare. "The Chinese are more civilized in that respect than the Russians. Occasionally someone might get his thumbs tied together with steel wire for stealing food, but the important thing was to break your spirit rather than inflict physical pain. The whole system was aimed at reducing prisoners to ciphers, getting them to admit their errors and throw themselves on the mercies of the Communist Party." Violence may have become more common since Kelly was released. Before Peking's Democracy Wall was closed down in late 1979, a wall poster described in graphic detail how eleven prisoners had been beaten to death and eight others seriously injured by sadistic guards at a Qinghai labor camp. (The facts were confirmed for us by a Chinese official we knew who said the melee occurred at the same Qinghai farm where Kelly was held.)

The poster writer signed himself "Member of the Chinese Communist Youth League who dares to reveal the truth." He described how a group of surly young prisoners from Peking had irritated one of the former inmates who had remained at the camp as a guard. On the pretext that he had to uncover the culprit responsible for a minor theft, the ex-convict, Qi Zhongxiao, and fellow guards herded these young prisoners into a compound and locked the gates. Then Qi and the others, armed with iron bars, pitchforks and sticks, turned on the prisoners. "The thud of iron bars was accompanied by abuse and shrieks of pain. The victims fell on their knees to beg for mercy. A strong smell of blood pervaded the compound. Some prisoners had their skulls split open with the brains spilling out, others had their chests perforated or their faces disfigured beyond recognition. Those who fainted were splashed with cold water, and once they came to, were beaten again. Prison officials watched the spectacle from the walls of the compound." The wall poster's author acknowledged that such incidents were commonplace during the Cultural Revolution, but noted, "It has been a long time since the Gang of Four was crushed. How could such an affair still happen in the new China and under the leadership of our party?"

The official press occasionally reports labor-camp brutality. A 1980 official broadcast from Jilin referred to three instances of death or injury suffered in beatings of "forced-labor team" members. A man named Zhang

Yong serving a three-year sentence for robbery tried to escape. That night, after he was recaptured, the leader and five members of the team beat him to death. The only sanction was temporary suspension for two supervisors of the team.

The Peking authorities always rebuffed our attempts to discover how many people had been consigned to Qinghai or the other labor camps scattered across the country. The official media sometimes hint that the number is steadily being reduced as old cases of political persecution left over from the 1950s and 1960s are reinvestigated, and old wrongs corrected. But former inmates insist that hundreds of thousands of people remain in labor camps, and the government has estimated in the past that 80 percent of all Chinese prisoners are in camps. The official press sometimes reveals a bit more about conditions there. In February 1980 a woman from Yunan province was rehabilitated and released after spending twenty-three years in a labor camp for shouting "erroneous political slogans." The *People's Daily* said her "crime" had occurred after her newborn baby had starved to death because of a milk shortage in her hometown. The newspaper hailed the party's decision to commute Li's life sentence as evidence that "the injustices inherited from the past are being steadily corrected." The clemency order also extended to seven Yunnan party cadres who had been punished for defending Li, including the head of the local public security bureau and a local prosecutor. For some, justice came too late: they had already died in prison.

The same labor camps that have released victims of earlier purges such as the Cultural Revolution and the 1957 anti-rightist campaign now appear to be refilling with delinquent youths, as well as with some members of the 1978–1980 democracy movement. So depressing was the prospect of a lifetime in the camps that a member of one democracy movement group in Kaifeng committed suicide on March 26, 1980. Mu Changqing threw himself under a train just as he and several other young government critics were about to be moved to a "re-education through labor" camp.

Benevolent Forest, the white-walled jail compound in northern Peking where we stopped briefly, seemed to serve as a way station for some youths going to labor camps. Jail officials there scorned the government's well-publicized commitment to open trials and due process. We acquired from people in the democracy movement the personal statement of a prisoner from Gansu province, Yuan Guoru. When Yuan insisted that he had committed no crime and had not received a trial, the jail officials scoffed at him. "We have five teams, one thousand policemen at Benevolent Forest," one cell-block director told Yuan. "We earn our living by arresting people . . . The newspapers that print so much about the constitution and the legal system earn their living by making propaganda. Those journalists and we policemen are two trains running on separate tracks."

The official rationale for dispensing with trials is that the labor camps are not prisons, only "a compulsory means of educating and transforming people," as the *Enlightenment Daily* argued. "Experience has shown that people can be transformed through work and political education . . . They can turn over a new leaf, follow the correct path and change from being idlers and mischiefmakers on the verge of committing crime to being law-abiding citizens." Although officials repeatedly stress the difference between "re-education through labor" and "reform through labor" (the latter term referring to punishment for convicted criminals), veterans of China's labor camps say that in practice there is no distinction. "We were all mixed together, doing the same work (usually farming and construction), living under the same conditions," a former Red Guard told us. He had been sent to an 8,000-man camp in Qinghai for five years' re-education after "mis-behaving" during the Cultural Revolution. "With the exception of a few of us who had political pull and got furloughed, nobody ever left the place," he said.

Under the published regulations, the maximum term for "re-education through labor" inmates is supposed to be four years. If previous practice is any guide, however, many of the youths sent away in recent campaigns can expect to spend the rest of their lives in the camps. A young writer we met in Peking said that if they were released, his friends in the camps found it very difficult to find jobs afterward or to marry. Work units see the blemish on their record. Families of young Chinese women and the women themselves know that the prospects of someone so marked are not good.

We met one former labor-camp inmate, Big Lin, in a Peking bungalow whose tenant, a generous and friendly worker we knew, sometimes enter-tained the city's down-and-out. We stopped by in the late afternoon and were introduced to a dark-skinned man in neat white summer shirt and dark slacks, and of a slender build that belied his nickname. He sat by the tiny stove, chewing sunflower seeds, sipping hot water and looking somewhat forlorn.

Big Lin had returned to Peking only two years before from the Teahouse Camp. We had heard first- and second-hand stories of life there and in other camps during the Mao era, but had not met anyone who had lived in that camp so recently. The experience had taken five years of his life. At age thirty-eight he had a bad leg and little prospect of marriage or children, all for something that would hardly have raised an eyebrow in the United States. Besides, he said, he didn't commit the alleged crime.

Being an engineer's son, Big Lin had seemed destined for a bright future as a technician at the printing plant where he worked if he could only curb his temper and stay clear of a few enemies. Then, in 1973, came one of the campaigns to stem ideological backsliding, and the workers at his factory were encouraged to expose any bad elements or class enemies. Someone accused Big Lin of calling his factory leaders "Chiang Kai-shek followers" and "fascists."

"They only had one witness who said I did that and he was not on good terms with me, but they sent me away anyway. We planted rice at the camp. I wasn't used to it, and when we went out in March to plant seedlings, it was just too cold," he said. He contracted phlebitis in one leg and when he was finally returned to his factory in 1978, he found it difficult to pick up where he had left off. His supervisors regarded him as rehabilitated, but "with a tail," meaning a black mark would remain on his record.

In some ways Big Lin had profited from the lingering embrace of the comrades in his old unit, even in prison. They sent him half of his $30 salary every month and gave him the other half in a lump sum when he returned. He had a job again and the same retirement plan as others in his unit, but the "tail" on his record clouded his future. He lowered his eyes to the bungalow's concrete floor. "China is different from other countries. I'm not married, so people are even more suspicious of me. They think I have some sort of sexual disability. I want to get this 'tail' erased, but I have had no luck."

Daniel Kelly said prisoners he knew "were used to the routine of the camps and they had such a blemish on their records from being sent to the camp that it would be nearly impossible for them to resume a normal life." A thirty-year-old democracy movement activist told us that some young men he knew in the camps had married women who had also been assigned to "re-education through labor." By marrying, such couples virtually guaranteed that they would become permanent exiles in the camps. They earned wages far below the minimum for such work and were allowed one leave a year to visit their families.

The labor camps thus became an integral part of the Chinese system. Today they offer a reliable supply of low-cost labor which can be moved about the country at will or put to work on massive public-works projects under inhospitable conditions. On the outskirts of Peking at least two of the camps, Teahouse and Clear River Farm, and probably many others, raise vegetables and fruits for city residents.

What Daniel Kelly remembers most clearly about Qinghai is that the work, usually reclamation projects, was never-ending and often quite pointless. "The authorities had some brilliant dreams for Qinghai. China was going to transform the wasteland. But the projects were doomed from the start. We worked for months digging ditches for a county-wide irrigation project, but the soil was nothing but sand and we had nothing to reinforce the walls with. So the ditches would eventually fill with drifting sand. The whole thing had to be abandoned."

Having survived Qinghai in the early 1960s when, he estimates, two thirds of the inmates died of starvation or diseases related to malnutrition, Kelly said he found Clear River Farm near Peking "not such a bad place." During his ten-year term there, a prisoner's ration was between 38 and 45 pounds of food a month, a considerable amount by Chinese standards. "A lot of peasants in Sichuan would have liked that ration, which may be one reason people were reluctant to leave," Kelly said. Former prisoners estimated that Clear River Farm still has about 20,000 inmates. Other suburban reform camps and factories under Peking jurisdiction include the New Capital Rubber Plant and the New Capital Tile and Brick Works.

In defense of the system, Chinese legal scholars said that because they are designed not to punish but to alter the attitudes of the inmates, the camps represent a humane solution to the problems of petty crime and internal unrest. Xiao Weiyou, a law professor at Peking University, answered when we pressed him on this point, "In every society there are always misfits, people who cannot be left at large because they jeopardize the public order. As long as such people exist, we in China feel it is essential to have 're-education through labor' camps too."

For many common criminals, city prisons offer incarceration more in the American manner. We were allowed to visit two large prisons in Peking and Shanghai. Both appeared to be clean and orderly institutions housed in very large, very old buildings. Prisoners had shaved heads and wore simple clothing. They made plastic sandals and socks and underwear for sale outside. Bao Ruo-wang (Jean Pasqualini), a Chinese-Frenchman jailed for seven years as an alleged spy, had complained that prisoners in the 1950s were never given a chance to leave such institutions. Bao said a request to leave at the end of a prison term meant the inmate's ideological remolding was not complete, for he was expected to ask for more of the party's hospitality. Those inmates who had finished their terms were forced to stay and continue as "free workers" in the prison factory, visiting their families only on weekends. Officials at both prisons told us they no longer follow such a system.

As is true of prison tours anywhere, China's official guides overlook the grittier side of inmate life and do not show visitors the worst jail areas. Yuan Guoru, the Lanzhou worker who spent time in Benevolent Forest, said the cell he lived in "was worse than a pig sty. We ate, slept and went to the bathroom in one barnlike, cold room with a wet concrete floor. People had been there one to ten years. There were insects. Meals were one bowl of vegetable soup and one corn cake a day." A beggar child who took an extra corn cake was severely beaten, as was a woman who tried to fetch a scarf she had left elsewhere in the prison. When a petitioner from Inner Mongolia broke a window, he was hung up by his wrists for three hours.

For misfits of higher rank, special places are necessary. A favorite dumping ground had been Qin Cheng Number One prison, a white-walled complex twenty-five miles north of Peking. It does not appear on any maps to which we have access. When a group of journalists interviewed Peking's chief prison administrators in 1980, the officials denied its existence. But several high-ranking Chinese, such as Peng Zhen; Bo Yibo, the Panchen Lama; former President Liu Shaoqi's widow, Wang Guangmei; and the

American Sidney Rittenberg, have spent many years there and left to tell about it. For long periods of time they were forbidden to talk to their fellow prisoners. Wang Guangmei, the object of particularly intense interrogations, torture and electric-shock treatments in the late 1960s, emerged "almost unrecognizable," one of her friends said. Some prisoners were denied food for days, then given a thick, rich noodle dish that caused them to throw up. Difficult prisoners were put in "peace suits," tight-fitting rubber uniforms that were inflated, making it painful to breathe. Rittenberg does not remember such bizarre punishment; he was a foreigner and was given special treatment. He does remember "being taken into Peking for a medical checkup and having two guards slam their elbows into me the whole trip."

Rittenberg was jailed in 1968, yanked away from the apartment where his four children slept on a chilly night as his wife, Yulin, thrust an old pair of long johns at him. He had to make them last for almost ten years. Rittenberg had been caught up in the Cultural Revolution, joining a small revolutionary group that ran Radio Peking for a while. Some high leaders —Rittenberg blames Mao's wife, Jiang Qing—saw Rittenberg as a convenient scapegoat. They labeled him an "American spy" and said he had been trying to overthrow Chou En-lai. In 1972, after the Cultural Revolution had wound down and its most powerful military backer, Lin Biao, had died in an alleged attempt to overthrow Mao, the jailers at Qin Cheng were replaced by a more reasonable crew. Prisoners were allowed to exercise and interact and given better food. Fewer cases of torture were reported.

Hundreds of thousands of party officials, scientists and artists in other parts of the country suffered imprisonment at places like Qin Cheng during the Cultural Revolution. We spent a morning in Shanghai talking to Yuan Xuefen, who in her glory had been a Chinese Judy Garland, the star of the Shaoxing operas which drew huge crowds delighted by the melancholy songs and tales of lost love. When the Cultural Revolution began she was taken from her family, including her one-year-old son, and detained in a Shanghai house. Several other important prisoners were locked in other rooms.

"I slept in my coat because I didn't know when I would be interrupted. They were always calling me names. They demanded that I write so-called confessions." They called meetings at least five hundred times to criticize her life and thoughts, she said. Later she was sent to a work camp, and then, in 1973, was freed but for a long time she was forbidden to perform.

As the older prisoners are released, new ones—including allies of the Gang of Four—have taken their place. As we were reminded continually during our stay in China, even with the commendable attempts at legal reform it remains a nation of men, not laws, and that has both its dark and its bright side.

Rittenberg was released in late 1977. In 1979, just before he took a trip to the United States, he was given his dossier as a sign that he had been completely cleared. At a banquet in his honor, hosted by some of the public security people, he asked if political prisoners in the future might be as roughly treated as he was. "Never!" said one burly man. Rittenberg asked how he could be so sure; after all, prison administrators like himself had erred before. But the man persisted. "You see, I was a prisoner in Qin Cheng myself. I know what it was like, and nothing like that is going to happen again."

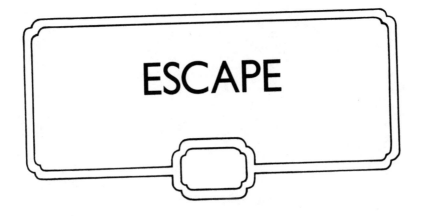

ESCAPE

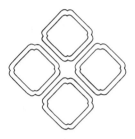

FOOD

For the people, food equals heaven.

—AN ANCIENT CHINESE PROVERB

A YOUNG HONG KONG–BORN CHINESE BUSINESSMAN WAS ELATED WHEN he closed a multimillion-dollar deal that would require him to live most of a year in Shanghai, supervising the construction of a modern electronics plant. His mother and grandmother, however, were horrified. "There's nothing for you to eat in Shanghai!" wailed the eighty-year-old grandmother, a refugee from a famine that devastated central China a generation ago.

She had no real cause to worry because China always makes ample provision for its foreign experts, tourists and other guests. But her genuine alimentary concern for her grownup grandson (who fights a weight problem five hours a week at a Hong Kong gym) betrays something fundamental about Chinese society: its perpetual obsession with food.

Probably no other people, not even the French, lavish as much thought and attention on food, its production, its distribution, its preparation and, most important, its consumption. The ritual of eating is linked so closely to well-being that, all over China, a standard greeting among friends is not "How are you?" but *"Chi fan le mei you?,"* interpreted as "Have you eaten?" Room attendants at the Peking Hotel greeted us that way no matter what time of day.

This fixation on food, besides producing a culinary tradition admired and imitated around the world, has affected everything from child-rearing practices to national import policies. Chinese babies and toddlers are often overfed: the choicest tidbits from the table are saved for the youngest. Affection is "expressed above all through giving of food," American Sinologist Richard H. Solomon has observed. "A proper Chinese baby is one so plump with nourishment that there can be no doubt about his good health."

The traditional obsession with food passed into the socialist era unchanged. John Roderick, the Associated Press bureau chief when we were in Peking, once dined with Mao Tse-tung in the Yenan caves in 1946. He remembers expressing surprise at how well the Communists ate. Mao answered, "Mr. Roderick, we may be Communists, but we are also Chinese and we love good food."

Prodigious amounts of manpower are required to feed China's billion mouths: 80 percent of the work force are peasants, working full-time in the fields. In the United States, by comparison, the farm population makes up only 3 percent of the total. Not surprisingly, China counts its population in terms of "mouths" instead of "heads." The Chinese word "population" comes out *ren kou,* literally "man-mouth."

Judging from the political language used in Peking, politicians and editorial writers often have their minds on their digestive tracts too. The *People's Daily* has described Europe as a "juicy piece of meat in the eyes of the Soviet gluttons," and the late Chou En-lai once boasted that the Russians wanted to "devour China, but find us too tough even to bite." Although that accomplished gourmet, the late Chairman Mao, warned his followers in 1927 that "a revolution is not a dinner party," he later turned to gastronomic metaphors to explain how the Communists defeated their Nationalist Chinese rivals. Eliminating the Nationalist regime, said Mao, "was a matter of eating it up, absorbing most of it and expelling the smaller part."

The most likely reason that the Chinese frequently resort to allegories about eating and being eaten is that for the last three millennia, millions of Chinese have often not known where their next meal would be coming from. Famines and floods have ravaged China so regularly that dynasties have been judged by how well they coped with these disasters.

As recently as 1943–1944, a combination of bad weather, greedy landlords and an inept central government led to the starvation and death of three million people in the central Chinese province of Henan, one tenth of the area's population. American correspondent Theodore H. White reported from the scene that hungry peasants had stripped the trees of their bark, and vendors were selling leaves for a dollar a pound. Even the green scum from the surface of village ponds was being consumed.

With some justification, the Communists claim to have eliminated the deadly cycle of famine-and-flood. But among Western farmers, agronomists and China scholars, who are only now gaining entry to the vast and impoverished countryside, grave doubts have begun to arise about whether the Communists adequately feed all their people. "In the countryside I saw beggars, people picking through scrap heaps for food, children covered with skin diseases—all the things that I thought had been banished from the new China," said a Chinese-American who had visited his ancestral home in Zhejiang province. "I wasn't prepared for it because you don't see that kind of thing in the big cities."

An American scholar who accompanied his Chinese wife to her native village on the northern plain in 1978 said the best-fed people, the strongest and most productive men, could count on two meals a day, usually a large soup bowl of wheat noodles. Each villager could buy three eggs a month; meat, usually fatty pork, was a once-monthly treat. Although the village lies close to the Yellow River, local people rarely eat fish because the catch must be diverted to the cities downstream. A professor at Anhui University in Hefei told us the landlocked province suffers from a stubborn pessimism about its future. "We've had seventeen bad harvests in the last twenty-four years, both from drought and floods," he said.

Chinese officials admit that despite the irrigation projects, land reclamation and sanitary improvements the Communist Party has so vigorously promoted over three decades, the average peasant is not much better off today than he was prior to the revolution. Farmers have only barely kept up with population increase, doubling their production of grain as the population doubled in the last thirty years. And they have paid a high price, clearing for grain production thousands of square miles of forests and grasslands which may now wash away with no more deep roots to hold them. At least one sixth of the arable land suffers from serious erosion because of the destruction of forests. The Yangtze River is now in danger of becoming as silt-laden by erosion as the Yellow River, having doubled its content of topsoil since 1958. The Yangtze carries away six hundred million tons a year. Heavy cultivation is also turning one fifth of the country's grassland into desert.

A late-1978 wall poster addressed to the "ladies and gentlemen of the Peking city government" complained that "tens of thousands of people do not have the wherewithal to clothe themselves or eat. What has happened to your Communist humanitarianism that you ignore this problem? The people need bread now to appease their hunger." Students at Wuhan University nearly rioted over the New Year holidays in 1979. Posters went up, lambasting the university cooks for failing to give them meat at the one time of year when plenty of meat is expected. "Do we have nothing but turnips and vegetables?" the posters said.

As if in answer to these attacks, the authorities have lately become more candid about the shortcomings of Chinese agriculture. "Food is the most fundamental problem of the economy," the *Enlightenment Daily*, the journal of China's intellectuals, admitted. "The problem of feeding hundreds of millions of people has not yet been wholly resolved." In 1978 the government admitted that average per capita grain production had shown no improvement since 1955, the output of meat, vegetables and fruit had stagnated, and the national fish catch had dropped by half.

Because the Chinese government rarely provides hard statistics, foreign experts are uncertain of the actual number of people who go hungry. Population expert Nick Eberstadt of Harvard University has estimated that as many as 170 million people in China may exist in a state of "semi-starvation," defined by the UN Food and Agricultural Organization as a daily intake of fewer than 1,550 calories. His conclusions, derived from the general statistical correlations between life expectancy and hunger in the Third World, have been challenged as guesswork, but no one disagrees that unless the Chinese slash their birth rate or manage to improve their agricultural output, they face disaster. From what we have observed, they waste so little of their food now that it is hard to see what they could give up if belt-tightening were ordered.

The Chinese government shows every sign of making the same calculations—and reaching the same conclusions. In reordering their modernization plans and readjusting the national budget, the leaders seem eager to make food a top priority. A new Food Ministry was created in mid-1979 to solve what the *People's Daily* dubbed "the eating problem." "Without an advance in agriculture, there can be no high-speed development for the national economy as a whole." Steven Butler, the young American scholar who spent six months in 1980 on a commune in southern Hebei, put it more bluntly: "I think there is a basis on which people in the villages measure their attitude toward the government, and it is what they eat."

Patience and ingenuity are lavished on the preparation of Chinese food, for key ingredients are often unavailable or in short supply. As shocked Westerners have discovered, a Chinese restaurant menu (particularly in the south) can include monkeys, dogs, cats, snakes, turtles and bear. The omnivorous southern Chinese are a source of amusement even to their northern brethren, who joke, "Down south they will eat anything with four legs, except maybe chairs." Our amah, Ah-Lin, as Cantonese as they come, was astounded to see the pigeons filling up Portsmouth Square in San Francisco's Chinatown during a vacation visit there. "You mean people just leave the pigeons here?" she said. "They don't kill them and eat them?"

A dedicated gastronome could spend the rest of his life cataloguing the sights, sounds and scents of markets in the cities and towns of China. With restrictions on private farming and marketing loosened, the variety and noise are at times overwhelming and fill mornings in cities like Peking with a purposeful, happy hum. In one Shanghai market we found lines of people at every stall, waiting for cabbage, potatoes, eggs or an interesting selection of tomatoes—small green ones from the state commune and big fat red ones from the private plots of a few local peasants. It was dawn, but people were everywhere. "I have to do this before I go to work, otherwise there is no time. I miss my exercises, but my wife and I have to take turns," one older, well-dressed office worker told us. Since few families have refrigerators (such appliances have just begun to become available to wealthy, well-connected families), people must shop every day. Young men whizzed by on bicycles with live chickens or crabs stuffed into plastic mesh bags. One man had a small frog on a string. At a bakery, people lined up for steamed bread, dumplings or fried pretzels for breakfast. Everywhere people were eating on the streets—buns, candied fruits or even small sticks of ice pops made from soybeans.

Chinese cook as they always have, making do with what is at hand. That system has not worked too badly in the past, for many of China's best-known dishes were born of necessity. Legend has it that Beggar's Chicken, a succulent dish celebrated in banquet halls in China and elsewhere, was concocted by a sixteenth-century hobo so poor he did not own a cooking pot. He stole the chicken, and without any utensils, cooked it by wrapping it in lotus leaves, coating them with mud and holding the package over an open fire. When the mud was knocked off, the chicken was fragrant with the flavor of the lotus. Approximately the same method is used today.

Stir-frying in woks, now so familiar to Americans, developed because food had to be cooked rapidly to save both fuel and cooking oil. Cooking oil is still rationed, and when we arrived in Peking the allotment was as little as 6 ounces a month. A hint of what this means can be gleaned from *Cookbook for the Masses,* a frequent gift to young brides which includes recipes that scrupulously call for one tenth of an ounce of lard or oil. The cooking-oil ration has since increased, due to an intense government campaign to cultivate oil-bearing crops; by the time we left it was slightly more than 16 ounces a month. Rationing of pork was suspended in 1979 in Peking and other cities, and plenty of pork was available at higher prices in free markets.

"Only Mandarins eat meat" goes an old saying that still rings true. Meat is still relatively expensive. To stretch this ration, Chinese often chop up bits of meat and fish, then mix them with vegetable fillings and stuff them into boiled, steamed or fried dumplings that are filling enough for a noon meal. Various combinations of pork, including the meat-and-vegetable-filled dumplings called *jiaozi,* also highlight holiday feasts. "I spent the whole day making *jiaozi,*" a friend complained when we asked if she enjoyed her holiday.

Varieties of meat taken for granted in the rest of the world do not appear on many tables. Steve Allee, an exchange scholar in Nanjing, fell into conversation with a Chinese student as they rested after a long climb to an old temple. "Do you have enough to eat in America?" the student asked.

"Yes."

"Do you eat a lot of beef?"

"No, it's pretty expensive. I eat a lot of chicken."

"Chicken! You eat chicken?" The young man was amazed. The Chinese have not developed the organization or skill for mass production of frying

hens; chicken was always the most expensive item on the menus we encountered in Peking. "After that it didn't matter what I said I ate," Allee
recalled. "If I ate chicken, in his eyes I had it made."

The Chinese talk for hours about the strange dietary habits of their
cousins in neighboring provinces, whereas foreigners tend to distinguish
two main divisions of Chinese cuisine—southern and northern. Northerners eat noodles, southerners eat rice. Southern cooking tends to be sweeter,
northern cooking saltier. The distinctions become more complex as a trav-
eler explores the varied regions of the south. Food from Sichuan and Hunan
is the hottest, Shanghai food the lightest, Cantonese food the most varied.
As the capital, Peking incorporates all regions and produces some special-
ties of its own. No region has a monopoly on grease. The Chinese like oil
and fat in their food.

The basic nutritional fact of China is that an overwhelming amount of
the food eaten—87.5 percent, according to the Joint Economic Committee
of the U.S. Congress—comes straight from the vegetable kingdom. Most of
this is grain: wheat in the north, rice in the south, millet or corn in other
spots. To the surprise of Americans, who are brought up to believe that
starches are fattening, the slim Chinese consume a staggering amount of
grain. In Canton, a male office worker can buy up to thirty-three pounds
of rice a month, i.e., more than a pound of dried uncooked rice a day, and
few young men have any trouble finishing their rations. "My mother has
many complaints about me, but she has never accused me of not eating all
my rice," asserted Xiao Weiguo, a Canton tour guide.

With grain as the staple, nearly everything else in the diet serves as a
condiment, to flavor bland rice or noodles. Hard times mean that a peasant's
supply of *fan*—rice or other grain—has been curtailed because of drought,
poor planning or other mishaps. The central government rushes in emergency supplies when necessary, but there is no minimum ration guaranteed
every peasant.

What makes this regimen tolerable is the vast array of vegetables that is
available, unregulated and cheap because so much of it is grown in private
gardens. Another saving grace is the ingenuity of Chinese cooks, whose
culinary skill and pride are so great that they have occasionally threatened
to create diplomatic incidents. Bowman Cutter, one of the staff aides on
Walter Mondale's 1979 trip to China, said he received an extremely chilly
response when he asked that a few courses be cut from what appeared to
be an overlong banquet scheduled at the Dong Fang Hotel in Canton. It
wasn't until after much delicate discussion with the hotel representatives
that Cutter got to the bottom of the matter. "The Dong Fang chefs knew
the American journalists had all visited the big restaurants in Canton. They
knew visitors looked down on hotel food, and if we cut out some course,
it would ruin their color scheme." To the Chinese, color and texture of food

are extremely important—in this case at least as important as Mondale's need for a small break in the schedule.

The Chinese take even more seriously the flagship of their international culinary reputation: Peking duck. They are every bit as passionate about *kao ya* (roast duck, as they call it) as Texans are on the subject of chili, as snobbish as the French when they discuss goose liver. Every step of its intricate preparation was developed by a chef to the Ming-dynasty Emperor Yong Lo in the fourteenth century.

Something called Peking duck is served everywhere from New York to New Guinea, but you will never convince most Chinese that the real thing can be had anywhere except on its home ground. "Outside Peking, duck leaves a lot to be desired," a well-traveled Chinese diplomat told us. He pronounced ducks bred in southern China "too skinny," those from Hong Kong "too fishy," perhaps because they are fed fish meal. As for the Long Island ducklings that often wind up in America's Chinese restaurants, "the less said the better." Taiwan duck is highly regarded by many overseas Chinese, and why not: when the late General Chiang Kai-shek fled the mainland he brought with him into exile some of China's finest chefs (we can testify personally to their skills). But in Peking, the Nationalist Chinese ducks are suspected of certain ideological deviations. "I hear they take all sorts of shortcuts in Taiwan," a waiter told us. "They hurry up the preparation for the sake of profits."

There is no chance of that happening in Peking, the Chinese insist, for every aspect of a Peking duck's existence from barnyard to dinner table is dictated by a thick government manual, the bible of duck tenders and duck chefs alike. The manual observes that ducks are perfectly suited to Chinese agriculture, for unlike temperamental turkeys or individualistic geese, they are "docile creatures" that "enjoy a quiet, collective life."

What is the secret of an authentic Peking duck? First, there is the duck itself. It must be of the snowy white Peking variety, a specialty of the dozen poultry farms that surround the city and raise about four million ducks a year. Ideally, the duck should be sixty-five days old when slaughtered and should weigh about five pounds. For the last two weeks of its life it will have been force-fed four times a day with a rich mixture of millet, corn, soybean cake and sorghum, gaining about two or three ounces a day.

We visited the duck farm at the Peace Commune outside Peking, a favorite source of fowl for the city's restaurants, and found life not quite as peaceful and free of ruffled feathers as the snowy-white ducks might have preferred. To come to a table as plump and succulent as gourmets the world over expect requires overeating so extreme that no sensible duck would acquiesce: the ducks are fed by machines every six hours, on the dot.

We watched, with stomachs somewhat unsettled, as one of the commune's expert duck tenders, Wang Derui, grabbed a duck by the scruff of its neck, forced open its mouth and thrust a plastic hose halfway down its throat. A large helping of mixed grain was pumped down the duck's throat from a grumbling machine that resembled a miniature cement mixer. The duck quacked indignantly, smoothed its feathers and waddled uncertainly back to its pen. Wang, who does about twenty ducks a minute as they come down a long, low corral, shrugged and turned to his next charge. All the older ducks we inspected in the holding yards outside had enormous hindquarters, as if the rubber hose had plunged all the way down and pumped them up like balloons.

So enamored are the Pekingese of their roast ducks that the city has opened a shrine to its best-known dish, a seven-story $5 million restaurant that seats 2,600 people and serves up every part of the duck except the quack. Its menu, consisting entirely of duck dishes, lists not only the standard Peking duck with pancakes, spring onions and *hoisin* sauce, the *pièce de résistance* of any duck dinner, but hundreds of variations. In the appetizer column alone there are fifty hot and thirty cold dishes, which are all concocted from the flesh, wings, liver, stomach and even the webbed feet of a duck.

This temple to the art of preparing and eating Peking duck was intended to augment three restaurants that had been overtaxed by the swelling demands of tourism and an ever-expanding local clientele. And when it first opened its doors in late 1979, this huge establishment was so besieged by patrons that reservations sometimes had to be made a week in advance. But later, prices rose so high (in some cases, $35 per person for foreign banqueters, half that amount for Chinese) that demand plummeted. The official New China News Agency, sensing a scandal at the duck restaurants, reported that unscrupulous managers had taken advantage of a late 1979 across-the-board increase in the price of meat and other food supplies to inflate all the prices on their menus. "Outlets that raised their prices in this disguised form have been criticized," the agency said. In response to complaints, the city dispatched inspection teams to all the duck restaurants and decreed that no one could charge natives more than $1.80 a pound for duck, putting the price of an average whole duck at $9 or $10. Since this represents about one quarter of an average Chinese worker's monthly salary, Peking duck remains a treat reserved for very special occasions.

There has been little relief, however, for foreign connoisseurs of Peking duck, who have always had to pay far more because of China's two-tier pricing system (discount rates for locals; whatever the traffic will bear for foreigners). An American businessman who tried to arrange a simple dinner at the new restaurant for $15 a head was scornfully told by the reservations clerk, "For such a small amount you can only buy ordinary food, not Peking duck." So the American took his business to one of the smaller, shabbier and more reasonably priced Peking duck restaurants, informally dubbed the Sick Duck. (All the Peking duck restaurants have nicknames bestowed over the years by faithful foreign customers. The Sick Duck got its name because it is located down the street from the Capital Hospital. A duck outlet less favorably situated, near a sewage treatment plant, is affectionately called the Stinky Duck, and the most venerable of the duck houses, opened in 1866, is named the Old Duck.)

The mammoth new competitor is usually referred to as the Wall Street Duck because it faces the street where the old city wall once stood, though its detractors insist on calling it the Monster Duck and contend that its quality suffers because of its size. When we dined there with Hou Baolin, China's premier comedian, he was openly scornful of the quality of the food, though he held his tongue when the headwaiter came by to see if all was well with his famous guest.

Ironically, Peking duck owes its fame to an outlander, a man who was middle-aged before he ever set foot in the big city. Yang Quanren, a peasant, arrived in 1835 with nothing but a knowledge of duck farming and a burning ambition to get away from it for the rest of his life. From a wooden plank placed across two stools, he started peddling ducks to the housewives of Peking. Eventually his sidewalk stall became a shop, and within a decade he had made enough money to convert the shop into a restaurant, the forerunner of the Old Duck restaurant. Using techniques developed by the chef credited with inventing Peking duck in the imperial kitchens five hundred years before, Yang established a reputation for serving the best duck in town. His restaurant, Quan Ju De (Repository of all the Virtues), was recognized as the country's leading duck palace. Its clientele included politicians, writers and actors, even the imperial family, and many years later, using the newfangled telephone, members of the royal family would ring up and summon the restaurant's top chefs whenever they felt a yen for duck. Another royal family, Japan's, patronized the duck restaurant for what is possibly the first recorded instance of Chinese take-out. Whenever Emperor Hirohito's cousin Saga Hiroshi (who was married to the younger brother of China's last emperor) visited Peking, she would take back to Tokyo with her a Peking duck, roasted by the Quan Ju De just before she boarded the plane and kept hot in a thermos-type container.

Soon after the Chinese Communist Party came to power in 1949, the Old Duck restaurant ceased to be an exclusive haunt for the well-to-do and was opened to working-class Chinese who had previously been able only to sniff the aromas from behind its heavily curtained doors. The clientele may have changed, but according to Zhang Wenzao, the seventy-four-year-old dean of Peking duck chefs, duck is prepared today exactly as it was six centuries ago. Zhang, the favorite chef of Deng Xiaoping, makes sure of that: practically every one of the capital's eighty duck chefs started as his apprentice.

Peking experts say it takes at least four days to prepare a duck for the oven. No part of the bird goes to waste; as it is cleaned and gutted, the feathers and down are saved (they are a top export item) and the internal organs are set aside for later use in the kitchen. Compressed air is then introduced between the skin and flesh. The duck, painted with a sugary solution, is hung up to dry for twenty-four hours, preferably in a stiff cold breeze. The point of these elaborate operations is to separate the skin from the meat and thus produce the crisp texture of the skin that purists demand. Then the duck's cavity is filled with boiling water, and the bird, head and all, is hung in a special oven and roasted over a fire of date, peach or pear wood, to impart the characteristic fruity flavor. A pound of fat usually drips off during the roasting, and although a healthy layer of fat remains directly under the skin, a perfect Peking duck is not supposed to be greasy.

Eating a Peking duck is almost as much a ritual as its preparation. The meal begins with cold appetizers, then hot, and moves on through dishes such as fried duck's heart in salt and pepper until at last the bird is carried triumphantly to the table to be admired before it is carved. Strict protocol calls for the skin to be served first, then the heartier flesh, though many diners, disdainful of tradition, mix the two. The routine is to pick up a few pieces of skin or meat with chopsticks, dip them into a special sweet bean sauce and tuck them into a paper-thin pancake. A few pieces of slivered scallion are added, the pancake is folded (so it looks like a taco), and the whole morsel is popped into the mouth. Duck soup made of crushed bones and cabbage usually follows for those not already sated.

Struggling to describe the attraction of a Peking duck to the Chinese, Americans who wrote the much respected cookbook *Chinese Gastronomy* said that in the way it marries crisp vegetables with rich meat, a traditional Peking duck dinner "most closely resembles a bacon, lettuce and tomato sandwich."

Their comment resembles the sort of backhanded compliment one hears often in China about the indelicate pleasures of Western food. All Chinese, even the poorest, seem united in the conviction that their cuisine is superior to all others. "In other countries, people seem to have no respect for their stomachs," sniffed a Peking journalist as he watched Linda enjoy a salad of raw vegetables and iced tea, both unthinkable to the Chinese mind. "Really, how can you eat those things?"

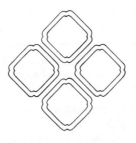

THE ARTS

CHINESE THINKERS FROM THE BEGINNING SAW ART AS A WAY TO INFLU-
ence behavior. Confucius even explored the ethical impact of good and bad
music. So when the Maoists set strict rules for painting, film, music and
dance in the 1940s and again in the 1960s, no one was very surprised. What
surprised us, however, was how quickly the older, simpler tastes reasserted
themselves after Mao died.

We could not really appreciate, until we lived there, how much people
in China looked to the arts for escape from the confines of life in an
overcrowded, bureaucratized society. It was one more part of the underground life everyone leads—getting better food through the back door,
getting better housing by *guanxi,* and finding relief from boredom in folk
arts that seep through the fabric of state-dictated culture. In many cases
these were simpler, more vulgar pastimes than either Confucius or Mao
would have publicly approved.

One evening, Linda walked into the hotel room and found our amah in
tears. When Linda asked what was wrong, Ah-Lin pointed at the television
set. A Peking opera was being broadcast, live. Somewhat relieved, Linda
said, "Has something bad happened?" "No," Ah-Lin sobbed, "something
bad is *going* to happen!" Like nearly every Chinese in the world past the
age of forty, and many even younger, Ah-Lin knew all the hackneyed plots
by heart. She thrilled as much in anticipation of disaster as to the event
itself, and like everyone else in Peking after Mao's death, she was ecstatic
at the revival of such artistic retreads. "They're not operas, they're folk
songs," said one overseas Chinese who had acquired a taste for Peking
opera. "They have one plot and four hundred variations."

It took us a while to become accustomed to a theater where the old, not
the new, drew the customers. The revolutionary operas, which Jiang Qing
encouraged, were mostly flops, surviving only because she permitted nothing else to be staged. The old operas held the hearts and memories of
Chinese theatergoers, and once Jiang had been arrested they came back

quickly, along with a complete set of artistic tastes for which we were unprepared.

The Chinese, we discovered, are crazy about electric organs and love ballads from Taiwan. Their favorite brand of humor makes gross fun of physical deformities and the dilemmas of life, using these devices to prick the Communist Party gently without leaving too many obvious scars. Love stories and tragedies predominate modern literature. If there is one place where politics still intrudes, it is in motion pictures. The Chinese react to this by flocking to movie theaters showing the most mediocre Western films. They take what they like, ignore the rest, and give only grudging praise to any of it. What little entertainment they get they feel more than entitled to.

Chinese behavior at public theaters, for instance, borders on rudeness. When we got tickets to the supposedly popular play *Newsboys* in Nanning in 1978, it was five minutes after the curtain went up before the chatter from the audience quieted enough so that we could hear the actors. When the curtain came down on the last act, nearly everyone rose immediately and headed for the exits, not bothering to applaud. This was par for the course. At a Shanghai circus, at a Shanghai dance drama, at a Guilin local opera, most of the applause came from foreigners. The Chinese responded with little more than a rattle of empty pop bottles, buzz of private chat, and a shuffle of feet. At the Gansu Provincial Theater in Lanzhou, where we spent an evening watching the opera *Story of the Plaque,* the favorite audience pastime was loudly chewing sunflower seeds and spitting on the floor. "I thought I was going to drown at the last performance," said an American teacher living in that northwestern town.

Cao Yu, a wise-cracking, plump little man considered China's best living playwright, grumbles about the Chinese reluctance to applaud. He once grabbed a member of the audience at one of his plays and asked what was wrong with the production.

"I loved it," the man said.

"Wasn't it any good?" asked Cao, unconvinced.

"The best I have ever seen. When I get home, I'm going to insist that my wife and children all go see it."

"Then why didn't you applaud?"

"I'm just not in the habit."

Rulan Pian, a scholar of Chinese music at Harvard, blames it all on Peking opera. Chinese operagoers often show up only for the high points, since they have seen and heard the story so many times before. When the villain dies, or the heroine commits suicide, people leave. No curtain call, no round of applause at the end, because few have sat through all the way. When Peking's number one opera troupe performed in New York in late 1980, they did not know how to take a curtain call, and each night had to adjust to the unfamiliar applause at the end of the performance.

The *People's Daily* once printed a Peking concertgoer's complaint that "the decorum in the concert hall was unthinkably bad and the influence on the evening extremely unpleasant." But Chinese audiences seem confident enough of themselves in the new era of "One Hundred Flowers Blooming" to remain casual and nonchalant, even when chastised. China's cultural reawakening offers many of them more opportunities to go out with friends at night and chat in air-conditioned theaters, as important to many poorly housed Chinese as the chance to appreciate whatever is going on onstage.

When something moves a Chinese audience, like the heroine's tragic death in a Peking opera, they respond with a buzz of warmth and excitement. A crowd packed into a sweltering movie theater in Canton laughed and cheered at a 1957 romantic operetta, full of boy-meets-girl winks and blushes. What the Chinese liked most seemed to us not much better than vaudeville. An evening's performance by a Hainan Island troupe in Canton included accordion solos, operatic arias and a big finale—a native dance with young women in red-and-blue caps, white tunics with blue polka dots, blue kilts with white cowboy fringe, red patterned leggings and sandals.

But what really worked was a plunge into comic sex, such as the night a local troupe in Nanning put on their new comedy, *The Sweet Life*. The play later became a national hit, and was made into a popular movie. The audience came late, chatted and left early, but they also laughed often and loudly at the antics onstage. The play's heroine, mother of four daughters but eager to produce a son, fights the official birth control policy. In the end one daughter marries a nice young laboratory technician whom the mother accepts as her long-desired son, but not before many misunderstandings have intruded. *I Love Lucy* has never been shown on Chinese television, but *The Sweet Life* relied on some of the same time-tested gags. At one point the weary husband of the heroine rushes to the hospital as the time for the birth of his fifth child nears. His office assistant uses the hospital telephone to arrange a study date with a young woman he has just met.

"Yes, I think I can meet you," she says, quite pleased. A nurse runs shouting past the hospital telephone. "Where are you?" asks the girl, puzzled.

"Oh, in the maternity ward," the young man answers.

"What?"

"Well, the baby's about to be born."

"Baby!?"

"Oh, I have to go, the time has come . . . Hello? Hello? Hello?"

When this underground Chinese thirst for the ribald and farcical goes too far, the official culture establishment sounds the alarm. Witness the reaction to the satire entitled *If I Were Real*. This 1979 play is a fictionalized account of Zhang Longquan, the Shanghai impostor who wined and dined in splendor for weeks because local officials thought he was the son of an important general. A private Shanghai production thrilled a packed audience with its vicious dissection of party officialdom. We saw a huge billboard advertising the play in Xi'an, and it was also produced in Canton. But the authorities in Shanghai banned public performances and persuaded Peking authorities to cancel a televised production at the last minute.

A somber official arts conference then put *If I Were Real* on its agenda. Some critics and playwrights complained that it was a distortion to have every official in the play misbehaving except for the general, who appears at the end to sort things out. Others said it was the best play they had seen in years. After much discussion, tempers cooled: the two sides agreed that the young authors should be encouraged to rewrite the play to put some officials in a better light.

The Chinese stand back from these literary battles and almost enjoy them as farce for their own sake. A favorite, perhaps apochryphal, story concerns the day Deng Xiaoping received a telephone invitation to a new Jiang Qing play. Sensitive to Deng's reputed distaste for revolutionary operas, Jiang's assistant heard Deng say *"Ji zuo!"* (Too leftist!) over the telephone. Deng's defenders contended that his Sichuanese accent had obscured the words *"Zhi zou"* (I'll be right over). In late 1979, arts officials held a dinner to honor the greats of drama, painting and literature, only to find that many dinner partners refused to talk to one another. It was impossible to avoid sitting near someone who had denounced you from one side or another during the campaigns of the 1950s and 1960s.

This underground, real-life Chinese theater of the absurd reached its zenith while we were in Peking with the intriguing debate over two nude women painted on a wall of the new Peking international airport.

Prior to the Communist takeover, the art scene was dominated by nearly interchangeable groups of painters who consciously emulated traditional masters of ink painting who had died centuries before. A few painters studying Western art had begun to experiment in the twentieth century. Experimenters and traditionalists both continued to work under the Communists, but all fell victim to the ravages of the Cultural Revolution. Huang Yongyu, the best of the latest generation working in the traditional medium, was forced to move from his apartment to a leaky hovel with no heat, electricity or running water. He had painted an owl with one eye open and one closed, which official critics took as a secret slap at government inattention to the masses.

By the 1980s Huang had been rehabilitated and socialist realism had begun to seem passé, even to the Chinese. One particularly well-connected artist, Zhang Ding, enlisted several experimentally inclined young artists to join him in painting murals for the new airport building. Zhang had taught at the old revolutionary base in Yenan in 1938. Under the post-Mao government, led by other old war veterans, Zhang's political credentials were impeccable. By contrast, Yuan Yunsheng, the artist who eventually painted the controversial nudes, was a forty-two-year-old renegade from Jiangsu with a mustache and whiskers, and a much different history. His career began with a year in a labor camp in the late 1950s when the political commissars at the Peking Fine Arts Academy, noting his interest in post-impressionism, labeled him a "rightist." Thereafter he spent sixteen years at Changchun in the cold and isolated northeast, teaching art to workers after hours at a "cultural palace," the Chinese version of the YMCA.

After his rehabilitation, in preparation for his airport mural, "Water Festival—Song of Life," Yuan spent six months sketching the activities of the Dai, a minority people living in the rain forests near the Burmese border. The nudes in the mural depict a traditional celebration in which clothes are occasionally shed. Their elongated bodies, Yuan told American art historian Joan Lebold Cohen, were inspired by Botticelli.

After the airport opened in October 1979, to approving notices from Western journalists, the comedic clash of official and popular tastes began. Some Chinese officials objected strongly to Yuan's work, saying it was inappropriate, bad art and offensive to the Dai people. But leading Chinese artists rushed to defend Yuan, and Party Vice Chairman Li Xiannian appeared to back them up. "Is that all they are afraid of people seeing?" said Li, well known for his appreciation of the female form, after a visit to the airport. The controversy grew so heated that then Party Chairman Hua Guofeng invited the Dai people to decide.

A delegation of Dai residents from Peking visited the airport and pro-nounced the mural suitable, except for a few minor errors: they did bathe in the nude, they said, but sarongs were usually worn over breasts rather than around waists. Then officials from Yunan, the home province of the Dai, wrote to the central authorities, complaining that the mural was an insult and a product of a Chinese anti-minority bias. The elongated figures were ugly, the letter charged, and the scene of a boy chasing a girl would never have been allowed if the youngsters had been Chinese rather than members of a minority. Armed with the letter, the critics of the mural managed to get the nudes covered with a makeshift curtain while they tried to persuade Yuan to revise the painting. The artist refused, which only added spice to the whole ridiculous affair.

The mural was located in the "foreigners-only" dining room at the air-port. When we stopped there for tea one day, a steady stream of Chinese looked in. Some peeked shyly at the curtain, not daring to touch it, but others walked in boldly and pulled the curtain aside to get a good look at the objects of dispute. Affecting ignorance of the affair, we asked one of the waiters why that part of the mural was covered. "It's being revised." Why? *"Bu tai qing chu"* (That's not too clear)—the favorite Chinese response to all sensitive questions.

The controversy sent a collective shudder through the art establishment. Arts colleges thought they had successfully finessed the fearful question of nude models. Some schools had found young peasant women whose families needed the money and so were willing to pose. Nobody objected, and many a young woman eventually married an art student who had admired her figure, but word of the airport controversy led one school to insist that all models henceforth wear garments. Eventually someone in the leadership, probably Deng Xiaoping himself, decided that enough was enough. The airport scandal was making China look silly, particularly to the foreigners who dined in the room where the mural was located. The curtain was removed and the controversy subsided, with one last fitting touch when the artists in the project objected that they had not received the customary bonus. Airport officials said that their free room and board while working on the project was enough of a bonus. Like all such disputes, this one had to go to a vice premier, who ordered the airport to pay.

If such efforts to throw some unpredictability and cheerful sensuality into Chinese art are to succeed in the long run, they may depend on the future of younger, unofficial artists, like the members of the "Xingxing" (Stars) group we chatted with at their first exhibit in Peking's Beihai Park. ("Stars" in Chinese has a Tinkerbell connotation, sparkling and bright, but *not* big and famous.) We studied a massive wood sculpture of a man's head, his face contorted by pain, one eye shut tight and a gag stuffed in his mouth. "This is my image of myself and of all Chinese people who have been oppressed," said Wang Keping, the thirty-year-old sculptor. "See, one eye is shut so we can't see much of what is going on around us. And the mouth is corked, like a thermos bottle, so we cannot speak. I've taken the cork out of my own mouth, for a while at least, but eventually of course, somebody may stuff it back in." Spectators crowded close, eying the statue and eavesdropping. They laughed nervously.

Wang and twenty-eight other young artists in his group celebrated an unexpected victory in the fall of 1979. They had been refused permission to show their work at the National Art Gallery, so they set up a sidewalk display near Democracy Wall which the police dismantled. A protest march followed, and a high party official allowed them to hold their exhibit in the park. In the summer of 1980 they displayed their works at Peking's Fine Arts Museum but still needled officialdom. Wang smuggled one of his favorite pieces, a wooden mask called "Idol," past the guards and into the exhibit after museum officials had made a last inspection. The "Idol" resembles Chairman Mao, looking like a Buddha with the star of the Red Army in the middle of his forehead.

When we interviewed these young men and women, they were indignant that the government had not seen fit to give them official commissions, and at the same time were pugnacious about official censorship. Ma Desheng, a young wood engraver, will occasionally hold out his arms as if he were handcuffed and talk about his willingness to endure arrest for his art. Ma is lame in one leg and uses crutches. He specializes in fine engravings and woodcuts, but he earns his living as a mechanic. Huang Rui, a painter born in the early 1950s, sweeps up in a leather factory. Wang Keping, the sculptor, writes scripts for Peking central radio and television.

Their artwork differs sharply from the billboard posters of smiling tractor drivers or the misty traditional landscapes that occupy most government-supported artists. They have tried abstract renditions of the imperial palace, impressionistic street scenes, nudes and sculptures, like the "Idol," which ridicule bureaucracy and other excesses of the Communist system. Some of the pieces are blatantly political, others more Chinese, more subtle. One pen-and-ink drawing, a paean to China's peasants, shows the tiny figure of a man prodding a team of oxen under the fierce sun. "They come into the world silent, depart the world unnoticed and leave behind only thousands of sweat drops to water the fields," an accompanying poem says.

Wang Keping prefers stark social and political parody. In his hometown of Tianjin he joined Red Guards during the Cultural Revolution, looting and burning a Roman Catholic church. These activities upset him even then. Picking up a piece of wood that had fallen off a chair, he decided to try carving out what he felt. He likes bits and scraps of wood. A wooden head swathed in chains is entitled "Love"; another head with an ugly growth on the cheek represents a bureaucrat ("they are a cancer"). Jiang Qing assumes the shape of a rifle ("power comes from the barrel of a gun").

When his symbolism does not seem to come across to his friends, Wang elbows them and asks, "You get it? You get it?" Some of the young artists' explanations are a bit thin. At the Beihai Park exhibit, Huang Rui had difficulty persuading visitors that his painting of a nude female symbolized "the spirit of freedom" rising from Tiananmen Square after the famous anti-radical riot of April 1976.

Many of China's older and officially connected artists support the young amateurs, if for no other reason than that the wider the boundaries of artistic freedom, the more they can experiment in their own work. The Peking Artists Association, the official artists group for the National Gallery, supported the "Stars" show. Many of its members protected the amateurs' works when the police broke up the original Democracy Wall exhibit. Huang Zhen, then the Culture Minister, was a Sunday painter himself who sketched scenes while a Red Army officer on the Long March, and he tolerated the young artists.

But on some matters, even the most provocative young amateurs step lightly. Most have resisted selling their work, especially to foreigners. "No Chinese could afford to buy any of our things," Wang said. "And while I don't know offhand of any laws or regulations forbidding us to sell to foreigners, there might be some secret regulation on the books. Why take a chance?" Some officials take heart from such caution, and write off the Xingxing group as a passing fad. One senior party official told Stanford University Professor Michael Sullivan, "They are young. If we allow them to exhibit, they will learn the error of their ways, and come back to the fold."

Like other parts of the society, China's artists are broken up into different generations. There is a group in their fifties and sixties who worked within the restrictive rules of the 1950s and gratefully accept today's limited freedoms. The very young people are impatient with any restrictions, and agitate as if there were little danger of a backlash. Members of another middle-aged group are bitter at having missed the chance to create during what might have been their most fruitful years.

Many of these artistic men and women seek refuge in the rhythm of daily work. For some this has become a deadening burden; the government has begun to milk the arts for all the income they can generate, so experimental work gives way to traditional ink paintings to feed the overseas market. Chinese artists keep up the old esthetic arguments in their spare time: What is Chinese painting? Should we use foreign styles? If so, which style? Can we develop a national style? Chinese artists, like their compatriots, seek consensus, and that stifles originality, leaving the banal and the familiar.

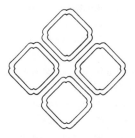

MOVIES

HAVING HAD THEIR FILL OF THE LATEST CROP OF GOVERNMENT-PRO-
duced movies, the two television comedians try a daring spoof on the
surprised viewers. One of them plays a brave peasant fatally wounded by
Nationalist invaders. His partner says, "You can't die yet—haven't you
forgotten something?"

"Oh, yes!" The wounded peasant's face is twisted in unbelievable anguish.
"Comrade, here . . . are . . . [gasp] my party dues! May I die now?"

"Not yet. You must say, 'How are the other comrades?' "

"Okay. How . . . [gasp] are the other comrades?"

"Fine. Now say, 'How are the villagers?' "

"How . . . [choke] are . . . the villagers?"

"Good, good. Now, you know what else to say?"

"Oh, yes—ready? We . . . [gasp] . . . *will have vic-tor-eeee!*" He topples
over, his audience laughing and nodding knowingly.

The world's largest movie audience (70 million people a day, 30 billion
a year, walking or bicycling to see some kind of film) has shown the same
impatience with the film propaganda and ritualized acting that they have
with committee-written music and revolutionary operas. Years after the
Communist Party purged Jiang Qing and other Maoist politicians who had
suppressed movies in the late 1960s and early 1970s, Chinese filmgoers
complain of *bangwei* ("the smell of the Gang") and turn up their noses at
much of what they see on the screen. Just how far the government will go
in reforming this unusually potent medium is uncertain, however. The
Chinese flock to the few grade-B American productions that have found
their way to China, but for a number of reasons there are not many of those,
nor are there likely to be many in the future.

China's filmmakers, too, are unusually candid about their failure to
overcome the old ideological influences. "Too flat and preachy, too talky,
too rough-and-ready and too black and white," commented seventy-nine-
year-old Xia Yan, probably China's most experienced screenwriter and a

man who suffered greatly during the Cultural Revolution. Ding Qiao, vice director of the Culture Ministry's film bureau, ridiculed what he called the "sky, ground and heart" syndrome, a series of stylized postures taken by the common Chinese movie hero in moments of great emotion (pointing at the sky, the ground and touching his breast). Jiang liked them: But even with Jiang in jail, they still survive.

The stilted gestures can be blamed in part on the pervasive influence of Peking opera on all dramatic training in China. In Peking opera, audiences prefer stock characters, and will watch the same operas over and over again, even though the characters fit into such well-worn niches that their make-up is color-coded: red for honest heroes, white for crafty villains, green for ghosts. Characters with both good and bad elements, constantly in search of themselves, may appeal to Westerners, but they make many older Chinese feel uncomfortable. Those Chinese see themselves as part of a group. They want to do the job assigned them, playing their role, and like to see this approach reflected in the old operas. But when this approach is carried into film, many Chinese do not find the results so pleasing. One teacher at the Peking Languages Institute sat through a private screening of an Alfred Hitchcock thriller. As the lights went back on, he turned to an American in surprise: "In our films we know who the villain is from the very beginning, but in your films, you can't tell who it is until the very end!"

Party pressure on filmmakers helped encourage these formula films, which fortified party stereotypes with the old opera techniques. The formulas existed long before Jiang Qing became a cultural czarina, and will probably survive her absence. At China's 1980 version of the Academy ceremony all the awards, called the Hundred Flowers Prizes, were presented personally by Zhou Yang, a slow-speaking, white-haired man in his seventies who has been a boss of party cultural matters since the 1930s. Zhou and his aides give no evidence of softening party control of directors, writers and actors. They promote "the scientific Marxist world outlook" and support artists who "reflect in their works the progress of the arduous struggle to achieve socialist transformation and modernization." In the time since we left China this emphasis, if anything, has increased.

The Hundred Flowers awards in 1980 revived a ceremony that took place in 1962 and 1963, then fell victim to the growing political demands of people like Jiang Qing who rejected prizes as propagating individualism and "awardism." Foreigners attending the 1980 festivities at the Friendship Hotel theater noticed immediately that most of the stars were in proper, subdued attire, though one of the leading starlets, Liu Xiaoqing, wore a sweater with a large red bow at the neck. The glossy color magazine *Popular Cinema* said 600,000 people sent in their votes for best movie, best actor and best actress, spurred on by full-page pictures of their favorite stars. But authorities made their own priorities known by decorating the stage with huge red banners that proclaimed "Workers of the world, unite!" and

"Long live invincible Marxism-Leninism–Mao Tse-tung Thought!" The movies receiving top awards were *Tear Stains*, the story of a political frame-up exposed; *Little Flower*, the tale of a girl cut off from her family during wartime; and *General Ji Hongchang*, about a Nationalist leader who switches his allegiance to the Communists. A romantic comedy involving sets of twins and much delightful confusion was rumored to have actually received more votes but had been stricken from the list because officials considered it too frivolous to serve as an example to the nation's film industry. Some in the audience found *General Ji* so stilted and boring that they left at intermission.

The filmmakers occasionally argue with the authorities over this political heavy-handedness. But even relatively enlightened leaders like Deng Xiaoping and Zhao Ziyang strongly endorse for the arts as well as other parts of society the "four basic principles," upholding socialism, the dictatorship of the proletariat, the leadership of the Communist Party and Marxism-Leninism–Mao Tse-tung Thought. The official press occasionally tries to discourage popular demands for lighter films by belittling Western movies. A *People's Daily* writer argued that the success of *Star Wars* in the United States reflected the "discontent of the American public and their hope to find consolation in the world of illusion . . . The American film industry is destined never to be able to find a true way out because the entire capitalist culture is decaying." The same newspaper characterized American films as "divorced from reality and devoid of thoughts, stressing only thrills and fun."

Which was, we discovered, exactly what Chinese audiences wanted. Several Charlie Chaplin films, such as *Modern Times*, have been shown to enthusiastic audiences. More recent American movies distributed in China have been less distinguished, the most widely shown during our stay being the science-fiction film *Future World* and Sam Peckinpah's trucker picture *Convoy*. Of *Convoy*, an American embassy cultural officer said, "That frightful film was nothing but sex and violence. The Chinese intellectuals I know were outraged. But the Chinese assistant I have, who runs the Xerox machine, liked those trucks and all the action." The film played to packed audiences, with some showings beginning at 5:30 A.M. "They would not show it or any other foreign films out in the countryside, however," the American cultural officer said. "They told us it would be too disruptive, too confusing."

Chinese film authorities found themselves in a dilemma in 1980 when they agreed to an American film festival in Peking. They delayed negotiations for six months to decide if they could risk screening films like *Breaking Away, Singin' in the Rain* and *Shane*. An American diplomat close to the talks enjoyed the Chinese dilemma over *Shane*, the classic tale of a lone cowboy, played by Alan Ladd: "Perhaps the Chinese were bothered that Shane was not operating in accordance with a central directive." The Chinese negotiators accepted *The Black Stallion* and *Snow White and the Seven Dwarfs* without much difficulty, but agonized over the rest of the available list: *Guess Who's Coming to Dinner, East of Eden, Patton, To Kill a Mockingbird* and *Raisin in the Sun.* They took *Guess Who's Coming to Dinner* only after it was pointed out that a Chinese theatrical company had done it on stage in Peking, using some actors in blackface. Grudgingly, the Chinese finally took *Shane* and *Singin' in the Rain,* but they clearly had their sights set elsewhere. "We know you've got other musicals," one of them said to the Americans. "How about *The Sound of Music?*" Songs from that Rodgers and Hammerstein hit musical are often heard on Chinese radio; it may be the most popular movie never to have been seen in a public theater in China. Jiang Qing got a print for her personal use from the American producers with the help of her U.S. biographer Roxanne Witke, but the Chinese have not paid for public distribution of the film.

The color and special effects of almost any U.S. production bowled over the Chinese. When they showed the seventeen episodes of the U.S. television series *Man from Atlantis* that were made before it was canceled, an American researcher in Shanghai told a Chinese friend that most people back home thought the series was trash. The friend hesitated, then explained that the Chinese like the science fiction and the swimming. Room attendants at the Peking Hotel seemed to disappear whenever *Man from Atlantis* was on; we found them clustered around the TV set in the lounge near the elevators. It was even difficult to find a taxi during that hour each week. Theater managers said their houses were deserted when the show was on the air.

Film has such enormous power in China. Tickets for the best movies, particularly the American films, are often hard to get. In big cities, young men can readily get a date just by waving an extra ticket to such a show. In provincial cities, scalping and trading of tickets go on at a frantic pace in front of some movie houses. We have seen at least two fist fights break out during arguments over movie tickets. The Chinese say that no one makes a profit. People simply want to sell tickets at face value when they cannot attend the performance, or find they would like to trade to see another movie. But we have heard bidding for higher prices. In one of the more candid new films we saw, a young pickpocket makes money selling movie tickets in front of theaters after he has lifted them from bus passengers.

Chinese filmmakers and party officials have had the same argument for the past twenty years: Should movies paint society as good and evil, black and white, in order to encourage socially acceptable behavior, or adopt the Western approach of giving villains and charlatans a certain human depth? The old Chinese tradition of moral stereotypes—each actor fitting a role—has almost always won out, supported by the party and by the distaste among all kinds of Chinese officials for what is considered Western excess.

In a letter to the *Peking Daily,* city Youth League official Xu Baolan echoed the sentiments of the Moral Majority in the United States:

> In the course of doing youth work, we have discovered that some units are showing certain unhealthy foreign films, which have already caused gravely evil results in society . . . and even caused some to embark on the road of crime. One murderer aged 17 has seen more than 100 foreign films in the past two years, many of which were films not shown to the general public, which depicted violence, sex, knights of ancient times, old-style acrobatic fighting and so on. He started by being frightened and scared of these films, but then gradually changed to a strong partiality for scenes of bloody murder, and ended up by committing a crime.

Ironically, government offices under pressure to raise money for the state have begun to use "internal" films both to improve morale and increase profits. A writer for the Peking *Market Review* complained that around New Year 1980 some theaters, in cooperation with local government offices, showed more than thirty internal films, probably obtained from Hong Kong brokers, to moviegoers eager to pay for such a treat. "Some offices lent the films for money, and some even showed the internal films in places holding more than 10,000 people so as to get more money."

One of the first Western movies widely shown after the death of Mao became notorious. It was an old British film, *The Million Pound Note,* in which Gregory Peck portrays a man given the huge single bill. He is able to live like a king by just waving it around. No one can change the bill, but everyone assumes Peck's credit is good. Most Chinese missed the subtle satire of capitalism. One newspaper said the film had inspired the young con artist in Shanghai who arranged to have himself wined and dined for free because he persuaded everyone he was the son of an important army general. Controversies such as these help explain the Chinese refusal to pay more than $10,000 for a Western film, especially one that might cause social trouble. Their rule keeps most Western films out; U.S. producers consider the maximum fee ridiculous when millions of Chinese will pay to see their films.

But when a U.S. film, acquired cheap, serves their own political purposes, the Chinese are not above promoting it for all it's worth. Consider *Nightmare in Badham County,* a made-for-TV film that was denounced by critics as inflammatory and gratuitously violent when it was first aired in the United States in 1976. The film tells the story of two college women who suffer false arrest, rape, torture and death at the hands of corrupt officials in a small Southern town. It provided a graphic device for answering the government's nettlesome critics abroad and in the democracy movement. And Chinese newspapers were full of favorable commentary on the film.

After Peking bought the film from a private distributor, the official information network leapt on the film like a new recipe for *jiaozi.* "Is it a nightmare? No, it is a bloody social reality," the special display outside one Shanghai theater announced. "In some people's eyes the United States is an ideal kingdom of human rights and law, but in the movie it is a human hell."

Far different is the Chinese-made *Xiao Zi Bei* (Those Kids) by the Changchun Studio of Jilin province, a Chinese *American Graffiti* about the loves and mishaps of youth—not young Californians cruising in hot rods, but young Shanghaiese who operate a public bus. The movie is full of pratfalls and pranks. A dreamy inventor cannot summon the nerve to tell the bus ticket taker he loves her until his friends make a tape recording of him practicing the words and play it under the couple's park bench.

Her fellow ticket taker is a genial laggard who closes the bus door on the leg of a woman rushing to get on. "Why the hurry?" he says, not the least bit nonplused.

"We must hurry to realize the four modernizations!" the woman replies, a rare moment of movie fun with one of the key political slogans of the 1980s.

All ends happily. The female bus driver ensnares the handsome young policeman who has been turning the lights green for her. Although too earnest in spots and showing a suspiciously clean and prosperous Shanghai, the movie provides the kind of light, aimless entertainment the Chinese prefer, and even has a few treasured sex jokes, if one listens carefully enough.

Screen kisses, however, still present a problem. Chinese directors treat them like fissionable material. Word spread widely about the liberties taken in a 1979 movie, *Love at Lushan,* so we went to see it. It was mostly tease: the audience's libido had to make do with one short kiss and the young heroine stretching seductively in her bright-colored sweater. The character was supposed to be a young Chinese-American woman (making her activities more acceptable to the censors), but the actress herself is from Shanghai and wore her ragged old Chinese cloth shoes on the set when the camera wasn't going to show her feet. The longest and most passionate screen kiss of 1980 was delivered by an Italian exchange student, Nicole Peyran, portraying a Chinese-Italian girl in the movie *Not for Love.* When the female characters are not entirely Chinese (even when the men they embrace are), audiences are supposed to forgive their indiscretions, though some Chinese see any movement in this direction as a bad trend. "I only hope that writers and directors will put such shots at proper places and not use them too much," one concerned viewer wrote to the *Peking Daily.*

Such difficulties evaporate when the Chinese plunge into their forte, cartoon animation, like the feature cartoon *Nezha Conquers the Dragon King,* a product of the Shanghai Animation Film Studio and the famous artist Zhang Ding. The sixteenth-century fairytale is an explosion of color and movement, with a touching story reminiscent of C. S. Lewis' *The Lion, the Witch and the Wardrobe*. The animation equals anything turned out by Disney Studios. When it appeared on television, our son Joe watched to the end, even though his Chinese was not good enough to follow the dialogue without subtitles.

Rudimentary filmmaking imported from the West began in 1895. By the 1920s and 1930s Shanghai had an active film industry, but the Communist troops fighting in barren mountain regions of the northwest had little time for such playthings. Ding Qiao of the Culture Ministry recalled that he could do only silent documentaries, with narrative read over a loudspeaker, but the Red Army troops were fascinated. When victory came, the Communist armies took over the big Japanese-run studio at Changchun and the sophisticated equipment still operating in Shanghai.

The Communist studios began to turn out a steady supply of features, some good enough to draw huge crowds even today. Talented actors like Zhao Dan captured the popular imagination with portrayals of historical heroes such as the ancient medical researcher Li Shizhen or Lin Zexun, the Qing official who tried to stop the European opium trade. When the Cultural Revolution began in 1966, Jiang Qing, who had acted in trite film romances in Shanghai in the 1930s under the name Lan Ping (Blue Apple), purged anyone she felt had ever slighted her. Qin Cheng prison, the detention center outside Peking for special political cases, began to fill up with actors and directors. They remained in solitary confinement with regular interrogations, but little exercise. When Zhao Dan emerged after several years of such treatment because of his differences with Jiang Qing, he couldn't speak or communicate or sit or stand like a normal human being. His wife, the actress and writer Huang Zongying, told us, "My children and I would go to another room and weep so that he wouldn't see us." Zhao died in 1980, after issuing a deathbed statement denouncing political meddling in the arts.

China now produces about one hundred films a year, but from 1966 to 1977 barely half a dozen new feature films were approved for release, and almost no new directors and actors were trained. As the film industry began to pull itself together after Mao's death and Jiang's arrest, the only experienced filmmakers were men in their fifties and sixties. Quality and innovation in films still suffer from that generation gap. As the Chinese say, *"Qing huang bu jie"*—meaning "The old crop has been consumed, but the new crop is not yet ripe enough to be harvested."

Young movie stars earn $35 to $45 a month, not much more than young factory workers—a cause for some private grumbling. Ma Ji, the comedy star, told us he would like something bigger than his two-room apartment. But older actors' monthly salaries often range above $200, and all enjoy a prestige not accorded ordinary workers.

An average feature film takes only a month to shoot and costs about $80,000. All Chinese films are dubbed. This speeds up filming and cuts costs, but dubbing makes the films appear stagy and unnatural to Western viewers. So, with considerable trepidation, the government has begun to experiment with films co-produced with Western companies—like the highly rated *Marco Polo* seen on U.S. television in 1982. "We cannot sanction any films that violate Chinese policies or contradict Chinese history or damage the image of the Chinese people," said Zhao Wei, a veteran actor and managing director of the new China Film Co-production Corp. At the time we spoke to Zhao, the Chinese were beginning work on the Sino-American production *The Marvelous Mongolian,* the story of a little horse's journey from Wales to Mongolia. Work was proceeding on a joint production of *Man's Fate,* the André Malraux novel of a Communist uprising in Shanghai in 1927, and on a film autobiography of Dr. Norman Bethune, a Canadian doctor who died in China while serving with the Communists during the Japanese invasion. These "friendship" projects were far from trouble-free. The Chinese were incensed that a small number of foreign Communists led by a half-Chinese, half-Japanese revolutionary were the heroes of Malraux's story. "The Chinese people led the revolution themselves," Zhao said. "There were representatives of other countries involved as advisers, that is true, but they were not the leaders."

Dr. Bethune caused even more trouble. In the Maoist canon, he is treated almost as a god—and as an inexhaustible symbol of the international appeal of Chinese Communism. Mao's 1939 essay, "In Memory of Norman Bethune," is enshrined in the Chairman's *Selected Works.* When the Chinese made their own movie of Bethune's life in 1964 with American expatriate Gerald Tannebaum in the title role, the good doctor was shown as a glorious, if balding, martyr. Canadian producer John Kemeny, who worked out a deal with the Chinese to co-produce a new version, and director Ted Kotcheff struggled for more than a year to convince the Chinese that their film, to be believable, ought to portray Bethune's human failings. Bethune had more than enough of those. He was reportedly a heavy drinker and something of a womanizer, and he had a terrible temper, which he thought nothing of unleashing on Chinese subordinates.

None of this was news to veteran Chinese leaders who knew Bethune, but the popular Chinese ignorance of Bethune's failings made it risky to authorize an honest portrayal. In the end, the Canadians seemed to be winning. Zhao, discussing the issue, seemed ready to welcome a new era for Chinese film and the Chinese audience's view of Dr. Bethune. "No one," said Zhao, "is one hundred percent perfect."

The enormous increase in the availability and variety of films, with more theaters open for longer hours, has brought attendance at theaters and outdoor showings up from 50 million daily in 1977 to 70 million in 1980. There are about 110,000 cinemas and an equal number of film projection teams showing movies on bed sheets in dusty village squares, and more and more films appear on television. One evening when we dined at a Chinese home, the children never appeared. They were glued to the TV set watching a new movie. And the movie mania has incited a capitalist-style commercial war that demonstrated, in the months just before we left Peking, how deep a hold the best made and least political films have on the leisure-time habits of ordinary Chinese.

In the first blush of the new movie era, the best Chinese and new foreign films were shown on television only weeks and sometimes days after they appeared in local theaters. Film studios complained that the showing of new films on television cut off about one third of their box-office receipts. But when film officials ruled that television would have to wait six months before showing new films, the Chinese public erupted in anger. Letters poured in to the *People's Daily,* complaining about long lines at theaters, or about new films not reaching theaters in remote areas.

One letter writer was particularly indignant when he heard film officials argue that in the United States and other countries new movies were also kept off television for long periods. Here was a Chinese government which had always insisted it kept a tight grip on moviemaking for the people's good, and yet once again what ordinary Chinese really wanted made no difference. "Films in a socialist country are to educate and serve the people," the letter writer argued. "Money should not come first, and this is a fundamental difference between socialism and capitalism."

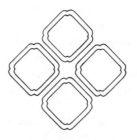

MUSIC

PEDDLERS SELL HER PICTURE ON PEKING STREET CORNERS WHERE FANS admire her pretty, babyish face. Police in Peking occasionally arrest young men for selling black-market cassettes of her wailing love songs. At friends' apartments we would listen to faint tapes of her recordings, usually copies of copies. Sometimes we brought a tape to the hostess as a special gift.

The singer is Deng Lijun, and to China's youth she is Linda Ronstadt, Barbra Streisand and Dolly Parton rolled into one. Yet Deng—or Teresa Teng, as she is known in Hong Kong—has no official Communist Party approval, and is not heard on the state radio. It is a small (and so far harmless) act of daring to listen to her music, for Deng Lijun is from that nest of counterrevolution, the island of Taiwan. Her saccharine, high-pitched ballads offer the Chinese one more delicious indulgence of common taste against the wishes of officialdom, the kind of guerrilla tunesmanship that allowed, as we shall see, the Chinese even to keep alive for years a favorite national anthem which they were forbidden to sing.

After decades of listening to recordings of thumping Communist marches and revolutionary odes to Chairman Mao Tse-tung, the Chinese—particularly the half billion of them under thirty—are turning more and more openly to what has been Chinese musical preference for years—the syrupy love ballads of Hong Kong and Taiwan. Songstress Deng is only the best-known exemplar of this triumph of popular taste, for the government recording studios now allow Chinese singers to copy her style. American country-western and East Indian dance tunes are also filtering in, such as the snappy Busby Berkeley–style dance music from a romantic 1950s Indian movie entitled *The Vagabond*. Taiwanese and Hong Kong songs can even be heard on city streets, despite occasional expressions of official alarm. Youngsters strolling in Shanghai, Peking and Canton play them on their tape recorders, huge models acquired from overseas relatives. If pressed by disapproving elders, the youths say they have bought the machines to "study foreign languages."

When popular foreign music—including such international disco hits as "Saturday Night Fever"—began to be played, while we were in China, at parties in the apartments of youths with affluent and tolerant parents, letters to Chinese newspapers heatedly condemned this as a sign of immorality— a haunting echo of the old Confucian insistence that music affects behavior. A reader of the *Peking Daily* said the sight of people "twisting their hips and shaking their legs" in the "indecent and decadent" manner of dancing at the Summer Palace "made me want to throw up." A Shanghai newspaper reader of the *Wen Hui Bao* said songs like Deng Lijun's, with their "live for today" philosophy, led young people to ignore work or study, and instead concentrate on dances and acquiring foreign tapes. Other letters defended the music: "If so many people like it, how bad can it be?"

While we were there, even Westerners who might otherwise have applauded this sign of independence from government preference for marches and patriotic folksongs began to question the emerging popular taste. Classical- and jazz-music devotees noted with alarm a growing affection among Chinese youth for Hawaiian guitars and the electric organ. Arrangements familiar to American cocktail-lounge habitués began to fill the Marxist-Leninist airwaves. Electric-organ concerts have become popular on television. One American scholar, appalled at the musical tastes of his many Chinese friends, commented, "They've gotten so sophisticated they've risen to the level of Muzak." But one of our Chinese friends shot back, "We like it because it's light music and you can relax."

Certainly the Chinese deserve a bit of musical relaxation. During the 1960s and 1970s, popular music revolved around rousing choral numbers like "Sailing the Seas Depends on the Helmsman." There were a few soft ballads, but the lyrics usually extolled the many ways the people loved Chairman Mao—not very conducive to romance on a summer night.

If there had been a Top 10 show in Peking, the number one hit of the 1960s would have been "Dong Fang Hong" (The East Is Red). It is a catchy tune that could have become popular at American family picnics and Girl Scout camps if given half a chance. Today the lyrics seem somewhat single-minded and out of date: "The East is red, the sun has risen. / China has produced a Mao Tse-tung. / He gives people happiness. He is the people's great savior."

During its heyday the song was ubiquitous, inescapable and oppressive. Factory, army and student dormitory loudspeakers started blaring it out at 5 A.M. Clock steeples chimed a few notes every hour. The first Chinese Sputnik beeped out the tune from orbit. "We had to sing it in the morning and then sing it again in the afternoon," groaned one Chinese official who preferred classical music. It is heard less often in the 1980s, predictably because it is associated with the now discredited policies of the Cultural Revolution, but government songwriters have had difficulty finding a suitable replacement. "The East Is Red" can still be heard in some Chinese cities whenever clocks chime out the hour.

While we were in China, supervisors of the official radio found the political atmosphere relaxed enough to reduce the amount of politically correct music and ply its listeners with foreign exotica. The Chinese craved, particularly, country-western music. "Kan-wei Te-wei-di" and "Da-lei Pa-er-duen" became featured singers on some Peking radio shows; visiting Americans turned on their radios and were startled to find they were listening to Conway Twitty and Dolly Parton. Many country entertainers do have a somewhat Chinese-style, singsong delivery. And many of the ballads are what the Chinese call "soft and mellow," a quality of leisure music keenly sought by Chinese retreating from streets full of cars and truck drivers honking horns. Country-western celebrates pervasive features of Chinese life: hopping freights, family trouble and getting up early in the morning. Some Chinese listening to country music complained that it did not improve their English. After hearing the song "I Don't Need No Man," an English-speaking Chinese friend of ours protested, "That's a double negative!" But the many Chinese enduring long separations from their families appreciated the song's lyrics: "The fastest train I ever seen was a hundred coaches long, and the only man I ever did love was on that train and gone."

This cross-cultural fertilization took some fascinating turns. When we tried to give a Chinese friend the English lyrics to "Auld Lang Syne" as we listened to it on the radio, the man insisted, "That's a Chinese song!" Indeed, it had often been played on the radio before the Cultural Revolution. Radio stations around the country regularly play the cowboy tune "Red River Valley," but somewhere in the foggy revolutionary past a friendly foreign leftist brought in lyrics from the Spanish Civil War. The Chinese lyrics now translate: "The national flags fly over the mountains. They protect Spain's freedom, vow to safeguard the country until death and kill the fascist swine." On a long train ride from Lanzhou to Xi'an, the loudspeaker softly woke us with that song, plus a series of pleasant Chinese adaptations of other tunes, including Gordon Lightfoot's "In the Early Morning Rain," and Rodgers and Hammerstein's "Edelweiss" from *The Sound of Music,* an extremely popular score in China despite the fact that the movie has never been publicly shown there.

The Chinese have also been ignoring committee-written ballads and seeking out a mix of their catchy foreign tunes and some of the Chinese folk music which goes back a few millennia. Tunes sung by peasants in the commune fields are thought to have changed little from those chanted when men first began cultivating the Hui and Yellow River valleys four thousand years ago. The demands of the emperor on the poor peasant are fixed for all time in one song: "I begin work at sunrise and rest at sunset. / Drink by singing a song and eat by plowing the soil. / What use to me is the imperial power?"

Even today, good tunes are those that can help Chinese workers pass long, boring hours in rice fields or assembly lines. In 1972, while on a long bus trip from Richmond to Washington, the Chinese national ping-pong team set about with lively interest to teach a few of these to the Americans on board, including Jay. A favorite was:

> *If you want to wear a flower,*
> *Wear a big red flower.*
> *If you want to ride a horse,*
> *Pick one that goes a thousand miles.*

The song, a vestige of the Great Leap Forward, was out of fashion by the time we arrived in China seven years later. The Chinese said it fell victim to the more modest economic goals of the post-Mao government, but different lyrics may some day rescue its rousing tune. When Jay tried on the bus trip to teach the Chinese "Row, Row, Row Your Boat," a rather stern party official in the group objected to the line "Life is but a dream." "Let's change it to 'Life is full of steam,'" he said.

That ideological, gung-ho bent is precisely what Chinese now avoid. Love songs have returned in great numbers. The lyrics are innocent enough in the Chinese context, though some might not pass muster with American censors:

> *People who pass her tent look back for one more glance.*
> *Her little pink face shines like the sun.*
> *I would give up everything to tend sheep with her,*
> *To see her small pink face and golden-laced clothes each day.*
> *I would be a lamb following her.*
> *I would let her whip me constantly and gently,*
>   *with a small whip.*

Young Chinese, mostly men in their twenties with thick winter coats and sometimes wispy mustaches, were usually jammed three deep trying to buy such songs at the record counter on the second floor of Peking's main department store when we stopped by. The big hits of the time were movie themes, particularly music from the tearjerker *Little Flower,* the story of a girl separated from her family during the Japanese invasion of the 1930s. Tian Yu, a helpful store clerk, played a bit of the thin blue plastic Chinese-produced record for us. Well-known female vocalist Li Guyi warbled: "The little girl looks for her brother, tears roll down her cheeks." The newly fashionable electric organ brought up the melody in the background. Some of the young men waiting to buy records hummed along.

"Actually, we don't have any of this one to sell right now," Tian said. "We got in two thousand copies yesterday, but they've sold out." The record cost thirty-five cents.

Farther down Wangfujing Street, in a side alley, the Foreign Book Shop Record Store was also doing good business in a makeshift hut while regular quarters were being remodeled. Despite the name, the store sells mostly Chinese records. Shun Zhongyong said his older customers still like Peking opera, but younger ones buy movie themes. Had he heard the Taiwanese songs of Deng Lijun? "Yes, they are very popular with younger people, but we don't sell them here. Her songs are much more emotional than the ones our Chinese singers sing."

Music fever became so intense that the official magazine of the Chinese music industry, *Songs,* polled its readers on their favorite tunes. Deng Lijun could not be mentioned, of course. Among the favorites listed was "Drink to Your Heart's Content, Friends," a stirring little number celebrating the fall of the Gang of Four. We heard it everywhere, even over the loudspeakers at the Tianjin docks. One courageous steelworker, Liang Hengjie, wrote to denounce three previous songs published by the magazine, "March on, Chinese Workers," "Song of Locomotive Engineers" and "All of You, Learn from Daqing," calling them an unhappy marriage of "political preaching" and "strident tunes."

On Peking's Dongdan Street we watched as young men crowded around a tape recorder listening to the antidote for such propaganda—another Deng Lijun tune:

> Can't tell if these are tears or rain.
> I remember, remember that it was raining when you said goodbye.
> Your tears fell, you cried at our parting.
> It will be hard to meet again,
> I hide your love deep in my heart.

Noting the fragile state of the people's morale, and with official newspapers openly acknowledging the ongoing crisis of confidence in Marxism, the government has been surprisingly tolerant of underground music like Deng's. It is a small pleasure that young people can enjoy. It suggests leniency and good sense on the part of the current government when compared to the days of the Cultural Revolution.

We met a man who had acquired a huge collection of records, mostly classical and jazz. During the Cultural Revolution, Red Guards found them and smashed them on the street in front of his house. Liu Shikun, the star pianist of the Chinese Central Philharmonic, had his right arm broken in two places by Red Guards, and was jailed for six years. He estimates that at least a hundred of the four hundred orchestra members were also jailed, confined to their homes or sent to the countryside. Many suffered public criticism sessions in which they had to bend forward with arms pulled back and out in the "airplane" position. Because he had participated in the Moscow piano competitions, and concerts in Eastern Europe and Hong Kong, Liu was accused of being a spy. He was not spared, even though he was the son-in-law of party leader Ye Jianying.

When this reign of terror ended, young Chinese flocked to foreign songs and Deng's love tunes, while older Chinese revived their obsession with Peking opera, and some of the other local opera styles—Shanghai, Canton, Hunan, Sichuan, and many more. We don't like Peking opera, or any of its provincial cousins, and so have been all the more curious why the Chinese are so attached to it. To our ears, the music has little melody. The singers perform in falsetto screeches, and the words are difficult even for Chinese to understand because they are often in local dialect. We can understand the lure of the colorful opera costumes, however. An audience of people forced by fashion and prudence to come to the opera in the drabbest gray and blue slacks and jackets can be expected to enjoy a stage full of fabulous designs—dragons of yellow silk, old sages with robes in peacock colors and long white beards, and kings in gorgeous raiments of red and yellow, goddesses in green and gold, all flapping and tucking their enormous sleeves. At a theater in Lanzhou, enduring a local opera out of politeness to our hosts, we suddenly realized our feet were tapping out the rhythm of the orchestra cymbals in spite of ourselves. Were we missing something?

Jay's former Chinese teacher, Rulan Chao Pian, said, "Those rhythmic undercurrents have a hundred different meanings and come to the listener in a hundred different ways. They tell a story, and after a few years of listening cannot be banished from the skull. Chinese opera—like Italian opera—is an acquired taste, but once one is addicted, there is no known cure. Whether in Taiwan or on the mainland, at well-lubricated celebrations such as wedding feasts, guests will get up and sing a few lines of Chinese opera. People immediately begin to bang on glasses to give the volunteer the beat, and imitate the gongs and drums." The rhythm carries everyone forward, and as Pian said, "It takes all kinds of Oriental social ingenuity to prevail upon these people that the audience has already been sufficiently entertained."

Peking opera is music carried forward by memory and gesture. As in Gilbert and Sullivan, traditional hand movements are followed. Few props are used. One man holds an oar and everyone knows he is in a boat. A whip means the man is riding a horse. Actors have more than three hundred ways of coughing and fifty-two distinct styles of wailing to delineate their character, all eagerly awaited by their audience.

Such passion for nuance may explain, in part, the most fascinating example of the musical underground we were to encounter—how for several years the Chinese maintained a national anthem they could whistle or hum, but which they were forbidden to sing.

The song was composed in the late 1930s during China's war against Japan. It was called "The March of the Volunteers," but it is most often referred to by its first staccato lyrics, *"Qi lai!"* (Stand up!) The man who wrote the original lyrics, Tian Han, was branded a counterrevolutionary when the Cultural Revolution began in 1966: Mao's wife held a grudge against him because he had slighted her when he was a Shanghai leftist impresario and she a budding actress in the 1930s. Everything Tian wrote, including the lyrics to "Qi Lai," became taboo.

The song's composer, a protégé of Tian's named Nie Er, drowned in 1935, a tragedy that in fact helped save his tune from later political attack because he had not had enough time to get into any serious disagreement with Jiang Qing. So in the 1960s this stirring song, which in tempo and spirit resembles the French national anthem, could be played at political rallies and state dinners, but nobody sang the words. In old films, wartime youths marching against the Japanese mouthed the familiar lyrics, but the sound track provided only an instrumental version.

For a while "The East Is Red" replaced "Stand Up!" as a de facto anthem; then the Mao cult lost steam in the late 1970s and a debate resumed over the Tian Han song. Even after Jiang Qing had been purged, some authorities argued that the Tian lyrics were outdated, written for a nation that had been flat on its back. Modern China, they said, was already standing up and marching. This view was not universally held. "It was the spirit of that day that mattered," said one young Chinese who left the mainland for Hong Kong after the Cultural Revolution. "The song helped the people remember. The lyrics of 'La Marseillaise' are outdated, too, but it makes no difference." Our acquaintances on Taiwan enjoyed the Communist discomfort. They suggested that the Communists simply didn't want a song calling for rebellion while they were trying to bring the country back under control.

In 1978 the National People's Congress tried to solve the problem by changing the old lyrics, which went:

> *Stand up, all you who refuse to be slaves!*
> *With our blood and flesh a great wall will be built.*
> *The Chinese nation now faces its greatest danger.*
> *From each comes forth his loudest call: "Stand up! Stand Up! Stand Up!"*
> *Millions as one, braving the enemy's fire, march on.*
> *Braving the enemy's fire, march; march on, march on and on!*

The new lyrics were clearly, as the government proudly proclaimed, "collectively written."

March on, brave people of our nation,
Our Communist Party leads us on a new long march.
Millions as one, march on, toward the Communist goal.
Build our country. Guard our country,
We will work and fight. March on, march on, march on!
Forever and ever, raising Mao Tse-tung's banner, march on.
Raising Mao Tse-tung's banner, march on, march on, march on and on!

Tian Han reportedly committed suicide after he was publicly disgraced during the Cultural Revolution. But many of his old comrades are back in power today. When we saw them standing at the front ranks in assemblies where the anthem was sung, we wondered whose lyrics they were singing. Sometime after we left China, we found out: the Communist Party leadership junked the new lyrics and restored "Stand Up!"

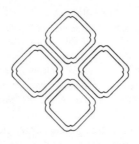

READING

ZHAO ZHENKAI, ONE OF THE YOUNG WORKER-EDITORS OF THE UNOFFI-
cial magazine *Today,* closed by the police in late 1980, had developed a
short-story style dedicated to the spirit of his generation—his footloose
characters, mostly former Red Guards, exuded an unbounded cynicism.
Zhao also toyed with flashbacks and stream of consciousness, and his name
spread in Peking. When the magazine closed down, some literary authorities in the party, impressed with the popularity of Zhao's work, took him
out of his factory and installed him as an editor of a new official literary
magazine, *New Observations,* one of the four to five hundred small journals
jamming China's post offices each month.

Some of his old colleagues from *Today* grumbled that Zhao had sold out;
their resentment was that much deeper because they yearned to do the
same. Few, if any of them, considered themselves rebels or dissidents. Like
other unofficial young artists—such as painters, musicians and comedians
—they dreamed of employing their craft and still staying in the system. "It's
a bargain: you allow yourself to be put under more control, but you widen
your audience—and are freed from factory work too," said one part-time
writer.

One of Zhao's *Today* colleagues, Lin Bing, put his first-person narrator
in a similar dilemma in a short story, "Star." The young worker has been
writing poetry that no one will publish. His wife wants him to accept a work
assignment so they can have a baby. "Well, my poet," she says, "have you
come closer to the Nobel Prize this time? Perhaps by the year 2000. You'll
be lucky if the archaeologists find you before the year 3000." The hero stares
at "the damned manuscript lying near the glass, soaked with some of the
beer that had overflowed. The postmark on the return envelope was fading
in the liquid. I knew what it said without opening it." His wife says, "A
poet, eh? How much is a kilogram of poet? You know the price? You'll
know you have the makings of a poet when you find yourself sleeping in
the streets." He agrees to see his father, an old writer from whom he has

been estranged. The father arranges for him to meet the editor of an official magazine. "You young men now have a great future," the editor says, scanning a few of his poems. "Such poems would have been a crime two years ago." He slaps the young man on the shoulder and says, "Bring all your poems to me from now on. With your permission, I will do some revision, of course . . ." No one else will publish his poetry uncensored. He throws the old poems into the fire and resolves to give the editor what he wants. "I felt like crying, I really did, but at the same time I realized that a new life was beginning."

Great Chinese writers have traditionally drawn money from the government, in the form of patronage. Chinese literature thrived in those periods, such as the Tang dynasty twelve hundred years ago, when imperial power, wealth, leisure and self-confidence allowed a few blessed talents to develop their skills. A street literature also thrived, with tales told by professional storytellers to children and adults that eventually found their way to printing presses. This tradition has remained so strong that it lives on in public parks and on the radio today, with the best storytellers enjoying the sort of fame accorded television anchormen in the United States. The eighteenth-century *Dream of the Red Chamber* may be China's greatest novel, a rich and rambling view of family life, but it had its genesis in a storytelling tradition considered somewhat undignified, so that most of its practitioners used aliases.

Early on, the Chinese decided that writing should be used for only the highest purposes. Essays and poetry were thought to promote correct behavior and reveal eternal truths. The beauty and complexity of Chinese characters gave them a religious aura. If a document happened to fall on the ground, it was considered an offense to step on the printed or handwritten characters. Certain taboo characters, such as the family name of the emperor, were not to be written at all. Emperors, acting much as the popes in Rome, were always on the lookout for literary heresy. The Qianlong emperor in the 1770s collected and destroyed 2,300 volumes containing seditious and abusive language. "None may remain to later generations, in order to cleanse our speech and make straight the hearts of men." A dictionary maker who printed taboo characters was executed; his two sons and three grandsons were sold into slavery.

Today works are withdrawn from circulation at the slightest change in official tastes. Library borrowing is discouraged. A person must ask for a certain book and then may not get it if he does not bring a letter certifying his need for it. Small matters of text must go to the very top for decision. According to one high official, Deng Xiaoping personally wrestled with the question of whether to lift a ban on the works of Chen Jo-hsi, a Taiwan-born, U.S.-based author. She had moved to the mainland to help build the new China, stayed through the Cultural Revolution, then left for America and later published a devastating collection of short stories, *The Execution of Mayor Yin.* The stories dramatize the fear and absurdity of the Cultural Revolution purges, but Chen later wrote an essay about overseas Chinese returning to the motherland which pleased many Communists, and so a re-evaluation of her work began. In the old manner of *guanxi,* if Chen herself could now be trusted, a ban on her previous writings was no longer necessary.

If some good writers of the past and present could display their talent, if the Chinese produced the remarkable poetry of the Tang dynasty and the lively novels of the Qing, why has the last century been such a cultural desert? Where are the Faulkners, the Solzhenitsyns? One twentieth-century writer, the essayist and short-story writer Lu Xun, seemed to write with exceptional clarity and emotional depth—just a simple Lu story about a man's lingering guilt over wrecking his little brother's kite reveals a great deal about families and pain. But Lu, who died in 1936, was plagued by political strife, ill health and an addiction to a cause that has distracted nearly every talented Chinese in this century—how to rescue China from its political, economic, military and spiritual doldrums. All questions but China itself seem insignificant to Chinese writers in this century. They have an ancient, Confucian compulsion to make everything they write socially significant. So issues dealing with family relationships, love and death are often ignored.

China was severely shaken by events in the nineteenth and twentieth centuries, but not in the way that the industrial revolution produced the urban, democratic upheaval which inspired the great novels of the West. China was and remains a rural, hierarchical society, but since there is definitely a demand for novels, China's own modernization campaign may someday awaken the industrial urge to examine the life of the common man and ease China out of its writer's block. For now, most Chinese novelists, even the best, still operate as Chinese writers always have, like doctors giving medicine: they lead their characters through politically prescribed morality plays rather than let them speak for themselves.

The frustration this produces is enormous. Although many Chinese like the stock characters in Peking opera, for their reading they seem to ache for more appreciation of life as it is, and they love to read. Bookstores sell out new shipments of novels, particularly translations of foreign authors, within hours, however long it takes the crowd to work its way past the sales counter. Many books never reach the front of the store; store clerks alert friends of new shipments and sell them out the back door. In nearly all major cities (except Peking—authorities there seem to think it unseemly), boys jam little bookshops where they can rent comic books for one cent and read about war heroes and spies.

The Chinese are drawn to Western literature in part because these books have been forbidden to them for so long and in part because of an old belief that literature is the heart of politics. Since, in the Marxist view, politics is the key to modernization, and since the West is so advanced, perhaps its literature is worth studying. Marx would blanch at the logic, but that is the way many Chinese feel. It grows from the time-honored urge to teach, like the old Confucian schoolmaster. Modern Chinese writers, for instance, still rely on the ancient device of using a narrator, breaking into a story the way the oral storytellers used to do, to warn the reader that the hero has just made a serious mistake he will soon pay for.

The Tang dynasty writer Han Yu wrote, "Literature carries with it morality," and with few exceptions Chinese writers have stuck to that. One of the most famous of the new writers, the youngest member of the Chinese Writers Association, is Wang Yaping, still in his twenties. During the Cultural Revolution he read the translated Western books his parents left behind when they were dispatched to the countryside. In 1977, shortly after Mao died and the Gang of Four was arrested, he wrote a short story called "The Sacred Duty" about a man framed during the Cultural Revolution and cleared by an honest public security officer. Wang submitted his story to many magazines; it attracted interest but no one would publish it until authorities received signals that direct attacks on the Cultural Revolution were permissible. The literary magazine *People's Literature* printed "The Sacred Duty" in September 1978. It won second place in the nationwide short-story contest and was made into a film, launching Wang's career. To a neutral observer the story remains a clumsy piece of work, with little more than good intentions to recommend it. By story's end, after the framed man has been cleared through a bizarre set of circumstances, his jailer, Chen, tells him, "The Gang of Four has been smashed. The injustice done to you has been righted." Wang concludes: "Chen's heart thrilled at the knowledge that the majesty of the law had been restored."

Writers in China have little incentive to stray from optimistic endings and "socially responsible" subject matter. For their carefully measured words they receive better housing, access to the latest Western novels, private showings of foreign movies, and travel to many exotic parts of the country.

Dabbling in realism and social criticism puts this stimulating and favored life at risk. One writer admitted, "I am afraid, but I try not to think about it." Young writers take care to avoid trouble by writing only of the abuses of the Cultural Revolution era, but it is often clear the artist is commenting on his own time. The further the Cultural Revolution recedes in time, the more immediate will be the message to readers, and the greater the chance of angry reaction from the party.

Chinese readers have always been accustomed to finding such hidden messages imbedded in poetry. The scholar-gentry class under the emperors was trained in the poetic forms of its day. It was customary to retire at opportune moments, such as on the occasion of the death of a parent, for months or years of thought and composition. The civil service examinations demanded poetry, of particular meter and style. Often the verses composed made sly fun of political enemies. The Tang dynasty poet Li Bai loved to indulge in politics, even to celebrate his own pacifism:

> Ravens and kites peck men's guts,
> And flying away, hang them on the boughs of dead trees.
> So men are smeared on the desert grass,
> And the generals return empty-handed.*

Li would probably have been executed as a subversive if he had not died young, reportedly from drowning after falling off a boat drunk.

In the twentieth century, even under the Communists, grave political debates were often disguised in literary squabbles which seemed no more momentous than an exchange of letters in the *New York Review of Books*. At the Tiananmen Square riot of 1976, the transgression that most outraged Maoist officials was a poem posted by some young men:

> Devils howl as we pour out our grief
> We weep but the wolves laugh
> We spill our blood in memory of the hero,
> Raising our brows, we unsheathe our swords.
> China is no longer the China of yore.
> And the people are no longer wrapped in sheer ignorance.
> Gone for good is Qin Shi Huang's feudal society . . .†

The "hero" for whom they grieved was the deceased premier, Chou En-lai. The reference to Qin Shi Huang, China's first great unifying emperor, was blasphemous, for all Chinese knew him to be a symbol for Mao Tse-tung. The government tried to counter with its own poetry contest, featuring lively verses like "Furnace flames reflect blazing wrath for Deng Xiaoping," but it did not work. Mao was soon dead and Deng was back in power.

Mao apparently thought his own love of poetry might seem too old-fashioned for the leader of a revolution and for a while would not allow his poems to be published. He advised young people not to copy his style, an irregular-meter verse form developed a thousand years ago during the Song dynasty.

The late Professor Hsu Kai-yu of San Francisco State, who talked to many Chinese writers, said that by tradition any man of consequence was expected to be able to write poetry. This had a strong impact on veteran revolutionaries, and many think Mao's own well-crafted verse, despite

*Translation edited by Robert Payne.
†New China News Agency translation.

Mao's fears of how it would be received, actually persuaded his countrymen that he would make a good leader. Later Mao's adversaries within the leadership countered with poetry. Former Foreign Minister Chen Yi composed this answer to the revolutionaries who attacked him during the Cultural Revolution:

> No food or drink for seven days,
> We die.
> No thinking at all for just one day,
> We don't die
> But are—dead.*

The man even the Communists acknowledge as the greatest Chinese writer of this century, Lu Xun, was a leftist, but he was also honest and blunt, carrying on a running feud with party literary czar Zhou Yang over Zhou's insistence that writers write only patriotic prose. A more compliant writer, perhaps the best of the post-1949 novelists, was Liu Qing, author of an epic called *The Builders*. It tells the story of a poor peasant, Liang Shengpao, who becomes the head of his local agricultural producers cooperative. In the book's last paragraph the author/narrator says of Liang: "After a life of slavery, he was at last able to carry himself as one of life's masters." The rest of the book is similarly optimistic and stilted. But *The Builders* provided realistic moments and some lively dialogue. In 1966 the book was labeled "a poisonous weed." The political attacks on Liu aggravated his asthma; he died in 1978 at age sixty-two. Chinese intellectuals say perhaps the most provocative writer they have today is Liu Bingyan, who works for the *People's Daily*. Liu's stories often expose bureaucratic bungling, but this is a fairly safe topic if the writer is careful about which bureaucrats he investigates.

Books in China, like everywhere else, remain a largely urban pastime, Few peasant homes have books, except for the works of Chairman Mao. The government calculated in 1980 that 140 million Chinese could not read or write, and that 120 million of those were under forty-five. Much of what the government publishes lies unread, for there is minimal regard for what people want to buy. In the Peking parks and in front of the New China Bookstore, we often found book stalls displaying neglected volumes, mostly propaganda novels and Marxist tracts. Book-hungry Chinese would not buy them, even when they were marked down to fifteen cents from a dollar. But in a back alley of Kunming, in the far southwest, we found a thriving free market where city youth could buy or barter used books, exchanging some popular titles for others.

*Hsu Kai-yu translation.

Such trade-offs are a way of life in Chinese universities. "Ten more minutes and it's my turn," one Fudan University student cautioned a friend poring over a Saul Bellow short story in translation. Government publishers estimate that each book they print reaches ten to twenty readers, all the more remarkable because libraries are few and crowded. A survey of university students in Canton found most of them spending at least five hours a week reading novels and short stories; some claimed as much as twenty-eight or thirty hours a week reading books that had little to do with their schoolwork.

People scheme to get copies of *Gone With the Wind, The Winds of War, Spoken English for Daily Use, Chemistry Self-Study, The Dream of the Red Chamber* and the *Three Musketeers.* Certain books sell at a premium. *The Count of Monte Cristo* cost 12 yuan at the Kunming free market, even though the book was marked at 4 yuan. Detective stories, such as *Sherlock Holmes,* are enormously popular, and the appetite for them has made mysteries frequent fare in evening newspapers and on television. John Ritter, an American teaching in Anhui, said his English students loved the *Sue Barton, Student Nurse* series. People with access to internal bookstores have also read works by Kurt Vonnegut, but one American professor who discussed Vonnegut with the Chinese concluded that they think of him "as they would of a pickled baby sea lion"—a bit of exotica that seems to have no useful purpose.

English students all over the country are diligently translating Western works into Chinese for the few extra yuan they can get from the hundreds of small literary magazines. Writers who look at the darker side of American life, like Joyce Carol Oates, have become favorites because they can be defended as critics of capitalist society. One Peking worker who was studying English kept his books dumped on top of a wardrobe. We found Ursula Le Guin's *The Dispossessed,* a science-fiction novel with Maoist leanings, alongside the works of Chairman Mao. The Chairman's sales have dropped off lately, but if past figures are to be believed, every person in Peking must have at least forty-two copies of the works of Mao and other Marxist writers.

The passion for books exacerbates the country's severe paper shortage. Newspapers regularly scold local government printing offices for using their presses, mimeograph machines and paper supplies to print books and make a little extra money; some government publishing houses in Peking have been printing Western detective stories, one newspaper charged. A Hubei newspaper said a city residents' committee was printing librettos, a hot item with the opera-loving Chinese. Other offices had been printing mathematical-game books illegally, often used in fortunetelling.

Party political officers would be happier if the passion for the printed word, and the government printers' new concern over profits, were not so great. In their view, some of the most popular Western novels now being sold have major weaknesses. The *Enlightenment Daily*'s Feng Jiayun complained that *Gone With the Wind* was a reactionary defense of the old American slave system, and objected to people buying it simply because it was fun to read. China's underground pornographers also present competition to official authors, who have tried to steal a bit of that market by writing more explicit sex; to protect themselves they use the current political villains so the racy material can be excused on political grounds. *How the Wall Was Breached*, by Cheng Dengke and Xiao Ma, purportedly exposes the amorous adventures of Lin Liguo, the notorious son of the former Defense Minister Lin Biao. The elder Lin's alleged plot to kill Chairman Mao was exposed in 1971, and Lin is said to have died fleeing to the Soviet Union, so he and his family have been popular scapegoats ever since.

In *How the Wall Was Breached*, Lin Liguo entices a poor young woman to his bedroom: " 'I never rape women. I ask them to submit to my requests . . . Hurry up, I only have a half-hour's free time today . . . You might feel badly for a while, but in a few days my name will be a part of history. Then you will feel proud. You will know your sacrifice was worthwhile. Get your clothes off. It gets easier after the first button.' " The young woman covers her face with her hands, not knowing what to do. "I awaited my terrible fate. I was like a rat under the paw of a wild cat. I could feel his panting, hot breath rushing from his nose onto my neck. His hands were forcing mine to unbutton my clothes.

"All of a sudden, the telephone rang. I don't know what gods were protecting me." The telephone caller informs Lin that his father's plot has been exposed, saving both the girl from a fate worse than death and the author from severe criticism for stepping too far over the Chinese line of propriety.

None of these stories pretend to much literary merit, but they have the reality and liveliness that the Chinese find most attractive in Western books. We often wondered what gifts might be most appropriate for our Chinese friends; eventually we found the most appreciated were books from Hong Kong, the best Chinese translations of Faulkner and Hemingway and Crane.

That gave our friends some of the best of the West to read, but we often felt that many Chinese—like men and women stuck in a long line with nowhere to go—would read almost anything that had a spark of interest. Cheng Ping, a young English-language graduate student in Anhui province, told us of the time during the Cultural Revolution when, while working as a railroad clerk, he found a twenty-eight-volume set of the 1947 *Encyclopaedia Britannica* in an abandoned library in Chengdu. He began to read it, bit by bit, through the hours and days when factional battles held up the trains and left him with nothing else to do. The older workers at the railway didn't mind, for he occasionally told them stories picked out from some of the *Encyclopaedia*'s histories and biographies.

And by the end of the Cultural Revolution, when the trains began running again and Cheng had found a young conductor to marry, he had read every last word.

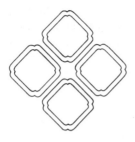

FUN AND GAMES

QIN GUOBAO, A SUPERVISOR IN THE SHANGHAI TOOL FACTORY, WAS STILL complaining about the cricket fights when we met him. Qin was a tall, stocky man with a graying crew cut, and as we talked in the little reception room, we became confused. Among the images that Westerners hold on to in order to make sense out of China is the idea that the Mao era was a time of humorless slogans and political purges. We, along with so many others, supposed that the fun only began after Mao died and his notorious widow was arrested. But again we overlooked the resourcefulness of the Chinese.

In the months before Mao died, the younger workers at Qin's factory had rediscovered the ancient sport of cricket fighting. They spent much of their working day running about nearby fields catching crickets in small woven boxes and organizing miniature battles, seeing which creature could force the other out of a circle. Scores of onlookers came around to bet on a winner.

The fad became so widespread that someone complained to Zhang Chunqiao, the Shanghai mayor who was purged after Mao's death. "Don't criticize the young people who catch crickets," Zhang replied. "The supervisors should go help the young people catch the crickets, and when they have got that experience they can encourage the workers to go back to work." Qin, recalling this, looked at us aghast: "Zhang openly advocated anarchism!"

By 1977, when we visited the factory, rules had been posted forbidding such behavior on company time. The post-Mao era was to be a time of purposeful production. But delays and dislocations still plague China's old rusting factories, and workers still take time off for fun. The Chinese have an insatiable thirst for games. They oil the wheels of *guanxi,* bring friends together and make possible a small wager now and then.

In back-alley shops in Peking, Tianjin and other cities, you can buy small wooden cups with snug caps. Puzzled when we found one, we asked what it was. The little woman who ran the Tianjin shop cheerfully explained,

"It's a cricket's winter home. You keep it inside your shirt to keep the cricket warm." She liked cricket fights. "The breed of cricket that really fights fiercely, you can't find them anymore," she said. "They still have lots of fights, particularly out on the commune, when there isn't much else to do. And people like to gamble."

In Hong Kong the Chinese penchant for gambling turned the local Jockey Club into one of the largest and most profitable corporations in town. Neighboring Macao has become a South China Sea Las Vegas. In Singapore, another small state composed mostly of Chinese, the race track packs in bettors even when it is only playing loudspeaker broadcasts of horse races going on in neighboring Malaysia. The Communists wanted to rid their new China of what they considered this mindless waste, so horse racing and gambling were banned. During the Cultural Revolution, some Maoists even tried to kill the competitive urge altogether. The motto for top athletes was "Friendship first, competition second." Young men and women who were medals winners of the 1960s could not revel in their victories or they would be accused of "careerist" urges. Lately the Chinese have returned to an old socialist pastime; now they want to prove the superiority of their system by walloping the rest of the world's athletes in such sports as ping-pong and gymnastics but with the renaissance of the competitive spirit comes the urge to gamble.

The *Peking Daily* complains that gambling has become rife in some areas and seriously affects the work, health and family relations. It reminds readers that gambling in any of the favorite Chinese pastimes—chess, cards and mah-jongg—is forbidden. Mah-jongg had such a bad reputation before liberation that it was banned altogether, whether played for money or not, but the click-clack of mah-jongg tiles can now be heard occasionally in Canton. The official press is full of reported abuses: private homes turned into secret gambling parlors; a tailor shop in an Anhui commune that lost $40,000 in 1979 because the workers spent most of their time gambling; a peasant woman who attempted suicide when she learned her husband had gambled away $300, more than three times their annual income. Police in one Shanghai district raided thirteen gambling clubs in early 1980; they claimed 80 percent of the people arrested for robbery in that district during the first ten months of 1979 were habitual gamblers.

But mostly police ignore the problem. Card games continue every summer night under city street lights. Our bus once stopped in Quanzhou (Tsinkiang), a seaport on the Fujian coast. Near the little pond in the town square we played a Chinese version of pinball, administered for a profit in broad daylight by a slim woman and her two daughters, aged five and seven. For about two cents we rolled a ball down an inclined board and let it fall into any of a number of holes. When we hit the correct hole we got a cigarette or wall calendar.

Chairman Mao understood the attractions of gambling, which may explain why some of his disciples were going so easy on Shanghai's cricket-fight promoters. Beneath the official censure of gambling there was some appreciation of its uses. While learning about peasant life in Hunan in the 1920s, Mao said he "went to teahouses and gambling parlors to meet everyone and investigate them . . . There was a peasant whom I invited to play Chinese dominoes." The man told Mao about class struggle in the village. He was willing to talk, Mao said, because Mao treated him as an equal and bought him dinner, and because "he would win some money from me."

Mao's adversary and successor, Deng Xiaoping, indulged his own passion for contract bridge. During the Cultural Revolution, his obsessive bridge playing was cited as among his principal crimes. The Red Guards said Deng had diverted government money to build a palatial club for high officials in Peking where he played bridge every Wednesday and Saturday night, Sunday afternoon and evening. Papers of state were brought to the club for his "stinking signature," the Red Guard journals said. Deng reportedly borrowed official aircraft to fetch his favorite bridge partners, including Wan Li and Yang Shangkun, during inspection trips. These two worthies disappeared during the Cultural Revolution, but have returned and are playing cards again. In 1979 the All-China Bridge Federation was revived, and Chinese teams have gone back to international competition.

Today, Western and Japanese sports figures pour in to help the Chinese hone their talents for all sorts of international competition. The "friendly" approach of the Mao era survives in one form: Chinese athletes usually praise the superior skill of their opponents. Then surprises follow: at a Sino-American diving competition in 1980 the Chinese insisted that all the judges be American so that the Chinese could learn from them. They proceeded to beat the much more highly rated U.S. team.

One of the diving stars is Chen Xiaoxia, a tiny, dark, quiet young woman who demonstrates Chinese competitive passion. She is from Dongguan County, Guangdong province, which is all you have to say to a Chinese to prove she is a potential champion. In the 1950s a swimming fad swept that rural county of 200,000 people between Canton and Hong Kong. Some say it began because so many young people wanted to learn to swim to Hong Kong, but whatever the reason, the Pearl River delta creeks were soon outfitted with bamboo lanes and brick starting blocks. The local authorities built fifteen Olympic-sized swimming pools and eight swimming schools. Dongguan became known nationally as the "home of swimming," providing nine of the twenty-nine competitors on the 1980 swimming and diving squad. Chen's family moved from Dongguan to Canton, and a swimming coach who met her when she was eleven suggested she switch to diving, which she did with some intensity. She began to try out dives that no Chinese, or hardly anyone else, had done before.

Since the mid-1970s Chinese athletes have been freed of most political constraints and diplomatic barriers, and can look forward to the Olympics in 1984 and most other international competitions despite the furor caused by the defection of tennis player Hu Na. They often display a loose, animal joy, a sense of fun for the sake of fun, that the official press rarely discusses. Wu Lanying, China's champion skeet shooter, talked about "fooling around" with some squirrel and bird shooting in Henan, where she works as an usher in a movie theater.

Mu Tiezhu, the 7½-foot, 300-pound center for the Chinese army basketball team, joked about his height. "Look your fill if you want to," he told staring passers-by when he first came to Peking in 1972. His name means "Iron Pillar." Meng Fanai, China's best female archer, was a stocky, well-muscled woman weighing 143 pounds and standing only 5 feet 4 inches tall. Her roommates' nickname for her was "Young Man," celebrating not only her build but her "straightforward" manner. She was a shot-putter to begin with, but switched to archery when she decided she needed therapy for her hot temper. Ma Wenguang was a weight lifter, at age twenty-three one of China's best, and like the others hoping to compete in the Olympics. We interviewed him in 1979 when he had already been to Pittsburgh for one meet, and seemed unlikely to return soon to his native Shandong. He ate about a pound of meat a day; peasants back home might see that much meat in a month.

All these athletes have been nurtured by a Soviet-style physical education system that has created physical culture schools in all the major urban areas and built up a corps of young stars. Many schools were closed during the Cultural Revolution, but their new students are coming back with special efforts to catch up in gymnastics, swimming, weight lifting, basketball, shooting and archery. All are dedicated to winning, but the physical activity also provides a pure escape from a crowded, routinized world.

At the Peking Amateur Physical Culture School, we stood and watched a gymnastics class on a cold fall day. Six- and seven-year-old girls dashed in, chattering and joking like mischievous monkeys. They tried out cartwheels, the sawhorse, the sandpit, gradually shedding layers of clothing as they warmed up. They never really stopped talking or working. A woman in a faded blue track suit sat on a rolled mat illuminated by a sunbeam from the skylight. Little girls came up and chatted and she smiled, dispensing advice and instructions without moving from her place. A tiny girl, no more than five or six years old, had run several laps of the gym and now stood before the woman. On command she bent over backward to an improbable angle, as flexible as a bit of wonton in a soup bowl. In front of us, small boys practiced spear play; the martial arts still lived. A nine-year-old overseas Chinese boy—a late starter in the Chinese training schedule—also attempted to bend over backward. "He's too stiff," his teacher commented. At the physical culture institutes in Nanning and Wuhan the regimen was much the same. Limber young people pranced about and did coordinated drills in unheated gymnasiums. Gymnasts and martial-arts specialists practiced side by side.

With the return to Olympic competition since the death of Mao, the good humor and friendliness that have characterized Chinese athletes occasionally wear thin. Janet Swislow, an American teaching in Wuhan, said she joined a basketball tournament at her university and found "none of that 'Friendship first, competition second' business. Competition definitely occupies first place." Her whole department officially protested one referee's decision in a game. "Another game was a case of mutual clawing and we bloodily staggered to a twelve-to-two victory. People play to win here." Frank Hawke, a Stanford graduate student, became the first American on the Peking University basketball team since the 1950s, when Korean War turncoat Morris Wills was a student. With his cowboy hat, shoulder-length hair and drooping mustache, Hawke drew many glances on campus. We wondered if he would bring the more physical style of American basketball to the Chinese game. But when we came to watch, we found the Chinese players getting into fights after some aggressive fouls, while Frank behaved himself. College basketball games are played on packed earth, outdoors, often in very cold weather. The authorities, sensing how boisterous Chinese fans can be despite appeals for "Friendship first," have ruled that no team can play on their home court. For the big game against crosstown rival People's University, the Peking University team had to board a bus to the Peking Teachers College.

Basketball is popular, but soccer is the favorite outdoor game. The Chinese occasionally claim to have invented it; a somewhat related sport called *cu-qiou* ("kick-ball") excited Han dynasty crowds two thousand years ago. Soccer was not played nationwide until after the Communist victory in 1949, though it had been introduced in many cities by travelers from Europe a century before. Soccer enthusiasts in China may not yet match the ferocity of fans in Britain or Central America, but they are working on it: fourteen young spectators were arrested after setting off firecrackers, cursing the referees, releasing pigeons and dropping bottles on the players from Britain's Norwich team. Three middle-school games in Shanghai in one month were disrupted when angry spectators rushed into the field to punch the referees, and one referee was virtually imprisoned in a car for four hours by the fans.

One day at an amusement park we saw a grandfather take a swing at a ticket taker who wouldn't let his grandson make a second "airplane" ride—the line behind them seemed endless. That is one of the annoyances of life in a village of one billion: even to find the delights of escape in games, one must get in line. The solution to this dilemma is the city park, the first destination of nearly any Chinese with time on his hands and a need for a good time. The importance of amusement parks to the morale of millions of Chinese began to dawn on us when we left our near-deserted hotel compound one evening in Beihai, a remote little town on the far southeastern coast not far from Vietnam. About two blocks from the hotel we found a small well-lit park, full of simple pleasures for a crowded country which needs lots of group entertainment.

"Beihai City General Labor Unions Public Park," the sign said. "Admission two cents." September weather was hot and wet; the park was mobbed. At least fifteen hundred people sat in concrete-and-wood bleachers listening to a man onstage sing a plaintive Cantonese folk song. A group of tall young men in shorts and warm-up sweaters practiced volleyball on a concrete court dazzling in bright spotlights. More people packed a crumbling assembly hall, formerly a church, to watch a 1950s movie, the film stained brown with age. About twenty men, young and old, read newspapers in a prefabricated library about the size of a house trailer. All its doors and windows were flung open to coax some air inside. Behind the assembly hall, another large, open-air amphitheater held about two thousand people enjoying a sudden evening breeze as two men, sitting at a table on stage, told fairy tales with noisemakers and Guangxi-dialect chants. Behind that stage, a small troupe of singers, actors and musicians rehearsed an opera, holding up their scripts. On a big stage at the back of the park, a full-dress Guangxi opera was under way. Curious children filled the back stage. Off to one side we found a workshop with young men sculpting heads and painting with charcoal.

In Canton we followed then Vice President Walter Mondale's teen-age daughter Eleanor on an evening tour of a big-city version of the little Beihai park. Admission was six cents. Big neon signs on the front announced the "Canton Cultural Park." It had a Ferris wheel, an airplane ride, a Canton opera show, and a minstrel stage with sixteen girls in turquoise costumes and peacock-patterned skirts singing "Oh, Susanna." Eleanor's favorite stop was the roller-skating rink. She "cracked the whip" with young Chinese women wearing red plaid skirts and blue polka-dot blouses, some of them professional dancers out on the town. In a little outdoor basketball arena, two women's basketball teams, Canton Air Force vs. Wuchang Physical Culture Institute, battled in T-shirts and shorts. The stands were packed—perhaps three thousand people in all. When we looked more closely we discovered that all of them, with the exception of Mrs. Mondale, Eleanor and their interpreter, were men.

At Peking's Dongdan Park, screened from the Avenue of Eternal Peace by billboards for Coca-Cola and other items of Western import, the clientele at midmorning were also mostly male, but they ogled cards, not women. The card players arrived after breakfast. They were usually young people without jobs, retirees, or men on vacation or "sick leave"—a disguised vacation. The origins of card playing in China are difficult to trace, but the Communists were known to be avid poker players at their base in Yenan during the Japanese and civil wars. *Pu-ke pai,* as the game is called in Chinese, is more popular than a bridgelike game, *pai-fen,* or even contract bridge itself. The Chinese press said Jiang Qing was unable to tear herself away from a poker game while inspecting the model village of Dazhai, even when word came from Peking that Mao was near death.

Whenever we visited the card players at Dongdan Park, we found fifty or sixty of them, usually in groups of six around low concrete tables. They played poker, and something called *Zheng Shang Yu* (Strive to Get Upstream), which resembles gin, war and pinochle. Three teams of two men each took turns lifting cards into the air with great flourish and slapping them on the table. "I've *bombed* you," they'd say. The Chinese don't trust dealers. The men would put a stack of cards in the middle of the table and take turns sliding off the top card in a natural cadence until the whole deck was gone.

Dong Yusheng, thirty-one, who works in a pharmacy, was enjoying a day off with his eight-year-old son, Haifeng. "This is good exercise for people, don't you think?" he said. An amateur historian accompanying us said the card game predated 1949 and had been popular in the emperor's court, where it was called Play the Queen. When the Great Leap Forward began in 1958, people worried that the game might be banned, so they adopted the new name, Strive to Get Upstream, from an important Great Leap slogan.

After some experiments we decided that the best way to surprise the Chinese at play was to take a long walk—or a pedicab ride—through back alleys. We found that sidewalk soccer, basketball and ping-pong were favorites with children. Some adults played baseball and softball (probably learned from the invading Japanese army before and during World War II). The rules and positions are about the same as the American game, except that the Chinese call the shortstop "the guerrilla." Children all over the country skip rope; they hop between or on top of two ropes held close to the ground in movements resembling hopscotch. Many play with a feathered shuttlecock they can bounce endlessly off the side of their foot. In Fujian, a rough brand of one-legged tag is popular. Children hold one leg and attempt to knock down their friends with their free hand.

Chinese children are incredibly adept at handling insects, since pets like cats and dogs are so rare in a nation starved for meat. During a long wait at a tiny rail spur in northern Shandong, a boy about Joe's age kept us entertained by tightly holding the wing of a huge bluebottle fly and making the creature do tricks. In Peking, children catch cicadas with long sticks smeared with pitch, then play with them.

In parks, lanes and backyards, a favorite morning routine is *tai ji quan,* the slow calisthenics that some Westerners have given the misleading name "shadow boxing." Peking authorities have been hustling to organize it as a stimulant to public health, boasting 138 *tai ji quan* training centers with 45,000 graduates. A recent report, impossible to confirm, said 196 out of 203 people with chronic illnesses had recovered or improved after practicing the morning exercises.

The ancient martial arts—the source of the *kung fu* craze that swept Asian and Western movie studios in the 1970s—suffered for a while under the antitraditional atmosphere of the Cultural Revolution. But in 1979, authorities allowed a meeting of martial-arts masters in Nanning. Experts from Hong Kong, Macao and all parts of China attended. Representatives came from the famous Shaolin monastery in Henan province, the subject of a hundred martial-arts movies and the U.S. television series *Kung Fu.* Some clever promoter even found a skilled martial-arts veteran from the 1900 Boxer Rebellion. The ninety-four-year-old expert, Liu Zhiqing, used the long-shafted dragon sword "with all the firmness of an ancient pine," China's *Sports Daily* said. We noticed in 1980 that martial-arts displays were even returning to movie screens.

Gentler pastimes—though also very group-oriented—have returned. During our shopping trips near the Peking Hotel, we could never park near the little shop of the China Stamp Company. Customers and kibitzers, up to two hundred or three hundred each afternoon, would fill up the sidewalk and spill into the street, buying, trading, looking and talking about stamps. Most were men, usually young students, but we saw some with gray hair.

Examining the wares, we got a sense of why stamp collecting did not fare well during the politically charged years of the Cultural Revolution. We found a 1968 stamp showing Chairman Mao attended by Lin Biao. The young man who sold the stamp to us for about $1.50 seemed unembarrassed by its content; in 1981, political flaws could be more easily overlooked, although Lin remained in ill repute. Another young man brought us what he said were four one-penny stamps from the Qing dynasty. "Two dollars?" he asked, hopefully. We said we didn't want to buy. "One dollar?" he asked.

Perhaps, to judge from such encounters, the hottest hobby on the rebound is not stamp collecting, but bargaining. Though no longer permitted in state stores, nor in many of the "free" markets, bargainers are welcome at the stamp company, as they are at the huge, impromptu, quasi-illegal bird market on Fu Cheng Gate Road, a busy thoroughfare in west Peking. The neglected construction site where the market convenes is always jammed, morning and afternoon, with young and old men looking at pigeons, sparrows and ducks. They even have an assortment of crickets, ready for battle, if only the price is right.

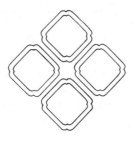

HUMOR

NOW AND THEN THE FOLLOWING STORY POPS UP IN PEKING: THREE prison inmates, slumped on the floor of their cell, tell each other how they got into such a fix.

"I am here because I supported Deng Xiaoping," says one.

"I am here because I opposed Deng Xiaoping," says the other.

The two of them look at the third man sitting in a dark corner. "I *am* Deng Xiaoping."

Whatever the political ups and downs, Chinese humor lives on—a subtle, sardonic and often backstage existence whose barb sometimes eludes the untrained ear. That may be why the Chinese have so often been perceived by outsiders as humorless. Much of their humor onstage is understated, for the very good reason that pointed jokes can bring the comedian a great deal of trouble. Much of it also is untranslatable; the Chinese have a language designed for complex puns.

If outsiders don't get the joke, that's fine with the Chinese. Their satire survives because it tweaks the authorities so gently that they can't be sure what's going on. Over the last few centuries, entertainers have developed a form of comic dialogue, called *xiang-sheng,* that seems to please everyone, from the highest authorities (Chairman Mao commissioned many private performances) to the most disgruntled young workers. *Xiang-sheng* performers almost always work in pairs, with a comedian and a straight man, as in American vaudeville. They skewer the absurdities of Chinese life and oppressive authority, and then, in a fashion that seems unique to China, bind the wounds before anyone notices.

Listen to Chinese comic dialogues and you can sometimes hear the opening bursts of an editorial in the Peking press six months hence. *Xiang-sheng* (literally, "face and voice") performers are often a little ahead of their time. Before the government went on its latest binge of decrying privilege and bureaucracy, one comedy team produced a dialogue in which a worker stumbles into a special dining room for high officials and asks for a bowl of noodles. He has to fill out forms giving his name, his work unit, his status, his class background, his relatives, his personal history—each demand producing more gleeful recognition from the audience. The skit climaxes when the director of the dining hall phones the provincial Party Committee, the inaccessible power center whose whims irk all Chinese, to see if the man can have the noodles.

Another dialogue involves a poor worker in a government canteen who complains, "You have nothing but cabbage—can't you give us a choice?"

"Sure. Eat—or don't eat."

One official Communist Party commentator, Gu Yewen, made a study of these skits in the early 1950s. They worried him: "Certain things that ought to be treated seriously are sullied by casual throwing together of some slippery and pointless language," he said. "The serious can seem unserious and bring counterproductive results."

Through clever use of ambiguity, most *xiang-sheng* performers managed to get through the political turmoil of the 1960s and 1970s with only a few years slopping pigs in work camps. After Mao's death, national stars such as Ma Ji, a sort of Chinese Buddy Hackett, spread their satiric wings again.

Party eminences without a sense of humor do not seem to know what to do about *xiang-sheng*. It is a runaway phenomenon; tens of thousands of people try their hand at *xiang-sheng* repartee at private parties. The satire cooked up by skilled amateurs in the company of friends and co-workers can be even more biting than that performed by Ma and other professionals. One dialogue making the rounds has one person play a soldier and the other his commanding officer:

Soldier: "Sir, I demand to see Chairman Mao."

Officer: "He's dead. You cannot see him."

Soldier (next day): "Sir, I want to see Chairman Mao."

Officer: "I told you yesterday, he's dead."

Soldier (following day): "Sir, I want to see Chairman Mao."

Officer: "I told you yesterday, and the day before, he's dead! Dead! Dead! Dead!"

Soldier: "I know, I just love to hear it."

Comedy enters other forms of entertainment: stage plays employ the old Shakespearean tricks of mistaken identity and slapstick for all they are worth. Television comedians do pantomimes. In the realm of literature, the stories of Lu Xun, which now have government approval and are widely read, can have a comic bite worthy of Mark Twain. But the burden of satire falls mostly on the *xiang-sheng* performers; no one else seems willing to risk the controversy.

"Sometimes we get letters from listeners. Some of them scold us," Ma Ji said. Critics aside, Ma has become a national institution, appearing with his lean, deadpan partner Tang Jieshong as host of big Chinese New Year's television specials, both men dressed nattily in Western-style coats and ties.

Chinese comedians like Ma try to devise safe ways to skewer their audiences' favorite target—the excesses of the Communist Party. The fall of the Gang of Four was a stroke of luck, because it not only loosened the restrictions on humor but provided a rich (and safe) subject of satire in the person of Mao's widow. In one popular routine, comedians perform an "autopsy" on Jiang Qing, reporting a second face on the back of her head and a demon attached to her back. They cut open her stomach with an imaginary scalpel, and find to their horror it is full of worms which they frantically try to stamp out all over the stage.

Making fun of the mental and physical deficiencies of people who don't quite conform is part of an old peasant tradition. Before the Communist victory in 1949, xiang-sheng routines frequently derided cripples and the mentally retarded. Such jokes do not appear so often in public now, except in light insults laid by one xiang-sheng performer on his partner. But underground humorists love to make leaders look stupid and tweak their physical deficiencies. The xiang-sheng form itself, with the comedy team often composed of a fat man and a thin man, milks physical differences for every possible ounce of humor. A favorite underground story about the 5-foot 2-inch Deng Xiaoping describes a Politburo meeting in the 1960s. Chairman Mao asks all objecting to his latest economic proposal to please stand. Deng jumps to his feet. "Since there are no objections," says Mao, "the proposal is adopted."

Physical impediments, after all, provide less controversial material than political deficiencies, but in a country like China, comedians find it hard to resist lampooning politics. Jiang Kun and Li Wenhua do a number called "The Photo Studio." Jiang can get no service when he comes in to have his picture taken. He sees a sign on the wall:

> Every revolutionary comrade who steps through the revolutionary entrance and wants to have a revolutionary photo made in this revolutionary photo studio must shout revolutionary slogans. If he or she does not shout the revolutionary slogans, then the revolutionary clerks will refuse to give revolutionary replies. With revolutionary regards.

So Jiang complies: "Serve the people! Excuse me, comrade."

Li: "Fight selfishness and repudiate revisionism! Yes, what can I do for you?"

Jiang: "Eliminate bourgeois ideology, foster proletarian ideology! I want to have a photo made."

Li: "Overcome selfishness and foster public spirit! What size?"

Jiang: "Revolution is blameless! Three inches."

Li: "Rebellion is justified! The money, please."

Jiang: "Give prominence to politics! How much?"

Li: "Get instant results from political studies! One yuan and thirty cents."

Jiang: "Repudiate counterrevolutionary authorities! Here it is."

Li: "Fight against putting money in command! Here is the receipt."

Jiang: "Sweep away all demons! Thank you."

The comics say they are lampooning the excesses of the Cultural Revolution, but they and their audience know that sloganeering lingers on.

Perry Link, associate professor at UCLA, who lived in Canton and Peking in 1979 and 1980, said in a paper on the phenomenon that "the point of a *xiang-sheng* joke is often ambiguous, and the reason for laughing perhaps different from the reason why a joke is officially approved." Link's interview with the great *xiang-sheng* master, Hou Baolin, was published in an official Chinese magazine, a sign both of interest in Link's work and of the reluctance of official writers to explore such ticklish territory as Chinese humor—it is easier to let the foreigner do it. Link collected scripts of at least fifty routines from radio, television, theaters and magazines. He found that *xiang-sheng* was a quick way for people to learn the latest boundaries of dissent and to work out some of the frustrations of life under an outrageously cumbersome bureaucracy. Sitting in a *xiang-sheng* audience, one often hears people exclaim "Exactly!" or "Couldn't have said it better myself!"

The relative outspokenness and easy humor which Chinese comedians have displayed since Mao's death have had an impact on private conversation. At a dinner with young Chinese we had not met before, a lively discussion began on the fate of dissident Wei Jingsheng, who had received a fifteen-year prison sentence for allegedly trying to sell state secrets about China's war with Vietnam to a foreign journalist. Jay, half teasing, asked if anybody knew any state secrets. "No, no, certainly not," replied all but one young woman. Rubbing together the fingers of one hand, she quipped, "Sure! How much money you got?"

The verdict against Wei was considered far too harsh by many Chinese. Few dared speak their minds openly, but after the trial, if someone lost a paper clip or misspelled a word, co-workers in a Chinese office would sometimes gasp in mock horror, "You'll get fifteen years for that!"

Chubby, bubbling Ma Ji and his partner, dour, slim Tang, have a routine that satirizes and, in the ambiguous way of *xiang-sheng,* also empathizes with the people's impatience with socialist rhetoric and values. In the rather cold-blooded fashion of Chinese romance, Ma is about to be interrogated by his girl friend. Tang demonstrates for him how to answer.

Ma: "What's on your mind each day?"

Tang: "I want to contribute more each day to the four modernizations."

"What's your goal?"

"I'm trying to get more technical information."

"What are your shortcomings?"

"I feel I don't have enough education."

"What are you doing about that?"

"I will study hard . . . What do you think of my answers?"

"No good, you haven't passed this test."

"Why not?"

"Those answers are not for lovers, are they?"

So Tang queries Ma: "What's on your mind?"

"I want to carry on our love each day."

"What's your goal?"

"To get a sofa and a wardrobe."

"What are your shortcomings?"

"My only shortcoming is I don't have enough money."

"What are you doing about that?"

"I want to borrow a little more."

Ma, now forty-six, was discovered in Hollywood fashion in 1956. A bookstore clerk, he entered and won a national *xiang-sheng* contest. He had learned the techniques on his own, listening to the radio. But after the contest, *xiang-sheng*'s master of masters, Hou Baolin, took Ma under his wing. Both Hou and Ma were criticized during the Cultural Revolution. Red Guards told Ma that a *xiang-sheng* he had written about a labor hero had actually vilified the man, and that another, satirizing taxes on Taiwan, had actually "beatified Chiang Kai-shek." He was sent to a work farm in Henan province for five years, where he collected manure and grew vegetables. When he could find a quiet moment, he composed new *xiang-sheng* in his head. He was released in 1972, and by 1974 had regained his stature sufficiently to be allowed to receive the famous visiting American comedian Steve Allen. Ma said he liked Allen but could not understand many of his jokes.

Chinese comics love puns. They come rich and complex in a language with at least eight separate dialects and an ancient literary language which, though dying from disuse, can occasionally be employed in a play on words. Audiences scream when Hou Baolin exploits the interesting fact that "shampoo" in Shanghai dialect is the same as "hit the head" *(da tou)* in Peking dialect. An unhappy Peking customer in Shanghai, told that everybody gets "hit," braces himself for the blow as his barber lathers up his hair.

Barber: "All done."

"All done? Why didn't you hit me?"

"I did."

"How did you do it so painlessly?"

Orville Schell, in his book *In the People's Republic,* repeated a joke told in Dazhai, the former model production brigade, based on the different meanings of the word *feng.* Someone asked Dazhai leader Chen Yonggui why he wore his towel-like bandanna inside Peking's Great Hall of the People, since the cloth was only designed to protect the head from the wind and sun of the harsh Shanxi countryside. There may be no *feng* (meaning "wind") inside the Great Hall, Chen replied, but there is a fair amount of *feng* (meaning "craziness").

That qualifies as Chinese peasant humor, broader and less funny and direct to a Western ear, but amusing to the Chinese. Some peasant jokes are intensely scatalogical, often unprintable. In her book *China Men*, Maxine Hong Kingston revives some of the Cantonese stories of Chan Moong Gut ("Fortunate Dream" Chan), whose favorite trick was defecating each morning on his neighbor's porch, then later betting the man he could eat whatever he found on the same porch. Chan places bananas dipped in brown sugar sauce on the porch, eats them, weeping and grimacing, and goes off with his neighbor's money, leaving the man satisfied he has taught Chan a lesson.

In Chinese jokes before liberation, clever peasants always triumphed over cruel but stupid landlords or warlords. A lot of these stories are still told, with stupid bureaucrats becoming the real, if unspoken, butt of the joke. One example: a Shandong warlord went to see a basketball game for the first time and sat watching for a long while, obviously perplexed. "Why do they use just one ball? I've got lots of money. I'll buy balls for *all* the players!"

This seems very mild to Americans, but then, the Chinese consider American humor excessive and too obvious. We once heard a Chinese wonder out loud "how such an unserious people could have come so far." American jokes fail to translate well in China, more because of the mysteries of capitalism than because of the language difference. Despite a lively and talented Chinese interpreter, several of Bob Hope's jokes to a Peking audience in the summer of 1979 fell flat:

"I spent a long time in the Hall of Longevity at the Forbidden City," Hope said. "I promised my insurance man I would . . ."

"The *maotai* [China's famous fiery alcohol] comes in three flavors—premium, regular and unleaded."

But Hope scored with a reference to Peking's frequent bicycle traffic jams. "They've got the road situation here well organized," he said. "The slow traffic is at the bottom."

China has developed few wise-cracking monologuists like Hope. The *xiang-sheng* teams are far more popular, largely because their routines are steeped in tradition; the Chinese distaste for standing out alone may also be a factor.

Some historians trace *xiang-sheng* back to dialogue plays performed at the court of the Tang dynasty, more than a thousand years ago, but a more obvious beginning seems to be the mid-nineteenth century, when a temporary ban on theater performances caused by the death of the emperor forced actors into the streets. Performers could collect small change if their routines were good enough. A system developed in which the two performers would sit on chairs facing each other while helpers put up benches for the audience all around them. Women were excluded because the jokes were considered too ribald. If a woman wandered into the area, the performers would rise in silence and bow until she left. We once asked Hou Baolin about this at a dinner. Like many of his American counterparts, he was cagey, suspicious of reporters and careful of his image. He declined to say very much about his off-color material. Some friends of his told such jokes at stag parties, he admitted reluctantly, and he himself was eager for new material from abroad. Someone was translating jokes from *Playboy* for him.

Over the decades *xiang-sheng* performers developed different styles, including the singing and mimicry that are still popular today. But rapid-fire exchanges have become *xiang-sheng*'s favorite technique of late. Abbott and Costello's "Who's on first" routine would be instantly recognized in China as skillful *xiang-sheng*. We heard Peking Radio broadcast a skit that seemed like vintage Abbott and Costello.

"I bet you can't repeat three sentences I tell you."

"I'm very smart. I can repeat them."

"Okay—I drink, you drink."

" 'I drink, you drink.' "

"I eat, you eat."

" 'I eat, you eat.' "

"You're wrong."

"What do you mean, I'm wrong? I said just what you did."

"No, the third sentence is 'You're wrong.' "

"I'm *not* wrong!"

Even just the lightning speed of the repartee offers *xiang-sheng* performers a chance to evade responsibility for material that might be politically risqué. An explanatory line at the end can sweeten the political venom, after the audience has had a brief chance to enjoy it. Two performers in the early 1970s spoke of an army squad leader who "leads the way in job performance."

"He struggles arduously and bravely assumes great burdens!"

"He leads the way in upholding discipline."

"He carries out the three great disciplines and eight items for attention!"

"He leads the way in eating."

"Huh? Leads the way in eating?" After a pause, to let the audience recall the goodies they have seen in army officer canteens, the comedians quickly explain that the squad leader had taken his men to Tibet, adding, "They were unaccustomed to the rarefied air and had to be trained how to eat and sleep."

Comic assaults on arrogant bureaucrats sometimes lack the softening twists at the end; in private, too, comedians don't bother to take the sting out. They have an assortment of jokes about party leaders that seem to go back decades. In some cases the jokes are identical to stories told about Nationalist officials under Chiang Kai-shek, and perhaps about leading generals of the Ming and Qing dynasties. In the early 1970s, a story was told of the Shanxi factory worker Wu Kuixian, whose loyalty to Mao temporarily had won her a high post in Peking. When a group of visiting Japanese health experts meet with her, they praise the traditional Chinese medicines that they have been importing and credit the work of Li Shizhen (a famous Chinese physician who died seven hundred years ago). Wu, the newly minted party leader, says brightly, "Well, well, I'll have my staff locate Dr. Li and you can thank him yourself." The Japanese are too polite to correct her. Later she scolds her staff for failing to produce the doctor. The Chinese revived the joke in 1980, but this time the confused official was Chen Muhua, a vice premier said at the time to be in a bit of political trouble.

By late 1980 the most irrepressible of official publications, the *Peking Evening News,* even dared lampoon a government minister who had come under heavy criticism for enjoying lavish meals at one of the city's finest restaurants, the Horn of Plenty (Fengziyuan), without paying for them. The offending official, Commerce Minister Wang Lei, was identified as the "mock commerce minister" and taken through a fanciful interview. What, for example, was his reaction to people's complaints about rising prices? "It's not as bad as people say," he replies. "When I entertain guests at the Horn of Plenty, famous dishes for eight people by the best chefs cost me only a few yuan, just the same as in the nineteen-fifties, so what's the problem?" What about complaints of long waits for tables and of bad service? That, he says, has never happened to him. "When I eat in restaurants not only the waiters but even the managers bring me tea and wine."

Like all art in China, humor is supposed to serve the system and to advance Communist causes; in the official press it often does. The new "Humor and Satire" supplement of the *People's Daily* provides a political diet of anti-Soviet cartoons and jokes. One example:

"What's the biggest country in the world?"

"China."

"No, Cuba."

"How come?"

"It has its government in Moscow, its graveyards in Angola and its people in the U.S.A."

Anti-Soviet drawings by the American cartoonist Herblock are particularly common, even though they are printed without permission. Occasional cartoons poke fun at bureaucracy gone mad, such as the party official who describes an artist's drawing of a chicken surrounded by many little chicks as "bad for family planning." More daring and ill-tempered was a cartoon that showed a porcupine, labeled "satirical literature and art," leaving an examination by "the higher level" with all his quills clipped off.

Some jokes lampoon the relentlessly materialistic side of Chinese life, although the government is currently condoning consumerism as good economic motivation. A friend of a pretty young woman named Wang asks, "I hear you're not dating Zhang anymore."

"Yes, my feelings toward him have changed."

"Then you will return his watch?"

"No, my feelings toward the watch have not changed."

We came across bits of unintentional humor in the official media, sometimes of a grisly sort. Radio Shanghai announced that a court had sentenced Shen Tuguan, a convicted murderer, to be deprived "of political rights for life." The item concluded: "Shen was immediately executed by firing squad." And we encountered remarks that probably seemed funny only to foreigners. An English-speaking tour guide in Xi'an, a veteran of other visits by Americans, said at the end of a long afternoon, "If you have no more questions, let's all mellow out." The provincial finance minister apologized at a Xi'an banquet for not drinking. He hoped we would not be offended, he said, but he could not drink because he had to keep the provincial budget figures in his head.

In the spring of 1978 some outstanding representatives of American show business visited China, intent on exploring the mysteries of Chinese humor. Along with Norman Lear and Mary Tyler Moore, the group included Carl Reiner and Larry Gelbart, who had just collaborated on the movie *Oh, God.* At Fudan University in Shanghai they watched an English class tell the story of how China's revered late premier, Chou En-lai, gave his parachute to a scared little girl who started crying during a bumpy airplane trip. Having cast George Burns as God in their movie, the Americans had no fears about toying with Chou En-lai. They got up and performed their own skit, rendered as if they were two students in the class who had not quite understood the lesson. By the end, they had Chou in tears and the little girl giving him the parachute. "Why are you crying?" asked Reiner in the guise of the child. "You've got the parachute!"

Reiner and company insisted, when we met them later in Hong Kong, that the Chinese thought this was hilarious, though there may have been a strong dose of nervousness in the laughter. (Sometimes we forgot, to our regret, how susceptible the Chinese were to giggles when faced with an embarrassing or difficult situation. Jay came close to killing a hotel attendant in Shanghai one evening. He had vigorously objected to the bad room that had been given Linda's interpreter, but the attendant did nothing but laugh in reply.) Still, Reiner seemed to have grasped the slippery edge of Chinese humor. When, during a briefing, a high official was questioned about the bad deeds of the Gang of Four, a subject the Chinese by then were as tired of as anybody, Reiner broke in, "I'd like to answer that for the minister. They were terrible, just *terrible!*" The Chinese laughed, this time evidently in relief.

Chinese humorists exercise the caution of people who know that what might be suitable as a target this month could be politically embarrassing the next. They also seem genuinely reluctant to make fun of people to their faces, though they regularly take well-aimed jabs behind people's backs. There are moments when a foreigner wonders if China isn't a nation of deadpan comics, skilled at the *xiang-sheng* method of quick, almost indiscernible digs, enjoying jokes without the victim's noticing. During a boat trip down the Yangtze River, we as usual peppered our guide, Mr. Li, with innumerable questions, often cutting into his tea time. At one point he remarked at the good behavior of two American children, not ours, who were on board.

"You should realize that those two children are very unusual," Linda said. "They are polite and quiet and say 'Please' and 'Thank you.'"

"Yes," Jay said. "Our kids aren't like that. They're nosy and loud, sometimes a little rude."

"Maybe they want to grow up to be foreign correspondents," said Mr. Li.

EPILOGUE

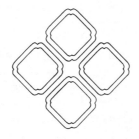

ARE THEY HAPPY?

THE CHINESE RARELY GET A CLEAR VIEW OF THE REST OF THE WORLD. They still hear of American streets paved with gold, a chicken in every pot. The old lies that relatives put in their letters from America a century ago still have currency. People wonder if they should believe foreigners who tell them they have things the West has run short of—frugality, modesty, idealism.

Ding Ling, the novelist who suffered terribly in the 1950s and 1960s, mentioned this in a speech in 1979: "I once asked a foreign friend, 'Of all the places in the world, which has the most hope?' He said China. It was changing, he said, and had people with democratic instincts, active minds and the daring to enter forbidden zones at great risk. In America and Europe, he said, people lead the good life and understand little. The young have no ideals. Drugs are a great problem. Feelings of emptiness bring individual and mass suicides. I agree with my friend, but we also have our problems, some quite serious."

Perhaps the greatest problem is the enormous gap between Chinese yearnings for political stability and material comfort and the ability of a still hidebound, heavy-handed government to meet these expectations. The problem is exaggerated because as in other societies, the young do not value the accomplishments of the past, do not appreciate how far their society has come. Dazzled by tales of the luxuries and liberties available in the West, they tend to undervalue their own honest, work-centered lives—the core of any productive society. One young man we knew received with gratitude an assignment in a city factory after eight years on a commune: "To my disappointment, the factory is not much better than the countryside. It has privileges for the few, and favor-trading. People boast, flatter and toady in order to get a promotion or a better job. Some leaders are gluttonous and lazy." Yet that same disillusioned worker now joins thousands of others who have bought special manuals to study new factory techniques. Like many young Chinese, he follows English lessons on the radio in his spare time. Like most of them, he indulges in vices no stronger than a pack of cigarettes and an evening beer.

Are they happy? Much of the time, whenever we pushed the Chinese we met to answer that unanswerable question, they said they were not. "Have you seen a Chinese kindergarten?" one young Communist Party member asked us. When we nodded he went on, "Then I don't have to explain China to you. If you want to eat, they tell you what to eat. If you want to read, they tell you what to read. If you want to wear something, they tell you what to wear."

The same young man then talked with enthusiasm of the beautiful old parks which were reopening in his native Shanghai. Now he could take his girl friend for a weekend stroll. He could buy more books, and he had more opportunities to meet people like us, people who might tell him things he did not know. He was openly contemptuous of his party's inability to inspire the nation, yet he said that he himself rose at six each morning, went for a short jog, practiced his English listening to the Voice of America, then bicycled to his office early so he could get a head start at work.

The Chinese we met were formal, polite, easily embarrassed, sometimes disarmingly droll, self-deprecating, suspicious and overburdened with office and home chores. In some limited ways, involving small personal achievements and family happenings, they can be happy. But the political wars of the 1960s and 1970s so dissipated their old national euphoria, going all-out for socialism and the motherland, that they no longer have the capacity to be exhilarated. It hurts too much to come back down from such peaks of emotion. They know the authorities may crush good moods as easily as they create them. "I'm happy when I can accomplish something, create something beautiful," one young writer working for the government said. "But I'm unhappy when the bureaucracy interferes. I had planned a trip, but they delayed it, so I'm not so happy now."

We made a list of some small satisfactions: family celebrations, tickets to Peking opera, the chance to write and paint and play a *pipa,* the chance to trade puns and gossip with co-workers, the chance to make fun of foreigners and revel in being Chinese. These safety valves help keep the Chinese serene in the face of an oppressive government. No matter how much people distrust the party and despise the middle-level bureaucrats who disrupt their lives, they do not strike back very often with violence or even very harsh words (except in odd times like the Cultural Revolution when the authorities themselves encourage it). The few strikes and demonstrations that do occur receive relatively little popular support. Richard Pipes, an American scholar of Russian history, agrees with the Soviet dissident Andrej Amalrik that the old humanistic traditions of Confucian China may explain this. "I know Russia infinitely better than China," Pipes told Willem van Kemenade, the China correspondent of the Dutch newspaper *NRC Handelsblad,* "but it is my impression that Chinese culture is much deeper than Russian culture. I mean culture in the broad sense. I was very much impressed, for example, by the appearance of Chinese villages, by the enormous work ethic, and organization of family life—all the things which make a society viable. This goes much deeper in China than in Russia." The Chinese have kept the teachings of Confucius, as well as the less intellectual principles of Taoism, alive for two thousand five hundred years. Recently they quickly repaired the monuments to Confucius damaged at his old home at Qufu, and the old sacred mountains—Taishan, Emeishan, Huangshan—draw thousands of visitors each day.

Like other people, the Chinese are never completely happy with change, even change from an era they would like to forget. After Mao died, they struggled to shake the guilt of moving back into an openly stratified society. For years they accepted the illusion that differences in status had been eliminated, and even now the government cannot completely repudiate the Maoist myth. "I think we [students] are particularly happy in comparison to our old friends back home," said Xiong Li, a third-year student at Peking Teachers College. He had spent six unhappy years in the Inner Mongolian countryside. "We have special privileges now. We get a three-month vacation, and later we get to work in the cities. I don't feel good about some of the friends I left behind. I hope they don't resent me."

The Chinese have no qualms about examining, endlessly and publicly, their own low morale, which may indicate that the problem is not as great as it sounds. They even dabble in public opinion polls, both official and unofficial. These give small glimpses into the Chinese soul, even if the most popular answers are often the most politic. An unofficial poll at Fudan University underscored why the Chinese seek pleasure in small successes rather than big ideas. Asked what they believe in, a quarter said "Nothing at all." Almost the same percentage said they believe in "fate" and a few even said "Christianity." Only a third said they believe in Communism.

An official poll by the Communist Youth League at the Peking Heavy Machinery Plant asked 482 workers: "What do you value most?" "Knowledge," said 15 percent; "a person of moral integrity," said 8 percent; "social stability," said 7 percent. Other random responses were: nature, adventure, friendship, meditation, literature and chess. One wrote: "My youngest son." "What do you hate most?" the poll asked. The landslide winner, at 45 percent, was, not unexpectedly, "the Gang of Four." Other favorites included "liars," "bureaucracy," "saboteurs of social order," "parasites," "toadies" and "arbitrary leadership."

"What do you want most?" About 38 percent said "knowledge and skill." Ten percent said "time." Others said "housing," "a good working environment," "will power" and "a sweetheart." "What troubles you most?" About 16 percent chose the safest answer: "Nothing." Twelve percent chose "housing," perhaps the most serious social issue of the day. Others mentioned lack of time, education, guidance, furniture, and care for aging parents. The answers to "How do you spend your free time?" help explain why time was such a factor in previous questions: about 30 percent said "study," 26 percent said "household chores." Some mentioned novels, films, television and foreign languages. About 4 percent (21 people) said they spent all their free time traveling back and forth to work!

These polls appear innocent of modern techniques like random samples and weighted responses. They may be no more valid than the poll our son Joe took of room attendants at the Peking Hotel. "Five said they like China and plan to stay," Joe said. "One guy on the eighth floor said he absolutely hates it."

By late 1980 the Chinese Institute of Psychology had embraced polling and conducted two surveys among workers in two cities. The questions were more political. Some of the answers reflected skepticism about the government's plans and a willingness to express disgruntlement in public.

Asked if they were hopeful about the success of the modernization of the country, 86 percent in one factory and 94 percent in the other said yes, but 10 percent said, "It's nothing to do with me," and 4 percent said no. About 52 percent said they wanted officials elected by workers, 38 percent called for "free competition for office," and 11 percent said officials should be selected by party higher-ups. Asked what motivated them, the workers responded in this general descending order: the need to modernize China, increase in pay and bonus, Communist ideals, career, happy home life, honor, fame and status, and promotion. A few answered: "Nothing." The psychologists also ranked responses to the question "What is the biggest obstacle to full use of your initiative?": 1) bad leadership, 2) low wages, 3) housing problems, 4) official privileges, 5) dull life, 6) job dissatisfaction, 7) factionalism, and 8) inadequate education for children.

We shared with pollsters an inability to measure accurately the depth of this discontent. The people we spoke to were often disgruntled to begin with. That was one of the reasons why they took whatever risks there were in talking to us. And, like the pollsters, we were not asking them innocuous questions about the weather, but forcing them to express their basic dissatisfactions, without giving them much of a chance to say whether they felt crushed or just annoyed by them. That having been said, the disillusionment with the Communists is still pervasive.

One young worker in Peking told us of his several years in Heilongjiang in the northeast. "We all volunteered to go. We were really enthusiastic about doing our part. We were told the place was a land of milk and honey, but we got there and found out it was a barren desert. But that isn't what turned us sour. It was the corruption of our leaders, who were dishonest. A lot of people became so disillusioned that they began to question Communism itself." Another young factory worker who had been reading in his newspaper about how the party had reformed and regained popularity said, "I made forty yuan under the Gang of Four. I make forty yuan under Deng

Xiaoping. What's the difference?" A well-traveled Latin American diplomat with several close Chinese friends said, "I don't know if there are any countries where people are more alienated than here. They aren't getting anywhere, so they trudge along."

Some Chinese say they expect morale to improve. Once it has sunk in that the government is no longer going to promise or demand huge annual increases in production, expectations may fall to more reasonable levels. Even today, said one overseas Chinese living in Peking, compared to the West "people expect so much less, they are more happy with what little they get." A woman in a Chinese publishing house said, "Few people are satisfied with what they are doing, and even if they like their work, they don't like their pay." But she added that some people were being allowed transfers as inefficient offices closed and new publishing ventures opened. Still, they needed the approval of their units to transfer and that remains difficult to get.

We met a young man in Chongqing, the son of an army officer, who seemed quite confident that he could change jobs when he got around to it. He was an official tour guide. Once he discovered we were journalists he questioned us for a half-hour about what we considered the most "prestigious" careers in China. "I'd really like something with a little more status than tour guide. I'd like to study to be a journalist." While traveling with a visiting U.S. health delegation, we met a Chinese doctor who was serving as an interpreter. He rather boldly explained to several Americans present that he was still suffering from persecution begun during the Cultural Revolution. His father had come under heavy criticism and had committed suicide. He himself had been exiled to a ninety-bed hospital in remote Ningxia, where his skills as a plastic surgeon were rarely required. He was rather open about his demand for a transfer. His confidence seemed born of years of despair. Having been down so long, he had nowhere to go but up. That reckless feeling may cut through some of the gloom and doubts of the Chinese in the 1980s. One foreign engineer said that many senior technicians told him, "What can they do to me after I've been cleaning toilets for ten years?"

The Chinese have been teasing, suffering and manipulating their government for centuries. It is the national sport. Magistrates working for the emperor rarely involved themselves below the county level. In the villages, local officials had some responsibility for collecting taxes, but families ran their own lives and the government interfered only when something went wrong. For the most part, families, not the police, watched other families and their own members, and handled crimes and incorrect thinking on their own.

The emperor was the keeper of the rites. He prayed the proper prayers so the harvest would be good. The idea of daily or even weekly civic involvement—studying the emperor's latest edicts, for instance—never occurred to the Chinese before this century. A peasant paid taxes to keep the government away.

The Communists wanted to change that, and to a large extent they have succeeded. Even the most remote and poverty-stricken Chinese villager understands in a vague way how policies in Peking affect his life, and knows personally the party branch members who represent the modern equivalent of the emperor. The villager may soon be able to sell the melons he has been growing in his backyard for much more than he gets today because of some decision in Peking, although such decisions usually filter down slowly and tortuously.

And still, the old distrust and avoidance of government lives on. The Chinese feel the farther you are from Peking, the less you have to worry about policy. During our first trips to China, in 1977 and 1978, we were struck by how friendly and casual people were in southern cities. Passers-by in Peking, on the other hand, would often look at us with suspicion if we just asked the time of day. By 1980, official policy toward foreigners had relaxed, so people in Peking were more at ease, but not altogether. James Thomson, curator of the Nieman Fellowship at Harvard, grew up in China and told us that even before 1949, people were more formal and restrained in the capital. In unguarded moments, people outside Peking will even lampoon its political pretensions. "I suppose you're very excited about the Congress," London *Daily Telegraph* correspondent Nigel Wade asked one woman after the National Parliament convened in 1978. The woman said no, then a look of mischief crossed her face. Imitating a delegate responding to the sixth straight speech on production targets, she applauded vigorously with an inane grin on her face.

Resentment of official absurdities often boils over when the government tries out a new idea. In China, this means meetings to explain the new policy to the masses, meetings to hear the views of the masses, and meetings to explain to the masses what they missed in the first round of meetings. We are convinced after much discussion of this matter that the Chinese like nothing less than sitting for hours listening to the views of the masses—themselves. For people who must spend hours getting to work and lining up for food at the market, or tending the private plot that is going to have to provide most of their vegetables, wasted free time is an agony. The post-Mao leaders cut down on meetings, but that seems to render the remaining meetings that much more difficult to endure. Both city and country Chinese make a habit of arriving late at meetings, knowing it is difficult to leave early.

One of the worst times, we were told, was in the spring of 1980, when the government decided to seek the views of the masses on who should get the pay raises promised to an undefined 40 percent of the urban work force. Our Chinese friends could talk of little else. They were exasperated rather than fascinated. The discussion leaders were unwilling to impose a time limit. The talk seemed to go on forever. One participant recounted the discussion: "Should the youngest people get it? No; while they are the lowest paid, many don't have families. Should the oldest get it? No, lots of them got the last pay raise. Should the best people get it? How do we tell who is the best?"

"Thirty years of meetings, and what have we got for it?" said one disgruntled office worker we met in Hangzhou. "The pay-raise meetings required political discussions. Some people said, 'I don't want to deal with it. I don't want a raise.' But the leaders wouldn't accept that. Everyone's first reaction was, let's have a secret ballot and vote on it and that's it. But the leaders said, 'You're going to do this and do it right.' We had to report on our work for the past three years, how we thought we ourselves and others had done. This threatened the personal relationships in the offices, making the meetings that much more excruciating. It was so complicated—keeping track of all that was said—that the cadres had to meet from six-thirty to eleven each night to get ready for the following day's group meeting." We even heard of suicides by workers mortified by personal attacks suffered at these meetings, something most people thought had ended with the Cultural Revolution.

This is the dark side of *guanxi,* the community spirit. People are so accustomed to operating in groups, checking with family, friends, co-workers and supervisors before making important decisions, that the pressure sometimes becomes too much. The Chinese enjoy the web of human relationships. The old ties make their days more comfortable and their futures more secure. But they dislike devices like the pay-raise meetings that force them to compare themselves to other members of the group.

The Chinese in Peking often debate just how much they are ruled by their urge for consensus, and how much by their individual needs. Foreigners, as well, go back and forth on this issue, changing their minds as they meet more and more Chinese. As an American teacher at Peking University said, "They are all so attentive I can hardly stand it. I'd be bored to death if I paid that close attention to everything I said. People come to China for two weeks and are so delighted to find the Chinese are human beings, warm, friendly, not blue ants. But after you've been here six months you realize they *are* blue ants. This isn't just because it's a Communist country, and the restrictions that puts the people under, it goes far back before that. It is the way they operate."

The word in Chinese for "freedom" or "liberty" is *ziyou.* It translates literally as "one's own motives" and to the Chinese has very selfish connotations. The Chinese themselves will acknowledge this, and joke about it, but they accept the anti-individualistic atmosphere, even though many long to escape from time to time. The pursuit of happiness to the Chinese begins with their group consciousness and pride at being Chinese. Nothing con-

tributed more to that feeling in this century than the collective loyalty to
Mao Tse-tung, so the way his memory has been denigrated since his death
has had a marked effect on morale.

In the popular imagination of the Chinese, Mao began as a mysterious
figure, a Robin Hood fighting in the hills of Hunan and Jiangxi like the great
rebel rascals of Chinese legend. He enjoyed the luck and supernatural
powers of the Monkey King, the fairy-tale hero, a comparison he did not
discourage. He seemed immortal, having been reliably reported dead several
times. Later, many Chinese saw him as a determined nationalist leader who
fought the Japanese while the Chiang Kai-shek Nationalists were hunkering
down in their southwest enclave. In any event, Mao united the country,
ended decades of war and famine, and installed a government so determined
to deal honestly and fairly with the lowest rungs of society that the Chinese
could hardly believe it.

Eventually, Mao became a kind of messiah. His name and exploits appeared in every child's textbook, newspapers printed his words in boldface
type, people watched his infrequent public or television appearances in awe.
Millions of young people, most of them now in their thirties, traveled all
over the country during the Cultural Revolution carrying Mao's gospel and,
in many cases, dying in his name. In the bloody battles of that period, all
sides claimed Mao's sanction, the fight always being over which of his
underlings had the true word. Politics in China proceeds much in that
fashion today. The Gang of Four trial showed the world one group, led by
Deng Xiaoping, tearing Mao's mantle off another, Mao's widow, Jiang
Qing, and her allies.

The myth about the Chairman has survived even among the young
democracy movement activists, who demand that Mao be accountable for
his bad deeds even while they express open admiration for his early revolutionary method. During a democracy movement demonstration in late 1979,
a young man from Shanghai named Hong Weixiu electrified the crowd with
a recitation of the government's failure to meet Marx's standards. Hong's
favorite pose, left hand cocked on hip, elbow out, cigarette held like a candle
with thumb and two fingers of the right hand, suggested Mao's posture in
a famous photograph of a Yenan speech in the 1930s. Hong later told us he
was patterning his life after Mao. He had left his factory job to travel
through villages in Anhui interviewing the peasants about conditions there.

There are people in the present Chinese leadership who would like to pull
down Mao's Memorial Hall and consign all his portraits to the flame
because he is an inspiration to ambitious young politicians who might wish
to wield power through mass campaigns and political purges. But today's
Chinese leaders appear to understand the political and emotional costs of
erasing all memory of a man so associated with the Communist Party in
the minds of the people. What would Americans think if a Republican
President derided Lincoln as a rabblerouser and closed his memorial in

Washington, or if a Democratic President labeled Franklin D. Roosevelt a warmonger and ended all reference to him in party speeches? The Chinese who see Mao's legend for what it is—a great danger to the future stability of any Chinese government—are dismantling it very slowly, like demolition experts defusing an old bomb buried near the foundations of a beautiful church.

The demystification process has proceeded on many fronts. In 1978 the *People's Daily* stopped putting Mao quotes in boldface type. The Chinese exchanged stories about investigations into Mao's sex life. Some insisted there was a building in northwest Peking called "12,000 House," holding at least that many works of Mao withdrawn from the stores and awaiting some final disposition. One American resident of Peking collected more than 1,500 different Mao buttons from Chinese friends who thought it impolitic to keep them and unwise to throw them away. Party leaders openly discussed his "mistakes" and rendered what they said was the "final verdict" on the Great Helmsman, praising his early triumphs and decrying his later excesses. Portraits of Mao were removed from walls and buildings all over the country, though many still remain in the homes of peasants and workers who honor his memory. They consider him essential to the very meaning of their lives, the remaking of imperial China into a modern, unified nation.

We found our visits to Mao's Memorial Hall eerie, both because of his pasty, deeply lined features preserved under glass and because of the many Chinese forming long lines to see him even while his legend diminishes in the official press. (By the time this is read, his Memorial Hall may be permanently or temporarily closed again.) For as long as four months at one point during our stay the hall was closed to visitors. We were told it needed repairs, but politics seemed to be playing a role.

The inscription above the main doors is in the handwriting of Hua Guofeng, Mao's appointed successor who was eased out of real power after the Chairman's death. The building is big and square, with graceful pillars. We watched visitors enter four abreast, then walk left or right, two abreast, around a huge embroidered landscape with a statue of Mao in front of it. Air conditioning chilled the red-carpeted room where the bier stood, surrounded by what were apparently plastic flowers (no one dared touch them). Mao's body, dressed in a gray suit of the style that took his name abroad, was completely wrapped below the chest in a bright red Chinese flag. His skin seemed old but lifelike; we had little time to stare. Political wrangling had delayed embalming of the body in 1976, and frequent visitors claimed the face had changed color and shape, indicating some mishap.

While we were inside no one spoke, or stopped moving. Outside again, foreigners made bad jokes about the "peasant under glass." The Chinese were not amused: they had seen the man who united them. His name would forever be associated with China and with some of mankind's great social experiments. Even if they do not love him, they are proud of him. He has helped make their generation immortal.

The old Chinese guarantee of immortality—the real key to happiness—was the family. Sons would carry on the family name and remember their ancestors with regular prayers and physical memorials. But in the 1980s, with Mao's national spirit diminishing, families now limited to one child apiece, with burial spots scarce and crowded, some Chinese are dabbling in other links of past and future. This explains in part the resilience and new life of religion in China, one of the phenomena of post-Mao China that are most easily misunderstood.

At the Southern Cathedral in Peking, where Chinese worshipers have begun to appear in numbers again in the last few years, American attaché Bill McCahill sat next to two old men in ragged clothes who looked like shepherds. Neither had a missal to follow the service. "But they were rattling off the litany of the saints in Latin," McCahill said. "You have to say the names of more than a hundred saints, in a certain order, but they knew the list by heart." When the authorities allowed ("arranged" might be a better word) the consecration of a new bishop of Peking in late 1979, the cathedral was packed with at least five hundred Chinese. Several hundred homemade rosaries sold out within minutes at a price of about thirty-three cents each. After the ceremony the tall distinguished-looking Bishop Fu came out to talk to scores of Chinese who had stayed behind. "I prayed for the motherland, the four modernizations and for workers of every belief," he told them. This is the message of the All-China Patriotic Catholic Association: be a Christian loyal to Peking rather than Rome. When an aide told the bishop's audience that they could kiss his ring, many rushed to do so. One man recognized a woman latecomer and pulled twenty rosaries he had bought out of his pocket. "You came too late," he said. "Look what they were selling today." "My God," she said, "I haven't seen one of those in twenty years."

The rebirth and resanctioning of religion impresses outsiders more than the Chinese, but to the government in Peking it is the impression on foreigners (particularly overseas Chinese) that is important. Despite the time and money spent in China by Christian missionaries before 1949, Western religions never won a following in China as large as that enjoyed by Buddhism, or even Islam. In 1949, by some estimates, there may have been two million Roman Catholics and perhaps another million Christians of other denominations in the country. Many of those escaped to Hong Kong, Taiwan, the United States or other parts of the Christian world. Courting good will overseas so that such Chinese might offer educational, financial and moral support, Peking now allows Chinese Christians to worship openly. We do not know how many practicing Christians there are, but we were occasionally approached by people who left small hints of their ongoing faith. "God bless you," they would say on parting. Bishop Fu told visiting Cardinal Franz Koenig that there are "several thousand" Catholics in the Peking area, and that three to four hundred Chinese attend services at his cathedral regularly. There are similar turnouts at Peking's Protestant Church. Churches have reopened to large crowds in at least two dozen cities throughout the country, particularly along the eastern coast, where missionary activity was greatest.

At one of these reborn churches in the remote east coast city of Fuzhou we began to wonder if, against all reason, Christianity might actually be offering some balm to the disheartened spirit of China in the 1980s. After some persistence and subterfuge, a group of us Peking-based journalists managed to locate and visit the Flower Lane Protestant Church, an old stone building tucked away at the end of an alley near the town's main shops. Old men in faded blue workers' clothes (the local clergy, we learned) were printing hymns and church notices and practicing choir selections for what was to be their first Easter service in fourteen years. One of the senior church staff, Ye Zhude, was at the piano practicing "Christ Our Lord Is Risen Today" in a strong baritone. The words for the hymn in Chinese were printed in the church program; few of the worshipers had their own hymnals and the church had none. Most hymnals and Bibles had been destroyed in the successive campaigns against religion in the 1950s, and particularly in the Cultural Revolution of the late 1960s.

Yet reportedly 1,200 to 1,400 people had jammed the church every Sunday since it reopened in late 1979. Many more shoehorned their way in for the Easter service. "People are thirsting for something spiritual," said Moses P. Xie, the seventy-seven-year-old Episcopal bishop. He said parishioners were demanding longer sermons than he gave before the Communists took over. At least one third of the congregation were people under thirty. He had conducted one wedding in the church and planned to begin baptisms of anyone older than eighteen who wished to accept the faith.

Some party officials may consider it helpful to let young people with religious family backgrounds pursue old ties to Christianity, Islam and Buddhism, as many seem to be doing. They may feel better, and become better workers. Bishop Xie knows it is illegal to proselytize religion, and religious leanings can hurt the career of any ambitious youngster. But Xie still promotes the productive benefits of love of God. "We should do something for the peace and security of our situation. People do look to the church as one place they can get help. The thirst is intense now."

It has to be a purely Chinese church. The foreign connections of the old Chinese Christian community helped accelerate its destruction. Xie, who had spent two years in Britain, suffered the usual accusations after 1949 that he was a foreign spy. During the Cultural Revolution he was forced to stop preaching altogether. Now he discourages foreign donations. The weekly collection plate and rent from old church properties bring in 1,500 yuan a month, more than enough to pay the church staff and finance repairs and improvements. He said the church may be stronger without the foreign missionaries, for "many of them did not think the Chinese were their equals."

To Chinese authorities, any foreign connections are like high explosives: sometimes useful, but extremely dangerous. Growing numbers of Chinese who think about the good life know things are better in the West. Authorities occasionally remind people of the history of unhappy foreign involvement in China, but these efforts don't seem to work. The young don't know what those foreigners—before 1949—were like. And for older people, memories of brutal Japanese soldiers and unscrupulous foreign businessmen are mixed with memories of American aid in World War II and the jobs they had and the friends they made in the British treaty ports. When Jay and Joe visited one of the most famous of the old treaty ports, Chefoo (now called Yantai), they found that the local citizenry had not even bothered to put up one of the museums of imperialist horror that exist in large Chinese cities. Jay's mother had lived in Chefoo when his grandfather was stationed there with a U.S. naval detachment, but Chefoo people such as an old rickshaw driver Jay found had few unhappy memories of the foreigners. China was a poor country, then as now, and then as now, foreign money helped.

One afternoon we were standing on Shamian Island in Canton, gazing at an old steeple, relic of a British empire we would never see again. A white-haired man in brown slacks and dirty undershirt came up and said, in careful English, "That was a church." It seemed an odd place for a friendly conversation, for Shamian had been a European enclave which for years had excluded Chinese, except those working for the foreigners. The old man liked it there. He had worked for the British customs office and in recent years had been working with a Chinese government agency that made a tidy profit from dealings with Westerners at the Canton trade fair. He looked nervously at some young men who were leaning against the fence and watching us. We spoke English and stood in what might be described as a historical neutral zone. In front of us was the old church built by the British. In back was the mansion that had housed the representatives of China's former socialist ally, Vietnam, its occupants unceremoniously ejected just a few weeks before, as the Europeans had been after 1949. "Chinese youths don't know anything about the foreign concessions or the church," the man said. "They don't remember, or else ignore, what it was like then."

A tour official in Canton told us his most vivid memory of foreigners on Shamian. One night just before the Communists took over Canton, he watched two Europeans get off their rickshaw at a hotel on Shamian, toss their money onto the ground and laugh as the rickshaw men scrambled in the dust for the coins made almost worthless by wartime inflation. The official vowed to tell his children some day about that moment of humiliation, and he eventually did, several times, "but they seemed rather bored by it."

Instead, young Chinese still nurture the century-old dream of an easier life across the sea. The United States retains the sort of image, despite official propaganda to the contrary, that led nineteenth-century Chinese to give San Francisco the name *Jiu Jin Shan,* "Old Mountain of Gold," still used in China. We spoke with dozens, perhaps hundreds, of Chinese who wanted to go abroad. We thought this was an urban phenomenon, found only among disgruntled intellectuals and Chinese who had relatives overseas or other foreign connections. But an American scientist working in a laboratory in Shanghai reminded us of what one of the peasant workmen temporarily assigned to him said when, after introductions, the peasant had presented his eight-year-old son. "When you go back to America, take him with you." The American had laughed. The peasant didn't.

We tried our best to discourage such talk. The quotas at U.S. Immigration were backed up anyway, and we began to realize that the lure of America could ruin any chances of a satisfactory life in China. That is what we think happened to Zheng Lianqun.

Zheng never saw his American father. His frightened Chinese grandmother burned the only picture when the Korean War broke out. But for years he made a number of unauthorized trips around the country in a desperate search for his past. Born in 1948, Zheng is one of the thousands of Chinese to whom normalization of relations between the United States and China meant more than a shift in global politics. The American embassy in Peking and the new U.S. consulates in Shanghai and Canton have been deluged with Chinese who have some American connection that they have kept hidden for years. When we met Zheng, whose light skin and freckles betrayed his heritage, he had made at least twenty trips to Peking and to his mother's home in Shandong, trying to prove his American citizenship. He had written to every high U.S. official he could think of, including the President, and methodically learned the name and address of every American journalist who happened to live in or visit Peking. He had sold his blood at least nine times to various Chinese hospitals to pay for the train tickets. He would ask anyone he met for further donations.

He said neighbors and relatives had revealed a twenty-year-old secret to him in 1972, after President Nixon's Peking trip. "I had it in my head before. [When I grew up] other children would tease me and call me a 'big old Yankee' because of the way I looked, but I thought it was a joke. All I knew was my adopted Chinese mother and father." They told him his father had been an American, a man named Louis George (or perhaps George Lewis) who served in the transport battalion of the First Marine Division in Tianjin from 1945 to 1946, when he married Zheng's mother, a twenty-year-old jute-mill worker named Li Shuzhen. Zheng said his mother succeeded in getting a U.S. immigrant visa in May 1947 and followed her husband to San Diego, putting Zheng in the care of another family because she thought the trip would be too hard on a three-month-old baby. She promised to send for him later.

Zheng's grandmother in Shandong received a picture of his mother with her American husband and two more small children about three years later. The husband wrote to his mother-in-law from Korea, but she burned the letter and no more letters came.

Zheng went to what was then the U.S. Liaison Office in Peking ten times before he got a letter from an embassy official that allowed him to actually get past the Chinese army guards and into the building. Embassy officials initiated unsuccessful searches for military records of his father back in the United States. Zheng stopped going to work at the construction company in Tianjin where he was a bricklayer. His wife received some disability checks from her own factory, and friends helped him.

Embassy officials eventually told Zheng his search was hopeless, but he refused to give up. The more time he devoted to his obsession, the more he cut himself off from Chinese society, without any real hope of finding his American past. Because of his avowed foreign connection, he was denied admission to the Chinese air force and was no longer allowed to read the special government bulletins circulated in his construction team. Zheng smiled and charmed people. He had no trouble persuading the guards to let him through the door of the Peking Hotel to see us. In late 1980, as we were packing to leave China, we got a letter from Zheng's wife in Tianjin. She had not seen her husband in a week. She was pregnant, the baby was due soon and she wondered if we could find Zheng and send him home. He turned up soon after on the trail of some visiting American dignitary, and we relayed the message. He nodded and grinned, then asked if we knew of any new American reporters in town.

In 1981, convinced there was no other way, he crossed the border illegally into Hong Kong, where he managed to charm U.S. officials who interviewed him in prison into letting him go to the United States. He is living in California, making regular trips to San Diego and San Francisco in search of his family.

China, like other countries, has plenty of young people with big dreams. It may take a great deal of disappointment to drag them back to reality. We met more than our share of these young people because we were often a part of their dreams. Any foreigners, particularly those who write and have articles occasionally printed in *Reference News,* seem to some Chinese to be a ticket to a big future.

But we also found many Chinese with simpler notions of their lives. They are probably the vast majority. The people who think of happiness in terms of a peaceful marriage, a modest salary raise or a new television set find this a fairly good time to be alive. Some of the sharp political edge of Chinese life has worn off with the death of Mao. People have a little more money to spend, and a little more to spend it on. Mindless bureaucracy and poor housing persist, but people are used to them. Many Chinese gain some small additional joy just from being Chinese. The nation enjoys respect and interest around the globe. We met an oil engineer sent out to the Bohai Gulf, a soldier back from the Vietnamese front, a scientist just returned from an international conference in Japan. All were happy to help China do things it has never done before. They come home adding to an ancient sense of national self-confidence.

When we lived in Hong Kong and talked to people who had left China illegally, we were surprised at the extent of that pride. Many refuges expressed sadness at leaving the mainland, despite its drawbacks. The pain and confusion of leaving China hits even those who despise Communism. An elderly peasant woman had been brought out to see her son, an engineer who had lived on Taiwan for several years. "Couldn't I go back to my village?" she told her husky, successful offspring. "I really don't know anyone here." Canadian diplomat Michael Frolic quoted an oil-drilling specialist, one of the technocrats who love China for the demands it places on what they know. His wife, an overseas Chinese, had made him leave, and he bemoaned giving up "my work, my life and my country" for an unknown future.

The vast majority of those who leave China do not wish to return, at least not permanently, but they still cheer on the sidelines, hoping that their cousins back home will acquire better leaders who can control the old fear of disorder and dissent so that at least private life may have some variety and refreshment. Huang Li, sent to New York to study sociology, began to help publish a journal calling for human rights in China, but told us, "I will go back if the situation changes."

"Chairman Mao turned out to be a terrible old man," said one sardonic young Red Guard who reached Hong Kong in a small rowboat. "But he gave some good advice: 'Trust the masses.' If the party could really learn to do that, to stop talking and listen to what people say, we might learn to forget Chairman Mao's worst, and remember his best."

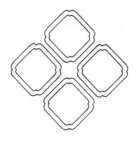

FUTURE

MARJORIE HUTCHISON, AN AUSTRALIAN INSTRUCTOR AT THE CANTON Foreign Languages Institute, asked her students to read Arthur Hailey's novel *The Moneychangers.* She wanted them to learn some idioms of the modern world. Words like "mortgage" and "credit card" she had some difficulty making clear to them. But when the novel described the complicated contest for leadership of an American bank, the students had little trouble understanding. "They know all about power struggles," Hutchison said.

In their infrequent attempts to predict the future the Chinese try to avoid unpleasant truths and imagine the usual socialist utopia—a soulless technological cornucopia. One of the new Chinese science-fiction novels, *The Fancy Future,* is full of video telephones, robots, flying taxis, computerized mines, spaceships, typewriters activated by thought and, a special Chinese touch, dozens of new fruits and vegetables created by biological engineering. The story, set in the year 2000, carries barely a hint of politics or human strife. But another novel about the year 2000, written by an unofficial writer and displayed on China's Democracy Wall in 1979, updates the cumbersome system of political intrigue and ideological infighting. In this novel an unnamed leader (suspiciously like Deng Xiaoping) dies in 1998. Many of his protégés also expire, apparently murdered. An investigation into the deaths gives power to a group of revived radicals, and the semicapitalist, decentralized management of the "Deng" years is overturned. A brave young wallposter writer tries to intervene, but he is arrested and killed, and the resulting protests help bring down the new radical government.

It is an amateurish attempt at literature, but the story conveys the compelling sense of a country that may not change much by the end of the century, despite novelties in the book like forty-seven-story apartment buildings, foreign newspapers sold in the streets and a population of 1.5 billion people. The author quotes a wall poster from the 1970s, which still describes China in the year 2000: "Control over political, economic, legal and other matters is monopolized by centralized leadership. As a result, the eating, drinking, toilet and sleeping habits of 900 million people, their emotions such as joy, anger, sorrow and delight, and their every act and every move are influenced by the physiological changes in these few people, their habits and preferences, their mental state and their ideological leanings. Thus, everything changes when an individual is removed from the scene, and the laws of a generation change with an individual's death."

That uneasiness over the prospect of more upheaval—something few Chinese thought about very often until the last century—affects everything that happens in China now. Newspapers and official publishers spin historic visions as spiritually and politically empty as taking a flying taxi to Tibet in *The Fancy Future*. But the people wonder how many more purges, changes of policy, and unexpected and arbitrary reappraisals and readjustments they will have to endure upon the death of Mao's successors.

The Chinese who have suffered the most from these sudden shifts, politicians like Deng Xiaoping, writers like Ding Ling and Cao Yu, express the most hope for the future. Their lives, nearing an end, have little meaning without some optimism. On a trip down the Li River in Guilin we first met an American who traveled in the same circles as these prominent Chinese and suffered as they did—Sid Rittenberg. Rittenberg came to China with the U.S. Army in 1946, but stayed to help the Communist revolution. He was jailed in the late 1940s as a result of an intrigue involving Russian attempts to defame his patron, American writer Anna Louise Strong. Rittenberg was accused of being a spy, and it took a while for his friends to discredit the charges. He was released in the early 1950s, then jailed again in 1968 when the Gang of Four decided he would be a convenient scapegoat. He spent a total of sixteen years in prison.

As the jagged, twisted beauties of the mountains around Guilin slid by, we told Sid we thought the Cultural Revolution had been an unmitigated disaster and expected him to agree. No, he said, something positive had come out of it. "I think what happened has inoculated the country against witch hunts," he said. Most Chinese share this view, or at least hope it is true, because so much of their future peace and prosperity depends on it. But we wondered if this optimism was very realistic.

In the last few years the Chinese have discarded Maoist ideals of equality and class spirit in favor of self-interest and order. But not all Chinese have approved of the dizzying change, and the Mao tradition still has enough of a hold on the Chinese people's image of themselves that it could reappear in potent form and force another struggle. Mao's China inspired Western interest in the same way the Communists won over the Chinese themselves, through seemingly unselfish devotion to duty and nation-building, to honesty and patriotism. In 1949, store clerks in Peking were astonished to see soldiers of the invading Red Army pay for what they needed, just as some foreign visitors told friends in the 1970s of hotel attendants running after them to return even the smallest pin left behind in their rooms. This law-abiding, ascetic characteristic, encouraged by Mao, reminded Americans and Europeans of their own Calvinist tradition of progress through hard work. Older Chinese saw it as a revival of the Confucian ideal of gentlemanly conscientiousness.

This obsession with integrity still survives in China. Our Chinese acquaintances seemed proud when we praised their work and said they were only doing their duty. Ideology has diminished, of course, and bonuses increased. Some Chinese will now accept small gifts, and some did not always return the items we sometimes mistakenly left in hotel rooms. But the urge for obeying the old Confucian code is there, and if the mild corruption of the 1980s grows worse, if economic inequities become too pronounced, a political faction with an eye to Mao could organize the resulting popular resentment in an assault on the government. The Chinese know this, and clearly remain ill at ease about their propensity for power struggle.

To read the seismograph of the Chinese social and political landscape—to detect the next great ideological earthquake and its possible magnitude—requires sensors in many different places. What causes rumbles in cities often goes unregistered in the countryside.

China's future will thus seem to unfold very erratically. Our own monitors—diplomats, journalists and scholars—will never be able to see much beyond the cities, or even much beyond Peking. In the countryside, life will change more slowly. But once the rules of change are understood—particularly the extent to which an individual Chinese can safely ignore the directives from on high—it is possible to see the outline of the next few years.

China cannot in our lifetime attain the efficiency and productivity of a Japan or a Germany. The lack of capital and technical expertise, the urge of citizens and bureaucracy to avoid responsibility, the unquenchable thirst for petty influence, *guanxi,* and the emotional need to do everything possible by the back door will take their toll. China in the year 2000 will still be poor and slow, but perhaps the government will be a bit more confident of its ability to deal with its own people humanely without risking the collapse of its authority.

The Chinese have done their most interesting work in the crevices of the system. Avant-garde artists have slipped their work briefly into official exhibit halls. The most interesting news has come on the grapevine. Private parties have enjoyed the best comedy dialogues. Taped music has offered an innocuous way to admire the mysteries of Taiwan. Lovers have found peace and privacy in long walks into unfamiliar neighborhoods. Any Chinese government is going to worry about people straying out of control, but the crevices will remain. They help hold the system together and keep morale from dropping to a critical level. The crevices are also apt to widen as the government follows its habit of alternately relaxing and tightening control, just as the cracks in mountain rock grow larger in the expansion and contraction of warm summers and cold winters.

Our teachers told us to view Chinese history as a whole, and look for two-thousand-year-old customs alive today; we journalists, focused on the latest trends, tend to take for granted the profound changes that have come in this century. Chinese society remains full of privilege for the few, but the gap between rich and poor is much narrower than it was fifty years ago. The countryside still hovers on the edge of famine, but peasant interest in birth control is deeper today—despite old misgivings—than it ever was before.

Perhaps the very top of the system has seen the most remarkable change. With the Cultural Revolution a horrible exception, the old Chinese habits of leadership succession by murder and assassination have been suspended. Even before the Cultural Revolution, Mao and other Chinese leaders had absorbed the modern world's disdain for star chamber trials and executions. They realized that curbing these old imperial practices would even be to their personal advantage—who could predict when the political tides might turn against any of them, even Mao? The new system has brought quick results of incalculable importance. Through Mao's intervention, Deng Xiaoping survived the Cultural Revolution, even though he was that campaign's second most important target. Where would China be today if the talented Deng had not been there to patch the government together after Mao's death? Mao's chosen successor Hua Guofeng was pushed aside by Deng, but was left alive and with an official position. Even the Gang of Four survives—under confinement.

Other changes will reveal themselves as the Chinese learn more and make new sense of their old traditions. But we should never overemphasize how much they may borrow from the West. The desire to be Chinese, to be close together, part of a family and a *guanxi* web, is just too strong. Americans should not be confused either by what lengths the Chinese will go to unlock the secrets of the modern world. The thousands of Chinese students who have recently reached the United States and Europe are probably a temporary aberration. Such exchanges, which lead young Chinese to question their heritage and the Chinese way of doing things, are threatening to the social order.

So, too, may fade the current Chinese passion for learning English. This craze has some of the flavor of the Westernization frenzy that swept Japan in the 1880s, when, for a while, all women of good families in Tokyo were taught European languages and ballroom dancing. In Peking today, elevator operators often do not even look up from their English phrase books while they push the button for the proper floor. Students regularly accost tourists in the street to practice their English vocabulary. A million copies of a government guide to the English language sold out within weeks, and the *Enlightenment Daily* decreed: "We cannot achieve any of our goals if we don't first learn the ABCs." "English is the most useful language in the world, by far. Even the Japanese speak English," said Wang Do'en, an English professor in Canton who returned to China in 1951 after studying at the University of Michigan.

A Canton hotel attendant told us, "I want to be able to understand the foreign books and movies that are becoming available again. The *People's Daily* said the movie *Star Wars* is about a fantasy world to which many Americans would like to escape because the realities of capitalism are unbearable. Naturally, I would like to see this for myself." At the Canton Foreign Languages Institute, near White Cloud Mountain outside of town, nearly 65 percent of the student body study English.

In time, the Chinese will begin to choose more carefully what they want from the West, just as the Japanese did in the nineteenth century. The Chinese talk a lot about Japan. A much copied wall poster in Canton in 1977 noted that in 1957 Japan produced 10 million tons of steel, about the same amount as China produced then. But by 1972, Japan's steel production had reached 100 million tons, while China's was only 20 million. "Does this mean," the poster asked, "that the Chinese people are less intelligent than the Japanese, that we are less diligent?"

The question was rhetorical. The Chinese find it hard to admit inferiority to a culture that borrowed so heavily from the ancient Chinese. By the same token, the Chinese are milking the Japanese of any advanced technology and management methods they can get, and Peking has encouraged Tokyo in its diplomatic battles with the Soviet Union, the other great power in China's neighborhood. But one day the Chinese will return to the principles of Sun-tzu, the ancient military strategist—one of the first proponents of a balance of power—and improve relations with the Soviets in order to offset the power of the West. There are good reasons for China's closeness to the West in the 1980s, but those reasons will not be good enough in the future. It may take another ten or twenty years for the leaderships of China and the Soviet Union to evolve to a point where better relations are pursued sincerely by both sides, but that time will come, particularly if the Soviets do not interfere too much in the most sensitive diplomatic question in Chinese eyes, the future of the independent government on Taiwan.

We have visited Taiwan several times. Each time it became easier to strike up conversations about Taiwan's future ties with the mainland, just as bit by bit the mainland makes itself more attractive to Taiwan. In 1980, due to improved air routes from the mainland to Hong Kong and on to Taiwan, Linda was able to travel from Canton to Taipei in a morning. At Chiang Kai-shek Airport, the immigration officer frowned at Linda's passport, full of People's Republic visas. "You have been to the mainland many times," he said menacingly.

"Yes, I have. I live there," said Linda, not certain what was going to happen.

The man smiled. "What's it like?"

Chinese and Taiwanese forces are closest off the coast of Fujian province. The Nationalist-held island of Quemoy sits within sight of the Chinese port of Xiamen. The Nationalist island bristles with underground bunkers and troops. Xiamen seems a beautiful, quiet little seaport recalling ancient glories, but it has its share of soldiers, and sometimes, as in the case of Zhang Qingfu in 1980, a man is executed there after being caught trying to sail for Taiwan. The Communists stopped bombarding the Nationalist islands with leaflet-filled shells on January 1, 1979, and without any formal agreement the Nationalists also ended their airborne distribution of propaganda papers. In addition, Xiamen's sea trade with the rest of the world began to improve. When we were there, a huge ferry cruiser from Hong Kong was disgorging overseas Chinese passengers who had come to see relatives. Even the informal bartering—and occasional smuggling—between mainland and Taiwan fishermen got a boost.

At a museum on Xiamen's Gulangyu Island, a residential part of town where the United States used to have a consulate, there was an exhibit in homage to the seventeenth-century hero Zheng Chenggong, better known by the name the Dutch gave him, Koxinga. In 1661 he invaded Dutch-held Taiwan with 900 ships and 25,000 men, and after nine months of fighting, expelled the foreign usurpers of Chinese power.

Today, Xiamen folk show little sign of gearing up for an attack on Taiwan. Instead, views of the offshore islands attract sightseers. Gulangyu has a spectacular crow's nest reached by climbing a winding stone staircase. From that height, the Nationalist islands look like lumps of cookie batter dropped into the smooth harbor. They are called Big Carrying Pole, and Carrying Pole Number Two, Number Three, Four and Five, with Quemoy and Little Quemoy islands just out of view. When the wind is right, often at two in the morning, Xiamen residents can hear the booming loudspeaker on Big Carrying Pole: "People of the mainland! Come over to our side!"

"Taiwan is like a treasure island because it is unknown," said Lin Yuru, a teacher at Xiamen University who voiced a common reaction. "I've read a little about it in books. It is not the life there that attracts youth. It is just the unknown."

The post-Mao government has put Taiwan on the top of its agenda for the 1980s. There is some urgency because Nationalist leaders from the mainland who still think of Taiwan and China as one will not be around much longer. The up-and-coming generation on Taiwan is full of bright native-born men and women who do not cling so tightly to the notion of reunification. If these Taiwanese try to declare the island an independent nation separate from the mainland, discarding entirely the convenient fiction of one China, the reaction in Peking will be extreme. But for now the Chinese leave their island kin alone.

The Chinese army is huge, perhaps 4.5 million people, but its equipment is primitive. Taiwan's air force might defeat it in the skies. The mainland navy does not have enough vessels to launch an invasion of the island. The Chinese incursion into Vietnam in 1979 showed that Peking might win ground with its numbers but lacks the modern equipment and skills to make a successful lightning assault and avoid heavy casualties. The Chinese nuclear force is still small. The Chinese cannot, even with a crash program, catch up militarily with the Soviets or the rest of the world in any foreseeable future. Everyone else is too far ahead. Any effort to produce a new weapons system would quickly be outstripped by some improved enemy defense. So the Chinese doggedly develop their factories and scientific laboratories, in hopes that in twenty years they will have the brains and equipment to build useful weapons and train a corps of army officers to use them. The nation's technological backwardness holds Chinese foreign policy in a vise. The leadership cannot easily break ties with the West because it needs Western technology and materials to speed economic development which leads to military security. In time, as the world changes, those Chinese ties to the West are likely also to loosen, if for no other reason than that there are enormous gaps between the two cultures, and then no one is quite sure where Chinese interests will wander. But whether or not Taiwan ever returns to the embrace of the motherland, mainland China will still be united, as now, just by the sense of being Chinese.

Muriel Hoopes, a remarkable Shanghai resident in her eighties, is a living demonstration of that feeling, and how much a Westerner had to sacrifice to be a part of China. She was a Philadelphia Quaker, working as a secretary when she met Chinese student Tu Yuqing, her future husband, on the New York subway in 1920. Over the next sixty years, after returning to China and raising a family, she learned a great deal of the country's emotional pull. In 1949 her husband, by then a prominent educator, asked if she thought they should leave Shanghai and go back to America. She resisted. She telegraphed him in Hong Kong, where he was on business: "You have studied for China, so you must come back and share what you know with China." She remembered how he cried whenever he came back from a trip and saw the yellow-brown waters of the Yangtze River. She did not want him cut off from those feelings. Both she and her husband argued strongly when their daughter and son-in-law seemed reluctant to return to Shanghai. Both were doctors, living a good life in New Jersey, but their father said to them, "Don't you want to serve the people?"

The Tus suffered for their loyalty to China. The grandchildren were forced by Red Guard harassment to stop speaking English. Hoopes and her husband were both detained in a makeshift prison. "I had to go to the toilet in the corner of the room, like a kid. I spent my seventieth birthday there, hardly believing what was happening to me." Much worse, her husband was imprisoned for more than four years, was badly beaten at one point and was left so numbed by the experience that he refused to talk about it after his release. He died in 1975, his spirit broken, and only his children could celebrate his rehabilitation in 1978. Today, Tu's children serve the new China, using their medical and scientific skills and fluency in English to make being Chinese something to be proud of again.

Will it work? The Chinese lean so heavily on the hope that things will go right this time that their immediate responses are nearly always positive. They enthusiastically embrace incentives, innovations, material progress and political liberalization, then caution that this must all be done carefully, with a few backward steps along the way for "reassessment." This is more than just honest caution. It is a daily struggle between a popular yearning to grasp material incentives and democracy, and stubborn resistance from an office-holding class stiffened by centuries of experience in holding on to power.

Thoughtful Chinese say that the popularity of the new incentives, the free markets, the loosened grip on literature and other facets of life guarantee that the people will never tolerate a return to single-minded repression and worship of a single leader's thoughts. But what power do the Chinese people have to guarantee that? Even as firm an optimist as Foreign Minister Ji Pengfei concedes: "There is no way that we can predict or guarantee that the second, third or fourth generation of successors will not guide China onto the wrong road."

The Chinese will continue to enjoy their food, tell jokes, take naps, spin tales and attend cricket fights no matter what the next few years bring, but their pride and confidence are at a critical point. Young people familiar only with internal power struggles must have some material gratifications, some exposure to the rest of the world, or their commitment to the system will evaporate. They are living in a period of breathless transition, risking political unrest, economic collapse and psychological despair as they move toward modernization. Even the old moderating virtues of Confucianism—brought back into vogue today—may not be enough to see them through.

But people like the Chinese who so skillfully slide through the barriers of their system can endure a great deal. They abide the excesses of the authorities and still eke out useful and often interesting lives. Just when we think the Chinese have again plunged into a bureaucratic, authoritarian dark age, we may find them crawling back on their roofs, secretly reconnecting their television antennas and pulling in signals from the rest of the world.

A NOTE ON SOURCES

THIS BOOK IS THE RESULT OF FIVE YEARS OF ACADEMIC STUDY OF THE Chinese and their language, followed by more than four years living in China and its environs. We spent three years in Hong Kong, with trips both to the mainland and Taiwan, and then about fifteen months in Peking, our base for travels throughout China. During that time we spoke to peasants, factory workers, officials, intellectuals, the young and the old. They told us what they could of their lives; they have provided most of the material in this book. We have added information and anecdotes from Chinese emigrants interviewed in Hong Kong, Washington, D.C., and California, but used only those insights confirmed by our conversations inside China.

We have used material from the official Chinese press—news articles, short stories, books and speeches, both public and internal—as well as unofficial stories and articles written by young Chinese who still occasionally publish, in circumscribed fashion, inside the country. We also owe a debt to several other writers on China, whose books we have sought to credit in the text.

Because this book is intended for general readers, we have not provided academic footnotes for our sources. We recognize, however, our debt to dozens of scholars who helped us before, during and after our time in China. We will be glad to provide more information about sources on request. Many of the people who spoke to us in China asked that their identities be protected, so we have often left them anonymous or altered names and locations, without changing the character of the story or the point the individual wished to make.

The *Los Angeles Times* and the *Washington Post* have permitted us to use in a different form some material first published in those two newspapers. We are grateful to our employers for that permission, as well as for the opportunity they gave us to go to China in the first place.

INDEX

ABOUT THE AUTHORS

JAY MATHEWS, the first Peking bureau chief of the *Washington Post,* and LINDA MATHEWS, the Peking bureau chief of the *Los Angeles Times,* are among the first married foreign correspondents ever given competing assignments abroad. Jay Mathews, a fluent Chinese speaker, earned a master's degree in East Asian regional studies at Harvard, while Linda Mathews graduated from Harvard Law School with honors in 1972.

The Mathewses reported for their separate newspapers in Washington, D.C., until they moved to Hong Kong in 1976, three months before the death of Mao Tse-tung. From Hong Kong they traveled extensively throughout China, and they moved to Peking with their two small sons in 1979, shortly after the normalization of relations between China and the United States.